BIBLICAL PATTERNS IN MODERN LITERATURE

Program in Judaic Studies
Brown University
BROWN JUDAIC STUDIES
Edited by
Jacob Neusner,
Wendell S. Dietrich, Ernest S. Frerichs,
Calvin Goldscheider, Alan Zuckerman

Project Editors (Project)

David Blumenthal, Emory University (Approaches to Medieval Judaism)
William Brinner (Studies in Judaism and Islam)
Ernest S. Frerichs, Brown University (Dissertations and Monographs)
Lenn Evan Goodman, University of Hawaii (Studies in Medieval Judaism) (Studies in
Judaism and Islam)
William Scott Green, University of Rochester (Approaches to Ancient Judaism)
Ivan Marcus, Jewish Theological Seminary of Americas
(Texts and Studies in Medieval Judaism)
Marc L. Raphael, Ohio State University (Approaches to Judaism in Modern Times)
Jonathan Z. Smith, University of Chicago (Studia Philonica)

Number 77
BIBLICAL PATTERNS IN MODERN LITERATURE

edited by
David H. Hirsch
and
Nehama Aschkenasy

BIBLICAL PATTERNS
IN MODERN LITERATURE

edited by
David H. Hirsch
and
Nehama Aschkenasy

Scholars Press
Chico, California

BIBLICAL PATTERNS IN MODERN LITERATURE

edited by
David H. Hirsch
and
Nehama Aschkenasy

220432
Library of Congress Cataloging in Publication Data
Main entry under title:

Biblical patterns in modern literature.

(Brown Judaic studies ; 77)
Essays originally presented at the First Annual Conference
of the Institute for Literary Research of Bar Ilan University,
Ramat-Gan, Israel, 17–20 May, 1982.
Includes index.
1. Bible and literature—Congresses. 2. Literature,
Modern—History and criticism—Congresses. I. Hirsch,
David H. II. Aschkenasy, Nehama. III. Universitat Bar-
Ilan. Institute for Literary Research. Conference (1st : 1982 :
Ramat-Gan, Israel) IV. Series: Brown Judaic studies ; no. 77
PN56.B5B54 1984   809'.93522   84–23641
ISBN 0–89130–813–X (alk. paper)
ISBN 0–89130–814–8 (pbk. : alk. paper)

Printed in the United States of America
on acid-free paper

The essays collected here were originally presented at The First Annual Conference of the Institute for Literary Research of Bar Ilan University, Ramat-Gan, Israel, 17-20 May, 1982. The Institute, under the directorship of Harold Fisch, and the University have been generous in their sponsorship and support of the humanistic studies generally and of this project in particular.

TABLE OF CONTENTS

TABLE OF CONTENTS (continued)

INTRODUCTION

The tradition of recreating the Biblical tale, adding epic expanse to its plot and dramatic complexity to its protagonists, started undoubtedly with the Hebrew Midrash. The Midrash exhibited a singular combination of literary criticism and literary creativity. In analyzing the Biblical text, the Talmudic sages revealed an amazing literary and aesthetic awareness, a sensitivity to subtleties of language, to techniques of foretelling, to verbal lacunae and redundancies. They deciphered the ancient text not only as moralists, intent on clarifying its message, but also as literary critics, alert to hidden signals enfolded in it. At the same time, the Scriptural story seemed to bring out in the sages their own artistic powers. With their imaginations invigorated by the beauties of the ancient yarn, they set out to tell their own tale, the Aggadah.

While the fundamental tenet of the ancient Jewish sages was the sacredness and intactness of the Biblical text, they still exercised a surprising measure of poetic license in their treatment of Biblical plots and characters. Indeed, the poetic nature of the Hebrew Aggadah was recognized early by the medieval philosopher Maimonides, who distinguished between the literary indulgence exhibited in the Midrash and the main intellectual activity of the rabbis, which was the study of Jewish religion and its law. He considered story-telling as a respite, a temporary diversion that the scholars allowed themselves occasionally. For him, this imaginative creation was not uniquely Jewish, but part of general poetic trends. Maimonides felt, correctly, that even when the tale was meant to be hermeneutical, its primary mover was the poetic mind.

The tellers of the Aggadah were motivated by two different needs. One was simple and self-evident: they had to reinforce the tradition of reading, studying, and discussing the holy texts. The other was more complicated: they felt called upon to respond to the changing cultural and aesthetic tastes of their own times, and to find the right equilibrium between the spiritual and religious tumult of the times and the indisputable authority and immutability of the ancient writings. Therefore, they re-told the Biblical story from two different angles and, in turn, the reconstructed Biblical tale served in two different capacities. In one, the intricacies of the tale itself and the motives of its protagonists occupied a central position; in the other, the sacred ancient text became a pretext for telling a different story, a story impelled by the needs of the times, whether political or aesthetic, in which the Biblical tale functioned as a source of energy and inspiration.

When the Talmudic sages centered on the Biblical story itself, they recognized its elliptical and terse quality as well as its dramatic potential. They embellished and expanded it to please the listener or reader who very often was already acquainted with Greek poetry and drama; at the same time they utilized the tale's tragic or comic elements to drive home the basic moral verities it imparted. In this instance, the impulse behind creating an expanded version of the Biblical tale can be labelled as aesthetic-didactic. But at other times, the attention of the rabbis was on the present, not the

- 1 -

past, and in those cases the Biblical story served as a parallel to contemporary events, or as an archetypal structure that underlay all human experiences and that made the present moment more plausible and life's predicaments easier to accept.

Thus when the Midrash filled in the details that seemed to be missing in the Genesis story of Cain and Abel -- the object with which Cain killed his brother, the nature of the brothers' quarrel, the dialogues that accompanied the deed and its aftermath, and Cain's changing emotions -- it clearly meant to enrich the story itself both for poetic reasons and in order to make the most of the moral lesson it contained. But when the Talmudic sages used the Cain and Abel story as a subterfuge that would enable them to comment with impunity on the murderousness of the Romans, or when Cain, as well as Esau, became code names for the cruel Roman rule, or when the argument between the brothers about the division of property was taken to allude to the Romans' attempts to appropriate Jewish land, then it is clear that they were telling a contemporary story and expressing feelings and concerns that they shared with their audience at the present moment.

But the Midrash tale was not only a political story in disguise. Though the tale was most likely intended as a parable that would explicate and elucidate the original text, it often happened that the parable eventually took over and drew attention to itself. These parables usually employ real-life situations and characters; thus the tension between the primordial Biblical couple is made clearer in a parable that tells of a domestic, everyday situation between a man and his too-curious wife. In these instances it is clear that what impels the storyteller is not so much the need to interpret the Biblical story, as simply the wish to tell a good story that combines a dramatic interest with an awareness of present-day reality. The Biblical tale in such cases serves as a frame of reference, an early precedent, or a prototypical configuration of all human experiences; but the impetus behind such stories (or "parables" as the Midrash calls them) is clearly literary and not exegetical.

In its use of the Biblical story as a starting point for new narratives, the Midrash thus opened up two methods of relating to the Scriptural material, both of which have been adopted by writers throughout Western literary history. The first method, in which the dramatic potentials inherent in the Biblical yarn are released, and the sparse tale is allowed to develop and expand, has been utilized in such different forms as the irreverent, secularized versions of the medieval "mystery plays," and Thomas Mann's solemn recreation of the saga of Joseph and his brothers. The second method, in which the Biblical material is a supporting structure for a new story, or in which Biblical images and connotations bring to light the subterranean layers of that story, has been represented in Western literature in works by the great masters such as Chaucer, Shakespeare and others.

For the most part, the works discussed in the present anthology represent the latter category, works that owe their vitality to the Biblical plots and images that underlie their surface structure. Whether they accept Scriptural tenets or question them -- as the Hebrew Midrash sometimes did -- these works may be seen as variations of the Midrash approach. May we propose, then, that writers from Chaucer to Garcia Marquez have been engaged in constructing Midrashim of their own and, as such, they belong to the Midrash tradition.

The essays gathered in the present collection deal with a variety of literatures, cultures, and periods. Since the Bible is the most pervasive "literary" influence in the Western cultural tradition, it would be virtually impossible for any single collection to cover all ages in all the languages and cultures of Europe.

The principal linguistic traditions represented here are English, French, and Hebrew itself, though there are also essays dealing with Russian, Spanish, and Yiddish literature. The introductory essay by Northrup Frye addresses itself to the question of the modern conflict between the logocentric and empirical tendencies in Western culture, and provides models of thinking by means of which these contradictions may be resolved.

In another essay of wide scope, Morton Bloomfield traces the attitudes toward, and the uses of "wisdom" as a ubiquitous societal phenomenon, fixing the place of Biblical wisdom literature in this larger social context. Harold Fisch's dazzling reading of Joseph Andrews presents a dual challenge to conventional criticism. First, he challenges the tendency of some critics to treat all Biblical allusions and imagery as "typological." Secondly, he challenges narrowly sociological and empiricist explanations for the rise of the novel. Henri Meschonnic presents a bold challenge to theories of Hebrew poetics that derive from Bishop Lowth's focus on "parallelism" as the governing figure of Biblical poetry. Meschonnic argues for the cantillation marks that govern the chanting of Scripture as a key to the meaning of the text.

Lawrence Besserman provides an excellent introduction to the literary uses of the English Bible in British literature with his analysis of Chaucer's attitudes toward the Biblical text. Noam Flinker takes up the influence of the Bible, specifically The Song of Songs, on Renaissance literature. Whereas Fisch and Besserman show the ways in which Biblical literature serves as a structuring device in British as well as European narrative, Flinker demonstrates the way in which Biblical literature and commentary generate allegorizing influences in British literature. W.Z. Hirst shows how intended parody of Biblical materials sometimes rebounds on itself. The invocation of the Biblical materials, even when intended to be parodic, leads to a reassertion of the Biblical world view. Although biblical influences in Shakespeare have been the subject of much commentary, Zvi Jagendorf presents an original and illuminating link between sexual type-scenes in the Bible and Shakespearean sex comedies, and then examines the implications for more recent sex comedies. Nehama Aschkenasy contrasts the ways in which Biblical structures modify and refashion tragic visions of a British writer (Thomas Hardy) and an Israeli (S.Y. Agnon).

Juliette Hassine illuminates certain aspects of Proust's Remembrance of Things Past by underscoring the link between Marcel's relationships to women and the biblical account of the creation of man and woman, along with the commentaries on that account. Lionel Cohn traces Camus's use of biblical motifs.

Menachem Brinker, Murray Baumgarten, and Hillel Barzel discuss various biblical influences on twentieth-century poets who wrote in either Hebrew or Yiddish, or, as in the case of H.N. Bialik, in both.

Marta Morello-Frosch looks into the ways in which Genesis provides an underlying structural frame for the Garcia Marquez novel, <u>One Hundred Years in Solitude</u>.

Efraim Sicher examines the rather surprising underlying presence of the Edenic paradigm in European and American dystopian literature.

Owing to the prominence of the Puritan tradition in American culture, the literature of the United States has, from its origins, been strongly motivated by biblical thinking and imagery. Emily Budick traces the interweaving of these patterns of thought into the works of three American writers; Sharon Deykin Baris examines Hawthorne's adaptation of the Daniel figure in what has been called the first great American novel, <u>The Scarlet Letter</u>. David Hirsch examines Henry James's use of the love imagery of <u>The Song of Songs</u> in what F.R. Leavis has called James's greatest novel, <u>The Portrait of a Lady</u>.

Essays by the following authors have appeared in different versions: Zvi Jagendorf, "In the Morning..." in <u>Prooftexts</u>, IV (May, 1984), 187-92; Nehama Aschkenasy, in MLS XIII (Winter, 1983), 101-110; Murray Baumgarten, in <u>City Scriptures</u> (Harvard U.P., 1982), Chapter 4; Emily Budick, in <u>The Hebrew University Studies in Literature</u>, X (Spring, 1982), 69-107; David H. Hirsch, in MLS (Fall, 1983), 39-60.

David H. Hirsch
Nehama Aschkenasy

VISION AND COSMOS

Northrop Frye
University of Toronto

Every human society, it seems, looks at its environment through a transparent cultural envelope of its own construction. There are no natural societies, in the sense of human groups living directly in and according to nature, able to dispense with such an envelope. There are no "noble savages," or completely natural men, for the same reason. A society's cultural structure normally consists of two concentric circles: an inner one which is peculiarly the "sacred," and an outer one which, though related to the sacred, has the less vigilantly guarded circumference that we describe as secular or profane. Writers on comparative cultural symbolism, such as Mircea Eliade, lay stress on the temenos, the drawn boundary that marks off the sacred area, and on the way that this temenos is reflected in, for example, the architecture of ancient cities. My own chief interest is in the verbal counterpart of the temenos, or what I call a myth of concern, the body of written documents that express what is of crucial importance to a given society. In the Christian culture of Western Europe, from the time of the New Testament down to around the eighteenth century, this central verbally sacred area contained the Christian Bible, assumed to be the definitive revelation to man of the essential knowledge concerning his historical past, his moral present, and his spiritual future or destiny.

Until the power of abstract verbal expression develops, the verbally sacred consists primarily of stories (mythoi), and after abstract thought has appeared, a good deal of it is expended on commentary, explanation and systematization of the sacred narratives. Before this takes place, however, most of the myths have consolidated into the kind of roughly unified, and certainly interconnected, construct that we call a mythology. The constructive principle of a mythology is the metaphor, the statement of identity, A is B, where two different things are said to be the same thing. Examples are in Genesis 49: "Joseph is a fruitful bough," "Issachar is a strong ass," "Naphtali is a hind let loose," and the like. If we ask what is the point of asserting that A is B when A is so obviously not B, we begin to get a clue to its importance in cultural development. A metaphor is not really a connecting of two things by forced and overstrained analogies. It is a way of setting up a current of verbal energy between subjective and objective worlds. It is not referential, in the sense of attempting to describe or set up a verbal replica of the objective world, but a way of absorbing the external world into cultural categories. The unit of metaphor, in most societies, is the god, the sea-god or sky-god or war-god who unites an aspect of nature with an aspect of personality.

A myth of concern is primarily a society's expression of what seems of immediate importance to itself: it deals with that society's views of its origin, its present obligations, and its destiny. It is not really a proto-science, or a primitive attempt to study the natural environment. But its impetus is normally imperialistic: after bringing secular culture into at least verbal consistency with itself, it goes on to deduce, from its sacrosanct writings, certain conceptions of the external world. At this stage the mythology has expanded to include a cosmology, the sense of a framework including the divine, the human, and the natural. But statements about the external world deduced from mythology are of course very apt to collide with what the actual observation of that world suggests. Hence what is often called, inaccurately, the conflict of religion and science, is really a conflict between mythological and empirical views of the natural order.

There have been two major conflicts of this kind: the heliocentric view of the solar system upheld by Galileo and Bruno in opposition to the social concern that demanded a geocentric view, and the evolutionary view of the origin of nature upheld by Darwin and contemporary geologists in the nineteenth century, which seemed to conflict with the doctrine of divine creation. These collisions have established a most important cultural principle. As one aspect of culture develops, science in our present context, the scientist becomes aware of a tension or polarization between the concerns or anxieties of society and the authority of his own discipline. Obviously he has to respect the concerns of society, otherwise he would have no social function at all; but increasingly, as time goes on, he finds he has loyalties and commitments to this science that he may have to defend even in the face of social threats.

This situation is generally admitted in regard to science, even though such things as the energy crisis, the deteriorating of the environment, and the lethal possibilities of atomic warfare indicate that social concern does have its own case. It is much more difficult for society to understand and recognize the fact that literature and the other arts also have an authority within themselves, and that the serious writer or painter must adhere to that authority no matter how much he may be condemned or ridiculed for doing so. Official Marxism (often called "vulgar Marxism" by Marxist intellectuals in the democracies) denies this authority in literature and the arts as a matter of dogma, and there have been startling outbreaks of hysteria nearer home. The reason for this state of affairs, apart from original sin, is that the origin and nature of authority in literature and the arts has not, to my knowledge at least, been investigated. Science's ability to appeal to verification and similar criteria make the question of its authority a relatively simple one; literature and the other arts are in a far more ambiguous and complex position. What follows is a tentative survey of some of the prolegomena needed for such a study.

Western civilization inherited a body of sacred stories, mainly from the Bible, and from the earliest days of Christianity this body of stories had already taken the form of what I have called a myth of concern. In a very short time, too, it had expanded into a cosmology, or view of the natural order. The Bible, as I see it, does not itself provide such a cosmology, but it does provide any number of hints and suggestions for one. It was inevitable, given the social conditions, that what Western Christianity derived from its sacred sources should have been a mythology and cosmology justifying a structure of authority. The metaphorical universe that persisted through the Middle Ages into and even beyond the Renaissance, in spite of all the cultural changes within society, was a structure on four levels. On the top level, of course, was God: the presence of God, or the real "heaven," was only metaphorically at the top, but the metaphor was usually taken as descriptive also. Below this came God's creation, the geocentric universe with the sky, the "firmament" of Genesis, forming the lower or visible "heaven."

The Biblical myth of creation is an artificial one in which God "makes" the world, instead of bringing it into being like an earth-mother. God being what he is, he could only have created a perfect world, with no sin or death or misery in it: this original creation was what God saw to be "good" in the Genesis account. The alienation myth of the "fall" was therefore necessary to account for the contrast between the model world that a good God must have created in the beginning and the world we live in now. The fall produced a third world, the world into which we are now born, where we are largely alienated from nature, including our own original nature. Before this fall, however, there must have been a fall among the angels, to account for the origin of sin and disobedience in the human mind, and the fallen angelic, or demonic, world constitutes a fourth level. Of these four levels, God is above nature, the demonic world below it, and the two levels of nature itself, or God's creation, come in between.

I have explained all this many times, but each context demands some repetition. World-constructs of this type have certain recurrent characteristics. One is that they rationalize the structure of authority in the society. The graduated four levels of the construct we are now discussing has the general model of the feudal conception of protection from above, obedience from below. Everything that is good in this construct comes from above in its origin, and everything good in our own lives comes from responding properly to such inspired impulses. The sacramental system of the Church, again, reconstructs our chaotic lives into a model imitating the form of what God originally intended man to be. In the Renaissance, with the rise of the secular prince, the analogy shifted to the king as the earthly representative of the One Person who was supreme in the universe.

A less interested function of the construct is to put man into a perspective in which his confused activity as a semi-conscious being striving for fuller consciousness can be made more intelligible. Our own view of things is blinkered by a schizophrenic subject/object split in which we are constantly stumbling over either/or dilemmas of our own making: we distrust the "subjective" as unreal (usually with excellent reason) and try to pretend that we can comprehend an independent objective world which is real, with very indifferent success. The conception of God is among other things an attempt to define a kind of existence which is free of all the limitations of the human intelligence. Thus Sir John Davies, in Nosce Teipsum, a wonderful grab-bag of epigrams setting forth common Elizabethan assumptions about the world:

But we that measure times by first and last
The sight of things successively do take,
When God on all at once His view doth cast,
And of all times doth but one instant make...

He looks on Adam as a root or well,
And on his heirs as branches and as streams;
He sees all men as one Man, though they dwell
In sundry cities and in sundry realms.

Our perception of time as a succession of three unrealities, a vanished past, an elusive present, and an unknown future, is reversed in God's mind into a single eternal present which includes past and future as well. Our ceaseless efforts to unite many things into a single form symbolic of our own unity as an "individual" does not exist for God, for whom the one and the many are merely aspects of the same thing.

One of the most important consequences of this mythological construct, for the understanding of the literature of the period at least, is its conception of two levels of nature. The original "good" creation included the garden of Eden, but with the fall of Adam this creation largely disappeared, and only the heavenly bodies, made of quintessence and revolving in perfect circles, are left to remind us of its original glory. The planetary spheres are the abode of the blessed spirits in Dante who have passed beyond the garden of Eden (which is at the top of the mountain of Purgatory in Dante), though Dante distinguishes between their manifestation in the spheres and their abiding place in God beyond the spheres. The use of the planetary spheres as the setting of the Paradiso is a spatial metaphor, but by no means an arbitrary or capricious metaphor. With the sin of Adam, man fell into a lower level of nature, the world of experience we now inhabit. This world is ultimately alien to him: animals and plants seem reasonably adjusted to it, but a conscious being cannot be. Man's essential quest, then, is to move from the world of physical nature in which he is born, and which he is in but not of, up to the second level which he was originally created to inhabit. The garden of Eden has disappeared as a place, but it is recoverable to some extent as a state of mind. Thus Chapman, in his long didactic poem The Tears of Peace:

So when the Soul is to the body given
(Being substance of God's Image, sent from heaven)
It is not his true Image, till it take
Into the Substance, those fit forms that make
His perfect Image; which are then impressed
By Learning and impulsion; that invest
Man with God's form in living Holiness,
But cutting from his Body the excess
Of Honors, perturbations and Affects;
Which Nature (without Art) no more ejects,
Than without tools, a naked Artisan
Can in rude stone, cut th'Image of a man.

The way upward from the ordinary to the genuinely human world is the way of morality, law, religion and education. This means that on the upper level of nature, the level that is specifically the level of human nature, art and nature are the same thing. Many things are "natural" to man, such as wearing clothes, obeying laws, and being in a state of social discipline and intellectual order, that are not natural to anything else in the order of nature. Chapman places this conception of two levels of nature within the framework of the chain of being, which is polarized by the conceptions of form and matter. The chain of being stretches from God to chaos, God being pure form and the "principles" of chaos (hot, cold, moist and dry) being as close as we can get to matter without form. The essential progress of man upward to his own original home is thus a purgatorial progress, whether an actual doctrine of purgatory is involved or not. Man was created in God's image, but that is not the image he is now born with, and recovering his own original form involves doing a good many things that our hazy post-Romantic superstitions would call "unnatural," such as quieting the mind.

The conception of two levels of nature, the upper one identical with art and the genuine home of man, is still going strong in, for example, Burke's Appeal from the New to the Old Whigs, written at the time of the French Revolution. It underlies Milton's Comus, where Comus attempts to seduce the Lady with arguments borrowed from what he calls the state of nature, where sexual intercourse is engaged in without self-consciousness. The Lady informs him that it is her chastity that is really natural, on her proper human plane. It underlies the critical views of Sir Philip Sidney, when he speaks of the poets expressing a golden age in opposition to nature's brazen one (meaning the lower level of nature). It underlies the complications surrounding the word "natural" in King Lear, where lower nature becomes Edmund's goddess, and thereby impels Gloucester's "natural" son into some very unnatural forms of behavior, such as betraying his father and brother. It underlies the last book of Gulliver's Travels, where we are informed that the "natural society" so much discussed in the eighteenth century might be possible for a gifted animal, like Swift's talking horses, but is certainly not possible for a "Yahoo" (i.e., man considered purely as an animal).

In God's mind, we saw, time is a pure present, and space would be similarly a pure presence: the "now" and the "here" that never quite come into existence in our own lives are realities for him. Man is the only being in creation who is out of his natural place ("kindly stead," as Chaucer calls it), and when he is in that natural place his experience of space and time become very different. Space in this higher world is a category that suggests a feeling of belonging rather than alienation: our word "home," suggesting as it does a space essentially related to ourselves, preserves something of the feeling. In fact the word "space," during the period we are examining, is usually expressed by "place," space there, emphasizing the importance of taking one's rightful position in the hierarchy of the created order. Time, again, on the second or genuinely human level, is more an expression of inward exuberance and energy than the compulsory succession of events symbolized by a ticking clock. The traditional symbol for this sense of time as inner energy is the dance, and more generally music, including the "music of the spheres" which symbolizes the harmony of the genuine creation. Thus Davies again, in the long poem Orchestra, an extraordinary vision of the world as seen as an interwoven cosmic dance:

> Since when all ceremonious mysteries,
> All sacred orgies and religious rites,
> All pomps and triumphs and solemnities,
> All funerals, nuptials, and like public sights,
> All parliaments of peace, and warlike fights,
> All learned arts, and every great affair,
> A lively shape of dancing seems to bear.

What Davies means by dance includes the element of ritual in human life, the sense of the sacred occasion or moment of time related to a spiritual reality. It also includes the vision of man as homo ludens, engaged in the play which is energy expended for its own sake and not for a further external end as work is.

We have emphasized the fact that this purgatorial upward quest of the soul, however central and significant, cannot be made on its own volition. In a universe of authority all initiation of essential action must come from the source of authority: grace must descend before merit can ascend. Even the revolutionary Milton does not think of liberty as anything that man wants or has a "natural" right to. Liberty for him is good for man because it is something that God wants him to have: man left to himself could not desire liberty, much less achieve it. John Donne, in an Eclogue, applies this downward-moving initiative to the temporal as well as the spiritual life:

> The earth doth in her inward bowels hold
>   Stuff well dispod'd, and which would fain be gold,
> But never shall, except it chance to lie
>   So upward, that heaven gild it with his eye;
> As, for divine things, faith comes from above,
>   So, for best civil use, all tinctures move
> From higher powers; From God religion springs,
>   Wisdom and honour from the use of Kings.

The figure employed here is one of the corollaries of the chain-of-being aspect of this mythological universe. Metals have been employed since Plato's day as metaphors for an aristocracy in the inanimate world with analogies (hence the word "mettle") in human life. They were enabled to "grow" out of the ground by the influence of the planets: The nearer or larger planets, the sun and the moon, brought out the "noble" metals gold and silver, and the smaller and more distant ones, Jupiter and Saturn, produced the "base" metals tin and lead. This gives Donne the illustration for his theme of all good coming from above, and for the social authority of a monarchy as representing by analogy the authority of God in the secular world. Monarchy is thus, for most people at the time in England (1613), the "natural" form of government for man, because it manifests the same kind of descent of order and law and harmony into a chaotic world that religion does. Such a view of monarchy is often dramatized in masques, especially those of Ben Jonson, where we move from a vision of disorder (the antimasque) upwards through society until we reach the person, often the king or queen, who is in the audience and in whose honour the masque has been held.

The initiative from above can generate a response from below, because, while everything in nature has an inborn tendency to death, it also has a tendency to return to its creator, which can be set free under the right conditions. In human beings, the soul is a substance different from the four elements that make up the body, and it struggles to liberate itself from the "mortal coil" surrounding it. Thus Marvell employs the figure of the drop of dew descending to an alien world and longing to return from it:

> Because so long divided from the Sphere,
>   Restless it rolls and unsecure,
>   Trembling lest it grow impure:
>   Till the warm Sun pity its Pain,
> And to the Skies exhale it back again,
>   So the Soul, that Drop, that Ray...
> Does, in its pure and circling thoughts, express
> The greater heaven in an Heaven less...

Marvell goes on to compare the dew drop with the manna of the Exodus, the food descending from heaven which was reabsorbed into its origin if not gathered. As in the apocryphal Book of Wisdom, manna is described as though it were snow.

In the period I am chiefly dealing with here (English literature from c. 1580 to c. 1660), perhaps the most illuminating portrayal of the four-level universe I am dealing with is to be found in the pendant to Spenser's Faerie Queene known as the Mutabilitie Cantoes. In this poem Mutability, a demonic goddess of the lower world of change and decay, the third and fourth levels we have been describing, claims jurisdiction over the world of the planetary spheres as well, on the ground that they revolve, and therefore change. Nobody questions Mutability's claim to be the supreme sovereign of the sublunary world, but Jove is the ruler of the upper part of Nature, and he resists her intrusion strongly. Mutability ignores him, or at any rate addresses him as "Saturn's son," stressing the degree of change that operates even in divine lives, and appeals to "the God of Nature," the Christian God, over the head of this minor functionary.

The Mutabilitie Cantoes are secular and not religious poetry: there are one or two Christian references, as we shall see, but the discussion itself keeps to secular terms. So it is simply the goddess Nature, who is supreme over both Jove and Mutability, to whom the appeal is brought. The evidence Mutability brings forward is evidence of change in the world below -- her kingdom -- which is caused or aligned with similar changes in the upper world, and so indicates that change, or mutability, goes on there as well. The evidence is chiefly that of the cyclical movements in nature: the months, days, hours, the cycles of life and death, and the like. Nature's decision is:

> I well consider all that ye have said,
> And find that all things steadfastness do hate
> And changed be: yet being rightly weighed
> They are not changed from their first estate;
> But by their change their being do dilate:
> And turning to themselves at length again,
> Do work their own perfection so by fate:
> Then over them Change doth not rule and reign;
> But they reign over Change, and do their states
>   maintain.

The effect of Nature's decision is to confine Mutability to the sublunary world, and to confirm the authority of Jove in "his imperial see." But that is not the real point of Nature's decision, which speaks of "all things," including evidently the things of this world as well. The cycles of nature are geared to two final movements, one downward into death and annihilation, the other upward into "perfection." The former is the direction of Mutability herself: "For thy decay thou seek'st by thy desire," Nature says to her. The latter is what we have called the purgatorial progression, where cyclical movement becomes the basis for a perfecting of form. In ordinary life repetition may be dull and mechanical, leading to nothing but more repetition, or it may be the basis of a growth in freedom, like practicing to play the piano. Hence there is a direction in change which is not simply into death, but is an upward movement into the oneness of being in which "all things" find their rest. Spenser concludes the poem with a pun on Sabbath, the final day of rest, and Sabaoth, multitudes or hosts. It is not a very good pun in Hebrew, where the two words do not even begin with the same letter, but in the Vulgate and English versions of the Bible that Spenser is using it is more convincing. Its significance for Spenser's society is indicated by the second part of the passage from Nosce Teipsum quoted above.

The Mutabilitie Cantoes are high metaphysical comedy, worked out in a secular context. We get an indication of the tone of the poem, and the mood in which it ought to be read, very early, in the description of Mutability's invasion of the sphere of the moon, the lowest point of the higher world over which she claims jurisdiction:

> Thence to the circle of the Moon she clambe,
> Where Cynthia reigns in everlasting glory,
> To whose bright shining palace straight she came,
> All fairly deck'd with heaven's goodly story:
> Whose silver gates (by which there sat an hoary
> Old ages sire, with hour-glass in hand,
> Hight Time) she entered, were he lief or sorry:
> Ne stay'd till she the highest stage had scann'd,
> Where Cynthia did sit, that never still did stand.

This is deliberate doggerel: the run-on fifth line in particular is a device Spenser does not employ in a serious context, and the bits of metrical putty in the seventh and ninth lines bring it closer, by Spenser's standard, to Sir Thopas than to, say, the descriptions of the Bower of Bliss or the Gardens of Adonis. It is consistent with such a tone that Spenser should incorporate into his poem a story of how Faunus the satyr bribed a nymph to allow him to see Diana naked. When he is discovered, he is hunted by his own hounds like Actaeon and finally both he and his nymph are turned into rivers. A stanza comparing Diana's rage with that of a farmer's wife who catches a "wicked beast" in her dairy-house tells us, by all the rules of Renaissance decorum, that we are still within the area of light verse.

The story of Diana and Faunus is obviously parallel to the main theme: the violation of Cynthia's sphere by Mutability is in counterpoint to Faunus' glimpse of the genitals of Diana. Diana and Cynthia are in Classical mythology both aspects of the threefold goddess whose infernal name is Hecate, and Mutability, though not identified with Hecate, is associated with her and comes from the same world. The theme of metamorphosis is one of the most popular in Classical mythology, and in the Christian centuries it became roughly a secular version of the fall of Adam. In terms closer to our present subject, a metamorphosis is a story of the dissolving of a metaphor into its original elements. That is, a being with personal qualities turns into a silent or at least unconscious object, a tree or bird or star or what not, the underlying theme being the reassertion of the gap between subject and object that all creative activity attempts to overcome. Metamorphosis stories are not common in the Bible: according to Sir Thomas Browne the story of Lot's wife is the only one it offers.

We have said that the decorum of this poem is secular, avoiding explicitly reference to the Christian framework which Spenser's readers would assume to contain both levels of nature. Mutability, brushing Jove out of the way, says that she appeals to the God of Nature over his head, and while contemporary readers would identify this deity with the Christian God, the latter does not appear, and Nature herself conducts the inquiry. There is however one exception, a stanza indicating that even Nature is subject to a greater power:

That well may seemen true: for well I ween
That this same day, when she on Arlo sat,
Her garment was so bright and wondrous sheen,
That my frail wit cannot devise to what
It to compare, nor find like stuff to that:
As those three sacred saints, though else most wise,
Yet on Mount Tabor quite their wits forgat,
When they their glorious Lord in strange disguise
Transfigur'd saw: his garments so did daze their
        eyes.

The fact that it is the Transfiguration episode that Spenser uses for almost his only Christian reference is doubtless connected with the fact that the word rendered "transfiguration" in English New Testaments is metamorphosis. This supplies the key to Nature's decision: metamorphosis moves simultaneously downward to the inevitable death of everything under the moon, and upward to the changeless being of the divine presence.

This use of a metamorphosis story, derived, in its general outline, from Ovid, is an example of the way in which Classical mythology had been adapted to a Christian framework by the poets of the Christian centuries. Strictly speaking, the Classical fables were to be regarded as demonic parodies of divinely revealed truths, especially when their similarity to those revelations was unmistakable. But in practice this view had been modified in a way indicated by Milton. In the Nativity Ode (a poem which is not about the Nativity but about the Incarnation), Milton describes the flight of the pagan gods before the coming of the true God. Our feelings about these deities are mixed: nobody wants Moloch back, but the "parting Genius," the "yellow-skirted fays," even the Lars and Lemures of the Roman household, leave a good deal of genuine nostalgia behind them. In Paradise Regained this situation is doctrinally clarified: there Jesus is offered the imaginative and philosophical riches of the Greek world, and refuses to have anything to do with them. This looks at first like an irritable obscurantism on Milton's part, but it is nothing of the kind. Because Jesus rejects the whole Classical tradition at that moment, before he enters on his ministry, he is safe from being taken over by it, deserting the prophetic tradition from a speculative one rooted in the theology of hell as described in the second book of Paradise Lost. But at the same time his rejection of it in the context makes it possible for his followers, including Milton, to accept so much of it: the "Genius," we note, has a very positive role to play in Comus, Lycidas, and Arcades. In short, Christ's rejection of Classical imagery redeems it, and creates two categories within it: the category of demonic parody, represented in Milton by Comus and his followers, and the category of positive analogy. Thus Giles Fletcher, in Christ's Victory and Triumph:

> Who doth not see drown'd in Deucalion's name,
> (When earth his men, and sea had lost his shore)
> Old Noah; and in Nisus' lock, the fame
> Of Samson yet alive; and long before
> In Phaethon's, mine own fall I deplore;
>   But he that conquer'd hell, to fetch again
>   His virgin widow, by a serpent slain,
> Another Orpheus was then dreaming poets feign.

Here the story of Deucalion in Ovid is a positive analogy of the story of Noah in Genesis, the fall of Phaethon similarly an analogy of the fall of Adam, and even the descent of Christ to the lower world to conquer death and hell and redeem his bride the Church is adumbrated by the failure of Orpheus to redeem his bride from the lower world. The last phrase in Fletcher's stanza indicates that Christian poets, for doctrinal reasons, had to express a conventional ingratitude to the Classical poets from whom they took their allusions; but the difference between the doctrinal demonic parody and the poetic positive analogy is clear enough.

The central conception of this analogy is that of Eros, the love that springs from the sexual nature of humanity. The word eros does not occur in the New Testament, where love means either agape, God's love for man reflected in man's love for God and for his neighbor, or philia, the kind of social cement that may be comprehensibly called gregariousness. And although the conception of Eros did enter Christian thought later, it is a fact of primary importance for the history of literature that Christian poets simply appropriated it as something that Christian doctrine had omitted and was of vital importance to them. The theme of metamorphosis itself is actually a by-product of Eros, a story of either the frustration or the fulfilment of erotic love. In the Mutabilitie Cantoes there is no question of the love of Faunus for Diana, his ambitions regarding her being pure voyeurism and nothing more, but presumably he does love the nymph he bribes, and the mingling of his streams with hers when he is changed into a brook is in the central tradition of such things, the best known example being the story of Alpheus and Arethusa.

It is well known that medieval poetry developed an elaborate parallel to Christian imagery in which the God of Love was not Jesus but Eros or Cupid. The parallel was extraordinarily detailed: the God of Love was both an infant in the arms of Venus and the power that created the world and held all the gods in subjection; he possessed the equivalent of grace; he had his saints and martyrs, his devotees and his heretics. We can see the parallel worked out as late as, say, Romeo and Juliet, where hero and heroine are obedient children going for confession to Friar Laurence, but who die as martyrs to another god whom Romeo describes as "my bosom's lord." Its imagery was by no means purely pagan: a lurking sexual element in the descriptions of Paradise, where Adam is the conscious presence in the garden and Eve's body is associated with the garden itself, is frequently employed, and this Edenic imagery modulates to "a garden enclosed, a fountain sealed" which is the body of the bride in the Song of Songs. Thus in a familiar poem by Thomas Campion:

> There is a garden in her face,
> Where roses and white lilies grow;
>   A heav'nly paradise is that place,
> Wherein all pleasant fruits do flow.
>   There cherries grow which none may buy
>   Till cherry-ripe themselves do cry...
>
> Her eyes like angels watch them still;
> Her brows like bended bows do stand,
>   Threat'ning with piercing frowns to kill
> All that attempt with eye or hand
>   Those sacred cherries to come nigh,
>   Till cherry-ripe themselves do cry.

Echoes of the garden of Eden, including the forbidding angels at the end of the story, and of the Song of Songs, mingle with echoes of the garden of the Hesperides and of the theme of forbidden fruit which underlies both the Biblical and the pagan myths.

The deeper significance of the poetic emphasis on Eros does not become really obvious, however, until towards the end of the eighteenth century, when the authoritarian four-level structure was beginning to cease to carry imaginative conviction and was dissolving as a context for poetry. Actually it had only lasted so long because it was a structure of authority and had the resources of spiritual and temporal authority to back it. The older structure, with its two levels of nature, obviously was one that put its main emphasis on the aspect of nature known as natura naturata, nature as a structure, order or system. An emphasis on Eros, then, would go much further than simply the inclusion of sexual love as a poetic theme: it would also bring into the foreground the natura naturans, nature as a process of growth, which in turn suggested that man was as much a child of nature as he was a child of God, and that many of his impulses had the moral ambiguity of nature when considered apart from humanity.

So from Rousseau through the Romantics, the framework of imagery behind poetry began to turn into something very different. Human civilization, with its laws, its reason, its social discipline, its clothes and its figures of authority, still sits on top of what in previous ages was the "fallen" or alienated world of physical nature. But the latter world is now thought of increasingly as something containing a non-human Other which is needed to complete human nature itself, and yet is not God. The relation of this natura naturans to ordinary human civilization may vary according to the poet's temperament: in Wordsworth it is profoundly benevolent for the most part; in others it may be sinister and terrible, even the kind of thing it is in the Marquis de Sade. Meanwhile, the stars in their courses can no longer symbolize the original divine creation with any real convincingness. In a post-Newtonian world the sky looks more like a mechanism than a product of divine wisdom. If it is a mechanism, of course, that leaves the organism as the highest form of creation we know of, and the world of "outer space" becomes increasingly a place of alienation, inhabited either by emptiness or, at most, by the idiot "immanent will" in Thomas Hardy which man has projected on it. But if nature contains an otherness that man needs to complete his own nature, the descent into it may be, as it was in pre-Christian times, thought of as a perilous but rewarding descent for the greatest of all buried treasures, the treasure of identity.

In the older model, themes of descent had survived mainly because of the prestige of Virgil, where a Classical Hades was substituted for the Christian hell. From Romantic times on, however, themes of descent take on an increasingly oracular quality, and are often associated with the world of dreams. In De Quincey's great mail-coach essay, for example, the dream world is the place where the fall of man is re-enacted each night -- a suggestion anticipatory of Finnegans Wake. In short, under Romanticism the old four-level cosmos is turned on his head, with a dead mechanical space above, a world of experience below it, a world of rapprochement between man and his natural origin metaphorically below that, and a world of final identity, sometimes, as in Prometheus

Unbound, associated with Atlantis, below that again. In the first poet of English literature who gives us this upside-down view of the old cosmos of authority, William Blake, it is interesting that once again all the imagery comes from the Bible, except of course that different proof-texts are supplied.

No human imagination can remain satisfied with an antithesis, and there have been many attempts to set up some outline of a cosmos that will escape from the overriding constraints of both authority and of revolution. Poe's Eureka was an early one, and it suggested to the poet and critic Valery that cosmology, as distinct from the areas explored by science and philosophy, was a literary product. Since then there have been many others, ranging from Yeat's Vision to Grave's The White Goddess, not of course new constructs, but new ways of rearranging traditional elements in the older ones. The subject has yet to be explored, though the immense contribution the Bible has already made to the subject suggests that it will remain central to all explorations. In any case one hopes for a vision of the imaginative cosmos that will show us our own imaginative creations against a background of equality and freedom rather than the limiting order provided both by a hierarchical vision and by the resistances made to it.

The Tradition and Style of Biblical Wisdom Literature

Morton W. Bloomfield

Harvard University

Central to the study of most early societies is the notion of wisdom -- the world view of most traditional societies and the source of its practical morality. It is the framework in which the world is viewed. It is a concept which shows amazing similarities throughout the world and must go back to the earliest stages of human consciousness.

Although there is some overlapping, wisdom may be divided into two major divisions.[1] The first and most basic, and indeed the one most ignored, is the fundamental outlook of most traditional societies -- the rationale of the universe as they view it. The second is prudence, which presents practical advice for the understanding of man and nature and which enables humans to find a general principle for the explanation of particular actions or rules of conduct to explain the past and guide the present and future.[2] When we speak of wisdom today we generally think of the latter -- the practical homey advice for living or for reconciling humans to life. Wisdom as philosophy is generally ignored or misunderstood. It may be, as it often is, partially categorized under other headings as science or religion, but even these activities are different and have a slightly different focus. They, however, do rest upon the notion of a rational universe which is of the essence of wisdom in its first and broadest sense. One of these two divisions is essentially an outlook, a philosophy of the world, a paradigm of paradigms and the other, prudence, is implicit in a mass of stories, praises, blames, proverbs, gnomes, exempla and so forth which apply that philosophy to concrete instances whether before or after the fact or which inculcate the principles of that philosophy.

As has often been said, something which explains everything explains nothing. This presents a problem to the student of wisdom literature: the notion of wisdom is so deeply embedded and so widely found in almost all early human endeavor that it is not easy to distinguish it from its background. As I hope to show, it is nevertheless a useful overarching concept for human understanding; one of the basic categories of under-standing early thought and early action.

We must understand that wisdom is man's first and most basic step towards rationality. Out of it came the fundamental world-view of science before statistical principles redefined the notion of science in our century and for many people it is still the basic view. It was the drive to overcome the arbitrariness of things that led to the discovery or, in some cases, invention, of order underlying the apparent disorder and chance of the universe. Repetition occurs in nature and life and thus some kind of order can encompass the apparent irrationality of things.

Historically speaking, rationality and reason have other significances besides order. These terms have been used by philosophers as a principle of understanding since Plato.

Plato, Aquinas, Spinoza, and above all, Hegel emphasized that reason is a cosmic principle. Another understanding of reason is that of the scientists who have made much of the rational or scientific method since Bacon in the 17th century. But reason as the notion of order predates the philosophical and scientific mode of thought and has not been systematically studied, perhaps because it is difficult to find order in human conduct. Unlike nature in general, human nature does not give us neat examples.

If G. H. Mead is right in his belief that one of the central questions of philosophy is the rise, transformation, and implications of the notion of reason, then a basic element in this development has been ignored.[3] Although Mead's concept of reason is too psychological and is oriented towards man's use of symbols -- both important aspects of the subject, of course -- he did recognize the anthropological aspect of the question. He and others, however, have missed the fundamental role of wisdom in the formation and creation of reason, human rationality, and science. As philosophical concepts, reason and science came out of the older concept of wisdom.

Wisdom is, thus, the root of both scientific and humanistic thinking and should be looked at in this light. All learning is at root and origin one. When we emphasize quantitative measurement, we come to a point of separation between the humanities and science; but when we emphasize their common origin in the notion of order and rationality, we tear down barriers and distinctions and see the unity of all human intellectual activity.

The ancient notion of wisdom may be conceived as the natural religion of early man. His myths and tales have as their presuppositions, no matter how fantastic the form, the idea of order and rationality. They attempt to answer the most basic question of all -- why? "Why" cannot be asked unless there is present the assumption of order and rationality. In other words, to ask why assumes that there is a why. It is this assumption that is basic and fundamental to all rational thinking, and it is called wisdom. When no simple universal answer is known or possible, myth and story fill the gap. Where they come from is of course another matter, but come they did. Wisdom is the root of all thinking about the universe whether propositional or metaphorical. It is the earliest intellectual and rational attempt to master and understand the universe and the formation of the results of that attempt. As the ancient maxim has it, "sapientia est ordinare."

Religion cannot be separated in most early societies from the wisdom perspective or indeed from almost any other early activity. It is so bound up within the culture of early societies that phenomenologically speaking, a division is difficult to make. Symbols help to maintain, as Dupré has remarked, "the rationality of our action as something that is connected with the past and directed toward a future accomplishment."[4] Without basically using the idea of wisdom, he defines religion as wisdom and recognizes its universality.

This new understanding is visible above all in recent Biblical scholarship, which finds that wisdom is ubiquitous and not confined, as it has traditionally been, to Proverbs, Job and Ecclesiastes.[5] Von Rad, a great Biblical scholar of our time, who has written the basic book on the subject, shows just how pervasive it is.[6] It is not accidental that both

Jesus and God as well as the Torah itself are ultimately linked with wisdom, for Logos, as it was called by Philo, is the principle of rationality that makes sense of the apparently irrational universe. Creation itself is the imposition of wisdom on chaos.

As we explore other cultures and their art we become more and more aware of the importance of wisdom. Nor is it merely confined to early societies. Most societies, except perhaps our own, still take the idea of wisdom as one of their basic concepts. As a philosophy of existence in both an extended and general sense and in the form of practical advice, wisdom is found almost everywhere. It has long been recognized that literature teaches as well as delights, but in the West in the past 100 years or so, the delight has been the center of interest and the teaching ignored or brushed aside. In most cultures, however, the didactic function of literature has not been ignored or brushed aside. Even in our Western popular culture, teaching is by no means ignored as comics, soap operas, romances and popular songs all reveal. The "art for art's sake" movement of the late nineteenth century still flourishes in high-brow art. Art must not be useful. This is not the assumption under which most of the world operates.

The unappreciative view of wisdom is that it consists of a mass of old saws and proverbs which were popular with our ancestors and which are boring, repetitive and useless. It is of course true that wisdom in one of its senses, as we have said, consists of proverbs, gnomes, meditations, and dialogues about human conduct and that some of it is boring, contradictory and repetitive. The moralizing which some moderns hate so much and which irritates those of the young who think it blocks merriment and joy is very characteristic of wisdom, for its subject, in the narrow sense of the word, is how to live so that one can get the best out of life as a whole. This is not a topic that appeals to those who are bent on immediate enjoyment or success.

Yet most cultures have praised and elevated wisdom and its manifestation in the sage. Perhaps the only subject which is universally admired is wisdom -- not only by Hebrews or by Greeks, but also by Hindus and Chinese, Polynesians and American Indians, Hausa and Xhosa. All peoples without apparent exception admire wisdom, hypostatize and personify it, practice or say they practice it, teach it to their children and use it to face or smooth away the irritations of everyday life. Perhaps the most admired man in all societies is the wise man, the Prospero who can explain and control things and who is the good magician, next only perhaps to the holy man who is often also the wise man.

Without gnomes and proverbs, traditional societies cannot exist. The Luo are a strong, intelligent, lively people of northwest and west Kenya who speak a Nilotic language. A Luo woman who wrote a thesis on women in her society not too long ago complained to her American director. She remarked that in order to really understand the Luo, one cannot get very far merely by studying their societal structure, as she herself was doing: only by studying their proverbs and how they use them can their real life be uncovered. Proverbs put things into perspective. Proverbs solve differences of opinion. Proverbs raise the specific up to the general and make sense of the world to people. A group of young Kamba people in another part of Kenya, as I was once told in Africa, wanted to know from their teacher what proverbs the Americans use. To know a people's popular proverbs and when and how they use them is to know that people.

The unexpected and the sudden are feared.[7] Wisdom manifested in all that is best in life, including language and law and art, enables us to control by either action or understanding the arbitrary and the unusual. Language provides us with a set of rules and vocabulary which permit us to grasp intellectually the world and encompass its novelty. Law is the embodiment of general rules for conduct, and ideally, lawyers are wise men. Practical wisdom is prudence, which enables us to act and to choose so as to move in harmony with the world. The craftsman-artist is the pattern of the wise man. Bezalel, the ancient Israelite artisan who created the tabernacle according to the plans of God, is always referred to in the Bible as a wise man. The smith who could work in various metals is the wise hero of many cultures, and his heavenly archetype may be found in Vulcan and Weyland.

Schools traditionally have existed for the purpose of handing on wisdom and knowledge, and teachers are at least theoretically the guardians and transmitters of wisdom. The Supreme artist is the Creator, and He, like his earthly counterparts, works all by wisdom. A knowledge of wisdom is an initiation into immutable knowledge -- not just into opinion. The ancient Sumerians believed all wisdom and science were gifts of the gods to man and hence sacred.

The notion of wisdom in the Western world rests not only upon rationality but also upon the idea of limits. Hell has no limits; heaven is limited. God made us all, as the writer of the Book of Wisdom puts it (11:20), by weight, measure and number. There is a rationale for everything that is good, and there is a proper place and time for everything. Things are normally located in their "natural" place and happen in their "proper" time or times. Here we have the concrete essence of wisdom: a knowledge of proper places and proper seasons. Included are those things or acts which are forbidden -- like those listed in the ten commandments -- for the most forbidden acts, no time or place is proper. Chapter 3 of Ecclesiastes, where we read about proper times for all things, provides an excellent example of the ancient Hebraic notion of proper times.

Hesiod's Works and Days gives us this kind of specific information -- a tradition continued in astrology, almanacs, and even in Aristotelian philosophy. St. Augustine speaks of everything in the universe as having its proper place. If anything is removed from its place, it seeks to return. Love and gravity are both forces which attempt to put things and people back in their proper places when they are moved or move out of them.

Religious law is an attempt to implement the concept. The Torah, for example, is the rule of how to do things in true wisdom -- the proper holy times (the sacred calendar), the proper places for doing things pleasing to God (the holy places and buildings), and the proper modes of doing things, both ritual and moral. God manifested Himself to His people in Law, which is supreme wisdom.

This concept of order is the foundation of divination and prophecy. Wisdom literature is frequently put into the mouths of sages, teachers or occasionally wunder-kinder (precocious or inspired children). Religion is not only ritual, belief and ethical conduct but also wisdom in ordinary life -- how to live and order one's being. The assumption is almost universal even if there has been some skepticism as to whether any human can successfully predict with exactitude the proper occurrence and location of events. The present king of Nepal chose the date and time of his wedding, as his predecessors had done, only at the advice of astrologers who told him when to go ahead. The ancient augurs looked at bones and livers to determine lucky, that is "proper" times.

Wisdom pertains to nature as well as to human relations and self-development. There are, as Kenneth Jackson has written, gnomes about nature as well as about humanity, but the wisdom of nature is related to man and is existential in import.[8]

Wisdom in its prudential aspect makes life bearable. One does not have to decide everything for oneself. There is, wisdom says, a traditional body of tested information which makes itself available for living. It provides a common ground for the settling of disputes and debate and enables man to make some sense out of a complex and difficult world. It says that there is a right and wrong way, time, or place to do things and provides some guidance towards the determination of these. Children and princes must be instructed in its basic principles, and man must live by it if he wishes happiness or at least if he wishes to know how to bear misfortune. It enables man to avoid, as Kierkegaard puts it, "the dread of infinite possibility." It not only assures us that things have some stability, but that in spite of the unexpected and the new, things will basically continue in a rational manner.

Closely connected with wisdom philosophy is, of course, the notion of tradition and ancestors. In sub-Sahara Africa, which I have visited several times, ancestors are involved in almost every action, public and private. They are present and watching every action, exhibiting pride or shame, rewarding and punishing. They show pleasure and displeasure. All men become ancestors, even if only metaphorically, and hence must not neglect their responsibilities towards ancestors when alive.

The degree to and the mode in which ancestors prevail in the world vary, and living members make diverse responses to these ancestral demands. The Japanese notion of on includes obligations towards ancestors. In Rome, Sallust speaks of "Quintus Maximum, Publius Scipio and other eminent men of our society" who "were in the habit of declaring that their hearts were set mightily aflame for the pursuit of virtue whenever they gazed upon the masks of their ancestors."[9] In the Judaeo-Christian tradition, we have Abraham, Isaac and Jacob and the other holy men who watch over the conduct of their physical and spiritual descendants, who plead for those present on the via, alive, to God, and who help the living to resist temptation and avoid difficulties. They may even bring us good luck, and God may be called the God of Abraham, Isaac and Jacob.

It must not be thought that wisdom and tradition are necessarily conservative forces. They may also be radical. Attempts to achieve harmony between the rules of wisdom and the world may result in change as well as in the maintenance of the status quo. The return to the past is not per se conservative; it depends where in the past one wants to go, how one interprets that past and how one uses it. Usually it may be said that the further back one wishes to go (where in other words there is less accurate knowledge), the more revolutionary the changes are. The man who wishes the world to return to the conditions of his childhood is usually more conservative than the one who wishes to return to the golden age. Wisdom as a motive force is in itself neither reactionary nor radical.

Traditional wisdom is based upon a rational view of the universe, but a rational view which encompasses the sacred. Inasmuch as there is a "right" way to do things and a "right" way in which the universe is ordered, the "right" is ultimately sacred. Neglecting to do the right thing is equivalent to violating the order of the universe. The sanctions which this "rightness" demands are the authority of the sacred. The ultimate rationality of things is grounded in the sacred and the holy.

The sacred has its paradoxes. Men need wisdom, both as a guide to the sacred and as a rein on its extravagances. The sacred, ambiguous and the mysterious, without the reins of wisdom, can lead to madness. There is a dialectical relationship between the two. The sacred without wisdom is madness; but wisdom without the sacred is barren. The Bible is the book of both the sacred and of wisdom.

As a book of wisdom, the Bible teaches the order men and women should follow if they are to gain salvation and obey the Creator. Certain of the books are singled out as wisdom literature because they deal with aphoristic and prudential advice as well as speculative attitudes towards existence dealing directly instead of indirectly with the question of order. Unlike most other religious traditions they all emphasize the power of God, an emphasis which differentiates Hebrew wisdom from that of other older cultures.

The three main wisdom books (in this specific sense) are Ecclesiastes, Job, and the Book of Proverbs. Two other "wisdom" books, Ecclesiasticus or Ben Sira and Wisdom are found in the apocryphal literature included in the Septuagint.

Biblical wisdom literature, like most literature, is not nationalistic. The notion of Israel is not central in these books. Nor are these books historical although they may be attributed to historical figures such as Solomon. Their international character is revealed by their borrowings from and similarities to the wisdom literature of other Near Eastern countries.

The literary form of wisdom is close to the colloquial -- both in vocabulary and in the use of language. The disjunctive mode comes naturally to its expression. Separation of concise truths is common just because that is the way wise men speak. They speak at moments and not continuously. Their sayings and brief speeches are made for pondering and long speeches are not suitable for pondering. They rise out of the oral and teaching tradition. Occasionally the teaching is encapsulated in stories such as fables, parables, and even jokes.

The wisdom tradition tends strongly in its style of presentation towards disjunction -- separate units often forced together without any clear link in meaning, except of the most general sort. A fair proportion of the Bible is presented in this fashion, and above all apodictic law. The unit is relatively brief and the point sharp and definite. The conditional law of the type "If -- then" is also disjunctive, but not to the same extent. And occasionally a second sentence of the normal declarative type follows the conditional statement. The mitzvoth and hukim (laws) are not presented in paragraphs but in sentences, often one, and occasionally two or three.

At times in narrative parts of the Bible and even more frequently in prophetic statement a similar type of disjunction appears -- both apodictic and conditional. Yet at times both in wisdom and in other types of literature, two apodictic sentences or even on occasion two conditional sentences on the same general topic follow each other. Yet the general feeling is separateness and disjunction. Unlike paragraphs, the sentences of which seem to flow into each other, the characteristic Biblical non-narrative style is rough-hewn; and, although several sentences may be linked by a parallelism or a similar theme, the general impression is one of jerkiness.

This tendency is abetted by the widespread use of parallelism in Biblical Hebrew. Parallelism forces sentences both into a kind of completeness and into a limited union with a following sentence or sentences. But this union does not continue over a long stretch of prose, occasionally over two clauses or phrases but rarely over a long stretch. The main linked type of Biblical language is to be found in narrative and to a lesser extent in the prophets. In other genres the language tends to be ejaculatory.

Why is this the case? I do not have enough knowledge of Semitic languages to be able to trace these disjunctive tendencies throughout the Semitic speech area, but, if I may judge from translations these tendencies are present in Sumerian, Akkadian and Assyrian materials, not to speak of West Semitic languages like Ugaritic.

Inasmuch as the alphabet as we know it was invented in the Semitic area, probably Phoenician, and (as in Linear B) primarily for business purposes, notes and jottings to jolt the memory would be natural; and wisdom, which for ages existed only on a moral level and concerned with teaching, would naturally tend towards short and pithy sentences which would stimulate but not burden the mind. As all teachers know, brevity is a valuable asset in teaching.

This tradition was carried over into Midrashic exposition. It is characteristic of both Talmudic and Midrashic style to present material in brief units, sometimes united by theme and sometimes not. I should like to call this style lemmatic because its unit of discussion is usually part of a sentence. It is focused on the lemma, not even the sentence and much less the paragraph. Although the present use of verse indications, not present in the original form of the Bible, tends to break up the Bible in its common present-day form, the paragraph as a unit does appear in its older form as in the Torah scroll. These paragraphs are probably originally rhetorical breaks rather than unified by a common theme.

The influence of wisdom literature on the Bible then, probably because of its universality, is not confined to its substance, but includes also its form. This principle is probably applicable to other writing cultures, but it seems certainly to be true of the culture of the ancient Hebrews, especially as manifested in the Bible. The popularity of disjunctiveness, with its conciseness and directness, and its emphasis on discrete units is due to the tradition of wisdom literature. Wisdom literature has not had its impact just on certain books of the Bible or on the other places where it has influenced the content of other parts of the Bible, but it has influenced to a great extent the very form of much Biblical and post Biblical literature in the Jewish tradition. The nature of narrative makes the formal influence of wisdom on story slight, but inasmuch as Biblical narrative tells the story of God's relation to the ancient Hebrews and the whole world of that time it is holy wisdom in action. As to form, however, the disjunctive technique of much Biblical style is the form in which wisdom teaching usually comes.

The notion of wisdom literature helps strongly to explain much Biblical style. The laws tend to this form to impress themselves upon the mind. The prophet falls on many occasions into this mode of discourse. Wisdom literature naturally seeks the brief and hence memorable form which will be impressed upon the hearer or reader's mind. It is didactic and hence pithy and intellectually graspable in length.

Ecclesiastes is a series of meditations on the theme of the vanity, shortness and determinisms of life. These are, as may be expected, presented disjunctively and arise as from a teaching or face-to-face situation. Sometimes they are rambling but more frequently are within their units emphatic and well-organized. Perhaps the most notable of these units is Chapter 3, 1-15 with its famous lines beginning "To everything there is a season, and a time to every purpose under the heaven." This concentrates on one of the central themes of all wisdom teaching: the notion of the proper time for all things and all actions.

Ecclesiastes is also full of proverbs, the common currency of the wise man. The Book of Proverbs itself contains meditations, especially the section on wisdom in Chapters 8 and 9. But it is much more proverbial in structure, with many more sharp breaks than we find in Ecclesiastes.

In Ecclesiastes and Proverbs we have, attributed to Solomon, the reproduction of pre-literate wisdom teaching, the oral ejaculation of wise men as they give us the discontinuous results of their pondering and of the pondering of earlier wise men. To the West, our clearest and most important source of ancient wisdom is the Bible and above all in these two works. Here, if we read them seriously, we are transported back into an oral culture, and a culture which although being reconstituted somewhat by the rise of the electronic media as Marshall McLuhan has made us aware of is still foreign to us. Although we are perhaps not as much a reading culture as we used to be, we are a culture which is both oral and written and because of this duality still very different from a purely oral culture. We are also a visual culture in a different sense than the visuality which comes from reading and travelling because we can see the whole world in our living rooms.

When we realize the extent of wisdom in older society and its presence in modern society from the advice we are flooded with on all sides and the consolations, true and false, we are offered for the sufferings of life, we must think it strange that we have in recent years seen it so little in our written tradition. There is indeed a link between an advice columnist such as Ann Landers and the Book of Proverbs although the latter contains a richer collection of helps for the disconsolate. The preacher, the psycho-analyst, the government pamphlet all perform an ancient function. America, perhaps because it is a "new" country, is more concerned with the articulation if not the living of wisdom than most Western countries. As far as the East and Africa are concerned, wisdom is bred into the very fabric of their cultures. In these areas as all over in the past, wisdom is associated with tradition. In America the tendency is to connect wisdom with science.

These two Biblical wisdom books, although indebted to their Oriental and universal predecessors, had, however, their unique qualities. They are, largely though not entirely, God-oriented unlike most of the other wisdom literature of the East. They are interrupted by passages of theorizing and speculation while continuing to emphasize their rather short units, especially in the Book of Proverbs.

The Biblical wisdom tradition found its greatest welcome in northern countries, especially in England. English literature has always had, until very recently, a strong wisdom aspect and some of it can be traced to Biblical sources. As we have pointed out, however, the notion of wisdom is so widespread that it cannot be said that the popularity of wisdom in literature is exclusively due to Biblical influence. Much of it, in Europe and America, however, is obligated to Biblical sources because of the wide-spread belief in the Bible as revelation and hence from God. With the decline in the influence of the Bible as revelation and with competing claims from psychiatrists and consultants, contemporary literature as a source of practical wisdom has declined.

Narrative in the form of parables, fables, myths and stories has until recently been a major source of wisdom. Since the rise of literacy and the novel, these forms contain truths directly and indirectly presented, and were frequently read as sources of wisdom. Directly we find proverbs and conclusions which give us information about human actions, needs and desires. Indirectly, we are given stories which reveal human needs. If wisdom sentences and moralistic stories are to be useful, they must often be contradicted by other sentences and stories. Human actions cannot be reduced to a science.

George Eliot provides a splendid example of a "wisdom" novelist. Her stories are not only didactic without preaching but they are interspersed with actual proverbs. A recent article about her realism clearly indicates the extent to which her ethical views are related to traditional wisdom such as we have been talking about. M. C. Henberg writes:

> Moral rules for Eliot can never be rationally justified by philosophical analysis. They cannot be constitutive of moral action, for following a set of moral rules does not guarantee morality in the way following certain rules guarantees that you are playing chess. But this denial that moral rules are constitutive does not mean that they must be discarded entirely. Moral rules can and do play a regulative role: in most instances obeying traditional moral precepts will in fact lead to a moral outcome.

The author goes on to write:

> According to Eliot, tradition encapsulates the hard-won moral knowledge of past generations.... Tradition, then, is a great organizing force and a person who ignores its precepts stupidly refuses to take advantage of the experience of authors.[10]

In her last great books, <u>Middlemarch</u> and <u>Daniel Deronda</u>, Eliot makes her persona a purveyor of wisdom in the traditional sense. The gnomic interjections increase, and she enriches her moral argument by the increased dignity and tradition of the authorial or persona voice. To take <u>Daniel Deronda</u> as an example, here are some of the comments of the voice. I take only a few brief and proverb-like remarks, proverbial in their worldliness as well as their morality: "But for complete enjoyment the outward and the inward must concur" I, 10, p. 132 (Penguin edition by Barbara Hardy). "Joy may be there, but joy, too, is terrible" VI, 47, p. 642; "Who that has a confidant escapes believing too little in his penetration, and too much in his discretion?" VI, 48, p. 657; "There is no escaping the fact that want of sympathy condemns us to a corresponding stupidity" VI, 48, p. 658; "Second-sight is a flag over disputed ground. But it is a matter of knowledge that there are persons whose yearnings, conceptions -- nay, travelled conclusions -- continually take the form of images which have a foreshadowing power" V, 38, p. 527; "The continual smile that discredits all expression" VIII, 59, p. 781; "There comes a terrible moment to many souls when the great movements of the world, the larger destinies of mankind, which have laid aloof in newspapers and other neglected reading, enter like an earthquake into their own lives" VIII, 69, p. 875.

This piling up of wisdom sometimes almost in bits and pieces indicates too clearly how it may enter into life, both giving advice and bringing consolation. The gnomic voice helps us over the rough spots by displaying sympathy and understanding. Here as elsewhere in the wisdom tradition, much wisdom is about wisdom. In the last analysis, wisdom must learn about the limitations of wisdom. To be truly wise, one must possess wisdom, but one must go beyond wisdom. "The authors of proverbs and those who strive for understanding" (Baruch 3:23) must still learn the lesson that wisdom though absolutely necessary is not enough. The road runs through wisdom in order to get beyond it. The greatest wisdom is to recognize its own limitations while at the same time recognizing its own truth.

But there is no way to avoid going through wisdom if one wants to understand life. Wisdom is created by rhythm and repetition, by order imposed on disorder, and by these principles understood in their broadest sense, man can imitate the wisdom of the universe. What is law, what is a calendar, what is poetic meter but rhythm and repetition?

If we turn to the history of English literature, we see a long line of writers, most named, some anonymous, all involved in purveying wisdom as well as pleasure. This pertains to Anglo-saxon and medieval literature especially, a situation not surprising, but it is also true of the sixteenth, seventeenth and eighteenth centuries, slowly diminishing in extent as the nineteenth century proceeds. Shakespeare, Bacon, Milton and many other names spring to mind. The eighteenth saw the beginning of the Enlightenment and with it came a diminished interest in the topic. Science or, more exactly, the scientific spirit, was separating wisdom from knowledge, but in the West it took a long time in dying.

Samuel Johnson is a fine representative of wisdom in the eighteenth century. The difficulty of placing him in the history of English literature is partly due to the dying of the tradition to which he belonged. He belongs to the category of wise men who as Keats said of Shakespeare, see "life as an allegory." However, unlike other hold-overs of this type, Samuel Johnson is preserved for us as the prototypical Anglo-saxon wise man by being the subject of a great biography. Boswell became his biographer in order to preserve the picture of a great man in action.

The famous stories Boswell tells indicate the anecdotal and proverbial side of traditional wisdom. They are complete in themselves. For example, Boswell wrote:

> (Johnson's) superiority over other learned men consisted chiefly in what may be called the art of thinking, the art of using his mind; a certain continual power of seizing the useful substance of all that he knew.... So that knowledge, which we often see to be no better than lumber in men of dull understanding was, in him, true, evident, and actual wisdom.

To show the roots of this wisdom both in Johnson's wonderful powers of mind and in his learning especially of the Bible is too large a task at present, but his wisdom lies in the tradition which all Western Europe lies under: the Classical and above all the Judaeo-Christian tradition of wisdom and salvation.

The violation of wisdom may lead to disaster and requires external and internal purification. The Greek word for sin, hamartia, and the Hebrew word for sin, chate, both probably come from roots which mean to miss the mark, to leave the right way. Ritual and ethical violations are both wide of the mark of the proper paths. Purification and confession enable man to return to the proper task.

The Bible then lives on in the Western tradition not only in its report of God's doings but also in its emphasis on wisdom which is practical, commonsensical and moral and which rests upon the notion of a universe governed by rationality and order. For us in the West, the Bible has not only given most of us our religious history and our path to salvation, it has also given and continues to give us our sense of spiritual and common-sensical order -- the wisdom of tradition.

Notes

1. There is much confusion between these two aspects of wisdom, in the scholarship on the subject. See for example Dalcourt (note 2 below); Keiran Conley, A Theology of Wisdom: A Study in St. Thomas (Dubuque, Iowa, 1963); Robert Preyer, "Victorian Wisdom Literature: Fragments and Maxims," Victorian Studies (1963), 245-62 (who does recognize the distinction between sophia and phronesis, wisdom and prudence, the one so high, the other so low and how to unify and distinguish them. If Conley is right, Plato recognized their close similarity whereas Aristotle divided them sharply. They are different aspects of the same virtue. For a short but useful summary of the notion of wisdom in the higher sense, see James D. Collins, The Lure of Wisdom, The Aquinas Lecture 1962 (Milwaukee, 1962).

2. See Gerard J. Dalcourt, "The Primary Cardinal Virtue: Wisdom or Prudence," International Philosophy Quarterly, 3 (1963), 55-79.

3. See W. Kang, G. H. Mead's Concept of Rationality: A Study of the Use of Symbols and Other Implements (The Hague and Paris: Mouton, 1976).

4. Wilhelm Dupré, Religion in Primitive Cultures, A Study in Ethnophilosophy, Religion and Reason 9 (The Hague and Paris: Mouton, 1975), p. 63

5. See Walter Brueggemann, "Scripture and an Ecumenical Life-Style: A Study in Wisdom Theology," Interpretation, a Journal of Bible and Theology, 24 (1970), 3-19; R. B. Y. Scott, "The Study of Wisdom Literature," ibid. 20-45, Hans Heinrich Schmid, Wesen und Geschichte der Weisheit, Beihefte zur Zeitschrift fur die alttestamentliche Wissenschaft 101 (1966); and R. N. Whybray, The Intellectual Tradition in The Old Testament Beihefte zur Zeitschrift fur die alttestamentliche Wissenschaft 135 (1974). An earlier book, Johannes Fichtner, Die altorientalische Weisheit in ihrer israelitischjüdischen Ausprägung, Eine Studie zur Nationalsierung der Weishiet in Israel, Beihefte zur Zeitschrift fur die alttestamentliche Wissenschaft, 62 (Giessen, 1933) is still useful. For an introduction to Babylonian wisdom literature see Johannes Jacobus Andrianus Van Dijk, La sagesse sumero-accadienne, Recherches sur les genres litteraires des textes sapientaux, Proefschrift ... Rijksuniversititeit te Leiden ... (Leiden, 1953) and W. G. Lambert, Babylonian Wisdom Literature (Oxford, 1960).

6. See his Wisdom in Israel (Nashville and New York: Abingdon Press, 1972). The German original was published in 1970. See also Harvey H. Guthrie, Israel's Sacred Songs, A Study of Dominant Theme (New York, 1966), especially Chapter 4.

7. See David Daube, Suddenness and Awe in Scripture, Robert Waley Cohen Memorial Lecture, 1963 (London: Council of Christians and Jews, 1963).

8. See his Studies in Early Celtic Nature Poetry (Cambridge: Cambridge U. Press, 1935), esp. pp. 127 ff.

9. Trans J. C. Rolfe in Loeb edition of The War with Jugurtha IV (p. 136).

10. M. C. Henberg, "George Eliot's Moral Realism," Philosophy and Literature, 3 (1979), 29.

BIBLICAL 'IMITATION' IN JOSEPH ANDREWS

Harold Fisch

Bar-Ilan University

Critics have paid somewhat perfunctory attention to the clear indications given early in Joseph Andrews that its hero is meant to recall the career of his Biblical namesake. When Joey is called to Lady Booby's bedroom early in the book, we are told that "for a good reason we shall hereafter call [him] JOSEPH"[1] -- the good reason being that he is going to act the part of Joseph in the Bible resisting the seduction of the wife of Potiphar. The second indication comes from Joseph himself in the second letter he writes to his sister Pamela after he is dismissed from his situation as a consequence of resisting Lady Booby's advances:

> I hope I shall copy your Example, and that of Joseph my Name's-sake; and
> maintain my Virtue against all Temptations. (Book I, chapter 10).

This puts the Biblical story on the same level as Richardson's Pamela as a shaping influence on the novel. The Biblically conscious reader (which of course means Fielding's average reader in 1742) would have seen Joseph from the beginning as fulfilling the role of the Biblical knight of Chastity. If he had been especially alert, he might even have noted that, like his Biblical namesake at the beginning of his career (Genesis 37:2), Joseph Andrews too was seventeen years old when he was promoted to be Lady Booby's footboy.[2]

Martin C. Battestin has given more attention than others to this dimension of the novel, noting that in this Fielding is following the pattern set by the latitudinarian divines of his day and earlier (notably Isaac Barrow and Samuel Clarke) who had proposed the Biblical heroes Joseph and Abraham as paradigms respectively of Chastity and Charity, or "Faith expressed in works."[3] Here we have the key to the twin heroes of Fielding's novel. Abraham Adams, like Joseph, is clearly linked to his Biblical namesake. In Book IV, chapter 8, with explicit reference to the trial of Abraham in Genesis 22, he will be morally tested by the reported death of his son Jacky. Like the story of Joseph and Potiphar's wife, this episode of the 'sacrifice' of Isaac too is handled in low-mimetic, the extravagant grief of Adams comically belying his earlier sermon on fortitude in the face of disaster. But surely Battestin is right in claiming that Fielding in drawing upon these figures from the Genesis narratives is developing a kind of "Christian epic"; the intention is not wholly or chiefly to burlesque the Biblical characters and episodes but to promote a Pelagian emphasis on the value of innocence and active philanthropy as a religion for ordinary folk in the world of everyday.[4]

Whilst pointing the way to a correct reading of the novel, Battestin has however failed to point out the true nature and extent of Fielding's use of the biblical analogy. The web of allusions is more sustained than one would suppose: as we shall see it goes far beyond the episode of Joseph and the lustful wife of Potiphar and encompasses the novel as a whole, its frame and composition. It may even be suggested that Fielding's use of the Biblical model has implications for the novel genre as such, of which Joseph Andrews is an early, crucial example.

I

Shortly after his dismissal from Lady Booby's service, Joseph, having set out on foot from their London home, is waylaid by two thieves in a narrow lane. They strip him naked and cast him into a ditch (I, xii). The parallel with the adventures of the Biblical hero (Genesis 37:23, 24) who is set upon by his brothers, stripped of his coat and cast into a pit is patent. The motif of the divesting of Joseph in Fielding's novel in fact begins with the (twice-mentioned) stripping of his livery earlier on (chapters ix, x). The livery will remind us of the Biblical Joseph's "coat of many colours." Indeed, the liveried servants of the town with whom Joseph had become acquainted in chapter iv are there described as "party-colour'd Brethren." After being beaten and left naked in the ditch by the robbers, Joseph is soon rescued (chapter xii) and given a ride in a passing stage-coach (though with great reluctance on the part of the travellers and the coachman). The stage-coach is surely meant to recall the caravan of Midianite merchantmen who "drew and lifted up Joseph out of the pit" and took him down to Egypt in the Biblical narrative (37:28). Joseph Andrews is now taken by his rescuers to Tow-wouse's inn where he is presumed close to death. His clothing is later discovered in a bundle which had been tossed to the side of the road and the livery which it contains is recognized by Parson Adams who thereby identifies the "dying" man, again reminding us of the continuation of the Biblical narrative where Jacob recognizes the coat of his supposedly dead son (37:33). This is not the first or the last time that Adams acts towards Joseph in loco parentis. But of course Joseph Andrews has a real father too, viz., Mr. Wilson, from whom he had been cruelly separated for many years, precisely as Joseph had been separated from his father Jacob. In Fielding's novel too the child had been kidnapped at an early age (like his Biblical namesake) "by some wicked travelling People whom they call Gipsies" -- the witty modern equivalent of the Ishmaelites or Midianites involved in the Biblical story of the sale of Joseph into Egypt. The reunion of father and son after the lapse of years and their tearful embraces (IV, xvi) will mark in the novel as in the Bible story (46:29) the happy ending of the narrative. But before that consummation is reached there are additional episodes, especially concerning the divesting and reinvesting of Joseph, which bear on the analogy.

In Book IV, chapters iv and v Joseph and Fanny are about to be committed to Bridewell through Lady Booby's machinations (Potiphar's wife all over again) when unexpectedly Joseph is raised to eminent social rank through the discovery that he is now directly related to Lady Booby through the marriage of his sister Pamela to her nephew. In this dramatic change of status, special emphasis is given to the matter of clothing. Joseph Andrews is invested in splendid clothing which Squire Booby produces from a Cloakbag; these include "Linnen and other Necessaries." Parson Adams's delight at Joseph's great good fortune is especially focused on the sight of his "new Apparel." Beholding it, he burst into Tears with Joy, and fell to rubbing his Hands and snapping his Fingers, as if he had been mad. (IV, v).

In the parallel episode in Genesis, Pharaoh had raised Joseph from prison to be his viceroy and as a sign of this had placed his own ring upon his hand, had <u>arrayed him in fine linen</u> and put a golden chain about his neck. (41:42). In fact the whole sustained motif of dressing and undressing, so central to Fielding's <u>fabula</u>, has its origin in the Bible narrative of the career of Joseph.[5]

So far the details of the analogy are fairly straightforward. There is however, one subtler application of the clothing motif in which the story of Potiphar's wife is again seemingly adverted to, though now from an unexpected angle. At first sight it seems to be an ironical inversion of the Bible story. In the final night-adventures in Booby Hall (IV, xiv) there is a great deal of coming and going among the ladies' bedrooms. It begins with Beau Didapper, the upper-class rake and scoundrel, who decides to make an attempt on Fanny's chastity by presenting himself to her in the dark as Joseph. He mistakes the room and leaps into bed instead with Mrs. Slipslop. She tries to capitalize on the opportunity offered but when Didapper, now made aware of his mistake, tries to escape the clutches of the aging but lustful Slipslop, she determines to prevent him and expose him, thereby seeking, like Potiphar's wife, to regain a reputation for her injured virtue:

> At that instant therefore, when he offered to leap from the Bed, she caught fast hold of his Shirt, at the same time roaring out, 'O thou Villain! who hast attacked my Chastity, and I believe ruined me in my Sleep; I will swear a Rape against thee, I will prosecute thee with the utmost Vengeance.' The Beau attempted to get loose, but she held him fast...

He makes his escape after the precipitous entrance of Parson Adams and the confusion which ensues. Later in the evening, Lady Booby, trying to sort out the tangle of misunderstandings, sees a fine pair of diamond buttons and the torn piece of a laced shirt on the floor of Mrs. Slipslop's bedroom. "To whom belongs this laced Shirt and Jewels?" she cries. All this will remind us not only of the angry wife of Potiphar but also of the coat which Joseph leaves in her hands before fleeing and which she later produces in evidence. Didapper, it would appear, has taken over the role of Joseph, as he wants to, but in an upside-down context where a far from innocent "Joseph" is involved in a sexual episode with a mistaken partner. One might want to argue that Fielding is not only echoing, but also exploding the Bible story of Joseph and Potiphar's wife.

This, however, is not quite so. For the truth is that this same inversion occurs in the Biblical source as well. For in the interpolated story of Judah and Tamar (Genesis 38), Judah (an antitype of Joseph) has relations with his daughter-in-law Tamar (the latter being disguised) and leaves behind him in pledge three items of his accoutrement: his signet, his bracelets and his staff. Lady Booby's question "To whom belongs this laced Shirt and Jewels?" in fact echoes Tamar's challenge to Judah when her "whoredom" is discovered: "Discern, I pray thee, whose are these, the signet, the bracelets and the staff." (38:25). The link between the two stories, that of Judah and that of Joseph, through the motif of the loss of clothing or other marks of identity is an important feature of this Biblical pericope. We are invited to see in the stories of the two brothers a pattern of symmetry and contrast which is more marked in the Hebrew than in the English translation.[6] What is for Joseph a mark of honour becomes for Judah a mark of shame. When Judah sees his personal effects in the possession of Tamar, he acknowledges that shame (38:26). Conversely, Joseph is only temporarily and outwardly disgraced through the loss of his coat: in the end he will be vindicated. Both in the episode of his being stripped by his brothers and his being falsely charged by Potiphar's wife he will shine out to the reader as the just man. Through his loss, he proves his rightdoing; through a similar loss, Judah proves his wrongdoing.

Fielding it would seem has sensed the dialectical relation between the two figures: he has Beau Didapper pretend to be Joseph only to reveal his true identity and shame through the loss of his buttons and lace garment. There is perhaps a wider, almost Marxist reverberation here. The stripping of the "Beau" is for Fielding and for us more than just one of the night's adventures in Booby Hall; it is the symbolic end of a type and of a mode of writing which have fallen into decay. All that is left of the Cavalier of an earlier day is his torn laced shirt and diamond buttons. He has departed in nakedness and ignominy. Joseph Andrews, whose rise he had sought to prevent and whose identity he had usurped, will gain the prize and he will do so without the need for false accoutrements. The loss of Joseph's livery in the early part of the book turns out to be no disgrace but the prelude to the disclosure of his true merit and standing in the world, a standing which will ultimately be confirmed by his being invested in appropriately honourable dress.

II

What all this suggests is that we have here a patterning of episodes by the well-known Augustan device of "Imitation". The reader enjoys recognizing the links with a classical source drawn from antiquity and given a witty but not entirely frivolous application to contemporary life. In like fashion, the eighteenth century reader enjoyed the systematic echoing of Juvenal's Third Satire in Dr. Johnson's "London" or the same technique in Pope's Imitations of Horace. Earlier on Dryden had wittily applied Biblical narrative material to a contemporary political situation in "Absalom and Achitophel". The pleasure was in recognizing the well-known contours of the Biblical story in the doings of people of one's own society. In the mode of realism that Fielding chose to practice, the device of "Imitation" was necessarily less direct, the borrowed episodes more deeply buried in the texture of his narrative. But they are there just the same. And it is more than a matter of detail: it is a matter of the total movement and shape of the source as Fielding and the latitudinarians understood it. He is writing a moral fable in which injustice and inhumanity finally will be overcome and Charity will prevail, in which the reviled and the lowly will be raised above their enemies, in which virtue will be rewarded, not in the next world but in this. Those were the directions in which the Genesis narratives -- indeed the whole Old Testament scripture -- pointed. Abraham Adams is in this respect the righteous man of the first Psalm who walks not in the counsel of the wicked nor sits in the seat of the scornful. His life bears witness to the notion that goodness will prevail and that it is the business of fiction to see that it does.

In its fashion Fielding's novel is a "Pilgrim's Progress" but, unlike Bunyan's master-piece, its relation to the Bible is metonymic rather than typological. Bunyan's heroes only seem to have adventures on the road -- that road is really a mystic path leading to the heavenly Jerusalem. Fielding's heroes by contrast occupy a narrative space similar to that of our own lives and yet they demand to be thought of in terms of the Bible. The Biblical heroes, Joseph and Abraham, are not seen as types of Christ but as exempla of virtue: every charitable man has a touch of Abraham and every chaste youth, a touch of Joseph. The Biblical heroes are -- it is hardly too much to say -- people like ourselves. This is not the way in which the Biblical images and figures function for Bunyan. In The Holy War he gives us the Old Testament imagery of battles, the noise of the soldiers and the shouting of the captains; he echoes Psalm 68 in the phrase "he hath led captivity captive" but these images are employed as trope, divorced from their physical and historical setting. There is no real war; the warlike doings of men are transcended, even condemned as vain and meaningless. Their only value is as symbols for the victory of Emmanuel (Christ) over Diabolus (the Devil). Metonymy works by a different way, not by symbolic substitution, but by the direct concrete relation subsisting between a master narrative and an unlimited number of derived narratives. The substantial reality of neither is transcended: they are rather beheld as parts of one another.[7]

There are of course Christian overtones in Joseph Andrews which bear a typological interpretation. Ignoring the more obvious parallel with the story of Joseph and his brothers, William Empson insisted that

> Fielding never made a stronger direct copy of a Gospel parable than in Joseph Andrews (I, xii) when Joseph is dying naked in the snow and an entire coach-load finds worldly reasons for letting him die.[8]

In that episode the postilion who gives Joseph his overcoat acts the part of the good Samaritan in the gospel-story (Luke 10:30f). That allusion is surely there. Moreover, by being associated with the story of the Good Samaritan, Joseph no doubt becomes here a type of Christ just as the Biblical Joseph, sold by his brethren, had become a type of Christ in some of the early writings of the Church. Nevertheless, the main narrative model here and elsewhere in the novel is the story of Joseph in the book of Genesis; the other stories are grafted onto that. A similar conflation of the metonymic and the typological is to be found in the final discovery of Joseph's identity. When Mr. Wilson identifies the straw-berry mark on Joseph's breast, Parson Adams rubs his hands and cries out, "Hic est quem quaeris, inventus est." The reference is to the story of the Prodigal Son (Luke 15) as well as to the meeting between Jesus and Mary Magdalene beside the empty tomb (John 20:15). But here again these are surely no more than overtones; the prime analogy is with the reunion of Joseph with his father Jacob which, whilst it could bear a transferred Christian meaning, retains in Fielding's text its substantiality as an object of "Imitation." It is not the union of the upper-case Son and the Father but of a lower-case son and father, i.e. any son and father estranged from one another and reunited by the well-known devices of romantic recognition. These devices are given added force by the Biblical vision which requires that good men are seen to prosper in an ill world.

Metonymy <u>versus</u> typology is in a way the point at issue between the latitudinarian divines and those of a more evangelical persuasion such as the Methodists, Whitefield and Wesley. To do good in the world was for liberal Anglicans (whose views went back to South and Jeremy Taylor) the way to heaven: one could be aided to it by reading the Bible as a collection of commands and moral <u>exempla</u> directly applicable to the worldly space we occupy. A more evangelical approach sees the earthly meanings of the Bible transcended in the interests of the doctrine of Grace. In Fielding this very issue of Works <u>versus</u> Grace is debated between Parson Trulliber and Parson Adams (II, xiv). That chapter should be read as a debate between Charity as symbol ("I know what Charity is, better than to give to Vagabonds") and Charity as practical command linking the doings of the figures in the Bible with those required of men in the world we know. It should also be read as a debate between two fictional models, the one aiming at a kind of inner integrity, the other seeking a correspondence between outer and inner events. We recall that <u>The Pilgrim's Progress</u> begins with Christian being warned against seeking salvation by way of Mount Sinai which is the path of Morality counselled by Mr. Worldly-Wiseman. He must instead pass through the little wicket-gate of the Covenant of Grace: his victories will be psychological victories. Parson Adams is Fielding's rehabilitation of Mr. Worldly-Wiseman for an audience which had learned from Tillotson, Hoadly and Clarke to prefer a rational, this-worldly model of salvation. One direction it would seem takes us forward to Emily Bronte, Conrad and James Joyce; the other points to Jane Austen, Dickens and George Eliot. Both can claim scriptural authority and indeed have their beginnings in two different kinds of "Imitation" of scripture practised at the beginning of the history of the novel.

In this connection, students of Fielding have overlooked an important item of bibliography. Five years before the publication of <u>Joseph Andrews</u>, the eccentric and highly unorthodox rational divine, William Whiston, a friend of Clarke and Hoadly and possibly the model for Goldsmith's Vicar of Wakefield, published his monumental translation of Josephus's <u>The Antiquities of the Jews</u>.[9] This together with <u>The Wars of the Jews</u> established itself quickly and would often be found standing on the shelf beside the Family Bible in good middle-class homes. It would be surprising if Fielding had not come across it and indeed a reading of the career of the Biblical Joseph as presented in Book II, chapters ii-viii of the <u>Antiquities</u> strongly suggests that Josephus's version as translated by Whiston was in Fielding's mind when he penned <u>The History of the Adventures of Joseph Andrews</u>....

Josephus gives an extended "novelistic" account of the story of Joseph and his brothers laying special emphasis on the episode involving Potiphar's wife which occupies a long chapter in place of the few verses devoted to it in the Biblical text. Josephus offers in fact a midrashic amplification of the episode giving special attention to "his beauty of body", his "virtue" and "chastity" -- all terms repeated several times in the course of the story of Joseph's life as told by Josephus. Josephus gives, like Fielding, two separate meetings between Joseph and his mistress. At the end of the first meeting, the effect of Joseph's refusal is summed up:

But this opposition of Joseph's, when she did not expect it, made her still more violent in her love to him: and as she was sorely beset with this naughty passion, so she resolved to compass her design by a second attempt. (iv)

The general similarity of the language to that of Fielding is notable. Potiphar's wife contrives an occasion for the second attempt on Joseph's virtue by pretending to be sick and is thus left alone in the house with him. Josephus says nothing about her being in bed -- this is Fielding's development of the hint -- but the notion of sickness had been introduced by Fielding also at the beginning of Book I, chapter v of Joseph Andrews. We are told that Lady B. after her husband's death remained "confined to her House as closely as if she herself had been attacked by some violent Disease."

The second and crucial meeting between Joseph and his mistress in Josephus includes a long speech by Potiphar's wife answered with an equally long statement by Joseph. Some phrases stand out as strikingly similar to Fielding. She tells him that "she was forced, tho' she were his mistress, to condescend beneath her dignity." (We may compare Joseph's reply to Lady B.'s invitation to kiss her: "I should think your Ladyship condescended a great deal below yourself" (chapter viii).) Potiphar's wife proceeds to warn him against "preferring the reputation of chastity before his mistress." Of Joseph's reply to this we are told:

neither did pity dissuade Joseph from his chastity; nor did fear compel him to a compliance with her; but he opposed her solicitations, and did not yield to her threatenings, and was afraid to do an ill thing; and chose to undergo the sharpest punishment, rather than to enjoy his present advantages, by doing what his own conscience knew would justly deserve that he die for it.

With less gravity, Fielding has his hero declare

that he would never imagine the least wicked thing against her, and that he would rather die a thousand Deaths than give her any reason to suspect him. (I, v)

(And in the continuation of Fielding's account in chapter viii: "What would you think, Joseph, if I admitted you to kiss me?' Joseph reply'd, 'he would sooner die than have any such Thought.'")

Joseph's speech in Whiston's translation of Josephus though detailed and well-reasoned (he introduces some advice about the pleasures she might enjoy by remaining faithful to her husband's bed) has little effect and Josephus continues:

Joseph, by saying this and more, tried to restrain the violent passion of the woman; and to reduce her affections within the rule of reason: but she grew more ungovernable, and earnest in the matter: and since she despaired of persuading him, she laid her hands upon him and had a mind to force him. (Emphasis added).

The conjunction of "violence" and "passion" occurs several times in Fielding's handling of the story but specifically in Lady B.'s exclamation following her second interview with

Joseph -- "Whither doth this violent Passion hurry us?" As for the notion of Potiphar's wife laying her hands on Joseph, this is a touch originating in Josephus; it does not occur in the Biblical text which only speaks of her seizing his garment. Readers of Fielding will recall that Lady B. in her first interview with Joseph "accidentally laid her hand on his" and in the chapter that follows, Mrs. Slipslop, a burlesque version of the wife of Potiphar, "prepare[d] to lay her violent amorous Hands on the poor Joseph."

Fielding remembers Josephus again towards the end of the novel in the scene describing the reunion of Joseph and his father, Mr. Wilson (IV, xv). Not being yet aware of the circumstances of their relationship, Joseph did not express at first the same "extravagant Rapture" as his father though "he returned some Warmth to his Embraces." This same distinction as to the intensity of feeling expressed by father and son respectively is made by Josephus (it is not in the Biblical account) who remarks that "Jacob almost fainted away" whilst Joseph, though he was likewise moved by the encounter "yet was he not wholly overcome with his passion, as his father was." (Josephus II, vii).

III

The details of the indebtedness to Whiston's Josephus are of less interest than the affinity itself and its implications for the kind of art-form that Fielding was developing. What was it that attracted Fielding about the version of the story given by Josephus? Why did he not just make do with the Bible story? We are here I think at the heart of Fielding's problem as a latter-day cultivated Englishman forging a new literary genre with the help of the narrative resources of the book of Genesis. The Bible is important, indeed indispensable, for the new middle class literary sensibility, and yet somehow it won't do. The whole tradition of epic and romance revolts against it. Longinus taught the men of the eighteenth century to appreciate the sublimity of "God said, Let there be light!" But what was one to do with "Moab is my washpot"? And how was one to handle the brutal directness of the Joseph story -- "His master's wife cast her eyes upon Joseph; and she said, Lie with me."? Tolstoy admired the simplicity and boldness of that verse. How much better it was, he remarked satirically, than the way of the modern writer who would feel it necessary to describe

> the pose and attire of Potiphar's wife, and how, adjusting the bracelet on her left arm, she said, 'Come to me.'[10]

All such details were, he claimed, superfluous. Nevertheless, in his novelistic procedure he provided a wealth of just such accordant effects -- they were evidently far from superfluous for him even when writing a simple tale like Father Sergius. The problem was to tap the power of the Bible story, what Auerbach calls "the intensity of the personal history" of Joseph who is, he says, "really in the pit"[11] and yet somehow overcomes its harshness. This harshness is a matter of diction but it is also much more than that; it is a matter of tone, sentiment and mores. There is an incompatibility to be overcome when the western sensibility confronts the undiluted text of scripture. That text is, in a word, too naked. Now Josephus had found a way of covering its nakedness. He had performed this service for the Hellenized Jews and gentiles of his time and in Whiston's translation with its Augustan flavour (Joseph we are told tried to "reduce [the lady's] affections within the rule of reason") he could help to do the same for Fielding's generation. In balancing the Bible story against the "midrash" of Josephus, Fielding had found a strategy for dealing with the essential dialectic governing the relation of the western writer to the Biblical text. For Josephus had introduced a certain opacity to reduce its glare, a certain smoothness to mitigate the harshness of its contours, a mode of amplification to arrest the suddenness of its transitions and a certain ease of manner to reduce the severity of its moral judgments. All this is of greater importance than the narrative particulars which Fielding evidently drew from Josephus. It is hardly an exaggeration to say that Josephus helped Fielding solve the main problem of designing a "comic epic poem in prose."

It may be worthwhile returning for a moment to that definition of Fielding's. It occurs of course in the "Author's Preface" to Joseph Andrews. What does he mean by a comic epic poem in prose? In its context the phrase is designed to make us think of the novel as a kind of comic version of the Odyssey (with heroes like mock versions of Achilles or Hercules); it may also rightly be explicated by reference to the mock-epic in Don Quixote, a model to which Fielding is demonstrably attached here and elsewhere. He announces on the title page after all that he is imitating the Manner of Cervantes. But the emphasis should surely be on the last word. The new form which Fielding (like Richardson and Defoe) was developing was essentially one that brought down the high matter of poetry and rhetoric to men's businesses and bosoms in the homely accents of prose. It was in this like the sermo humilis of the early Middle Ages. And this mode, as Auerbach has so well illustrated, provided a way of shedding a Biblical significance on the matter of everyday.[12] It represented in this a decisive break with the high rhetoric of the classical world: it showed also the challenge of the common man to the world of upper-class artificiality -- an aim identical with that of Fielding in his fiction. And behind this sermo humilis, legitimating both its style and its revolutionary social view, is the pattern of the Bible and its narratives.[13]

And yet Fielding does not quite give us the sermo humilis. It is there and it is not there. His narrative voice is not really like that of the unknown author of the martyrdom of Perpetua quoted by Auerbach. Nor is it like Augustine's who tells us in his Confessions that when he became a Christian and turned his mind to the scriptures he had to learn to "bend down [his] neck to its humble pace... for the swelling of my pride could not bear its humility."[14] Fielding does not bend his neck. His humility is tempered with the archness of the mock-sublime. If we examine his definition carefully we shall see that it contradicts itself. The new kind of narrative will be "prose" but it will also be "poem"; moreover, the term "comic epic" suggests that there will be both inflation and deflation. Immediately after offering us his definition, he finds it necessary to qualify his insistence on prose. It will not be quite Wordsworth's "language of men." Whilst excluding the high manner from his sentiments, he will reintroduce it into his diction he says in the form of Burlesque. All this suggests a certain ambivalence towards the sermo humilis as well as an ambivalence to the text of the Bible as its source and authority. That ambivalence finds its expression in the way that Fielding leans simultaneously on Josephus and the Bible itself.

There are other ways of expressing this dialectic. We should consider in this connection the foregrounding of the motif of dress throughout the novel. At all points we seem to have to do with the putting on and putting off of clothing. Early in the story we have Joseph being stripped of his livery and soon afterwards, as we have noted, he is left naked by robbers; the novel ends with Fanny putting off her garments as she prepares herself for her bridegroom -- "for as all her Charms were the Gifts of Nature, she could divest herself of none" (IV, xvi). As in King Lear nakedness signifies vulnerability, but also truth, authenticity and... Nature. The sight of Edgar's nakedness had been Lear's fundamental anagnorisis -- he confronts "unaccommodated man" himself. And yet dress is necessary too for authenticity; often it is the only evidence of our true identity:

Allow not nature more than nature needs,
Man's life is cheap as beast's

-- declares Lear. This is true of Fielding's novel also. Joseph Andrews achieves his true place in the world when he is invested in appropriate garments. Beau Didapper will be stripped of his false honours whilst Joseph will be clothed in scarlet. That is in a way the culmination of the story. It may be suggested that we have here a reflexive use of this metaphor, Fielding seeking through it to resolve the dialectic of the sermo humilis (nakedness) and the lofty style (ornament) which is at the heart of the genre he is seeking to shape. In the same Author's Preface, Fielding actually speaks of "the Dress of Poetry" in analogy of "the Dress of Men." It need hardly be said that such terms as "ornament" and "nakedness" were an inseparable part of the discussion of prose rhetoric both in Fielding's day and earlier. In the oft-quoted passage from Thomas Sprat's History of the Royal Society (1667) we hear of the Society requiring from all its members "a close, naked, natural way of speaking... preferring the Language of Artizans, Countrymen, and Merchants, before that of Wits, or Scholars."[15]

It will be seen that we have here something like a four-term homology in which natural is to artificial language as nakedness is to dress. We could go further and suggest that they both correspond to a further antinomy, that between Artizans (and Merchants) on the one hand and Wits (or Beaux) on the other. In short there is a class distinction implied in the passage from Sprat as the new middle class appropriates to itself the style of nakedness and the upper classes are condemned for their false ornaments. That sociological distinction is present in Fielding's novel also as an aspect of the confrontation of styles but it is not as simple as that. Didapper and Joseph also exchange roles. If at one point Didapper aspires to take the place of Joseph, as we have seen, so Joseph aspires to take the place of Didapper, assuming some of the dress and symbols of the upper class. In this inevitably he will betray the ideal of simplicity. Like Shakespeare, Spenser and Milton before him, Fielding has been caught in the inevitable dilemma of the Hebraic versus the Hellenic components of the western literary tradition.[16] Milton's hero in Paradise Regained, Book IV condemns Greek ornament and lavishes his praises on Hebrew nakedness but he does so in all the lofty terms of art. If Milton could not resolve the paradox, we should not expect Fielding to resolve it either.

However if Fielding ultimately leaves us with a paradox, we should be grateful to him for having defined the terms of it as clearly as he does. His ultimate statement comes by way of the pastoral mode. This is the mode evoked in the description of Fanny stripping for bed in the final chapter of the novel:

> She was soon undrest; for she had no Jewels to deposite in their Caskets, nor fine Laces to fold with the nicest Exactness. Undressing to her was properly discovering, not putting off Ornaments; For as all her Charms were the Gifts of Nature, she could divest herself of none. How, Reader, shall I give thee an adequate Idea of this lovely young Creature! the Bloom of Roses and Lillies might a little illustrate her Complexion, or their Smell her Sweetness: but to comprehend her entirely, conceive Youth, Health, Bloom, Beauty, Neatness, and Innocence in her Bridal-Bed; conceive all these in their utmost Perfection, and you may place the charming Fanny's Picture before your Eyes. (IV, xvi)

The irony of this passage is that the language puts on its finest dress, its ornaments of style, whilst at the same time and at exactly the same pace Fanny divests herself of her dress and ornaments. The language is here the most brocaded, the least naked in the book and we should add that it is at the greatest remove from the simplicity and directness of the Hebrew narrative from which the story of Joseph had been taken. Pastoral here brings art to the aid of Nature. The passage seeks to deceive us by the cunning inversion of its signifiers, but we are not deceived. Perhaps in this it acts out the nature of dress itself which half reveals and half conceals. Even as it denies Fanny's need of them, the passage piles up before our enchanted gaze the riches of Caskets, Laces, Charms and Gifts. We know it is the triumph of words only, but we revel in it as we escape the self-denying ordinance which the Royal Society had imposed on its members or which the Puritan orators had imposed on themselves.[17] The climax of inversion comes in the magnificently self-contradictory sentence:

> Undressing to her was properly discovering, not putting off Ornaments: For as all her Charms were the Gifts of Nature, she could divest herself of none.

The ambiguity of "discovering" is a master-stroke. It signifies uncovering as well as revealing. What we thought to be uncovering we "discover" to be the displaying of treasures. We have exchanged Fanny for "the charming Fanny's Picture," i.e. Fanny fixed and immortalized in a literary tradition which she can share with all those shepherdesses who always turned out to be ladies in disguise. Through her, Fielding defines a nakedness which will not require us to divest ourselves of Charms, Gifts or Ornaments. They are all in the passage. Indeed, like Fanny, we have not put them off, we have put them on. We have put them on even more grandly than before because from now they will be signs not of Artifice but of Nature. As such, they can be draped charmingly over the horns of our dilemma.

Notes

1.   Henry Fielding, The History of the Adventures of Joseph Andrews..., ed. Douglas Brooks (London: Oxford University Press 1971), p. 24. All subsequent quotations from this edition.

2.   Noted by Douglas Brooks, ibid., p. 370.

3.   Martin C. Battestin, The Moral Basis of Fielding's Art: A Study of Joseph Andrews (Middletown Conn.: Wesleyan University Press 1959), pp. 26-35.

4.   Ibid., pp. 41, 95 and passim.

5.   Robert Alter (Fielding and the Nature of the Novel, Cambridge, Mass.: Harvard University Press 1968, pp. 126-128) writes insightfully on the "dialectical reversals" of the theme of clothing and nakedness in the novel but he surprisingly fails to link this with the story of Joseph and his brothers and the wife of Potiphar.

6.   See Midrash Bereshit Rabba, 85, sections 2 and 9. The Rabbis find a number of links between the story of Judah and Tamar on the one hand and the story of Joseph on the other. In both there is mention of a kid of the goats -- in Judah's case it is payment for services rendered; in the case of Joseph, his brothers slay a kid and use it to bloody Joseph's coat. In both stories we have the expression "haker-na" -- "discern, I pray thee" in reference to the identification of personal effects.

7.   Cf. Herbert N. Schneidau, Sacred Discontent: The Bible and Western Tradition (Baton Rouge: Louisiana State University, 1976), pp. 289-291 on metonymy as the characteristic mode of the Bible itself.

8.   William Empson, "Tom Jones" (The Kenyon Review, XX, Spring 1958) reprinted in Fielding: A Collection of Critical Essays, ed. Ronald Paulson (Englewood Cliffs, New Jersey: Prentice-Hall 1962), p. 129. I find no reference to snow in the chapter. Empson was evidently misled by the reference to a brief hailstorm in the previous chapter.

9.   The Genuine Works of Flavius Josephus, The Jewish Historian..... Translated from the Original Greek....by William Whiston [folio] (London 1737). Subsequent quotations from this edition.

10.   Leo Tolstoy, "What is Art?" (1898), chapter xvi, trans. Aylmer Maude. Reprinted in The Great Critics, ed. J. H. Smith and E. W. Parks (New York: Norton 1951), p. 686.

11.   E. Auerbach, Mimesis, trans. Willard Trask (New York: Doubleday 1957), p. 15.

12.   E. Auerbach, Literary Language and its Public in Late Latin Antiquity and the Middle Ages, trans. Ralph Manheim (New York: Bollingen Foundation 1965), Chapter I, p. 27 f.

13.   Ibid., pp. 51-53.

14.   St. Augustine's Confessions, or Praises of God.... Newly Translated into English... (Dublin 1807), Book III, chapter 5 (p. 67).

15.   Edition of 1734, p. 113.

16.   My work to date has been much concerned with precisely this tension. See Jerusalem and Albion (London: Routledge and Kegan Paul 1964), passim and Hamlet and the Word (New York: Ungar 1971), passim.

17.   See Harold Fisch, "The Puritans and the Reform of Prose-Style", ELH, XIX (1952), pp. 229-248.

CHAUCER AND THE BIBLE: PARODY AND AUTHORITY IN THE PARDONER'S TALE

Lawrence Besserman

Hebrew University

In the last two decades of the fourteenth century, when Chaucer was at work on the Canterbury Tales, a central and most contentious subject in English religious and intellectual life was the role of the Bible: what were to be its legitimate uses? might it be translated into English? by what authority could it be interpreted? For the orthodox, of course, there was, and had always been, the Pope, at the head of the Church, to arbitrate and render final judgment in such matters. The Church came, in a sense, before the Bible. This was what John Henry Newman concluded almost 500 years after Chaucer, when he converted to Catholicism: the Bible all on its own could not withstand the ravages of what Newman called, in a marvelous turn of phrase, "the wild living intellect of man" -- and so the church must have the authority to decide the matter of validity in biblical interpretation.

But things were more perplexing in Chaucer's time than in Newman's. For in Chaucer's day there was a Great Schism in the Catholic Church; there were, in fact, two churches, and two popes, one at Rome, one at Avignon. Each pope had anathematized the other. When Chaucer says, in Troilus and Criseyde 2.36-37:

> For every wight which that to Rome went
> Halt nat o path, or alwey o manere...,[1]
> [Every person going to Rome
> Doesn't take the same road, or travel in the same manner]

his sophisticated, anticlerical (this doesn't mean irreligious) audience would surely have laughed at the thought that one way to get to Rome was to go to Avignon.

And there was also Wycliffe, whose first translation of the Bible into English appeared in the 1380's, and whose second, more elegant version was completed in the early 1390's (we are fairly certain now that Nicholas Hereford and John Purvey deserve the credit for these translations, and not their master, Wycliffe). These were the first complete English Bibles -- Old Testament, Apocrypha, and New Testament -- ever to appear; they were roundly attacked by the Church, and especially by the Friars. By 1408 it had become a crime to own an English Bible without a license from the local bishop, and Wycliffe and his followers were branded as heretics.

Wycliffe's answer to the corruption of the Church was a fundamentalist one: all power to the Bible, back to the words of Christ, back to the early, undivided Church of the New Testament. Chaucer, we may infer (I shall say more about this in a moment), was skeptical of the Wycliffe fundamentalist solution. The Bible was, after all, a book. If he had seen a few manuscripts of the Vulgate -- and with access to the libraries of his courtier friends he would have seen many -- then he knew that the manuscripts varied, in small details mostly, but sometimes in greater ones, too; controversial marginal glosses were not uncommon. The stability of the text, let alone its interpretation, was uncertain, a frail thing.

We should have this in mind when we find Chaucer twice worrying aloud about the accurate transmission and preservation of his own works:

> And for ther is so great diversite
> In Englissh and in writyng of oure tonge,
> So prey I God that non myswrite the,   1795
> Ne the mysmetre for defaute of tonge.
> And red wherso thow be, or elles songe,
> That thow be understonde, God I b4seche!
> (Troilus and Criseyde 5.1793-1798; Robinson, p. 479),

> Adam scriveyn, if ever it thee bifalle
> Boece or Toylus for to wryten newe,
> Under thy long lokkes thou most have the scalle, [a scabby disease]
> But after my makyng thou wrtye more trewe;
> So ofte a-daye I mot thy werk renewe,   5
> It to correcte and eek to rubbe and scrape;
> And al is thorugh thy negligence and rape [haste].
> ("Chaucers Wordes unto Adam, His Owne Scriveyn";
> Robinson, p. 534).

These passages make it quite clear that Chaucer knew, as did Newman, that a book may fall prey to the "wild living intellect of man." Or, perhaps worse, it may even fall into the hands of a lazy or -- worst of all -- an imaginative scribe.

In Chaucer's poetry -- mainly in the Canterbury Tales -- there are over 500 allusions to the Old Testament, Apocrypha, and New Testament, including hundreds of translations of verses that are Chaucer's own, not citations of the Wycliffite Bible, but original work translated directly from the Latin. Almost all the characters in the Canterbury Tales wield biblical verses and interpretations or glosses of biblical verses, for all sorts of strange and usually self-interested (not so strange) purposes. The terms glose and glosynge ('gloss' and 'to gloss, to interpret') almost always mean, in Chaucer's usage, 'to interpret falsely, to misinterpret'). The sharpest instance of this is seen in the Squire's Tale, when the "strange knight" who lists the magical properties of his sword claims "This is a verray sooth, withouten glose" (V 166) -- here 'truth' and 'gloss' are antithetical terms.

The Wycliffites and the Friars had each laid claim to the Bible; they each found support for their conflicting positions on major social and religious issues in the interpretation of key biblical texts. Chaucer's skeptical poetic response to this great Battle of the Book going on about him was not to choose sides, but rather to embody the strife in the Canterbury Tales. If one insists on asking "Whose side was Chaucer on?" then the answer must surely be that he was far more sympathetic to the reforming Wycliffites than he was to the Friars and other functionaries of the established Church. But his real interest was the disinterested, artful rendering of what he obviously must have regarded as great material. The Bible, to Chaucer, was a book, and, as W. Meredith Thomson says,[2] like any other book (be it by Ovid, Boethius, or Boccaccio), it was grist for Chaucer's poetic mill.

Let me illustrate this point, before passing to the Pardoner, with three instances of Chaucer's use of the Bible as a gloss to his poetical fictions.[3] First, from Troilus and Criseyde:

> I passe al that which chargeth nought to seye.
> What! God foryaf his deth, and she al so
> Foryaf, and with here uncle gan to pleye...
>
> (3.1576-1578)

These are the words of the narrator, the morning after Troilus and Criseyde's first night together. Criseyde is still in bed after Troilus has left, Pandarus has lifted her sheet, jokingly offered her a sword to cut off his head, and kissed her. As Robinson notes (p. 287, n. 1577), the expression "God foryaf his deth" had become proverbial, a way of saying just how far forgiveness could be carried. Its ultimate source is Luke 23:34: "Iesus autem dicebat: Pater, dimitte illis: non enim sciunt quid faciunt...." The narrator's daring analogy makes Criseyde into Christ, betrayed by Judas-Pandarus, put to "death" by Troilus. To explicate all the implications of this analogy -- the various ways in which it does or does not hold true to our sense of the narrative -- would require too lengthy a digression. Suffice it to say that it is at once playful and profoundly serious; approached from one direction it seems frivolous, comic, and even blasphemous, while from another it is weighted with pathos, foreboding, and sober religious sentiment.

The next two examples come from the Canterbury Tales. First, from the General Prologue:

> For this ye knowen al so wel as I,
> Whoso shal telle a tale after a man,
> He moot reherce as ny as evere he kan
> Everich a word, if it be in his charge,
> Al speke he never so rudeliche and large, [freely]
> Or ellis he moot telle his tale untrewe,   735
> Or feyne thyng, or fynde wordes newe.

He may nat spare, althogh he were his brother;
He moot as wel seye o word as another.
Christ spak hymself ful brode [freely, frankly] in hooly writ,
And wel ye woot no vileynye is it.   740

Here Chaucer, in his persona as poet-creator of the entire fiction, anticipates objections from those squeamish members of his audience who might be offended by the dirty words. His defense is on moral grounds: to be true to one's sources is to be honest; and then Chaucer invites an extraordinary comparison. Since Christ spoke brode 'freely, frankly' in the Bible, so will he, Chaucer, in the Canterbury Tales. But in what sense is the Canterbury Tales comparable to Scripture? And how are Christ's "frank" words in the New Testament comparable to the words of the Miller of the Shipman, scoundrels born of Chaucer's imagination? This we are left to ponder.

My third example, also from the Canterbury Tales, occurs in the link between Sir Thopas and the Tale of Melibee. Chaucer again uses the Bible as an explanatory gloss on his poem, but now he speaks in the fiction, as the diminished poet-pilgrim who takes orders from Harry Bailey:

...ye woot that every Evaungelist,
That telleth us the peyne of Jhesu Christ,
No seith nat alle thyng as his felawe dooth;   945
But nathelees hir sentence is al sooth,
And alle acorden as in hire sentence,
Al be ther in hir tellyng difference.
For somme of hem seyn moore, and somme seyn lesse,
Whan they his pitous passioun expresse--   950
I meene of Mark, Mathew, Luc, and John--
But doutelees hir sentence is al oon.
Therfore, lordynges alle, I yow biseche,
If that yow thynke I varie as in my speche,
As thus, though that I telle somwhat moore   955
Of proverbes than ye han herd bifoore
Comprehended in this litel tretys heere,
To enforce with th'effect of my mateere,
And though I nat the same wordes seye
As ye han herd, yet to yow alle I preye   960
Blameth me nat; for, as in my sentence,
Shul ye nowher fynden difference
Fro the sentence of this tretys lyte
After the which this murye tale I write.
(VII.943-964)

Here Chaucer the pilgrim-poet asserts that his Tale of Melibee stands in relation to its source as the Gospel narratives of the Passion stand to one another: not identical in every detail, but in the "sentence", that is, the "meaning." And the author of Melibee, Chaucer himself, stands, for a moment at least, by analogy, in the role of Evangelist. Again, we are left to puzzle over the dizzying implications.[4]

In each of the preceding three passages, Chaucer's use of the Bible to gloss his poetry is both playful and at the same time thought-provoking and profoundly serious. All three instances are not only self-ironic, but rich in important thematic and stylistic overtones. Nevertheless, in so far as they point outside of their fictional contexts, I think that they are meant to parody the current scene in biblical exegesis and interpretation. To put it simply: Chaucer mimics, for our amusement, the unashamedly and ingeniously selfish uses to which the Bible was being put by both the Wycliffites and their opponents, especially the Friars.[5]

II

There are some 25 biblical allusions in the 630-odd lines of the Pardoner's Prologue and Tale, making it almost as richly biblical in texture as the Wife of Bath's Prologue (with some 50 allusions in around 850 lines). But here Chaucer's handling of appeals to biblical authority and analogy is very different from the comical excesses of the Wife of Bath; it is very different, for that matter, from his handling of the same material in the examples I have cited from Troilus and Criseyde and the Canterbury Tales. The primary difference is that the laughter in the Pardoner's Tale is grim, and the parody is the darkest in Chaucer -- so grim, and so dark, that an otherwise temperate and subtle critic like Kittredge was sufficiently unsettled by the character of the Pardoner to declare that he was "the one lost soul among the Canterbury pilgrims" (a judgment worthy of the Parson, if of anyone, but surely not the literary critic's work).[6]

What was it about the Pardoner that upset Professor Kittredge so? And what made Harry Bailey so angry with the Pardoner? Their confrontation entails what is undoubtedly the moment of greatest verbal violence in the entire Canterbury Tales. To the Pardoner's suggestion that the Host be the first to buy one of his relics, Harry Bailey replies:

"Nay, nay! ... thanne have I Cristes curs!
Lat be ... it shal nat be, so theech! [so may I prosper]
Thou woldest make me kisse thyn olde breech, [trousers]
And swere it were a relyk of a seint,
Though it were with thy fundement depeint! [stained]   950
. . . .
I wolde I hadde thy coillons in myn hond
. . . .
Lat kutte hem of, I wol thee helpe hem carie;
They shul be shryned in an hogges toord!"   955
(VI.946-955)

We are no more likely to find out for certain what made Harry Bailey angry than what made Kittredge angry. But my reading of both the critic and the fictional character leads me to an inference: both the critic (master scholar and editor) and the character (master of ceremonies) were men who loved order -- things, facts, and people in their proper place or station, and the Pardoner, Chaucer's only fully drawn invert, is the master subverter of order. Inversion is the tonic note of the Pardoner's portrait in the General Prologue (he sings to the Summoner, "Com hider, love, to me!"; he has "heer as yelow as wex;" "No berd hadde he, ne nevere sholde have;" and the narrator says outright, "I trove he were a geldyng or a mare").

Inversion is the dominant note of the Pardoner's Prologue and Tale, too. He boasts that he poses as a saver of souls when he is really a destroyer of souls; he is a layman (we know this from circumstantial evidence: no tonsure, and he says that he preaches like a cleric) but he usurps the duties and powers of a priest (preaching and granting absolution). In his tale, three young men, seeking to find death and kill him, kill one another instead; an old man seeking to die can't manage it; a very moral exemplum is put to a most immoral use: extortion; and, finally, biblical allusions are used to hide or distort biblical truths.

In a sudden outburst of diabolical honesty, the Pardoner admits that he is the quintessential anti-biblical man:

> I wol noon of the apostles countrefete;
> I wol have moneie, wolle, chese, and whete....
>
> (VI.447-448)

Yet the biblical exempla come rolling easily off his tongue (VI.485-555 et passim). Throughout the Prologue and Tale, the Bible serves the Pardoner as a disguise; it is the cloak behind which he goes about his work as a self-proclaimed apostle of Antichrist. To distract and deceive his victims, he flaunts his knowledge of out-of-the-way scriptural authority:

> And over al this, avyseth yow right wel
> What was comaunded unto Lamuel--
> Nat Samuel, but Lamuel, seye I;
> Redeth the Bible, and fynde it expresly...
>
> (VI.583-586)

You may have heard of Samuel, he chides his listeners, but I'm talking about Lamuel (Proverbs 31:4ff,); you don't remember him? Repeatedly he encourages his audience -- it would be more accurate to say he dares or taunts them -- to read the Bible and see for themselves (cp. VI.483, 578, 742). All great victories in battle, in the Old Testament, were brought about by abstinence and prayer, he claims. Do you doubt it?

Looketh the Bible, and ther ye may it leere.

Looke, Attilla, the grete conquerour,

Deyde in his sleep, with shame and dishonour,

Bledynge ay at his nose in dronkenesse.

(VI.578-581)

It's all in the Bible; even the story of "Attilla, the grete conquerour."

Though these and other biblical allusions in the Pardoner's Prologue and Tale have received a good deal of critical attention, they could well stand further scrutiny in light of Chaucer's practice in citing the Bible elsewhere in the Canterbury Tales, and with due attention to the controversy about biblical authority raging between the Wycliffite reformers and Church apologists, especially the Friars -- a controversy whose significance for understanding Chaucer we have not yet properly measured. The task that lies ahead for Chaucer scholarship is large, and far beyond the scope of this paper. But to facilitate the larger task we must first have an accurate inventory of Chaucer's biblical allusions. I shall conclude by drawing attention to a hitherto unnoticed instance of the Pardoner's inverted use of biblical authority.

It occurs in the passage in which the Pardoner boasts about the salubrious effects of a shoulder bone from a "holy Jewes sheep" that he has in his possession. First he claims that the water in which this sheep's bone has been dipped will cure sick cattle (VI.353-360). Then he reveals that if the owner of the sick cattle drinks a draught of the same water, every week (he neglects to say for how many weeks!) before cockcrow, fasting, then his livestock will multiply (he neglects to say how fast!). He concludes:

And, sires, also it heeleth jalousie;

For though a man be falle in jalous rage,

Lat maken with this water his potage,

And nevere shal be moore his wyf mystriste,

Though he the soothe of hir defaute wiste,

Al had she taken prestes two or thre.

(VI.366-371)

This "cure" for jealousy is an inversion of the judicial ordeal to which, according to Numbers 5:11-31, a wife suspected of adultery must submit:

And the Lord spake unto Moses, saying, Speak unto the children of Israel, and say unto them, If any man's wife go aside, and commit a trespass against him, And a man lie with her carnally, and it be hid from the eyes of her husband, and be kept close, and she be defiled, and there be no witness against her... And the spirit of jealousy come upon him.... Then shall the man bring his wife unto the priest.... And the priest shall take holy water in an earthen vessel; and of the dust that is in the floor of the tabernacle the priest shall take, and put it into the water.... Then the priest shall charge the woman with an oath of cursing, and the priest shall say unto the woman, the Lord make thee a curse and an oath among thy people, when the Lord doth make thy thigh to rot, and thy belly to swell; And this water that causeth the curse shall go into thy bowels, and make thy belly to swell and thy thigh to rot.... And he shall cause the woman to drink the bitter water.... and if she be defiled... the water that causes the curse shall enter into her and become bitter.... And if the woman be not defiled, but be clean; then she shall be free, and shall conceive seed. This is the law of jealousies, when a wife goeth aside to another instead of her husband.... Or when the spirit of jealousy cometh upon him, and he be jealous over his wife, and shall set the woman before the Lord, and the priest shall execute upon her all this law. Then shall the man be guiltless from iniquity, and this woman shall bear her iniquity. (my italics; King James version)

Though he never refers to it explicitly, the Pardoner inverts the biblical ritual in a most ingenious way: the problem of adultery has been solved without any inconvenience to the parties involved -- it is the husband instead of the wife who drinks the potion, and there is no waiting to see if his belly swells or his thigh rots; the adulterous woman's ordeal has become the cuckolded husband's surefire cure.

Notes

1. See The Works of Geoffrey Chaucer, 2nd ed., F. N. Robinson (Boston: Houghton Mifflin, 1957), p. 402. All subsequent citations of Chaucer's poetry are from this edition.

(This is a very lightly edited version of a paper I read at the Bar-Ilan University conference on "Biblical Patterns in Modern Literature," May 20, 1982; I have included some documentation not offered in the oral presentation.)

2. "Chaucer's Translation of the Bible," in English and Medieval Studies Presented to J. R. R. Tolkien, ed. Norman Davis and C. L. Wrenn (London, 1962), pp. 192-193.

3. For discussion of these passages in a different context see my earlier paper, "Glosynge is a Glorious Thyng: Chaucer's Biblical Exegesis," Revue de l'Université d'Ottawa, 53 (1983), 333-334.

4. For further discussion, see D. W. Robertson, Jr., A Preface to Chaucer (Princeton, 1962; rpt. 1969), pp. 367-368.

5. See Penn R. Szittya, "The Antifraternal Tradition in Middle English Literature," Speculum, 52 (1977), 287-313.

6. George Lyman Kittredge, Chaucer and His Poetry (Harvard, 1915), p. 180.

"IN THE MORNING, BEHOLD, IT WAS LEAH":
GENESIS AND THE REVERSAL OF SEXUAL KNOWLEDGE

Zvi Jagendorf

Hebrew University

Genesis, the book of all beginning, is also about the beginning of sex and love. Both begin in the Garden: the first as a blessing given equally to animals and humans -- "Be fruitful and multiply", and the second implied as the reason why a man shall "leave his father and his mother, and (shall) cleave unto his wife; and they shall be one flesh." These are the ways Genesis talks about sex and love before the Fall. The former is a blessing given without differentiation to the as yet not clearly separated human pair. Both are addressed. Both are equal subjects of the twin verbs -- be fruitful and multiply. The latter, love, is more specifically the motive of a man. And here the text, looking forward towards civilisation and a peopled world, makes a general statement about the way the human community grows; by sons becoming lovers and by two people becoming one.

Before the tasting of the fruit, then, both the unspecific recipients of the blessing of sex and the more specific pair -- Adam and Eve -- are more like each other than different. Their natures and tasks are not yet distinguished from each other though their bodies are. If procreative sexuality of necessity demands a pair with a difference, then this original pair is understood to have the maximum of identity with the minimum of difference; but of this they are not yet aware.

The awareness of sexual difference is the fruit of knowledge and after the Fall Genesis imagines sex in a new and striking way: "And Adam knew Eve his wife." The metaphor of sex as knowing cannot in this context be accepted as a euphemism, "modesty of language" as some commentators have called it. For as Cassuto points out the Hebrew word "YADA" (knew) has behind it the full weight of the drama in the preceding chapters.

In them primal innocence is lost through the stealing of knowledge and clearly the first post-paradisal sexual act, called an act of knowing, is to be distinguished from the innocent, instinctual sexuality of Paradise by this new catastrophic element of awareness. In the first chapters of Genesis the same verb "YADA" means to know and distinguish between moral categories and to be aware of one's own and another's physical difference (nakedness). Underlying all the first instances of knowing is the concept of distinction rendered physically immediate by the image of the opened eyes.

If knowledge is the awareness of difference, then this awareness in sex separates the original twin-like innocent and instinctively sexual pair into a knower and a known, a subject and an object; one the male who acts and experiences and the other the female who is experienced and acted upon. Before the phrase "And Adam knew Eve his wife" the verb "YADA" is not found in the singular form. It is always THEY, the human pair, who

220532

know or are forbidden to know -- they knew they were naked. So this first description of a historical sexual encounter appropriates for the man both poles of the metaphor of knowledge, that of consciousness and that of sense, that of the mind and that of the body. He possesses mentally and physically that woman whose difference he recognises and uses.

Yet this striking fusion of body and mind in the verb to know contains the seeds of its own reversal. For there is no way in which this pristine clarity, this strict division into sexual subject and object can withstand the facts of human experience in the world, the deviousness and duplicity, the lies and illusions that mark the relations and especially the sexual relations between people. As the world fills up with men and women, as they compete with other and fight against the obstacles of nature, each sex exploiting its own natural advantages, relationships between them become more complicated. As the narrative of Genesis soon shows the initial simplicity of man's claim to mental and physical possession of his mate is relatively easy to undermine.

A man may know a woman (physically) and be mistaken about her identity. He may even know her carnally without any awareness whatsoever; he may be drunk. On the other hand, a woman being possessed in sex, apparently the object, may yet be the subject, the only possessor of the volatile element of awareness. She may know the man who mis-takes her. Thus the poles of the metaphor may be separated to great ironic effect. Sense and awareness may be divided up between the pair with the crucial controlling element of awareness going to the woman who was originally man's object.

Now Genesis never says that a woman "knows" a man. Hebrew, it seems, could not say that (though it could in the negative as Lot's daughters are said not to have known man, Gen. 19:8). Yet as the story of men outside Paradise begins to be told, the formal syntax of male knower and female known is famously subverted. In central examples, one of them the first love story in Genesis, the roles are reversed and ironic though benign comedies of sex are set out. These are comic episodes because they deal with man as l'homme moyen sensuel, a creature of his body and a slave of his instincts. They are also comic because they overturn the conventional authority of the male and uncover the blindness and weakness of the would-be knower. They are comedies finally because they enact a benign trick which exploits a natural observable difference between men and women in their sexual roles.

The man is true master in sex only temporarily -- unless he loses himself in the sensual ecstasy, his orgasm. Then his mastery is gone and he has nothing to show for it. Now power goes to the woman who bears the witness of the deed. She holds the seed in her womb. She is changed, in some cases, from virgin to wife. The comedy then lies in the contrast between man's claim to sexual mastery (knowledge) and the facts of common experience which show this claim to be based on the unfounded hubris of a creature who is in fact a slave of his biological role, his women, and in Genesis his God.

Lot would be a simple, maybe grotesque, example of this comic reversal. After the destruction of the cities of the plain he flees to a cave with his daughters. They are seemingly the only survivors of the cataclysm. In the strange seduction that follows, knowledge -- and therefore guilt -- are specifically and grotesquely taken away from him.

He is drunk and asleep and the text tells us in each incestuous instance "and he perceived not (VELO YADA) when she lay down nor when she arose" Gen. 19. 33, 35. On the other hand the conventionally male qualities, both purpose and knowledge, are given to his daughters who turn their father into a passive creature to be possessed and exploited for his seed. There is no guilt in this text and no recognition. Unlike Shakespeare's Bottom, Lot does not wake up to tell us about his strange, erotic dream. What has happened is that procreation has started again after a catastrophe and an escape. The rape of Lot is an act of desperation, a forced parody of that other act of sexual beginning outside Paradise when Adam knew his wife. But it is also proof that the world can be peopled again and a family saved out of a woman's initiative, a woman whose combination of cunning and instinct dwarfs the male, whoever he may be, into a role of passive dronelike service.

Genesis is interested in this kind of reversal. It has a tension and irony about it that the straightforward couplings of everyday procreation lack. The text, whose laconic qualities and reticence are famous, will not of course imagine any sexual encounter in detail, and the thoughts of the protagonists are not available to it, but this very restraint, in certain contexts, adds to the irony as the reader contemplates the implied interplay of presence and absence, awareness and illusion in situations which harness a man's passion and intentions to a purpose greater than itself. Saying this we must explicitly acknowledge the transcendental principle that works mysteriously through these webs of illusion and cunning. In biblical narratives the desires, needs and conflicts of men are subordinate to the power that shapes history by instigating and exploiting them. In the episodes considered in this study that divine power seems to be working specifically through the reversal of sexual authority and appears to be promoting the affairs of families and nations through the happy and natural combination of male weakness and female intelligence, resourcefulness and fertility.

Jacob's wedding night (Genesis 29) is one of the classic examples of the reversal in Genesis. It is both the climax and anti-climax of the Bible's first love story. (We will remember that the verb "AHAV" to love is used here only for the second time in Genesis with reference to the feelings of a man for a woman.) It is an episode given its shape by the purpose and desire of its protagonist Jacob who chooses one sister over the other, works for her, turning seven years into a few days by the force of his expectant will, and who demands her on the last day as the only wages of his labour. Here, then, is an intended moment of perfect possession in which Jacob will finally know and taste the unique object of his desire and love. He does. That is the sharp irony of the text's reticence. What this reticence implies is this: (and the traditional commentators and the Midrash say it in so many words) in the dark Jacob knows Leah sexually, but he knows her as Rachel, for the image in his mind prevails over the presence of the woman at his side.[1] On the other hand Leah knows Jacob truly and by imitating the woman he loves undergoes the change from virgin to wife, a change as real as Jacob's passionate ecstasy in the night is illusory. The hubris of the lover is thus destroyed. The light of day mocks his passion, his purpose of seven years, and reveals his error. To a reflective reader it also reveals the comic logic of measure for measure which repays Jacob in the same false coin he used to cheat his blind father. In the episode of the stolen blessing (Genesis 27) which is as fully sensual and as detailed as the wedding night is modest and laconic the same tensions are at play.

The parallel is famous. The two tricks mirror each other and their closeness in the text has suggested a causal connection to commentators. But what interests us is how the fullness of the rendering of one trick, the blessing, can spill over into a reading of the emptiness of the other. For the episode of the blessing is able to put into words the actual interplay of sensuality, awareness and illusion that cannot out of modesty be described in the wedding night.

There in his darkness is the blind, passionate male, Isaac, the father, the figure of authority whose gift of blessing via kissing, smelling and touch is so akin to the sexual gift. Moved by desire (hunger) and love of Esau, he presumes to <u>know</u> the object of his passion through all senses but sight. Opposite him is Jacob, like Leah in his own bed later, the unloved one playing the part of the loved one (Esau), imitating his brother's sensual presence, the smell, the hair, the clothes; even the taste of the desired food is an initiation. The blessing itself is like the sexual gift of the passion-blinded virgin groom to his open-eyed virgin bride. It changes the status of both the receiver and the giver. For once given it cannot be repeated in the same way. Like the receiver of the blessing (Jacob), the bride (Leah) carries in her womb the sign (a son) whose presence and effect only time will reveal. But the father, like the groom, gives this precious gift to an illusion communicated by his senses. Sensual knowledge has turned out to be the opposite of true knowledge.

The motif of the passionate male duped in bed by a cunning woman is a basically comic motif in folklore and secular literature. And it is so in Genesis where male purpose and authority are shown to be fragile and illusory. The man's intention, whether it be simply to sleep and be left alone like Lot, to make love to his bride like Jacob, or to lie with a harlot like Judah amounts to nothing. He is, to borrow Isabella's phrase from <u>Measure for Measure</u>: "Most ignorant of what he's most assur'd" -- his intimate sexual purpose.[2] But such ignorance is not in these cases destructive, whatever the disappointment, for a woman who possesses knowledge exploits his sex for good reason and for natural ends. Substituting her purpose for his, she does nothing worse than conceive children, often righting a wrong and certainly peopling the world -- which in those days was a good thing.

Not a love story like Jacob's, nor on the other hand a primitive tale of the victory of procreation over consciousness like the story of Lot, the tale of Judah and Tamar (Genesis 38) is in many ways the most complete working out of the motif of sexual mis-taking in Genesis. This story is more like the secular comic treatment of the bed trick because it takes place (unlike the Lot episode) in a detailed social setting of village and family like and (unlike Jacob's story) it carries the plot through to the all-important scene of recognition which justifies the woman.

Unlike Leah, who is passive and manipulated by Laban, Tamar is the sole arbiter of her own fate, the prime mover and protagonist of her own story. She uses her sex in a cunning way to capture for herself something wrongly denied her -- the desired status of a mother. Like the heroine of a Shakespearean tragi-comedy (indeed like Helena in All's Well) she knows how to exploit the natural weakness of her man by playing the degrading part of a loose woman at the roadside. But she turns this shameful episode of accidental sex into a serious obligation by taking pledges which eventually serve as proofs of paternity.

While our other examples of the trick give unequal weight to the various elements of the situation, the story of Judah and Tamar is worked out with grace and proportion giving each element its due. The reasons for the deception are there -- Judah's failure to keep his promise to give her his third son in marriage. The scene of bargaining between harlot and client at the roadside is imagined in detail. In it the man's importunate desire is offset by the woman's logical, cunning argument that draws out of Judah the pledges (signet, bracelet and staff) that will eventually justify her. Then comes the complication of the plot when Judah cannot find the harlot again to redeem his pledge. By separating the various strands of the plot, leaving Judah shamed without his pledges and having Tamar melt back into her widowhood, the story makes possible the all important, climactic scene of discovery and recognition.

In this scene the woman's shame only implied by Tamar's disguise as a harlot is made explicit as her pregnancy becomes public and is condemned. She is exposed and sentenced to death. Here as in countless final scenes of comedy to which indeed it is related, signs, identifying marks and objects come into play to establish names and relationships, discover the truth and solve riddles. Recognition of objects, of persons, above all of responsibility is the topic here as Judah the figure of authority and the stern judge of whoredom is confronted with the tangible evidence of his breach of promise as head of a family, his blindness as a lover and clearest of all -- his fatherhood.

This is such a classic and perfect recognition scene because it does not limit itself to the mechanical discovery of identities through signs. It is a scene of true moral recognition, for in its course Judah recognises his own guilt in his failure to provide the widow with a husband and justifies the woman whose apparent sexual sin was to be punished. So, as in comedy, at the very last moment in a scene of tense confrontation, the truth of past deeds comes into the open and an accidental wayside sexual impulse is transformed retroactively, into an act of natural compensation which establishes a family.

The story's order and unity may be summed up in the way the text is arranged around the crucial terms of knowledge and recognition. When Judah goes in unto Tamar by the roadside we are told that he "knew not" that she was his daughter-in-law. Judah's ignorance is the condition for this act of apparently wild, accidental sex. In the climactic scene Judah's recognition of his pledges justifies the woman. In this way honourable recognition redeems the potential harm of the blind act of passion. Finally, in a coda, the text returns to the denial of knowledge by the roadside. "And he knew her again no more", but now in a specifically sexual sense. Just as lack of knowledge originally made sex possible so knowledge and discovery finally forbid it. Unlike the protagonists of secular comedy the partners of this story must rémain separate. The happy end is children for Tamar rather than marriage. Salvation as so often in the Bible lies in the birth of sons.

The lines of tension we have found in these biblical episodes between sense, consciousness and recognition, between motive and consequence, all focussing on the crux of the use men and women make of sex, form a fundamentally comic pattern which we meet again in secular comedy and specifically in Shakespeare's tragi-comedies, Measure for Measure and All's Well that Ends Well, both plays which turn on the device of the exchanged partner.[3]

It is certainly not chance nor is it simply a feature of comic convention that there is so much ado about knowing in both the elaborate recognition scenes of All's Well and Measure for Measure:

> Duke: Know you this woman?
> Lucio: Carnally, she says. (Measure for Measure, 5.i.212-213)

It is not chance for these plays focus on the absurd, potentially dangerous pretensions of would-be knowers, lovers whose sexual authority and power are subverted by unrecognised women who, submitting to their man's lust and playing the whore, rob it of its sting. For Shakespeare the biblical usage is firstly a weapon of irony with which to chasten his young men's empty claims to the freedom of their desires and to knowledge of what they are and who they want. Yet given to the woman, this combination of sense and awareness, of physical and mental possession becomes a means of justification unfolded in a final scene to witness how a man's evil purpose is transformed unconsciously into a benign act. For here knowledge of the truth rests firmly with the women. Rejected like Leah, wronged like Tamar, Shakespeare's Helena and Mariana imitate their desired rivals, tolerate more or less consciously the degradation of being loved for someone else and work a kind of salvation out of an ambiguous sexual encounter.

The ambiguity of this encounter is at the heart of Shakespeare's perception of tragi-comic sexuality. Never, understandably, shown on the stage but imagined before-hand and contemplated afterwards, it is the unseen focal point of both plays. By rigidly separating the lustful ignorance of the male predator from the cunning knowledge of his apparent victim, Shakespeare loads the deed with significance. It both ties and unties the tragi-comic knot. It is an illusion and a reality, a crime in purpose and a lawful act in practice. It damns and saves the man, branding him liar and lecher; yet it is the one act that can lead him to recognize his true status which is like that of Judah -- a promise breaker, a mis-taker of a woman, a future father and a knower of himself through an acceptance of his misdeeds. Of course the Shakespearean pattern demands a wedding and the secular comedy's symbol of promise is not the pregnant woman but the pair united in marriage.

In our analysis of the biblical episodes we noticed differences in the amount of awareness granted the various protagonists. Jacob is terribly mistaken on his wedding night but the excited awareness of a bridegroom must in his case be imagined as well as his blindness. Leah on the other hand is mistaken about nothing but the text dampens our interest in her awareness, though it is a fact of the situation, by making her so clearly a counter in her father's plot against his nephew. The dramatist, although far freer to disclose his characters' thoughts, also chooses to whom he will grant greater degrees of consciousness. In Measure for Measure this belongs mostly to the man, Angelo, the sinning judge who is afflicted by the awareness of his sin -- but before and after the act -- although blind and ignorant in the bed. The women he mis-takes is by contrast passive in her knowledge, unbothered by its ambiguities and content to play her role according to the book:

> Duke: No? You say your husband.
> Mariana: Why just, my lord, and that is Angelo,
>> Who thinks he knows that he ne'er knew my body,
>> But knows, he thinks, that he knows Isabel's.
>> (5.i.200-203)

In All's Well on the other hand the shallow, rather trivial young protagonist Bertram, indulges unthinkingly in what he imagines to be a trivial, soldier's seduction. There the awareness is solidly with the rejected wife Helena who sleeps with him as his mistress and takes his ring as a pledge. Her sense of her ordeal, after the fact, is very different from Mariana's impersonal cleverness in the recognition scene of Measure for Measure. Shakespeare makes us understand in Helena's words what Leah might have thought in Jacob's arms:

> But, O strange men!
> That can such sweet use make of what they hate,
> When saucy trusting of the cozen'd thoughts
> Defiles the pitchy night; so lust doth play
> With what it loathes for that which is away.
>> (4.iv.21-25)

Such words come very close to imagining the reality in the conventional situation, here the disturbing mixture of passion, disgust, participation and observation that is the woman's burden as the knowing partner in the bed-trick. In language reminiscent of Sonnet 129 Helena grapples with the lust that feasted on her body. She participated in it. She was used sweetly but she was also abused. She was aware of the hatred for her in the man coupled in intimacy with her. Helena is making us think here not of the saving fact of her impregnation which is the point of the biblical episodes, but of the ordeal of consciousness that accompanied the moments of pleasure and of the defilement that her successful impersonation made her undergo.

It would be more than the fabric of the comedy could stand if this perception were taken any further. Helena is not moved from now on by disgust or the desire for revenge.

On the contrary, once the consummation is over, the bed-trick takes on its conventional magical property as a device of resolution and the source of recognition.

Consciousness has its limits in the comic structure, for as this play's title says and as the biblical stories show, it is the end that matters. The means may be ambiguous, disturbing and as grotesque as Lot's rape, but they are of less weight than the providential outcome. Such sanctifications of "ends" in the person of the justified, often pregnant woman has a religious quality to it even in secular comedy. In All's Well, as in Shakespeare's Romances an aura of the miraculous envelopes the unmasking and the riddle solving of the recognition scene when the apparently dead are found to be alive and the rejected are shown to be with child.

As in the recognition scene of Judah and Tamar, the woman holds one side of the stage unravelling the web in which the man has been caught. For the man opposite her, the would-be sexual predator, the ironies in the Hebrew metaphor of knowledge are pieced out in great and painful detail. For in the light of his failure to know carnally the woman he desired, the whole edifice of his pretences and betrayals is split wide open. For him the elaborate stages of the recognition process with its atmosphere of courtroom and auto da fe are in essence a slow and painful return to the bed in which he knew his wife without knowing it. Caught in this shame, known by all those around him, judged by those above him, the man cannot but face the true, unflattering image of himself. Recognition is harder in this comedy than in the biblical episode because we demand more than the acceptance of responsibility through redeeming pledges. We demand an inward movement which may in the end be a matter of faith -- our own. Shakespeare's young man in All's Well makes it a condition of knowledge:

> Bertram: if she my liege can make me know this clearly
>   I'll love her dearly, ever, ever dearly.
>   (5.iii.309-310)

Although the permissibility of bedside lights and full-voiced conversation in the bedroom made the device of the substituted partner harder and harder to take after the seventeenth century, the irony of physical closeness and mental distance which underlies it persists in the modern understanding of sex and is perhaps given its clearest and most schematic treatment in Goethe's novella Elective Affinities. This has been closely analysed recently by Tony Tanner in his book Adultery and the Novel but I would like to draw attention to the connection between Goethe's work and the texts I have already discussed.[4]

Goethe's essentially modern contribution to the ancient tension of sense and awareness in sex is to grant equally to his man and his woman full and destructive consciousness. To use the terms of Genesis: their eyes are open and they knew each other. In this episode a man and his wife come together in sexual embrace but each is aware of the ghostly presence of another beloved one in the bedroom. As Goethe says this is a kind of bridal night. The wife, Charlotte, has retained the youthful modesty of a bride, but in reality it is a painful parody of the consummation of a marriage, for the bride wishes her husband were not there and he, seduced by darkness and his feverish imagination, holds another woman in his arms.

In our earlier examples the seductive imagination controlled only the man. His was the error, the hubris of the would-be knower, and this error faced the true knowledge of the woman. In Goethe's scene there is no actual mistaking, no real sin, but that is just why the act is so destructive and tragic in its consequences. For error is pardonable and in the comic structure of our other examples a man's mistake can be balanced by the benign purpose of the woman. But this mutual, open-eyed sinning of the mind is irredeemable just because it is entirely mental. The illusion of lust that in some of our earlier examples is revealed finally to produce a saving act is here an act of damnation because its guilt is firmly rooted in the mind, is more real than what the body does. In the biblical tales the mind is weaker than the body just as man is weaker than woman and the end is of more weight than the means. In Goethe's tale the guilt of sinning intention makes for the most tragic consequences. The child conceived in this bed bears the shape of the imagination of his parents. He is a changeling possessed of the features of the absent partners, a child of the thought of sin and of death.

In Goethe's secular hell of unfulfilled passions we have perhaps come as far as is possible from the essentially benign mechanism of sexual trickery found in Genesis and in Shakespeare's tragi-comedy. Consciousness which after Paradise becomes a playful and volatile element in the sexual game is no longer playful in this bedroom of a constricting marriage. When awareness is total and illusion is mutual, and when there is no difference between the stance of the man and that of the woman there is no room for a benign providence to work. There is indeed no providence, but only a kind of moral determinism which produces the changeling child and then demands his death.

"Adam knew Eve his wife" is the first move in a game of mind and body in which the permutations and shifts are many. Goethe's couple of open-eyed, trapped escapists are caught in an endgame in which there is nowhere to move. The true rhythms of their bodies act out a lie. Married, living rational lives, far removed from the primitive cunning and passionate blindness of the old sexual encounters they pay the price exacted by the facade they maintain, lacking even the indulgent cynicism of Shakespeare's modus vivendi in Sonnet 138:

Therefore I lie with her, and she with me,
And in our faults by lies we flattered be.

The Zohar's commentary on Jacob's wedding night may serve as our epilogue.[5] For the Zohar the image in the mind is primary to all action in the world. All things in the world, it says, are consequences of thought and mental activity and this holds true of sexual activity. A man who makes love to his wife while his mind is possessed by another's image is said to sow false seed and the child is considered a changeling, its birth open to evil influence. In its reading of Jacob's wedding night the Zohar concentrates on the effect of the mental image on the act of generation. Was Reuben this kind of changeling child? Was Jacob this kind of man? Surely not. This is where Providence intervenes to make all well that ends well. The biblical time scheme is large, far larger than the life span of a couple in a novel. The Zohar finds a text in Chronicles I.5 that says the birthright went from Reuben, Leah's son, to the sons of Joseph, Rachel's child. Here, then, is proof of the primacy of thought. The seed that left Jacob's body under the control of the thought of Rachel achieves its aim, finally, in spite of all the body's weakness. Thus the Zohar, having to accept the fact of the trick, defeats it by making Rachel pregnant with a thought. The Patriarch is saved from sin. The night is not defiled. The man, for a change, wins the game.

Notes

1. The Midrash takes pains to give the situation vraisemblance. We are told, for instance, that the lights were extinguished against the suspicious Jacob's wishes, that Rachel connived with Leah giving away certain signs agreed between her and Jacob and that Jacob called his 'bride' by the name of Rachel all that night and that Leah answered to her sister's name. This material is collected in Louis Ginzberg: The Legends of the Jews, 7 vols., The Jewish Publication Society of America, Philadelphia, 1909-1928. The legends about Jacob are in Vol. I, pp. 355-361.

2. Measure for Measure, Arden Shakespeare, ed. J. W. Lever, Methuen, London, 1965.

3. All's Well That Ends Well, Arden Shakespeare, ed. G. K. Hunter, Methuen, London, 1959.

4. Tony Tanner, Adultery in the Novel, Johns Hopkins University Press, Baltimore, 1979, pp. 187-199.

5. I have used the authoritative modern Hebrew collection of Zohar texts: I. Tishby, The Wisdom of the Zohar, 2 vols., Bialik Institute, Israel, 1961. The passage I refer to is in Vol. 2, pp. 646-649.

CANTICLES AND THE JUXTAPOSITION OF HOLY AND SEXUAL
IN SEVENTEENTH-CENTURY ENGLAND

Noam Flinker

Ben-Gurion University of the Negev

Allusions to Canticles in Renaissance English literature generally suggest an implicit reading of the biblical text echoed. In many cases this interpretation corresponds fairly accurately to the generally accepted allegorical understanding of Canticles as a love song between Christ and his Church. Such allusive texts establish a contextual norm to be compared with less predictable allusive approaches to the Bible.

The allegorical reading of the Song of Songs was responsible for a great many habits of thought and association during the Renaissance and earlier periods. Even a cursory glance at paraphrases and commentaries from this period make evident the allegorical way in which readers of the Bible perceived the significance of the Song of Solomon. The male speaker is generally identified with Christ and the female expresses the spiritual love of the Christian Church.

The orthodox regularity with which such interpretations translate the sensuous immediacy of the sexual language of the Canticles into allegory is somewhat remarkable for the modern reader. Thus when the Song of Songs speaks of kisses ("Let him kiss me with the kisses of his mouth: for thy love is better than wine"[1] [1.2]), Thomas Brightman explains:

> The Church then desireth to be instructed with the words of her Bridegroome, which she calleth Kisses, as the most assured pledges of the bridegroomes love; neither can any thing be compared with this love; therefore she preferreth it before wine, which is chiefly esteemed among those things which taste most pleasantly: for the comparisons of this song are taken from such things which do chiefly tickle up the sences: because our infirmity is such, that we commonly feele no greater pleasure in this life, then in those things which pertaine to these inferior sences."[2]

The woman in Canticles speaks of having her lover "lie all night betwixt my breasts" (1.13) and John Trapp comments:

> This is Christ's proper place.... But too often he is shut out, and adultery found between the breasts (as Hosea ii.2); there they carried the signs of their idolatry (as Papists now do their crucifixes), to testify that the idol had their hearts.... As the wife will keep her bed only for her husband, although in other

things she is content to have fellowship with others, as to speak, sit, eat, drink, go, etc.; so our consciences (which are Christ's wives) must needs keep the bed -- that is, God's sweet promises -- alonely for ourselves and our husband to meet together, to embrace and laugh together, and to be joyful together. If sin, the law, the devil, or anything would creep into the bed, and lie there, then complain to thy husband Christ, and forthwith thou shalt see him play Phinehas's part, etc.[3]

These commentators are insistent upon the spiritual significance of the fleshly metaphors of the Bible, even though they do not choose to follow the lead of more cautious writers who avoided the entire issue of sexuality in dealing with Solomon's Song. George L. Scheper quotes such Protestant exegetes as James Durham or Nathanael Homes as examples of commentators who, "when the sexual aspect of the union tends to surface ... avert their eyes and allude to the dangers of lewd interpretation."[4]

These comments suggest that for many Renaissance readers, the metaphors of the Song of Songs helped to break down conventional barriers between the holy and profane. Biblical metaphors that involve sexuality were assumed to concern a relevant correspondence with the spiritual, but the exact nature of the relation between body and spirit was open to significant individualization. The commentators range from the cautious (such as Durham or Homes) to the more direct and bold (such as Brightman or Trapp), but the essential differences between them are slight. Men of letters, however, are considerably more divided. Robert Aylett's The Bride's Ornaments (1621, 25) is allegorical and conventional in its cautious imitation of the commentators. Poets such as John Donne, John Milton, and Andrew Marvell, however, used the conventions to achieve a striking degree of poetic creativity. Donne's use of holy and sexual imagery may derive from allegorical readings of the Song of Songs but this is by no means certain. Aylett, Milton, and Marvell, however, all allude to Canticles so that an examination of the function of the echoes in each poet will help to focus upon specific ways in which the biblical text affected seventeenth-century English verse.

Robert Aylett's The Bride's Ornaments combines a very ordinary conception of the allegorical force of the sexual tensions in Canticles with a programmatic organization of Protestant meditations on a series of religious values perceived as allegorical woman such as Charity, Humility, Joy or Zeal. The meditations are preceded by a verse translation of the Song of Songs which thus serves as an introduction to the theological material. Many of the meditations later allude back to the introduction and inevitably echo the orthodox interpretative tradition about Canticles, the allegorical nature of the nuptial metaphor. A few examples of Aylett's method should suffice to illustrate.

As he proceeds to describe spiritual or heavenly love, Aylett's narrator refers to conjugal relations as an image of Christ's love for this Church:

Behold! by all these Names, he doth inuite
Vs to embrace his mutuall heau'nly Loue,

He calls vs. Friend, Child, Sister, Spouse, Delight;
His Seruants sends vs curteously to moue,
    To royall Banquets and sweet beds of Loue,
    By grace adopting vs, to be Coheires
    Eu'n with himselfe, of glorie great aboue,
    No cost or paines, not his owne Blood, he spares,
But like a Father, Husband, Friend, for vs he cares.[5]

Aylett's summaries of chapters three and four of Canticles are relevant here, along with his translations of sections of these chapters. Terms such as "Spouse" or "bed" are taken directly from the Bible. Aylett summarizes chapter three:

The Church her Spouse in bed doth seeke, not find:
Shee doth arise, and seekes him in broad way. (p. 4)

Invitation, friends and delight are all central to chapter four:

Christ here the graces of his Church commends;
His rauisht heart with loue to her doth show:
Into his Garden he inuites his friends,
Where in abundance all delights doe flow. (p. 6)

Although the entire chapter is relevant, Aylett's rendition of 4.10 is most to the point:

My Spouse, my Sister, how faire is my Loue! Christ.
Oh, how much better are thy brests than wine! (p. 7)

The "royall Banquets" are described in chapter two:

        Oh how I long
    Vnder his pleasing shadow to abide!
    His fruit delightfull is vnto my tongue,
    He sets me at the banquet by his side,
And with sweete loue as with a Banner doth me guide. (p. 3)

Throughout his translation, Aylett makes the allegorical significance of the sexual images clear, yet he does not try to avoid the sensuous frankness of the original Hebrew. His point is that man's sexual nature is, properly understood, a hint of the sweetness of Christ's love. Love is all of a kind if we understand it rightly and its sexual roots are totally misapprehended if regarded as mere physical or earthly pleasure.

    In his meditation "Of Zeale and Godly Iealousie" Aylett's speaker employs violent images of fire, passion, and anger as he elaborates upon the significance of jealousy. He

concludes with a sense of past sinfulness and a desire for future salvation in terms of
negative and positive (i.e. holy) sexuality:

> Oh were mine head a conduit full of teares,
> Mine eyes two rocks continually to run,
> As well to cleanse foule <u>Lusts</u> of youthfull yeeres,
> As coole the zealous flames in me begun;
>   Had I thus once my Bridegrooms presence won,
> I never would let goe my well laid hold,
> Till hee into my <u>Mothers</u> chamber come,
> With sweet embraces ay, mee to infold,
> His ardent <u>Loue</u> would neuer let my <u>zeale</u> grow cold.[6]

It is significant that Aylett chose to refer to Canticles 3.4 here. His own translation of
this passage is less sexually explicit than the conclusion of the meditation above:

> I would not let him goe, but held him fast,
> Vntill him to my Mothers house I wrought,
>   And to her Chamber, that conceiu'd me, brought.[7]

Aylett's speaker identifies in the meditation with the Church who speaks allegorically in
Solomon's Song. His desire for Christ is presented in lushly allusive references to
Canticles. There is a paradox here in that the allegorical allusion is more explicitly
sexual than the passage itself but this is almost to be expected since the sexual metaphor
has an unmistakably spiritual reference in the meditation, whereas a parallel stress of the
sexual in the translation of Canticles might have suggested too much sexuality and thus
have proved undesirably distracting.

Aylett's attitude towards sexuality is uncompromising in condemning fleshly
experience. He is careful to distinguish between his allegorical understanding of the
metaphors of Canticles and fallen human desire. His treatment of Zeal in terms of the
metaphor of passion makes the distinction most explicitly:

> Oh <u>blessed fire</u>! If kindled aright,
> It burne with Loue of Heauen, and holy things,
> Retaining in our hearts, both day and night,
> His sweet imbraces, who is <u>King</u> of <u>Kings</u>,
> Loathing the worlds vaine wanton wicked dallyings.
> . . . .
>   O see the force of Loue and Zeale doth moue
> All powers that in <u>Heau'n</u>, <u>Earth</u>, <u>Hell</u> transcend;
> Grant <u>thee</u> alone I zealously may <u>Loue</u>;
> And let thy <u>Iealousie</u> me safe defend,
> That neuer to <u>strange</u> Gods I my affection bend.[8]

On a conscious level, then, Aylett's speaker goes to considerable trouble to distinguish between his metaphors and "vaine wanton, wicked dallyings." This, of course, is well within the Protestant tradition about Canticles.

It is of note that the sexual identity of the speaker in the Bible does not affect the speaker's choice of metaphor. Surely Aylett could have found a passage in which the man is speaking of his passion for the woman. Sexual roles are irrelevant to spiritual readings of their significance. Human sexuality is a metaphor for something beyond itself and as such the most passionate appeals to sexual longing and "ardent Loue" are meant to indicate the true meaning of these human experiences. Although it is clear that Aylett is sublimating his own sexual energies into the spiritual metaphors of the poem, it is important to see that the relevance of the sexual metaphor stops short of sexist role playing. The meditation opens with a desire for holy fire to ravish the speaker's soul and it concludes with the allusion to the passionate words of the Bride. In other parts of the meditation, jealousy is presented from the point of view of male and female. Thus it is human sexuality rather than the more limited sexism of male domination that informs Aylett's imagery.

Although Aylett's treatment of Canticles corresponds quite closely to the ideas and outlooks of most seventeenth-century theologians, it does not necessarily follow that such a context is adequate for reading all allusions of the period. Milton provides a relevant illustration. One might have expected that the Protestant traditions shared by Milton, Aylett, and Spenser, not to mention a number of striking parallels between The Bride's Ornaments and Paradise Lost, would also have found its way into Milton's epic. This however, is not the case. Whereas right use of passion for Aylett meant "Loue of heauen, and holy things" as opposed to "vaine wanton, wicked dallyings," Milton's address to "wedded Love" (Paradise Lost IV. 750 ff) sets up the conditions whereby this "perpetual Fountain of Domestic sweets" (l. 760) takes on central importance in the cosmos. After insisting upon the prelapsarian sexual relations between Adam and Eve, Milton's narrator alludes to Canticles as a means of describing this explicitly sexual love. Adam awakens at the beginning of Book V and whispers to Eve:

> Awake
> My fairest, my espous'd, my latest found
> Heav'ns last best gift, my ever new delight,
> Awake, the morning shines, and the fresh field
> Calls us, we lose the prime, to mark how spring
> Our tended Plants, how blows the Citron Grove,
> What drops the Myrrh, and what the balmie Reed,
> How Nature paints her colours, how the Bee
> Sits on the Bloom extracting liquid sweet.[9] (V. 17-25)

The echoes of Canticles 2.10, 13 and 7.12 have been pointed out by various scholars.[10] The male speaker in the Song of Solomon addresses the woman:

Rise up, my love, my fair one, and come away. (2.10)

Later on he suggests:

> Let us get up early to the vineyards;
> let us see if the vine flourish,
> whether the tender grape appear,
> and the pomegranates bud forth:
> there will I give thee my loves.   (7.12)

Adam's language applies very similar patterns from Canticles to his own human love for Eve. Perhaps it would be more accurate to say that Adam's love song to Eve here was later imitated by Solomon in his Song so that the original version is recorded in Paradise Lost. In any case, it is plain that Adam's view of his song is hardly allegorical. He is singing to Eve and the language of Canticles must therefore be understood on a literal, sexual level, the theologians notwithstanding.

In the prelapsarian world of Paradise Lost there is nothing surprising about such a natural or sexual interpretation of Canticles. Raphael assures Adam that

> Whatever pure thou in the body enjoy'st
> (And pure thou wert created) we enjoy
> In eminence, and obstacle find none
> Of membrane, joynt, or limb, exclusive barrs:
> Easier then Air with Air, if Spirits embrace,
> Total they mix, Union of Pure with Pure
> Desiring; nor restrain'd conveyance need
> As Flesh to mix with Flesh, or Soul with Soul. (VIII. 622-29)

Thus the commentators on Canticles are not necessarily contradicted by Milton in the earthly, implicitly sexual allusions to Solomon's Song. Christ's love for the Church might indeed be akin to Adam's love for Eve before the fall. However, the undivided cosmos of God's creation makes no poetic distinction between physical and spiritual, so that the experience of love for both Adam and Raphael is similar in nature. The angel is merely considerably more refined. Nevertheless, the reading of Canticles that is implicit in Adam's speech is not an allegorical one. The fear of the theologians that "our Carnalness makes it hazardous and unsafe, to descend in the explication of these Similitudes"[11] is ignored as Solomon's Song becomes a model for Adam's fleshly love for Eve.

Paradise Lost thus provides at least one instance of a literal view of Canticles. Adam as poet was not bound by the understandings and clichés of traditional exegetes as was Aylett's narrator. This suggests that the seventeenth-century poet may have had considerably more freedom to interpret biblical texts than is generally indicated by modern scholarship, at least with regard to Canticles. The case of Andrew Marvell is most striking. Given a choice between the allegorical interpretations of Aylett and the literal allusions of Milton's Adam, it is hardly a foregone conclusion that Marvell must have accepted the more orthodox view of Solomon's Song. A consideration of the choice between Aylett and Milton suggests a third possibility as well: ironic ascription of Aylett's method to a speaker who is less than conscious of the implications. This, I suggest, could have been Marvell's approach to his "Nymph complaining for the death of her Faun."

The echoes of Canticles in Marvell's poem have attracted scholarly attention since Muriel C. Bradbrook and M. Gwyneth Lloyd Thomas pointed to the allusions and suggested that "the love of the girl for her faun is taken to be a reflection of the love of the Church for Christ."[12] In 1945, Douglas Bush suggested that if the poem has "any ulterior meaning, it may be an Anglican's grief for the stricken Church,"[13] although this comment was not included in his second edition. In response to Edward Le Comte's objections to Bradbrook and Thomas,[14] Karina Williamson pointed out "that the poem certainly has 'religious overtones,' even if they are not sufficient to justify a cohesive religious interpretation."[15] She went on to claim that "the cardinal reason for supposing that the poem is intended to have religious associations is that the central passage seems so clearly to draw on the Song of Solomon." Other scholars such as Ruth Wallerstein, Geoffrey Hartman, Rosalie Colie, and Donald Friedman also relate the relevance of Canticles to Marvell's poem.[16] Of the scholarship that I have seen, however, only the work of Earl Miner suggests the possibility of a less allegorical understanding of Solomon's Song here: "It seems possible to conclude, however, that Marvell sought in the Garden passage a glancing, witty, but serious parody of The Song of Songs that reveals more about the innocence lost by the Nymph and more about her solemnity concerning the Faun than any patterning of the Nymph upon the Church and the Faun upon Christ."[17] Milton's example of a literal approach to the Song should be seen as a definite alternative to the spiritual readings that so many scholars have required of Marvell. Stanley Stewart's admirable scholarship in The Enclosed Garden: The Tradition and Image in Seventeenth-Century Poetry leads him to insist upon a view of the Song of Songs that is too narrow: "For the context of the Song of Songs, as Marvell received and used it, was, above all other things, distinctly allegorical."[18]

The scholarship that has pointed toward the allegorical traditions available to Marvell about the Song of Songs cannot tell us what the poet thought about these materials. The tone of the Nymph's lines that echo Canticles makes it clear that something more complicated than Adam's echoes of the same biblical poetry is involved. This, however, does not mean that Marvell shared the views of Aylett and the allegorists. The Nymph may see her Faun as a Christ figure and deliberately echo Canticles to add to her sense of its importance but if so, there remains an ironic gap between her understanding of her condition and the poet's. Since there is no way to prove the existence of such a gap, I can only suggest its dimensions in an effort to establish a reading of the poem that will attend to some of the problems raised.

The Nymph opens her "Complaint" with a description of the violent act of the "wanton Troopers" who have shot her pet. Although she claims that she wants to forgive the murderers, she fears that "Heavens King" will not allow this. Her logic, however, soon becomes irrational as she assumes that the Faun is somehow Christlike in its power to redeem:

> Though they should wash their guilty hands
> In this warm life blood, which doth part
> From thine, and wound me to the Heart,
> Yet could they not be clean: their Stain
> Is dy'd in such a Purple Grain.
> There is not such another in
> The World, to offer for their Sin. [19] (18-24)

She is confused and moves from an unarticulated sense of the Faun as Christ to the absurdity of the troopers wanting to wash their hands in its blood in order to cleanse themselves. Of course, were the Faun equivalent to Christ, the Nymph's arguments would not necessarily hold in any case, since then the sacrifice would apply even to the crucifiers (if only they accept him).

The Nymph's story then proceeds with an account of her "Unconstant Sylvio," the gift of the Faun, and her regard for its love:

> Thy Love was far more better than
> The love of false and cruel men.   (53-54)

In her description of the garden where she would play with the Faun, the Nymph refers to familiar aspects of the landscape from Canticles:

> I have a Garden of my own,
> But so with Roses over grown,
> And Lillies, that you would it guess
> To be a little Wilderness.   (71-74)
> . . . .
> Among the beds of Lillyes, I
> Have sought it oft, where it should lye;
> Yet could not, till it self would rise,
> Find it, although before mine Eyes.
> For, in the flaxen Lillies shade,
> It like a bank of Lillies laid.
> Upon the Roses it would feed,
> Until its Lips ev'n seem'd to bleed:
> And then to me 'twould boldly trip,

And print those Roses on my Lip.
But all its chief delight was still
On Roses this its self to fill:
And its pure virgin Limbs to fold
In whitest sheets of Lillies cold.
Had it liv'd long, it would have been
Lillies without, Roses within.   (77-92)

In the Song of Songs, the woman tells those who ask of his whereabouts that her

>   beloved is gone down into his garden
> to the bed of spices,
> to feed in the gardens,
> and to gather lilies.
> I am my beloved's,
> and my beloved is mine:
> he feedeth among the lilies.   (6.2-3)

Elsewhere the man describes his beloved as one "that cometh out of the wilderness" (3.6, 8.5) and the woman charges the daughters of Jerusalem "that ye stir not up, nor awake my love, till he please" (2.7, 3.5, 8.4). The Faun, then, feeding in the gardens among the lilies and hiding from the Nymph is compared to the lover in Canticles who is sought by his beloved, and finally found and brought to her mother's house and bedroom (3.1-4). Some of the Nymph's lines should be read as deliberate attempts on her part to establish parallels between her situation and that of Canticles. Motifs such as "Wilderness" or the hiding Faun provide explicit echoes of the Bible in an oblique manner that has attracted the attention of numerous scholars.

Although the imagery is obviously taken from Canticles, the significance of the echoes remains elusive. If we merely understand the Nymph on a literal level, she seems to be setting up a slightly perverse comparison between the Faun and a lover, like Catullus's Lesbia and her sparrow (II, III) or Skelton's "Philip Sparrow." Many scholars have preferred to take the allusions to the Song of Songs more allegorically and have then been faced with the enigmas such an allegory imposes upon the rest of the poem. A less problematic solution would limit the allegorical relevance of the Nymph's allusions to her own somewhat befuddled sense of the world. She may confuse her pet with a lover, but she goes beyond the ladies in Catullus or Skelton and makes her pet into Christ as well. From this point of view, the poet remains highly critical of his heroine who becomes more and more hysterical as the poem proceeds.

The Nymph's hysteria reaches a climax as the Faun actually dies. She exclaims:

>   O help! O help! I see it faint:
> And dye as calmely as a Saint.   (93-94)

She then proceeds to mourn her pet and prepare for her own consequent death. The Nymph is out of control of herself and deliberately allows allegorical language to inflate her description of her pet with corresponding exaggeration and ridiculousness. The images from the allegorical tradition associated with Canticles elevate the Faun to the level of Christ and the Nymph thus sees herself as somehow parallel to the Church. We need only go one step further to recognize the poet's rejection of all this as absurd and the ironic vision shifts the tone here from enigmatic to ironically dramatic. It is as if Marvell were recalling the dullnesses of poets like Aylett and subjecting them to critical ridicule. The Nymph echoes Canticles to suggest an allegorical pattern that reader and poet reject as unwarranted on any level.

The significance of allusions to the Song of Songs in the poetry of Aylett, Milton, and Marvell is thus complicated and individualistic. These analyses and comparisons posit a tension between the allegorical understanding of the biblical text and a more literal, essentially earthly reading. The issue would have been much further complicated by the addition of examples from more exclusively devotional poets such as Herbert, Vaughan, Crashaw, or Taylor, but that is a subject for further study. My concern here has been to provide poetic documentation of very explicit use of allegorical tradition in Aylett's allusions to Canticles and then juxtapose these rather simple poems against passages from Milton and Marvell that are considerably more supple and complicated. Theological assumptions about the allegorical nature of Canticles need not be accepted as valid for the creative poets of any period. The aesthetic and poetic differences between the verse of Aylett and that of Milton or Marvell are thus reflected in the way in which they accepted or rejected theological commonplaces.

Implicit in this discussion has been the initial assumption that biblical allusion in general and echoes of Canticles in particular carry with them interpretive views that the reader is expected to hear. The context in which we must read the poems thus demands literary analysis of the Bible, including a critical and highly individualistic skepticism about theological commonplaces ordinarily regarded as authoritative. In Milton's case we have his De Doctrina Christiana to document his unorthodox approach to biblical interpretation. Marvell left no such document, but the sophistication such a view ascribes to him is surely not unwarranted.

Notes

1. All biblical citations are to the King James Version, Reference Edition (New York: American Bible Society), unless otherwise stated.

2. A Commentary on the Canticles Or, The Song of Solomon, in The Workes of that Famous, Reverend, and Learned Divine, Mr. Tho. Brightman (London, 1644), pp. 981-82.

3. Solomonis, Or, A Commentarie upon the books of Proverbs, Ecclesiastes, and the Song of Songs... (London, 1656), rpt. in A Commentary on the Old & New Testaments by John Trapp, ed. Hugh Martin, III (London: Richard D. Dickinson, 1868), 229.

4. "Reformation Attitudes Toward Allegory and the Song of Songs," PMLA, 89 (1974), 558.

5. The Song of Songs, which was Salomons, Metaphrased in English Heroicks by way of Dialogue, With certayne of the Bridges Ornaments, viz. Poeticall Essayes upon a Diuine Subject... (London, 1621), p. 40, stanza 54. [STC 2774]

6. The Brides Ornaments viz. Fiue Meditations, Morall and Diuine (London, 1625), p. 20, stanza 36 [my numbering]. [STC 1004A]

7. The Song of Songs... [STC 2774), p. 5

8. The Brides Ornaments... (STC 1004A], p. 18, stanzas 28, 29.

9. All citations from Paradise Lost are to The Complete English Poetry of John Milton, ed. John T. Shawcross (New York: New York University Press, 1963).

10. E.g. Howard Schultz, "Satan's Serenade," PQ, 27 (1948), 24-25; Merritt Y. Hughes, ed. John Milton: Complete Poems and Major Prose (New York: Odyssey Press, 1957), pp. 302-3); Alastair Fowler, ed., Paradise Lost in The Poems of John Milton, eds. John Carey and Alastair Fowler (London: Longmans, Green & Co. Ltd., 1968), p. 675.

11. James Durham, Clavic Cantici or an Exposition of the Song of Solomon (London, 1669), p. 401 as quoted by George Scheper, p. 558.

12. Andrew Marvell (1940; rpt. Cambridge: University Press, 1961), p. 50. More recently, in "Marvell Our Contemporary," Andrew Marvell: Essays on the tercentenary of his death, ed. R. L. Brett (Oxford: Oxford U.P. for Univ. of Hull, 1979), p. 111. Bradbrook has commented that she and Ms. Lloyd Thomas "had done no more than note the analogies with 'The Song of Songs' and the overtones associated by biblical gloss with that ancient love poem."

13. English Literature in the Earlier Seventeenth Century (1945; rpt. New York: Oxford U.P., 1952), p. 161.

14. "Marvell's 'The Nymph Complaining...'," MP, 50 (1952), 97-100.

15. "Marvell's 'The Nymph Complaining': A Reply," MP, 51 (1953), rpt. in Andrew Marvell: A Critical Anthology, ed. John Carey (Harmondsworth: Penguin, 1969), pp. 282-83.

16. Cf. Ruth Wallerstein, Studies in Seventeenth-Century Poetic (1950; rpt. Madison: Univ. of Wisc. P., 1965), pp. 335-36; Geoffrey Hartman, "'The Nymph Complaining for the Death of Her Fawn': A Brief Allegory," Essays in Criticism, 18 (1968), 121; Rosalie L. Colie, "My Ecchoing Song:" Andrew Marvell's Poetry of Criticism (Princeton: Princeton U.P., 1970), p. 146; Donald M. Friedman, Marvell's Pastoral Art (London: Routledge & Kegan Paul, Ltd., 1970), pp. 102, 108-9.

17. "The Death of Innocence in Marvell's 'Nymph Complaining for the Death of her Faun," MP, 65 (1967), rpt. in Marvell: Modern Judgements, ed. Michael Wilding (Nashville: Aurora Publishers, Inc., 1970), pp. 278-79.

18. (Madison: University of Wisc. P., 1966), p. 154.

19. All citations from Marvell's verse are to The Poems of Andrew Marvell, ed. Hugh Macdonald (London: Routledge & Kegan Paul, Ltd., 1952).

THE REASSERTION OF BIBLICAL VIEWS IN EUROPEAN ROMANTICISM

W.Z. Hirst

University of Haifa

If, as Harold Bloom has explained, literary history is a battleground on which great poets "wrestle with their strong precursors" by "misreading" them in order "to clear imaginative space for themselves," special resistance will be offered by Biblical narrative, in which (to use Erich Auerbach's words) "Doctrine and promise are incarnate."[1] But the loss of what Northrop Frye has called the "distinctive authority"[2] of Scripture in the Romantic period encouraged writers to rework Biblical themes more radically than before. While poets attempted to impose new meanings on stories taken from Holy Writ, they also made wider use of non-Biblical myths and of popular legends (which had long been freely reinterpreted) both in order to adopt and to revise Biblical viewpoints. Meyer Abrams draws attention to the exceptional scope of "assimilation of Biblical and theological elements to secular and pagan frames of reference... in the period beginning in the 1790's."[3] On the other hand, it has frequently been claimed, recently again by Paul Cantor in an essay on Byron's Cain, that "Romantic poets set out to subvert the religious tradition from within: and successfully "inverted the orthodox values."[4] I will try to show that when these poets retold story from Scripture in order to alter or reverse Scriptural doctrine, the traditional standpoint retained some of its former authority and tended to reaffirm itself, sometimes even proving to be inseparable from the tale, whereas under the cover of recreating non-Biblical stories writers achieved a more thorough-going revision of Scriptural themes.

In Byron's Cain the revision of the Biblical point of view is apparently so funda-mental that the play has almost universally been regarded as running counter to the spirit of Scripture. Granted, Cain voices Byron's own protests as a Romantic rebel, and his onslaught on divine benevolence receives no convincing refutation from Adam and Abel, the representatives of the orthodox position. But, as I have shown elsewhere,[5] Cain's (and Lucifer's) sacrilegious indictment, though not dismissed through debate in the dialogue, is rejected by means of the tragic pattern of irony, conflict, peripeteia, and anagnorisis. The ironic overthrow of the hero constitutes a dramatic or poetic (though not a logical) rebutal of his self-righteous accusations by exposing him, the murderer, as traitor to his own humanitarian aspirations. Although no argument is vitiated by its advocate, in a drama the ironic situation of a blinded protagonist tends to undermine his case. Despite Cain's late outbursts of former recalcitrance (III.468-469, 509-510), his newly gained insight restrains him from repeating his earlier insinuation (I.72-79) that God trapped man in order to mete out merciless punishment; and the play leaves us with a sense of the danger of futile revolt against the human condition and against the mystery

of the cosmic order. After we have read Genesis and pondered the questions implied --
and Scripture raises the central problem of innocent suffering explicitly in the Book of
Job -- the Bible challenges us once more, by means of Byron's drama, to reconsider the
same questions, which now are formulated as the caustic attacks of Cain's and Lucifer's
reasoned rhetoric. These reasoned attacks fail to subvert traditional values. Byron called
Cain a "Mystery," but the classic irony of the play's tone and structure reminds us of
Oedipus Rex, for example, which suggests that man's limited reason is an inadequate
guide in a world ruled by inscrutable power. Cain is thus closer to Milton's justification of
God's ways to men than to an impious vindication of man's rebellion against a malignant
deity, though the latter view has been widely accepted over Byron's own repeated
objections.

The Biblical spirit pervading Cain, so foreign to Byron's habitual iconoclasm, his
relativism, and his profound scepticism, results primarily from the ironic pattern of
rebellion and punishment already inherent in the Cain story of Genesis. Once Byron
chooses to rewrite this story he is tied to its pattern unless he decides to reverse it
completely by disculpating his hero or even rewarding Cain's heresy. Conjectures about
what a writer might have done will clarify what in fact he did do. In as far-reaching a
reversal of the traditional pattern as the reward of Goethe's Faust for his heretical
aspiration or the repentance of Shelley's Prometheus and the overthrow of his Jupiter,
Byron might, for example, have represented the introduction of death into the world as a
new stage of freedom from the anxieties and miseries lamented by Cain, with Abel's life
as the necessary price, or he might conceivably have depicted the killing as an act of
self-defence. Byron did not go so far: he adhered to the Biblical pattern of murder
followed by pariahdom. But even in a work faithful to its Biblical model, Byron's
rebellion, paradoxically, remains as fundamental as Goethe's or Shelley's, for while Cain's
and Lucifer's vitriolic formulations of the unresolved dilemma of theodicy are in
character and appropriate to the expected peripeteia, they also give expression to the
poet's own desperate frustration. Nevertheless a sense of verisimilitude seems to have
constrained Byron to imitate his source's basic downward movement casting his hero from
sin and pride into retribution and humiliation, unlike Goethe and Shelley, who felt free to
reverse this pattern by raising their heroes for a reunion with their long-lost loves after
Faust's soul prevails over Mephistopheles and Prometheus over Zeus-Jupiter. For despite
the Bible's loss of prestige as a body of dogma a Biblical story yet retained a distinctive
authority as a story, which was conceded neither to the German "Faustbuch" nor to a
Greek myth. In the nineteenth century poets no longer hesitated to reverse the doctrines
inherent in most Biblical stories, but a change in attitude towards Cain's universally
condemned killing of his brother could only be effected if, as in the case of Goethe's
Faust and Shelley's Prometheus, the story itself were radically altered.

Cain, however, is concerned with the consequences of Adam's expulsion from Eden,
a Biblical story whose doctrinal implications had apparently long ceased to be taken for
granted, since Milton had already found it necessary to reassert them. The transfer of the
Fall theme from Adam to Cain tends to restore the Bible's authority by moving the focus

to some extent from the question "Are God's ways justified?" to the question "Is rebellion against God's ways justified?" Unlike the argument of Cain, Adam's arguments against God's arbitrary temptation and excessive punishment would not have been undercut by the advocacy of a spokesman who, inflicting unmerited pain on his brother, commits the very injustice against which he inveighs; moreover, Cain should have been forewarned by his parents' error, ever-present to his eyes, and, in addition, he is repeatedly reminded of the parallel between the serpent's temptation of Eve and Lucifer's offer of knowledge to him (II.403-409, III.92-93). Byron may have projected his own yearning for lost Eden and his obsession with the temptation of man, mortality, heightened consciousness, and "fury against the inadequacy of his state to his conceptions"[6] into Cain rather than into Adam because of the former's appeal as outcast doomed to endless wandering, a prototype of the branded Romantic hero-villain who glories in his isolation, because of the potential for conflict and irony inherent in the Cain episode, or because he feared to meet Milton on his own ground. Or perhaps it was a vestigial Calvinism that unconsciously propelled the iconoclastic poet towards a story with sufficient authority to force him into a dramatic repudiation of his own blasphemies, just as his cult of sin and his self-portrayal as a damned soul may have relieved him of the torture of having to indict a God Whose ways his reason failed to justify. (A residual Calvinism may also have prevented him from completing Heaven and Earth, his play about the Deluge, in which the polemics against the Biblical position would have been more devastating because, unlike her ancestor Cain, the heroine Aholibamah, Byron's mouthpiece for his rebellion against innocent suffering, does not disqualify herself through murder.) Whatever the reason for the shift of the Fall motif from father to son, the logically irrefutable arguments against God made in the name of absolute justice cease to have dramatic validity if voiced by a spokesman who sheds the blood of his innocent brother. The Byron who chooses to express his futile cravings for perfection within the framework of a play retaining the Bible's sense of divine mystery has moved beyond the limited human perspective of the Byron who projects his legitimate protest against unexplained suffering into the indignant and furious allegations of a glorified Romantic rebel.

The force of such a reassertion of the Biblical world view is highlighted when seen against attitudes reflected in the poet's non-Biblical works, especially the uncompromising posture of rebellion exhibited by the Byronic hero of the Turkish tales, Childe Harold, "Prometheus," or Manfred. Whereas in Cain the tragic-ironic pattern resolves the tension between man's state and his conceptions into a recognition of divine inscrutability, "Prometheus," for example, triumphantly defies an "inexorable Heaven" to the end. Don Juan, however, indicates that neither baffled resignation nor unflinching defiance represents Byron's most fully developed position: both are here subordinated to a wider context. Lacking the authority of a Biblical plot to compel the story to an anticipated conclusion with its built-in message, the Don Juan legend leaves Byron free to choose his own. The many playfully serious references to Adam and Eve give evidence of Byron's continued preoccupation with the Fall theme, but the poet's ironic detachment neither attacks nor endorses the accompanying doctrine. Since the sin of Adam, unlike

Cain's, is no longer accepted by the Romantics as indisputable, its treatment puts less pressure on a rebellious poet to convey a sense of the Biblical view. Such a view would have decisively altered the meaning of Don Juan. But Byron easily adapts the Fall theme, together with a magnificent variety of other themes, to the shifting poses of his epic satire.

Like Don Juan, Goethe's Faust imports certain Biblical motifs into a non-Biblical popular legend, but here they have the effect of reasserting Biblical attitudes against the general reversal of doctrine. (Faust is "non-Biblical" in the sense that the story does not occur in the Bible, but the legend contained Biblical motifs from the beginning.) Like Don Juan, Faust not only produces a typically Romantic revaluation of ideas but inverts the traditional story pattern: Juan is pursued by women and Faust's soul is saved. From the start Goethe prepares his audience for the reversal of the well-known ending by letting the Lord of his "Prologue in Heaven" vouch for Faust's basic goodness, and implicitly for his ultimate salvation. The Faust legend, which Goethe first encountered in a puppet play, was still, as it had been in Marlowe's time, an allegory of the road to Hell. The story of the devil-compact denounced that pride which, blind to human limitations, thirsts for forbidden knowledge leading to an enslavement to evil; but indirectly it warned against all knowledge pursued independently by prying into the secrets of nature instead of relying on divine revelation as expounded by the teachings of the Church. Goethe's reversal of these traditional values is complete. Faust's self-reliance replaces reliance on dogma; and his pact with Mephistopheles, which he treats as a wager that the devil will never satisfy him, is pressed into the service of the Lord (Who has given His sanction to it) and into the service of Faust's ceaseless aspiration, the means of his redemption. The legend's pious admonitions to be humble and resigned yield to Goethe's plea for striving after the totality of experience, the unattainable goal which condones even calling the devil in aid. Thus Goethe exploits a story which had served as an ecclesiastical exemplum in order to reverse the ecclesiastical message, and such a reversal works towards a radical revision of the underlying Scriptural standpoint. Unlike Byron's Cain, Goethe's Faust is no less a justification of man's own ways than of God's ways to man. While Byron's retold Biblical Cain story retains the spirit of his source in spite of the hero's blasphemies, Goethe achieves at least a partial revision of Biblical sentiment by adapting the non-Biblical Faust legend. In contrast with the Bible's call to resist temptation and to sin no more, Goethe's secular doctrine of incessant "streben" (striving, aspiration) exhorts to ever-renewed trials of activity though they inevitably involve new guilt, for "Man errs as long as he will strive" (1.317). As in Cain, in Faust reason rebels against the notion of forbidden knowledge. In Byron's drama, however, the Scriptural apperception, the sense of divine inscrutability inherent in the Biblical narrative, reasserts itself against Lucifer's (and Byron's own) insinuation that acquisition of reason -- the "One good gift" (II.ii.459) -- justifies disobedience of a divine command. In Faust, on the other hand, reason ("Venunft"), that "light of Heaven" which fires man to transcend his mortal bounds, in vindicated against the ridicule of a cynic who sees only the futile jumps of a cicada (ll.284-290).

But although Goethe does invert an ecclesiastical lesson and revises Biblical sentiment, the poem abounds in Biblical motifs,[7] and the unexpressed doctrines lurking in these motifs indirectly reafffirm Biblical attitudes. While in Don Juan the sustained irony of the authorial voice neutralizes views ingrained in Biblical episodes, in Faust, as in Cain, such views remain uninhibited by the tone of the play, which must be distinguished from opinions expressed by the characters, from Mephisto's constant and Faust's occasional cynicism. It is the Bible that, paradoxically, provides the device for reversing the traditional ending of the Faust legend with its warning against deeds and alliances not sanctioned by the Church. The wager offered by Mephisto to the Lord, Who calls Faust "My servant" (l. 299), is modelled on the dialogue in the first chapter of the Book of Job. Both Satan and Mephisto are accusers of man before God and both ultimately function as instruments through whom He justifies His trust in man. Satan even displays some of Mephisto's scepticism about human nature when he asks: "Does Job serve these for nought?" (Job 1:9). Goethe's transformation of the puppet-play devil into a being who rightly defines himself as "Part of that force which would/Do evil evermore, and yet creates the good" (ll.1335-36), the spirit of negation indirectly inciting individuals to renewed activity whenever they are in danger of relaxing their efforts, is in keeping with the Jobian idea that even the infliction of suffering is sanctioned by God for some inscrutable purpose, and remains inaccessible to the limited mind of suffering humanity. The description of the hero as the servant of God, while reversing the Church parable of damnation for an independent investigation into nature's secrets, also affects Goethe's own agnostic position, which offers Faust's autonomous search after the purpose of existence as an alternative to the Christian faith. The "Prologue in Heaven" is not merely a technical contrivance ensuring Faust's salvation: it relates his doomed endless striving on earth to the higher purpose of representing it in the Biblical guise of a human duty towards God. Like Job's unorthodox outbursts demanding his vindication, Faust's heretical aspiration brings him, unknown to himself, closer to the Lord. Although Faust remains "a secular theodicy,"[8] and although the hero is unconcerned about the hereafter (ll.1660-70, 11442-48) and rightly confines his quest to life on earth past and present, the Jobian prologue would seem to provide transcendental validation of this quest.

Faust's frustration at finding nothing under the sun that grants him lasting satisfaction is the taedium vitae of Ecclesiastes. Koheleth furnishes the model not only for the opening soliloquy, Faust's reasoned pre-judgment on life, which is to be corrected, near the end of the work, by his unreasoning experience, but for the one side of the hero's nature which reminds him day after day that all is vanity. This is the coldly analytical intellect (reason as Kantian "Verstand," not "Vernunft") objectified in the cynicism of Mephisto. The scepticism predominating in Ecclesiastes is in conflict with the spirit pervading most of the Bible, but in the last chapter this scepticism gives way to an injunction to "Fear God and keep his commandments: for this is the whole duty of man" (12:13)."[9] While Goethe's iconoclastic hero of course does not preach submission to rules established by divine decree, his scepticism repeatedly undergoes a similar reversal: a suicidal despair at the meaninglessness of existence is induced by his Mephistophelian logic and then overcome by his irrational but essentially human reaffirmation of faith in life. Although Faust upholds that aspect of reason ("Vernunft") which causes man to aspire beyond his limits, as in Cain the acquiescence in the failure of analytical reason ("Verstand") to penetrate ultimate mysteries is inspired by Scripture, here it is undermined obliquely through Job and Ecclesiastes.

The analogies between Faust and Moses, another "servant of the Lord" (Deut. 34:4), have sometimes been overstated,[10] but the parallel situation in their dying moments is obvious: both heroes enjoy a final vision of the goal they have sought nearly all their lives and never won. Goethe adopts the unentered promised land as symbol of the eternally pursued ideal, Wordsworth's "something evermore about to be," which Novalis thought of as an elusive blue flower and Tennyson as the destination of an endless voyage undertaken by an unyielding mariner, who "cannot rest from travel" and would "sail beyond the sunset" after an ever-receding horizon.[11] The end of the Moses story also constitutes an unfinished journey, a quest frustrated, but this frustration falls just short of final fulfillment as the aged lawgiver catches sight of his goal. Faust's hope, had he lived, would have been disappointed like all ideals when translated into reality, but the Biblical image conveys the impression that he has nevertheless progressed towards some definite objective, and supports those readers who feel that he is justified in calling the vision his "highest moment" (l. 11586). Faust's eternal dissatisfaction is finally assuaged when he sees in his mind's eye his own unwearied endeavor renewed in the ceaseless activity of his fellow-men. The amoral striving of this Nietzschean superman, well illustrated by his ruthless victimization of Philemon and Baucis in the preceding episode, now gives way to an anticipation of selfless action motivated by a communion of interests. At this point Faust is no longer beyond good and evil. The last picture beheld by the Hebrew leader who has sacrificed his own happiness for his people inspires the scene in which Faust's erring striving is replaced by a vision of unflagging activity within a more conventionally ethical frame. And the question of the hero's redemption is finally taken out of its secular context. Critics are not agreed to this day whether Faust is saved only through his own striving or also by an act of grace expressed as love "from above" (ll. 11936-39). The "mater gloriosa" briefly appearing at the end of Faust (ll. 12094-95) is far removed from the standard picture of the mother of Christ,[12] but, like Moses' vision of Canaan and the various other Biblical echoes with their unstated inherent themes, she leaves her mark on Goethe's iconoclastic drama. The subversion of Church and Scripture becomes ultimately less radical than the reversal of the Faust parable suggests.

Whereas Goethe's Faust effectively adapts to a non-Biblical figure the motif of the unfulfilled longing of Moses in sight of his goal, probably the most famous Romantic poem about Moses himself, Alfred de Vigny's "Moise," makes remarkably little of this motif. Although the subject of the poem is Moses on Mount Nebo and the view of the Holy Land is described in some detail, there is only the briefest reference (l. 22) to the divine edict prohibiting the entry, and, unlike his model, Moise makes no complaint about this prohibition. The silence of Moise on this point is all the more surprising because fifty-nine out of the poem's hundred and fifteen lines consist of his address of various grievances to the Lord. By not mentioning the longing to enter the promised land and scarcely alluding to the divine edict that frustrates this longing, the poet deflects attention from the act of disobedience that provoked the edict. Vigny's picture of an unfailingly obedient servant anguishing over his fate constitutes a veiled attack upon God. As against the beautiful description of Moses' death at the end of the Pentateuch, where God's burial of His faithful servant conveys love and appreciation and His final words provide a fitting conclusion to a life-long dialogue, Vigny leaves us with his hero's insinuation of the ingratitude of a jealous and wrathful deity, followed by a cruelly brief factual announcement of the leader's disappearance ("Bientot le haut du mont reparut sans Moise," l. 113), three sparse words of human tears ("Il fut pleure," l. 114), and divine silence, a silence to be developed in Vigny's later poems.[13] In contrast with the frontal blasphemous attacks of Byron's Cain, which are undermined by the dramatic patterns, the unanswered oblique indictment of God's ways by Vigny's Moise is supported by the tone of the narrative, so that a far-reaching revision of the Biblical standpoint is achieved.

Nevertheless the Bible retains a firmer grasp on the poet than he seems to realize. In a letter written much later,[14] while stating his more obvious revisionary intention of using the Biblical figure as mask for the man of genius weary of his grandeur and isolation, Vigny completely dissociates himself from his source. The reader, however, easily recognizes the repeated death wish as Jobian[15] and the sigh over wisdom (l. 61) as the Preacher's increased knowledge which "increaseth sorrow" (Eccl. 1:18). We may also sense an irony in the yearning of Moise for the ignorance of common mankind (l. 58) as we remember that no one after Adam and Eve's eating of forbidden fruit can ever regain the blissful unawareness of Eden. The poem generally approximates the Biblical atmosphere by reproducing the Biblical landscape and cramming echoes from differing parts of Scripture, whether associated with Moses or not, into the final moments of Vigny's hero.[16] But even the motif on which the poet is focussing, the curse of election leading to a weariness with the glories of greatness in isolation from humanity -- the typically Romantic theme which comprises Vigny's revisionary treatment of his subject -- is ultimately inspired by the call of various Biblical prophet figures, including the call of Moses himself, in which the human will vainly resist the divine. Jeremiah's prophetic mission is already thrust upon him before his birth. Even the implacability of human destiny conveyed by the concluding reference to Joshua's election is not un-Biblical in tone. Vigny's implied rejection of God's ways runs counter to the spirit of Scripture, but not, paradoxically, his depiction of the harshness of the human lot. The poet would have given us a more anti-Biblical picture if he had strengthened the impression of divine ingratitude. He might, for example, have invented a deity who refuses to grant the wish for death. But Vigny is tied to the Biblical story. Despite his eclectic treatment of Scripture, and even despite the deviation in his account of Moses' last moments and death, he remains faithful to the basic plot structure of the episode he has chosen: at God's command Moise ascends Mount Nebo leaving his people behind, beholds the promised land, dies, and is succeeded by Joshua.

While the subversion of the Biblical standpoint in a Biblical work like Byron's Cain is more apparent than real, and even in Vigny's "Moise" there is a clear limit to the poet's revisionism, Shelley's and Keats' fundamental departures from their Greek sources in Prometheus Unbound and Hyperion[17] achieve more radical transformations of Biblical ideas, as Goethe does in his reversal of the Faust legend, but without Goethe's Jobian mitigation of anti-Biblical sentiment. By overthrowing Jupiter Shelley reverses the Greek myth, which could only have ended with Prometheus' surrender to or at least reconciliation with Zeus, for Zeus spelled irresistible power to the Greek mind. But at the same time Shelley also reverses the Biblical concept that man is bound to an omnipotent God, against Whom rebellion is futile. Shelley represents Prometheus, the champion and symbol of mankind, as temporarily enchained by his own mind-forged manacles, and Jupiter as a creation of this mind. More unequivocally than in Goethe's Faust human redemption in Prometheus Unbound depends on humanity alone. Considering in the Preface to his drama the two rebels against divine authority, Prometheus and Satan, Shelley claims he rejected the latter because of "taints of ambition, envy, revenge, and a desire for aggrandisement." But if so, why did he not change Satan's character in order to make him the harbinger of a Messianic age? Such a change would have gone no more against Biblical tradition than the sudden forgiveness of the defiant Prometheus and the downfall of omnipotent Zeus-Jupiter go against Greek tradition. Unless we are prepared to conjecture that, his explicit statements to the contrary, Shelley unconsciously recoiled from the sacrilegious notion of overthrowing the Biblical God, we must assume that it was the distinctive authority which the nineteenth century still granted to the Biblical story as story that protected it from this ultimate transformation. Shelley's version of the Prometheus myth must have strained his contemporaries' willing suspension of disbelief, but the choice of the Biblical story as his vehicle for the reversal of Biblical doctrine would have brought him up against an insurmountable barrier of implausibility.

The fragmentary nature of the two Hyperions does not prevent us from recognizing the sweeping alterations that the myth undergoes in Keats' hands. In the earlier fragment Apollo, god of poetry, will replace (and perhaps absorb) Hyperion in an age that sees the dethronement of Saturn-Time (kronos being identified with xronos); and in the second version the deifying imagination of a poet overcomes "his own weak mortality" (i.389) by retrieving immortals from a timeless realm hewn in stone and thus breathing new life into them. Beauty is to conquer time, the artist conquers mortality. Keats, who admits only that he is imitating Milton's style, is in fact rewriting Paradise Lost. For Milton's fideistic answer to the theological dilemma of evil, suffering, and death in a universe created by a benevolent God, Keats attempts to substitute another optimistic proposition: that timeless beauty and a poet's imagination can save a mortal from time. The completed epic would have constituted a revision of Biblical doctrine with faith in the beautifying power of the artist as the surrogate for faith in Christ. But it would still have been a faith! For Keats, however, it is an empty hope belied by his experience of reality. Keats' recognition of this (and not the "Miltonic inversion")[18] causes him to abandon the poem.

But what if Keats had retold the Bible story without disguising it as a Greek myth? He might then have completed the work, even though his thesis is contradicted by what he has felt on the pulses. He might, for example, have re-adapted Milton's Biblical story with Christ assuming the part of Apollo and Satan that of Hyperion. The plot structure of such an epic would have corresponded to traditional versions of the Biblical tale, and the distinctive authority of the well-known story as story would then have put pressure on Keats to satisfy the expectations of his audience. Thus he would have conveyed an idea he wanted to believe in though his heart told him that it was false. Just as the un-Keatsian wish-fulfillment ending of Endymion resulted from the poet's fidelity to the in-built theme of a revered classical myth that immortalizes a mortal, so he might have been happy, at a time when the odes were expressing his shattering sense of mortality, to feel constrained to submit to the still greater authority of a Biblical tale in order once more to say to the end what otherwise he was only allowed to dream. Such a hypothetical revision of the Biblical story would have constituted a less radical break with the Bible than the renunciation of faith demonstrated by his failure to complete the epic. And still more extreme (but probably truer to his innermost feeling) would have been the representation of a fall symbolizing the hopelessness of the human condition in the face of blind cosmic forces. The Hyperion myth would have supplied such a theme of despair as readily as the far more optimistic (though also tragic) themes of Keats' two unfinished versions. The Biblical story would have offered more resistance to the theme of hopelessness.

In the Romantic revaluation of ideas poets on the whole launched their most effective assaults on Biblical sentiment when they were not retelling a Biblical story. Only Blake, the most persistent revisionist of Scripture, seems to have been equally undeterred by the distinctive authority of Biblical doctrine and Biblical plot. Blake revises and sometimes reverses the Scriptural standpoint in his constant introduction of Biblical figures and concepts into his own idiosyncratic mythology, where, for example, Job's leviathan reappears as a tiger and the God of Genesis as Urizen, Nobodaddy, or Starry Jealousy. But his views are no less revolutionary when he rewrites a Biblical story. Since he knows no limits to changes in the plot, the source story virtually disappears and with it the doctrine once inherent in it. Little of the original warning against fratricide is left in "The Ghost of Abel," and the Jesus of "The Everlasting Gospel" "will not do,/Either for Englishman or Jew."[19] The revisionism of other poets, however, tended to be inhibited by a Biblical plot. Whatever people's attitudes to the teachings of the Old and New Testaments, as a work of literature the Bible still retained an unrivalled authority. Bible stories were freely enriched, but they were usually changed only up to a point. The inhibiting force of Biblical stories as stories, and the accompanying residual pressure of the doctrines which were originally incarnate in them, probably contributed to the relative paucity of Romantic works which retold Bible stories in contrast with the pervasiveness of Biblical allusions, images, and themes. More eager than previous generations to conquer the castle of Scripture, the writers of the Romantic period may have sensed a danger when "they set out to subvert the religious tradition from within," not threatened by the dragon of orthodoxy (whom they no longer feared) but by the compelling fairy power of the fable.

Notes

1. Harold Bloom, The Anxiety of Influence: A Theory of Poetry (London: Oxford University Press, 1973), p. 5; Erich Auerbach, Mimesis: The Representation of Reality in Western Literature, trans. Willard Trask (1953; rpt. Garden City, New York: Double- day, n.d.), p. 12.

2. Northrop Frye, The Secular Scripture: A Study of the Structure of Romance (Cambridge, Mass.: Harvard University Press, 1976), p. 7.

3. Meyer H. Abrams, Natural Supernaturalism: Tradition and Revlution in Romantic Literature (New York: Norton, 1973), p. 66.

4. Paul A. Cantor, "Byron's Cain: A Romantic Version of the Fall," KR, n.s., 2, (No. 3, 1960), 50.

5. Wolf Z. Hirst, "Byron's Lapse into Orthodoxy: An Unorthodox Reading of Cain," KST, 29, (1980), 151-172.

6. In the Wind's Eye (vol. 9 of Byron's Letters and Journals), ed. Leslie A. Marchand (London: John Murray, 1979), p. 54.

7. See Osman Durrani, Faust and the Bible: A Study of Goethe's Use of Scriptural and Christian Religious Motifs in Faust I and II (Berne: Peter Lang, 1977).

8. Abrams (p. 95) thus describes Wordsworth's Prelude.

9. Bible critics might object that chapter 12 is an interpolation, but just as I discuss Faust as a complete entity and not as a series of scenes composed in stages over the poet's life-time, so I treat chapter 12 of Ecclesiastes as an integral part of the text handed down to us and see in the pious conclusion an ironic reversal of what precedes.

10. E.g. by Konrad Burdach in "Faust und Moses," Sitzungeberichte der koniglichen graussischen Akademie ler issenschaften du Berlin, 1912, I, 358-403; II, 627-59, 773-789.

11. William Wordsworth, The Prelude, VI, 606; Novalis (Friedrich von Hardenberg), Heinrich von Ofterdinger; Alfred, Lord Tennyson, "Ulysses," ll. 6, 60.

12. See Durrani, pp. 171-173.

13. In the collection Les Destinees, especially "Le Dont des Oliviers."

14. Letter to Camilla Kaunoir of 1836 quoted by Leon Seche in Alfred de Vigny, 3rd ed. (Paris: Mercure de France, 1913) II, 1780179. "Moise" was written in 1.22.

15. David Rice McKee, "Alfred de Vigny and the Book of Job," MLN, 45, (1938), 244-2,6, suggests that the allusion to Job (3:18) might have come to Vigny via Chateaubriand.

16. See Hernande Artfeld, Vigny et la figure de Moise (Paris: Lettres Modernes, 1969) and her annotated edition Vigny: "Moise" (Paris: Archives des Lettres Modernes, 1967).

17. A more detailed comparison appears in my "Shelley's and Keats's treatment of their source myths in Prometheus Unbound and Hyperion" presented at the third international Shelley Conference (August 1982) and the two Hyperions are further discussed in my John Keats (Boston: G. H. Hall, 1981), pp. 25-26, 92-103, 143-150.

18. The Letters of John Keats, ed. Hyder Edward Rollins (Cambridge, Mass.: Harvard University Press, 1958), II, 167.

19. Epilogue to "The Everlasting Gospel" in The Poems of William Blake, ed. John Sampson (1913; rpt. London: Oxford University Press, 1960), p. 156. Professor Harold Fisch drew my attention to this work.

BIBLICAL SUBSTRUCTURES IN THE TRAGIC FORM:
HARDY, THE MAYOR OF CASTERBRIDGE;
AGNON, AND THE CROOKED SHALL BE MADE STRAIGHT

Nehama Aschkenasy
University of Connecticut

Bringing together Hardy's The Mayor of Casterbridge (1886)[1] and Agnon's And the Crooked Shall Be Made Straight (1912),[2] a novella not yet translated into English, may seem an arbitrary yoking of different social milieus, cultural frames of reference, and verbal associations. But the apparent gap between Hardy and Agnon, and especially between these two particular works, is reduced considerably once we become aware of striking similarities in a number of artistic motifs and dramatic coincidences, as well as in the central tragic vision. Though both stories first appeared in serialized forms, they manifest an unmistakably Aristotelian "unity of action" in their unremitting focus on the decline and fall of their respective protagonists. In both stories, an initial act of "shame and horror", to use Dorothea Krook's tragic formula,[3] triggers a series of dramatic coincidences that, abetted by forces of fate and chance that have been let loose, contribute to the inevitable tragic catastrophe.

While it is impossible to establish a direct influence, the glaring affinities between the two works call our attention to the sometimes mysterious ways in which folk motifs and literary patterns travel across countries and cultures and find themselves in different settings.[4] The fair as a grotesque reflection of moral and social chaos, and as the actual and symbolic backdrop for the protagonist's intoxicated surrender to temptation, is a powerful vision in both stories. A wrongful, immoral "business transaction" is at the heart of the tragic entanglement in both. In Hardy's story, the selling of the wife in a moment of drunken rashness, with which the novel starts, sets off a series of coincidences beyond the protagonist's control. In Agnon's tale, the "act of shame and horror" is not one single episode but rather a protracted state; it starts with the protagonist's ill-advised departure from his hometown and wife for the purpose of collecting alms, and culminates in his selling the letter of recommendation given to him by his rabbi. In both stories, the protagonists' financial failures are tied to the obscure vicissitudes of the business world as well as to the uncertainty of harvest. The reappearance of a person thought lost and dead, the mishandling of letters, the motif of the "double", and the case of the wife who is married to a second "husband" while her lawful first husband is alive are elements of fateful significance in both stories.

But it is not only in the plot that the similarities between the two stories are so provoking. In fact, in terms of plot line alone, Agnon's tale seems to be a prose version of Tennyson's poem "Enoch Arden" (1864).[5] Like Enoch Arden, Menashe-Hayim, Agnon's protagonist, comes home to find his wife nursing a child by a second husband whom she married when the first husband was declared dead. Like Enoch Arden, Menashe-Hayim chose to spend the rest of his life in self imposed exile and complete anonymity, away from human community, rather than ruin the happiness and reputation of his wife, who is unaware of the sinfulness of her second marriage. But while Tennyson's hero does not offer any philosophical observations regarding his personal experience, both Henchard, the deposed mayor of Casterbridge, and Menashe-Hayim, Agnon's hapless protagonist, comment on the moral and theological implications of their tragic predicament. The central situation is similar: in both cases, the first marital union, sanctified by God and community, was fruitless. Henchard's child died in infancy, and Menashe-Hayim's marriage never produced an offspring. However, the wife's second marriage, though impure and unlawful, seems to have been blessed by nature; the wives of both protagonists bear children to their second "husband". In both works, the bewildered protagonists question the moral order of the universe in words which reverberate with Jobian echoes. Hardy says of his protagonist: "Part of his wish to wash his hands of life arose from his perception of its contrarious inconsistencies -- of Nature's jaunty readiness to support unorthodox social principles."[6] Agnon's protagonist expresses a similar sentiment while at the same time accepting God's verdict.[7] In fact, the Jobian stature of both protagonists, while not fully developed in either story, is quite apparent; Hardy's Henchard "cursed himself like a less scrupulous Job",[8] while Agnon's hero is described in words taken from The Book of Job (14:1): "Man that is born of a woman is of few days, and full of trouble."[9] Moreover, both Henchard and Menashe-Hayim find solace in The Book of Psalms, and see in it a reflection of their own predicaments.

Both stories are saturated with Scriptural citations and references that are not just isolated allusions that illuminate individual episodes. In both, a specific Biblical pattern provides the structural meaning of the total work, and serves as a scaffold that supports the entire narrative. The main dramatic situation in Hardy's novel, the conflict between Henchard, the old mayor of Casterbridge, and Farfrae, his successor, is described as analogous to the Saul-David conflict in 1 Samuel. In Agnon's story, the protagonist who leaves his home and wanders among strangers is seen as reenacting his nation's destiny of dispossession and exile, a major Biblical theme. But the differences between Hardy's and Agnon's treatment of the Biblical structures are of great significance. Let us first see how the Biblical materials are evoked in these two stories and incorporated into the narrative.

On several occasions in The Mayor of Casterbridge Hardy likens his protagonist to specific Biblical characters. At times, it is only the writer who is aware of the analogy, while his protagonist remains oblivious to the Biblical dimension of his own predicament. In addition to the reference to Job, Hardy also tells us that Henchard felt "like Saul at his reception by Samuel",[10] and at another point he depicts him as "Samson shorn".[11] On other occasions, it is Henchard who suggests the similarity between himself and a Biblical character: "I -- Cain -- go alone as I deserve -- an outcast and a vagabond";[12] and, "I felt quite ill... and, like Job, I could curse the day that gave me birth."[13]

But the only parallelism that extends to the entire plot and is sustained throughout the story is undoubtedly that between Henchard and Saul.[14] To delineate briefly the major features of this analogy: Henchard is a Saul-like figure in his potential of greatness as well as in his lapses into rages and depressions. Gloomy and lonely, he is drawn to the younger man, Farfrae, who, like his Biblical counterpart David, possesses musical skills. But the loving relationship between the two men deteriorates into suspicion and animosity when their fortunes change. Henchard loses his business, his social position, and even his daughter; while Farfrae gains the admiration of the townspeople, prospers financially, and marries first Henchard's fiancée and then his beloved stepdaughter. Eventually, the younger man will inherit the older man's position as the mayor of Casterbridge. The Biblical parallels are obvious. Saul, too, felt betrayed by people whose loyalty he demanded on the basis of their natural ties to him: his son Jonathan and his daughter Michal. The loving friendship between the two Biblical characters also sours when the older man is threatened by the younger man and sees in him the potential usurper of his title and power. Henchard's secret visit to the weather caster parallels Saul's nocturnal trip to the witch who raises the prophet Samuel from the dead. It is in this scene that Hardy himself draws the readers' attention to the parallelism between Henchard and Saul. In the modern story, as well as in its ancient counterpart, the encounter with the prophet bodes ill for the seeker of the future and marks his financial doom.

Since Hardy's focal point is Henchard and not Farfrae, the correspondence between Henchard and Saul is much closer than that between Farfrae and David. While Farfrae possesses David's good looks, fine voice and social charm, he ultimately emerges as lackluster, a pale reflection of his glamorous counterpart in the Bible. Furthermore, while in the central conflict Henchard's role parallels that of Saul, Hardy attributes to Henchard some of the qualities of David. In one instance, Henchard fights with Farfrae, yet at the last moment he refrains from destroying him; this is reminiscent of two Biblical incidents in which David has a chance to kill Saul, yet decides to spare the king's life. In another scene, Henchard identifies with the "Servant David" and asks the church choir to recite Psalm 109 to him.[15]

Henchard, then, incorporates in his character a variety of Biblical figures: the ill-fated Saul, the strong Samson rendered powerless, the puzzled sufferer Job, and the prototypical sinner, Cain. While each Biblical figure illuminates one aspect of Henchard's personality, the most dominant is that of king Saul.

At the same time, a different frame of reference that becomes apparent in the novel links the mayor of Casterbridge to another ancient king, Oedipus of Thebes. While the Biblical parallelism is established by the actual naming of Biblical figures, the analogy between Henchard and Oedipus is done mainly through a series of incidents as well as imagery. One of the first scenes in the novel portrays the arrogant mayor confronting the embittered townspeople who complain about the damaged wheat that the mayor had sold to the bakers and that produced debased bread. The theme of pollution and the protagonist as responsible for it suggests an analogy with the first scene in Oedipus Rex, in which the people of Thebes complain about the plague to Oedipus, who turns out to be the source of it. Hardy, then, draws the image of the diseased monarch from both Hebraic and Hellenic sources.[16] The analogy with Oedipus reinforces the tragic framework of the novel and suggests the existence of malevolent forces in the universe. Henchard's one act of violence has unleashed those irrational forces and, no matter how much he tries to make amends for his initial act of "shame and horror", those forces, in the form of chance coincidences, fatal reappearances of people, and the vicissitudes of nature, will finally defeat and destroy him. "Tragedies end badly," says George Steiner; the tragic personage "is broken by forces which can neither be fully understood nor overcome by rational prudence."[17]

On the other hand, the introduction of the Biblical pattern takes the novel away from the exclusively tragic domain and anchors Henchard's predicament in a sphere that emphasizes human responsibility and free will, and calls for a just punishment for man's sin. If the analogy with Oedipus implies that Henchard's universe is a vicious circle in which he is trapped regardless of what he will do, the Biblical dimension offers another vision that sees human life in terms of progress and change and views time as a healing mechanism.

The Greek conception of time recognizes no historical development, says Tom Driver, "and the changes come about not through the guilt of man but through the will of the gods."[18] The Judeo-Christian consciousness of time, on the other hand, emphasizes "the significance of action taken in the historical present".[19] The Hellenic element in Hardy's novel would suggest that Henchard's tragedy lies in his imperfect human nature, in his inability, as man, to alter or control the powers around him. And the novel offers many instances of Henchard's sense of entrapment. The Hebraic presence, on the other hand, sees Henchard's predicament in the context of a dynamic moral frame in which human suffering is a consequence of the wrong human action. Henchard accepts his role as sinner and understands the nature of his punishment in Biblical terms when he likens himself to Cain and adds: "...But my punishment is not greater than I can bear".[20] The Hebraic conception of human life as determined by human action is certainly present in the story. Hardy, who read Matthew Arnold,[21] was undoubtedly acquainted with the chapter "Hebraism and Hellenism" in Culture and Anarchy (1869) in which Arnold sees the polarity between Hellenism and Hebraism as that between pursuing knowledge ("right thinking", in his words) and choosing moral action ("right acting").[22]

It is hard to say which vision ultimately wins in The Mayor. Both the Hellenic and the Hebraic are present as optional conceptions of man and his place in the universe; one is stark and uncompromising, the other demanding but reconciliatory. It is not surprising that there is no critical consensus as to whether Hardy's novel achieves full tragic proportions.[23] The Biblical figures who function as the archaic prototypes of Henchard are remote from the tragic sphere.[24] However, one may wonder why Hardy chose Saul as the main counterpart of his protagonist. While the Biblical vision as a whole is non-tragic, as Steiner explains, it is undeniable that there are tragic moments in the Bible. Moreover, of all Biblical characters, it seems that Saul comes closest to the tragic.[25] In fact, the tragic potential of the Saul story has been fully utilized by the Hebrew poet

Tchernichovsky in two ballads which emphasise the heroic stature of Saul, the starkness of his fate, and the sense of doom that accompanies him. In one ballad ("Shaul BeEin Dor"), Tchernichovsky recreates the sense of Saul's painful confrontation with the ghost of Samuel the prophet. The king emerges as an appealing figure, attempting to understand his fate, trying to impose order over chaos. The prophet speaks in the name of an irrational, obscure power, the laws of which are arbitrary and inscrutable. This episode is reminiscent of the Oedipus-Tiresias bitter exchange in Oedipus Rex. Interestingly, Hardy has also anchored the analogy between Henchard and Saul in the protagonist's attempt to gain knowledge with the aid of a soothsayer.

It seems that while Hardy used the Biblical prototypes for the non-tragic dimension that they would introduce in the novel, he singled out the character of Saul as Henchard's ancient counterpart because of an intuitive perception of the tragic potential of this particular Biblical figure.

The protagonist that Agnon has chosen to carry the weight of the tragic predicament is different from Hardy's hero. Henchard's personal traits immediately suggest that he is likely to come under the tragic pall: he exhibits a capacity for great rages as well as a hubristic defiance of the laws of nature and man; yet he is not evil. Agnon's protagonist, Menashe-Hayim, is colorless by comparison. While Agnon couches his story in an archaic idiom and sets it in an old-fashioned, dying folk culture, he seems to offer the modern idea that even the "little" man, the man of no special "character", is capable of the tragic experience. Indeed, Menashe-Hayim's act of defiant impiety, the selling of the letter of recommendation, is not less outrageous than Henchard's selling of his wife, especially in the light of the dramatic events that it triggers: Menashe-Hayim will lose his wife, who will unwittingly enter a marriage that is sinful and defiled in the eyes of Jewish law.

Unlike Hardy, Agnon does not name any Biblical figure as the ancient prototype of his protagonist; nor does he recreate a particular Biblical episode of dramatic potential in his story. Instead, the Biblical language of exile and redemption that suffuses the narrative, and that is implied in the title itself, suggests that Menashe-Hayim reenacts his nation's entire historical destiny of punishment and restoration. Menashe-Hayim thus relives not an isolated Biblical episode, but the main drama that underlies the total Old Testament vision. The title, which is an exact quotation of Isaiah 40:4 ("...and the crooked shall be made straight, and the rough places plain"), sets the tone; it offers an eschatological vision of national redemption, and establishes the Biblical terms of the story.

However, the Biblical structure is only one of several layers of verbal and cultural associations that exist in the story. In fact, the nineteenth-century protagonist and his milieu serve as the middle point of a number of concentric circles of ideas and concepts. The other prominent layers are: the Talmudic, marked by the use of Aramaic as well as of legal-halachic terms such as "deserted wife" ("^{C}agunah"), "halachic problem" ("sugiah"), "borrower" ("shoel"), "legal evidence" ("siman"), "testimony" ("^{C}edut"), "transgression" ("^{C}abeirah"), "adultery" ("issur ^{C}arayot"); the Literature of Ethics, identifiable by wise sayings and ethical aphorisms which are either quoted from actual Rabbinic texts, or imitate their style; the Hasidic-mystical, made up of tales of miraculous, last minute rescues, in which words such as "faith", "salvation", "miracle", and "fate" are predominant; and the popular layer, which represents the ambiance of the contemporary folk culture and is marked by the language of superstition ("the devil", "shed mishahat"), premonitions (the protagonist kissing the empty mezuzah space, the ballads sung in the fair), and the callous, mocking voice of the community that sometimes intrudes into the tale.[26]

The Biblical layer of the story cannot be read in isolation; it is inextricably tied to the other circles of associations which, together, exhibit the mutation, transformation, and even corruption of specific Biblical concepts. For example: the most predominant concepts within the Biblical orbit are those of redemption and exile. Indeed, the root g'l, to redeem, is the most frequently used in the story; the root glh, to go on exile, also appears quite often. The husband's departure from his home and wife is described as going on exile, and his return is viewed as the redemption of both himself and his wife ("ki yavo veyig'al", he will return and redeem).[27] The concept of redemption in this context echoes the prophetic language, hence Menashe-Hayim is reenacting his national destiny. But the word "redeemer" is later used in the narrow legal meaning in which it appears in the Bible (i.e. the kin who redeems the blood, or the property, or the wife, of another family member). Ironically, it is not the lawful husband who will be the redeemer of his wife, but the second husband ("nimṣa lah go'el", a redeemer was found for her)[28] Furthermore, the verb "to redeem" is used within the Talmudic-halachic context, too, when the rabbis try to "redeem", or free, the wife from the limbo status of "'agunah" ("Lega'olah mikablei ha^{c}iggun", to free her from the bonds of "^{c}iggun").[29] Again the irony is apparent: the rabbis think that they redeemed the woman, while actually they have enabled her to commit adultery. As the story moves towards its resolution, words deriving from the root g'l, to redeem, appear in greater frequency. At this point, Menashe-Hayim wishes for the redemption of his soul in mystical terms;[30] yet the word redemption is now stripped of all its associations and narrows down to one meaning only -- death.[31]

A similar mutation occurs in the root glh, to go on exile. Initially, Menashe-Hayim's wife prepares for him "the gear for exile", a phrase repeatedly used in the Book of Ezekiel chapter 12. This prophetic phrase creates the grand setting for the protagonist's departure from home, and anchors his private experiences in the collective, national destiny. Together with the title of the story, that describes the return of the exiles, the Biblical echoes suggest the Hebraic quality of historical remembrance of past events, and the conception of the future as open and redeemable, that Tom Driver sees as the main traits of the Judaic consciousness of time.[32] As the story progresses, however, the relationship between the wandering of the exiled nation and the begging from door to door of our protagonist becomes merely satirical. Menashe-Hayim deteriorates into a greedy, gluttonous vagabond, and Agnon marks this change in his protagonist by adding the Biblical phrase that describes Cain's wanderings: "a fugitive and a vagabond" ("na^c vanad").[33] At this point, the wandering of the protagonist no longer parallels that of the nation's, since it does not mean an expiation of sin but, rather, sinking more and more into sin. Furthermore, to justify his failure to return home, Menashe-Hayim uses the excuse that he deliberately "exiles himself" ("^{C}oseh golah"). He is thus distorting the concept of "exile" as used in the Literature of Ethics and in Hasidic sources. In the former, it is suggested that an individual should temporarily leave his family and wander among strangers in order to perfect his soul. In Hasidic tradition, the Zaddik, spiritual leader, goes on exile as a way of preparing himself for his leadership role. Menashe-Hayim, however, corrupts the Biblical, Rabbinic, and Hasidic meanings of the concept of exile, thus revealing both his depravity and comic pretentiousness.

Towards the end of the story, Agnon abandons altogether the verbs that derive from the root glh, go on exile, and uses repeatedly the verb "wander" ("na^C vanad"), associated with Cain. This time, it is the protagonist, in a moment of illumination, who views himself not in terms of the individual who fulfills his nation's destiny, but as the sinner Cain. He asserts that, just as he has been wandering in this world, so his soul will continue its restless wandering in the other world.[34] Thus the theme of the return of the exiles, described in the title of the story, comes full circle in an ironic reversal of its Biblical meaning; instead of restoration into harmony, we have the vision of Menashe-Hayim's tormented soul, forever in exile, eternally wandering.

Agnon's story abounds with many other Biblical allusions that introduce motifs from Genesis, Lamentations, the Psalms, Job, and the Book of Esther. Generally, the biblical language creates a comic discrepancy between the sublime and the mundane, as when the grotesque musicians in the fair are described in the language with which the psalmist envisions the return of the exiles.[35] In other instances, a Biblical verse is quoted word by word, or slightly paraphrased, and incorporated into the language of the narrative only to reinforce the protagonist's estrangement from the Biblical world, and to foretell disaster. For example: Menashe-Hayim expresses his wish to visit the fair with the phrase used by Moses when he begs God to see the promised land: "...let me go over and see" (Deuteronomy, 3:25). Besides the inherent irony, these words suggest Menashe-Hayim's eventual failure to enter his own promised land, i.e., his home.

The reversal of the Biblical context is a satirical device; the Biblical idiom dwarfs the protagonist and exposes his faults and pretensions. At the same time, the Biblical dimension reveals the tragic loneliness of modern man, cut off from the ancient source of meaning and comfort.[36] While the Biblical language in the story creates a world filled with the promise of redemption, the actual plot, especially the ending in which the protagonist acts against Biblical law and dies a sinner, reveals a world empty of the main Biblical premises.

On the other hand, Agnon's story does not commit itself totally to the tragic vision. While the tragic structure of the plot is undeniable, Agnon rejects the Hellenic conception of man as a plaything at the hands of the gods. The first chapter of the story uses repeatedly various words that signify "fate" (such as "mazal" -- fate, "gzeirah" -- predestination, "galgal" -- the wheel of fortune), and creates the impression that the protagonist is exposed to the capriciousness and irrationality of a malevolent force that governs human life. Yet it soon becomes clear that the term "fate" is used as an excuse by a protagonist who is unable to face up to his own inadequacies. Furthermore, the Hasidic stories inserted early into the narrative prove that it is man's own inner resources that determine the happy outcome of events, not outside forces. Therefore, Mena-she-Hayim's predicament cannot be fully defined in tragic terms since he is not controlled by hidden, evil forces; nor is he seen as gaining dignity and nobility by spitefully challenging the injustice of these forces. Thus, at the end of the story, Agnon's prota-gonist is not only denied redemption in Biblical terms, but is also deprived of the grandeur of the tragic hero.

And yet, Menashe-Hayim does ultimately achieve a measure of redemption, though it takes place outside both the Hebraic and the Hellenic orbits. A "dissociation of sensibility" occurs at the end of the story that allows us to separate the concept of "sin" as a Biblical-legal term, from the idea of "guilt" as a psychological state. In the Biblical sphere, within which Menashe-Hayim still moves, he continues to be a sinner; yet he rids himself of his guilt feelings and experiences an emotional tranquility at the end of the story. His redemption is defined in psychological terms as that of a man who has made the courageous decision to sacrifice his own life for the happiness of another human being. His reward is also emotional. He dies convinced of his wife's love and assured of being buried in the grave, and under the tombstone, designated for him.[37] If the crooked is being made straight at the end, it is not in Biblical terms, but in modern, secular, psychological terms. Redemption is located in the subjective consciousness of the individual who has finally made peace with himself, but it is not bound up with his fulfilling the divine destiny of his community.

It is quite apparent that while the Biblical presence functions as a supportive substructure in both works, the two writers differ in their use of the Biblical material. For Hardy, the Scriptures serve as a large storehouse of archaic legends that contain prototypical characters and situations. The relationship between the Biblical universe and the Wessex environment is, therefore, metaphorical: Henchard felt _like_ Job, acted _like_ Saul, etc. Furthermore, for Hardy the architect the Biblical plot offered a structure that could be used as a direct parallel of the modern plot-line. The symmetrical neatness and the almost geometrical precision of the analogy are essential to the narrative form of Hardy's novel. There is no structural tension, no paradoxical or satirical relationship between the Biblical story and its nineteenth-century counterpart. True, the Saul-David precedence expands the insular, regional story both spatially and chronologically; thus the Henchard-Farfrae conflict is the Biblical tale writ small. But the architectural support that the Biblical frame offers Hardy is mechanical, imposed by a skilled artisan to perfect his fictional creation.

In Agnon's story, the Biblical element is embedded in the language itself and is thus inseparable from the very fabric of the narrative. While Hardy's plot is independent of the Biblical structure, Agnon's tale has no life of its own but that which is inextricably tied to the Biblical dimension. The language of exile and redemption places the individual story in a larger framework of universal significance where the personal and the historic meet and creates expectations that are eventually defeated. The crux of the narrative is the constant tension between the Biblical frame and the modern plot. Thus the language of absolute justice and eschatological promise constantly challenges the temporal, relative, and enclosed reality of the protagonist and is, in turn, challenged by it. Both the Biblical and the modern are tested against each other; the correlation between them is simultaneously direct and reverse, genuine and ironic. Agnon does not need the adjective "like" because the Biblical presence asserts itself as an organic part of the verbal life of the tale, rather than as a structure extraneous to the actual dramatic web. For Agnon, the Bible exists not as an archaic layer that the artist can draw on to reinforce his narrative, but as a ubiquitous presence, constantly claiming attention and provoking the imagination.

Notes

1. Hereafter, The Mayor. All page references will be made to the Harper edition (1950).

2. Hereafter, The Crooked. All page references will be made to Schocken's 1971 edition, volume "Elu VeElu".

3. Elements of Tragedy (New Haven: Yale University Press), p. 8.

4. Agnon was an avid reader of German letters (See: S. Y. Agnon, NeAtsmi El Atsmi, Schoken, 1976, pp. 113, 115, et passim). It is possible that he became aware of the works of Hardy through critical reviews that appeared in Germany before he left for Israel (in 1907). It seems that Hardy was popular in Germany even before the turn of the century. Carl J. Weber, in The First Hundred Years of Thomas Hardy 1840--1940 (New York: Russel and Russel, 1965), lists works on Hardy that appeared in Germany as early as 1889, 1894, 1901, 1902, and 1903. An indirect source through which Agnon could have heard of Hardy's works was the Hebrew writer Y. H. Brenner. Brenner spent some time in England and, as Agnon himself testifies (MeAtsmi El Atsmi, p. 121), was a voracious reader. Brenner read also English and used to have long talks with Agnon on world literature.

5. "Enoch Arden" was translated into German by Carl Hessel in 1874 (?) (Leipzig: P. Reclam jun). Another translation, in an illustrated edition, appeared in Berlin in 1883, published by G. Grote.

6. The Mayor, p. 368.

7. The Crooked, p. 122.

8. The Mayor, p. 330.

9. The Crooked, p. 123.

10. The Mayor, p. 214.

11. The Mayor, p. 373.

12. The Mayor, p. 361.

13. The Mayor, p. 90.

14. The close parallelism between the Henchard-Farfrae drama and the Biblical story has been closely studied by Julian Moynahan in "The Mayor of Casterbridge and 1 Samuel", PMLA, 71 (1956), 118-30.

15. The Mayor, p. 269.

16. See D. A. Dike, "A Modern Oedipus: The Mayor of Casterbridge", Essays in Criticism, 2 (1952), 169-79.

17. The Death of Tragedy (London: Faber, 1961), p. 8.

18. The Sense of History in Greek and Shakespearean Drama (New York: Columbia University Press, 1967), p. 27.

19. Driver, p. 39.

20. The Mayor, p. 361.

21. See Carl J. Weber, Hardy of Wessex (New York: Columbia University Press, 1965), p. 42.

22. Matthew Arnold, Culture and Anarchy (New York: Bobbs-Merrill, 1971), p. 109.

23. See John Paterson, "The Mayor of Casterbridge as Tragedy", in A. J. Guerard (ed.), Hardy: A Collection of Critical Essays (Englewood Cliffs: Prentice-Hall, 1963), p. 95.

24. Milton, of course, treated Samson as a tragic character in "Samson Agonistes". The Book of Job was also "rewritten" as tragedy.

25. On the tragic dimension of Saul's figure and career see: Hillel Barzel, "Moses: Tragedy and Sublimity", in R. R. Gros Louis (ed.), Literary Interpretations of Biblical Narratives (New York: Abingdon, 1974), pp. 125/6.

26. This is not an attempt to differentiate between the historical layers of the Hebrew language used by Agnon, but rather, between the areas of cultural connotations and symbols present in this story.

27. The Crooked, p. 112.

28. The Crooked, p. 116.

29. The Crooked, p. 113.

30. Gershom G. Scholem shows how the concepts of exile and deliverance have been converted in Kabbalah, and later in Hasidic thought, into terms denoting personal-psychological processes or mystical-cosmic ideas. See Major Trends in Jewish Mysticism (New York: Schocken, 1974), pp. 286, 305, 341 et passim.

31. The Crooked, p. 123.

32. The Sense of History, p. 39-66.

33. The Crooked, p. 88.

34. The Crooked, p. 127.

35. The Crooked, p. 99 offers a comic paraphrase of Psalm 126:6 "He that goeth forth and weepeth, bearing precious seeds, shall doubtless come again with rejoicing, bringing his sheaves with him."

36. The idea that Agnon's troubled protagonists represent modern man's tragic predicament and sense of estrangement is one of the main premises that runs through Baruch Kursweill's works on Agnon. See Massot ᶜAl Sipurei Agnon (Tel Aviv: Schoken, 1963).

37. Arnold Band argues that the ending of the story takes it away from the tragic sphere. See Nostalgia and Nightmare (Berkeley: University of California Press, 1968), p. 87.

THE CREATION OF EVE IN THE WRITINGS OF MARCEL PROUST

Juliette Hassine

Bar-Ilan University

Every layer and motif in Proust's A la recherche du temps perdu ("Remembrance of Things Past") reflects on and reveals the meaning of the work as a whole, which for our purposes it would be useful to review here.

The work, written between 1909 and 1922, consists of seven parts. The first part is called Du côté de chez Swann ("Swann's Way"). This book opens with an account of the narrator's deep sleep, his awakening awareness, and, by way of that, the world's coming into being. At the center of the book is the first artistic revelation. Subsequently, the love of the Jew Swann for Odette is related. Swann's côté (his estate) is called the côté of Méséglise. (In French, the word côté -- side, way -- is etymologically identical with the word côte, rib.)

The second part, A l'ombre des jeunes filles en fleurs ("Within a Budding Grove"), tells of the narrator's love for Gilberte, his friendship with the painter Elstir, and his long conversations about the sculpture work over the portals of the Balbec church. The third part, Le Côté de Guermantes ("The Guermantes' Way"), relates the narrator's love for the Duchesse de Guermantes, a French noble family of Christian knightly origin, and speaks of the Dreyfus affair and of anti-Semitism. Here is an attempt to shatter the myth of francité, Frenchness, that is rooted in knighthood and Christianity. The fourth part, Sodome et Gomorrhe ("Cities of the Plain") is about the loves of the Baron de Charlus, member of Guermantes' family. The fifth part, La Prisonnière ("The Captive"), tells of the narrator's love for Albertine. He decides to hold her captive in his house as a way to cure his jealousy; this part contains lengthy discussions of the works of Vermeer, Wagner and Balzac. Speaking about those artists, the narrator expounds on the idea of totality of vision in their work taken as a whole. The aesthetic conception that emphasizes mission and totality of vision with respect to an artistic creation turns the creator into an omnipotent being, like God. The narrator interprets the works of Dostoevski in that light. In that interpretation mention is made of the biblical motif of the creation of Eve, and that interpretation will be the focus of our discussion here. The sixth part, La Fugitive ("The Sweet Cheat Gone"), tells of Albertine's escape and death in a riding accident. The seventh part, Le Temps retrouvé ("Time Regained") tells of the narrator's return to the house of Guermantes. He has a sudden artistic revelation and realizes that his life had been guided by a destiny. The narrator discovers the means of expression by which the events of his life gain coherence. He calls that creative characteristic "Wisdom" ("'Sagesse'"). The end of the work is also its beginning. In fact, Proust wrote the work and its conclusion at the same time, its structure and all its parts laid out in advance.

- 95 -

It should be noted that the first title given to the work as a whole, L'Adoration perpétuelle, is a Christian expression related to the seven sacraments. It may be asked what induced Proust to give a work that is totally devoid of religiosity, piety and sacrality, a title taken from a Christian rite. Indeed, the French Catholic author, Francois Mauriac, criticized this immense work for the total absence from it of God. The reason for that title can be found only by reviewing the works that preceded the magnum opus and which reflect the author's spiritual biography. We shall undertake that in order to properly assess the biblical motif in general, and specifically the creation of Eve.

His youthful work, Les Plaisirs et les jours, was published in 1895. Its title recalls the work by Hesiod, Works and Days (in French, 'Les Travaux et les jours'), in which the Greek poet tells of the creation of the races of man. That same author also wrote the Theogony, about the beginning of the world's creation. In Proust's youthful Les Plaisirs et les jours there is a story called "The Confessions of a Girl". This story is suffused with the "confessions" of St. Augustine, who is referred to explicitly in the story.

It can be said that these two elements -- Greek mythology by way of Hesiod and Homer (the Homeric hymns), and the works of St. Augustine -- are the principal influences on Proust's work. It should be borne in mind, too, that Augustine interpreted the Bible, especially the Book of Genesis and the creation of Eve, and that his view contributed a great deal to the crystalization of medieval Christian exegesis.[1]

From 1899 to 1905 Proust devoted himself to the translation into French of the works of John Ruskin. Among the works he translated and edited is The Bible of Amiens. Stories from the Bible and New Testament are depicted in the statuary of the Amiens cathedral, and for more than five years Proust devoted himself to very intensive study of the Bible, Christian art and Christian biblical exegesis. In this he was aided by Emile Male's studies of medieval Christian art.

It should not be forgotten that Augustine's theological points and interpretations, and especially his Civitas Dei, received broad expression in the art of the Middle Ages. We shall consider Civitas Dei at the end of this essay.

Proust has sharp criticism for Ruskin's "idolatrous" approach. The English critic often lapsed into unauthentic art criticism, in that he contended that the beauty of the works of art depends on their embodiment of Christian truth.

For Proust the creative faculty lies beyond religious consciousness and Christian actualization, and in that he differed from Ruskin and even more so from Augustine, who saw no salvation for mankind outside of Christianity. Indeed, his work is a reply to Ruskin and to St. Augustine; the title L'Adoration perpétuelle is undoubtedly ironic, and he replaced it with another title apparently because it was too provocative.

Before proceeding with the discussion of our subject, we should quote the verses of Paul, which are the source of the Christian interpretation, one of whose founders was St. Augustine:

"Husbands, love your wives, even as Christ also loved the church... So ought men to love their wives as their own bodies. He that loveth his wife loveth himself. For no man has ever yet hated his own flesh, but nourisheth it and cherisheth it even as Christ the church. For we are members of his body... For this cause shall a man leave his father and mother and shall be joined unto his wife, and they two shall be one flesh. This is a great mystery, but I speak concerning Christ and the church (ecclesia).

Epistle of Paul the Apostle to the
Ephesians, 6:25-33

Several important points emerge from this passage:

1. The figure of Eve prefigures the church.

2. The faithfulness man owes the church.

3. The dimension of mystery (anagogy), which cannot be challenged and is binding on the world as a whole.

4. Man's goal and purpose is his integration in the church.

The overture of the work speaks of the creation of the world and the awakening of awareness, and there the influence of Hesiod's Theogony is discernibly greater than that of the first chapter of Genesis. In writings that appeared under the title Contre Sainte-Beuve, which are a preliminary sketch for the magnum opus, the dream of Eve's birth is located in an associative context together with the birth of Christ. In the final version in A la recherche du temps perdu, the birth of Christ has disappeared.

"Sometimes, too, just as Eve was created from a rib of Adam, so a woman would come into existence while I was sleeping, conceived from some strain in the position of my thigh. Formed by the appetite that I was on the point of gratifying, she it was, I imagined, who offered me that gratification. My body, conscious that its own warmth was permeating hers, would strive to become one with her, and I would awake. The rest of humanity seemed very remote in comparison with this woman whose company I had left but a moment ago: my cheek was still warm with her kiss, my body bent beneath the weight of hers. If, as would sometimes happen, she had the appearance of some woman I had known in waking hours, I would abandon myself altogether to the sole quest of her, like people who set out on a journey to see with their own eyes some city that they have always longed to visit, and imagine that they can taste in reality what has charmed their fancy. And then, gradually, the memory of her would dissolve and vanish, until I had forgotten the maiden of my dream."

The same passage appears in Contre Sainte-Beuve, but in A la recherche du temps perdu Proust added the sentence:

If, as would sometimes happen, she had the appearance of some woman I had known in waking hours, I would abandon myself altogether to the sole quest of her, like people who set out on a journey to see with their own eyes some city that they have always longed to visit, and imagine that they can taste in reality what has charmed their fancy.

In the sketch the passage ends with "I had forgotten the maiden of my dream, as if she were a true love." (In A la recherche du temps perdu, the narrator quickly forgets his loves and begins new loves; we will take up the motif of faithfulness below). By means of the sentence Proust added in the final version, the theme of Eve's birth is interwoven into the work's tapestry. In this passage Eve is described as being born from the sleeping narrator's thigh rather than as coming from his rib. Here we may consider the source and reason for the change. Eve's creation from Adam's rib, with the addition of the verse "male and female He created them", left room for the reflections in Midrash Rabbah and in the Kabbalah on the primal androgyny, reflections which made their way into Christian hermeneutics. We may recall that the subject of androgyny is discussed in Plato's Symposium, which was well-known to Proust. In Proust's work the perspective of androgyny with respect to the narrator is rejected, for androgyny or hermaphroditism would place the narrator in the category of creature and would thereby deprive him of his "godliness". Within the work, the narrator's body is the space for all creation and all unfoldings. The birth from a thigh recalls the birth of Dionysus from Zeus' thigh, as related in the Orphic and Homeric myths. The goddess Semele, while pregnant with Dionysus, was killed by a thunderbolt hurled by Zeus. Hermes saved the six-month old fetus, sewing it into Zeus' thigh and releasing it when it had come of age. Hence, the meaning of the name Dionysus, "the child who was born twice", or "the son of the double gate". Thus, too, the Orphic-Dionysian dimension of the work. The narrator grants everlastingness to his figures only on the second round, when he awakens memory from his own inner depths. The Eve who emerges now in a dream is lost. He will find her anew by means of artistic recollection. The birth of Eve from the narrator, in a world devoid of divinity and providence, recalls the creation of the earth by Gaea in the Homeric and Orphic myth, which is mentioned in Proust's work. Gaea emerged from the ocean and gave birth to her son Uranus (the sky) while asleep. The presence of parthenogenesis, or self-fertilization, eliminates any assumption of hermaphroditism or androgyny, and does away with any dependence on Christian theology, which maintained that the advent of Jesus Christ, by virtue of the holy logos fulfilled in his flesh, heralded the union of the two essences that were separated in the act of Creation, the spiritual essence represented by Adam, and the essence of the "animal soul" represented by Eve, two different essences that cannot be fused except with the grace of the revelation of Jesus Christ. Eve, or the narrator's dream-girl, like all his true loves, is not of an essence different from or opposed to the narrator's. In the opening pages of his work Proust already denies any association with the birth of Christ, for in Christian hermeneutics the birth of Eve prefigures the birth of the Church (about which we shall have more to say below).

The second dimension in the process of Eve's creation in Proust is that of deep sleep, corresponding to the deep sleep in the biblical tale. Augustine regarded this stage as ecstasy in which there was an inner awareness of what was taking place. In contrast, midrashic legends regard this stage as one of non-awareness ensuring the secret and mystery of the creation of woman. That is what makes love possible. Adam Kadmon (primordial man) was unable to live with Lilith because he was present at her creation. In Proust's work the mystery in which the beloved is enwrapped is what impels the narrator to ravish her, and to hold her captive in order, perhaps, to unravel her secret. However, after he imprisons Albertine, the narrator discovers that she has no secret. He comes to the conclusion that in their lives men do not guard any secret and that mystery is the exclusive property of the work of art. Albertine the captive, says the narrator, is not a work of art for me. In La Prisonnière, in the overture, Albertine's and the narrator's slumber are described at length, foreshadowing Albertine's sleep in the later books. In La Prisonnière, Albertine's repose provides respite for the lover who suffers dearly for not being able to discover the secrets of a "being who is always elusive and in flight". Asleep, she becomes like clay in the artist's hand. The narrator describes her sleep at length, like the long hours he spent at the seashore in order to hear the rumblings of the deep.

> Then, feeling that the tide of her sleep was full, that I should not ground upon reefs of consciousness covered now by the high water of profound slumber, deliberately I crept without a sound upon the bed, lay down by her side, clasped her waist in one arm, placed my lips upon her cheek and heart, then upon every part of her body in turn laid my free hand, which also was raised, like the pearls, by Albertine's breathing; I myself was gently rocked by its regular motion: I had embarked upon the tide of Albertine's sleep.

Here it is important to observe the meeting with the biblical text. While Albertine is asleep the narrator can produce from her a kaleidoscopic play of metaphors and forms, and can speculate about her being without fear of resistance or opposition. In Genesis, too, Adam's sleep is the time of Eve's creation. According to the midrash, man must set out in search of the lost pearl (or treasure). The search for that lost pearl was not taken up by Christian exegesis, which preferred the moral allegory with respect to Eve's creation. (In the Christian view, she represents sin and prefigures the Virgin Mary.)

It can be said that in fashioning the motif of Eve's creation, Proust departs from Christian theology and we can speak of a point of encounter with Jewish hermeneutics, an encounter that can be attributed more to Proust's liberated vision and intuition than to any prior knowledge. In the work, sleep makes possible the act of creation, or the act of "wisdom" as Proust calls it. Any participation or presence by matter in the process of its realization as form is liable to endanger the creative process. The non-involvement of the material in its realization as form is fitting in a work that relates an odyssey of Memory. The narrator's body is the material space for the memory's indwelling, or for form's. The narrator is not aware of Eve's birth from within him or of the presence within him of fertile memory that rises benevolently.

In the Proustian anthropology, three forces can be discerned: The body, which serves as the space for the memory's odyssey; memory which will become form; and the creative wisdom that oversees the realization of the form in the matter, but is free of both the matter and the form. Here we find the basic principles of Proustian creation.[2]

The essence and qualities of wisdom remain a mystery, and we have already emphasized the meaning of that conception as opposed to the Christian view (of Richard de Saint V.) about the holy logos fulfilled in the flesh that brings about the fusion of the two forces: Adam-Eve or Spirit-animal soul.

In Proust the wisdom is not part of any theological ontological hierarchy and is not dependent on any mystery of Incarnation, and may even fertilize itself. The desire to restore the loss (the search for the lost pearl) features in all the love affairs in A la recherche du temps perdu, and especially in the books La Prisonnière and La Fugitive. But after he takes and imprisons Albertine, he comes to the conclusion that he does not love her at all. Albertine's presence fills his heart with emptiness and sterility. In this context, the association which more clearly represents his relationship to Albertine appears in Le Coté de Guermantes, namely, the memory of the biblical version of Eve's creation which decorates the Balbec church and which is retold by the narrator in a tone both derisive and humorous.

> Certainly I was not in the least in love with Albertine; child of the mists outside, she could merely content the imaginative desire which the change of weather had awakened in me and which was midway between the desires that are satisfied by the arts of the kitchen and of monumental sculpture respectively, for it made me dream simultaneously of mingling with my flesh a substance different and warm, and of attaching at some point to my outstretched body a body divergent, as the body of Eve barely holds by the feet to the side of Adam, to whose body hers is almost perpendicular, in those romanesque bas-reliefs on the church at Balbec which represent in so noble and so reposeful a fashion, still almost like a classical frieze, the Creation of Woman; God in them is everywhere followed, as by two ministers, by two little angels in whom the visitor recognises -- like winged, swarming summer creatures which winter has surprised and spared -- cupids from Herculaneum, still surviving well into the thirteenth century, and winging their last slow flight, weary but never failing in the grace that might be expected of them, over the whole front of the porch.

The reductive (and slightly ironic) attitude to the biblical text is understandable in light of the fact that it clashes with the perspective of Proust's work. A serious approach to the biblical text was liable to endanger the structure of the work, which in all its parts resembles the church at Combray, a fictional cathedral which is, as it were, a symbol of A la recherche du temps perdu. This church differs from the one in Balbec, and we shall consider that difference.

All these things made of the church for me something entirely different from the rest of the town; a building which occupied, so to speak, four dimensions of space -- the name of the fourth being Time -- which had sailed the centuries with that old nave, where bay after bay, chapel after chapel seemed to stretch across and hold down and conquer not merely a few yards of soil, but each successive epoch from which the whole building had emerged triumphant.

The church in Balbec is the subject of a lengthy discussion between the narrator and the fictional artist, Elstir. Over the portals of the church, Christian history from Adam and Eve to Jesus and from Jesus to the Apostles is represented. Elstir, the fictional artist who represents Ruskin, and to a certain remote extent, also Augustine, relates to the biblical text by the canons of Christian interpretation (the literal meaning, symbol, allegory, anagogue or mystery). For Elstir the portals of the Balbec church comprise a tremendous theological poem constructed of concentric circles, with the heavenly Jerusalem on the outermost circle. The narrator discreetly rejects the dogmatic interpretation. His response is embodied in the construction of the church, which has a unique other time, utterly different from Christian theological time which is described by Elstir as time stemming from Creation and rising to the heavenly Jerusalem, as in the "Civitas Dei" described by Augustine.

In the Christian historical conception developed by Richard de Saint-Victor, the second Eve, that is, the Virgin Mary, heralds the utter and total end of the sinful Eve of the Old Testament. In this view, the Torah is merely one level of an all-encompassing hierarchical system. As opposed to Christian theology, the Proustian Eve, Albertine, does not cancel out all the Eves who preceded her. Proust's church in A la recherche du temps perdu points to a substantial change from Ruskin's The Bible of Amiens and Augustine's Civitas Dei by way of Eve's birth from the thigh instead of her creation from the rib; and that, no doubt, was intentional. Augustine maintained that the creation of Eve, as described in the Old Testament, prefigures the creation of the Church, which emerges from the rib or side of the dying Saviour. This appears in the miniatures of Emblemata Biblica, and in a painting called "The City of God and the City of Saint Augustine", a fifteenth-century work that appears in a manuscript of Augustine's Civitas Dei in the Sainte-Geneviève library in Paris.

In the first circle of this picture stand Adam and Eve. To the left of Adam are figures from the Old Testament. To his right is Eve and to her right stand the Church Fathers and the Apostles, all in keeping with Augustine's interpretations. The portals of the Balbec church also depict a view of the City of God (Civitas Dei), and it may be supposed that that work, along with pictures on the subject from the Middle Ages, were the sources of the description of the church of Balbec in A l'ombre des jeunes filles en fleurs.

The biblical theme of Eve's creation depicted on the façade of the cathedral in Orvieto in Italy is mentioned by the narrator in a conversation he has with Albertine in La Prisonnière about the works of Dostoevski ("In my view," says the narrator, "all his books can appear under the title 'Vengeance and Expiation'"), and on that occasion he lingers over the meaning of the actions of the elder Karamazov who rapes Smertchaïa, the crazy woman who, impelled by a maternal instinct, returns to the Karamazov garden to give birth.

> I know very few of his books. But is it not a sculpturesque and simple theme, worthy of the most classical art, a frieze interrupted and resumed on which the tale of vengeance and expiation is unfolded, the crime of old Karamazoff getting the poor idiot with child, the mysterious, animal, unexplained impulse by which the mother, herself unconsciously the instrument of an avenging destiny, obeying also obscurely her maternal instinct, feeling perhaps a combination of physical resentment and gratitude towards her seducer, comes to bear her child on old Karamazoff's ground. This is the first episode, mysterious, grand, august as a Creation of Woman among the sculptures at Orvieto.

For the narrator, Dostoevski, in The Brothers Karamazov, reiterates the myth of the creation of woman as depicted at Orvieto, that is, in accordance with the Christian reading of the Bible. In the narrator's view, the works of the Russian author could all be collected under the single title "The Story of a Crime". The fatal return of Woman to Man (The Brothers Karamazov) relates itself closely to the three levels of the imaginary in Proust, namely, The Story of a Crime, Vengeance and Expiation, and the creation of Eve.

And thus, for him, the creation of woman according to the Bible is the story of the first crime, perceived as the foundation of all crimes powering the imagination and psychology of the culture of the West. Following the taking of the rib from man, he is compelled to set out on a search in order to restore the loss, which for the narrator is the "restoration of stolen property". Proceeding to the bitter end, that sometimes ends in the death of the woman.

Interpretation of the Monumental Frieze of the Orvieto Cathedral:

We will attempt to interpret the frieze from Proust's point of view as reflected in the passage on Dostoevski's work and as understood with reference to the monumental frieze that extends along the entire wall of the Orvieto cathedral. There, three stages in Eve's creation are depicted: (1) the taking of the rib; (2) the creation of Eve from the rib; (3) the presentation of Eve to Adam.

The depiction of the taking of the rib is of special interest. It shows a figure in the role of the Divinity incising Adam's side with a scalpel, and creating a rather wide opening. Adam is in a deep sleep, as if from great fatigue, with his face to the ground. He is asleep in an orderly and well arranged garden, like that of a house. He is lying in a niche of the garden wall (and here the association with the Karamazov garden is clear; all the ambushes and all the crimes take place in a niche under the windowsill that looks out over the garden). In a different representation of the taking of the rib, from the same church, two additional figures are present, angels apparently, of much broader dimensions than the representation of God performing the deed in awe, almost furtively. The expression of the frightened divine figure in action is almost what would be appropriate in a case of breaking and entering, with the wide-dimensioned figures standing guard over the clandestine scene. All those present are very frightened and seem repelled by the deed which seems more like an instance of burglary.

While in his work Proust does recreate and embellish the myth of Eve's creation which also appears in Dostoevski's works, he does so only in order to refute it. The repetition of the crime and of the myth, which had had broad resonance in western art and culture, is out of place in Proust. True, Albertine is ravished and held captive, but in the end she leaves the narrator on her own free initiative and meets her death in a fall in a riding accident, by sheer chance, in a way that has nothing to do with her previous life with the narrator. Proust's work does not contribute one whit to the valorization of myth, especially the myth of the creation of woman. In the last book, Le Temps retrouvé, Albertine emerges from the narrator's memory, or artistic "sagesse" free of memory of the sinful and forced relations of the past, of the narrator's fleeting emotions, and appears as the goddess of Time by means of the picture of the "sun setting beyond the seas" not destined to return to any destination, free of all the illusions, idolatries and myths that theretofore had sustained the narrator. By way of conclusion it may be said that Proust's work describes the process of liberation from the Christian dualistic-antagonistic outlook and announces new psychological and anthropological principles.

The fixed hierarchical concentric circles of Augustine's Civitas Dei become in his work kaleidoscopic circles moving endlessly, in opposition to the fixed Christian hierarchy, and as such Proustian Time is already made manifest in the overture. That was made possible by Proust's comic view. The creator even takes a humorous view of the odyssey of the memory he created and which appears as necessarily so and as a totality of vision only to someone who does not know how to read between the lines. Creative wisdom lies beyond the myth of the complete creation that seemingly emerges from necessity. Proust's work contributes to the demythologization of any drama of Creation, especially any drama of conversion and inspiration deriving from mission and necessity (as in the case of Augustine).

The story of Eve's creation contributed greatly to the establishment of the myth of the "Ecclesia", the Church whose mission, according to Christianity, is to bring the communities of men into it. Whoever abuses his goal, namely the return to the mother of all, the Mother Church, may be likened to a withered branch (such as the Jews).

In the first book, Swann's Way is called Méséglise. The source of the name is a district near Combray called Mèréglise (Mother Church). By exchanging the "r" with an "s", Proust creates an opposing concept. Méséglise is the contrary of Mèréglise. By this change Proust reveals his opposition to the Jew Swann's entry into the lap of Christianity. Here we may be aided by a detail from his biography. Proust's mother was a Jewess, and in his work he did not want the memory of the Jewish mother to be lost in the lap of Christianity.

If we turn to other mythologies we read of the creation of a mass of men at one and the same time, of the creation of an entire race. For example, Hesiod's Works and Days speaks of the creation of five races of men by Zeus (the generation of gold, the generation of silver, the generation of copper, the generation of brave warriors and the generation of iron). Hesiod's mythology did not emphasize the creation of one man as the father and archetype of the entire human race. The birth of men in a monogamous or monandrous situation provided a broad field for the theological establishment of the Christian totalistic conception, with its historical, artistic and spiritual implications. For that reason the Eve born out of the narrator's dream is figureless and has no archetypal dimension. Every woman he meets thereafter differs from the one before and causes all the previous loves to be forgotten. The absence of a sacramental ritual, or of an oath of faithfulness (l'Adoration perpétuelle) with regard to the bond of love is what frees the Proustian world of the tragic mythic conception. And so that we, the readers, do not slip into a totalistic myth or tendentious conception with regard to Proust's view of the biblical spectacle, he extols the act of Creation and his being a man able to leave a woman; he does so at the beginning of La Prisonnière, at a time when he is living with Albertine calmly and peacefully, totally ignoring the dramatic era of Eve's creation with all the meanings it has within A la recherche du temps perdu. The biblical motif is interwoven with other mythic levels, and neither is it the most dominant; and that is part of a ceaseless process of demythologization, which is at the core of a work which is a response to the greater Christian commentator, Aurelius Augustinus, who was also the founder of the Christian empire.

Notes

1. Of Augustine's works, the Confessions, which relates the "history of a soul, could well have had most influence on the young author. A theory of memory occupies a prominent place in that book. The faculty of memory is rooted in the recollection of God. In his saga of memory, A la Recherche du temps perdu, Proust, taking issue with that view, defines the quality of memory as the quality of remembering "metaphors".

2. Here we may mention the exegesis of the Midrash on the verse "And the rib, which the Lord God had taken from the man, made He a woman" (Genesis 2:22), which says that God endowed woman with elative intelligence (or wisdom) (binah yeterah), which is akin to what Proust refers to as sagesse when speaking about artistic understanding. But it must be noted that this intersection of interpretation is incidental and stems from a free reading of Midrash Rabbah or of Proust. It must also be noted that the transcendental dimension of the "sagesse" is not posited in Proust's A la Recherche du Temps perdu.

MOTIFS BIBLIQUES DANS L'OEUVRE D'ALBERT CAMUS

Lionel Cohn
Bar-Ilan University

Essayer de parler de motifs bibliques dans l'oeuvre d'Albert Camus exige, au préalable, deux réserves importantes: parlant de Bible, il sera exclusivement question de la Bible hébraïque, sand référence au Nouveau Testament, et d'autre part, il ne peut s'agir, chez Albert Camus, d'une référence essentielle, mais bien plus tôt, accidentelle. Le terroir culturel de Camus, c'est l'hellénisme, non le biblisme et encore moins l'hébraïsme. Il n'y faut pas voir de réserve à l'égard de cette source d'inspiration, mais une tendance naturelle méditerranéenne que lie cet algérien à la culture grecque. Il est cependant intéressant de relever quelques motifs bibliques qui apparaissent dans les écrits de l'auteur de La Peste. Ces motifs, il faut en distinguer trois composantes: tout d'abord, des schémas bibliques, utilisés à dessein des images bibliques apparaissant presque inconsciemment, et enfin des thèmes bibliques intervenant dans les textes camusiens théoriques.

x

x   x

Schémas bibliques utilisés consciemment d'abord: dans cette première catégorie, il faut commencer par citer le thème le plus célèbre, le thème de la Peste. La Peste n'est pas nécessairement un thème biblique, mais le sujet de l'épidémie évoque les épidémies relatées dans la Bible, et Camus nous invite lui-même à nous relier à cette référence, puisqu'il cite ses sources bibliques dans ses Carnets:

> Bible: Deutéronome 28, 21; 32, 24 - Lévitique 26, 25. Amos 4, 10 - Exode 9, 4; 9, 15; 12, 29 - Jérémie 24, 10; 14, 12; 6, 19, 21, 7 et 9. Ezéchiel, 5, 12; 6, 12; 7, 15.

Il apparaît donc -- de ces 4 citations -- que c'est dans la Bible hébraïque que Camus a essentiellement puisé son inspiration pour le thème de ce livre qui devait être appelé à une telle notoriété. Il sera donc important de comprendre les raisons qui ont motivé Albert Camus à utiliser ce thème et à en faire le sujet essentiel de son second roman.

La peste, tout d'abord, est une plaie imposée par Dieu en Egypte aux ennemis d'Israël. La dimension métaphysique de ce thème est donc immédiatement apparente. Il s'agit, en effit, d'une punition céleste, et c'est ainse que Paneloux agence, son prêche qui est nettement influencé par les prophéties bibliques. Camus le dit d'ailleurs clairement dans ses Carnets:

Pour le prêche: "Avez-vous remarqué, mes frères, comme Jérémie est monotone." (Carnets II, 67)

Jérémie est donc, entre autres, l'exemple de Paneloux. La première dimension est donc clairement vouée et exprimée par Albert Camus: il s'agit de refuser, en premier lieu, l'idée biblique de sanction, de lien entre l'acte de l'individu et les malheurs dont il est la victime. Cette idée, biblique s'il en est, de l'intervention d'une Autorité Supérieure dans l'histoire de l'homme, doit être rejetée: c'est le sens du deuxième prêche de Panelous qui a changé de ton depuis son premier discours: il n'est plus certain de la punition, et il n'est plus le prophète qui avertit d'en haut. Impliqué dans l'épidémie, et ne comprenant plus son sens, il change de style:

Chose curieuse, nous dit le narrateur, il ne disait plus "vous" mais "nous" (I p. 1399)

La notion de sanction laisse la place à la notion de responsabilité collective. L'attitude du "prophète Paneloux" se fait plus hésitante, et, loin de tenter d'imposer une doctrine toute faite, Panelous se veut, en ce deuxième prêche, moins dogmatique et davantage enclin à découvrir la leçon qui jaillèt de la souffrance. Si, au début de l'épidémie, le fléau est un effet de la miséricorde divine,

"il vous élève et vous montre la voie"

il lui faut reconnaître, dans le deuxième discours, que

"l'amour de Dieu est un amour difficile".

C'est une autre attitude biblique qui nous est proposée ici. A la figure de Jérémie succède l'image de Job: l'admonestation laisse la place à l'acceptation difficile de la souffrance.

Ici, se profile la deuxième signification du thème biblique de la peste: ce n'est pas seulement le problème de la sanction qui est posé, mais une second interrogation sollicite les victimes de l'épidémie: l'espoir est-il permis? La Bible insiste sur la dimension temporelle de la souffrance: Moïse guide les enfants d'Israël vers la sortie d'Egypte, et l'arrivée en Canaan, David et Salomon préparent et construisent le Temple, les prophètes annoncent la venue du Messie, l'avènement d'un monde meilleur. La perspective biblique implique une espérance, et cette espérance, c'est ici l'espoir de la fin d'un fléau. Mais là aussi, Camus tient à distinguer deux temps: la première phase, pendant laquelle les séparés, nous dit Camus dans ses Carnets (II, p. 74) espèrent encore quelque chose, et

c'est seulement dans la deuxième phase qu'ils n'espèrent plus.

La peste brise donc l'espoir. La perte de l'espérance terrestre est un jalon de plus dans le refus d'une certaine vision biblique de la réalité. Camus l'exprime à propos d'une citation relative à Kafka:

> On doit frapper à mort l'espérance terrestre, c'est alors seulement qu'on se sauve soi-même par l'espérance véritable (Ibid)

Lier ainsi le salut au refus de l'espérance terrestre et à l'attente de la "véritable espérance" est évidemment adopter un schéma biblique. Cela ne signifie évidemment pas que Camus accepte cette attitude et s'identifie avec cette espérance: ce serait plutôt la nostalgie de cette espérance qui assombrit les derniers jours des condamnés de la Peste. Ici aussi, comme dans le cas de la sanction divine, l'absence d'espoir est une présentation a contrario d'une image biblique. La révolte métaphysique que symbolise la difficulté pour Paneloux de faire accepter par Rieux la mort de l'enfant, cette révolte remet en question l'ordre du monde, tel que le voit le croyant, par l'intermédiaire de la Bible. Le cri de colère du médecin:

> Je refuserai jusqu'à la mort d'aimer cette création où des enfants sont torturés,

ce cri exprime le refus de la punition qui est sans objet, et de l'expoir qui est sans signification.

Mais le thème de la peste implique une troisième dimension: il ne faut pas seulement voir dans l'épidémie une sanction, ou essayer de se rattacher à un vain espoir. Le caractère collectif de l'exil, la séparation qui définit les victimes de l'épidémie, le lien entre l'individu et la collectivité, telle est la troisième dimension, elle aussi liée à l'imagerie biblique du fléau. L'histoire biblique est, en effet, l'histoire d'un peuple, d'une collectivité et la responsabilité qui lie entre eux les victimes de l'épidémie, n'est pas sans évoquer, ainse, les punitions qui frappent par exemple la génération du déluge, les révoltés de Babel ou encore les habitants de Ninive. Et c'est ainsi que nous arrivons à une seconde utilisation par Camus d'un schéma biblique: le thème de Jonas. Le prophète biblique, chargé de faire revenir à Dieu, les habitants de Ninive, a donné son nom, nous le savons à une importante nouvelle d'Albert Camus. La comparaison entre le Jonas biblique et le peintre à succès de l'Exil et le Royaume va permettre de jeter une nouvelle lumière sur les liens entre l'imagerie camusienne et la thématique biblique.

Qui est Jonas? Quel lien rattache le héros de la nouvelle de Camus au personnage biblique du même nom? Pourquoi Camus a-t-il précisément choisi cet exemple pour le but qu'il s'est proposé? Il met en exergue de sa nouvelle le verset 12 du permier chapitre du livre de Jonas:

> Jetez-moi dans la mer..., car je sais que c'est moi qui attire sur vous cette grande tempête,

et il est légitime de s'interroger sur la signification de cette citation. Est-ce l'artiste au travail -- sous-titre de la nouvelle -- qui attire cette grande tempête sur la collectivité? Quel lien, en fait, entre l'art du peintre et l'inspiration du prophète? Ici, il faut relever, une fois de plus, les significations diverses de la symbolique biblique. Dans un premier temps, le personnage de Jonas est chargé de signifier les difficultés de l'artiste, happé comme son homonyme biblique, par le succès, et conséquemment victime de ce triomphe, et dans un deuxième temps les hésitations d'un homme, inséré dans une société, qui recherche la solitude. Le problème de l'artiste se double de celui de l'homme, et il apparaît ici que l'imagerie biblique reçoit tout son sens.

Pour comprendre la signification du thème biblique de Jonas, il apparaît que la lecture de l'histoire de Jonas -- qu'il appelle Jona -- par M. Henri Meschamic est extrêmement instructive. M. Meschamic ne se réfère nullement à Camus, mais son interprétation -- qui n'occulte nullement la lecture traditionnelle -- illustre bien le double problème du héros de Camus. M. Meschamic écrit:

> (Jona) ne fuit pas par peur. Bien qu'il risque d'être mis à mort, plutôt que d'être écouté, dans la ville du mal. Moïse, Jérémie avaient refusé à Dieu, par peur. Jona refuse parce qu'il sait d'avance. Ne veut pas jouer le jeu de Dieu...Job reconnaît que Dieu a raison. Jona se tait. Le livre finit sur le silence de Jona non-réponse à la question de Dieu... la question en clausule de tout le corpus-Bible est une question suspensive. Mais ce n'est plus le silence de Dieu, c'est le silence de l'homme...Une des valeurs de Jona initiatique serait de représenter la prophétie même du fonctionnement langage-histoire... hors du piège ancien qui opposait l'universel au particulier...vers le singulier qui est le même que le pluriel, la condition de l'universel dans le particulier concret. (p. 81-82).

Se retrouvent expressément soulignés ici les termes de la difficile tâche de l'artiste dépeint par Camus: le Jonas camusien, à l'instar du prophète biblique, ne peut assumer la mission dont il est investi; il eût dû jouer au maître face à ses admirateurs, à sa famille, à ses disciples.

> Jonas maintenant faisait école. Il en avoit d'abord été surpris... mais, bien vite, il se débarrassait sur son étoile de cette incommode maîtrise...

Maître malgré lui, le peintre est semblable au prophète malgré lui. Il ne croit pas en la mission qui lui semble imposée, de même que le Jonas biblique est sceptique sur l'efficacité de ses efforts. Mais si leur mission leur apparaît ainsi dénuée de sens, nos deux héros cherchent semblablement une diffcile synthèse entre ce que Meschamic nomme "l'universel" et le "particulier". L'exergue choisi par Camus dans le texte biblique -- expliquant que le prophète est responsable du malheur des marins dans le bateau -- souligne clairement le problème que notre auteur veut soulever: l'individu et la collectivité sont séparés par des intérêts opposés, mais la plainte de l'individu ne se traduit pas par une révolte mais par le silence. Jonas n'a pu fuir l'appel divin, et le voici arrivé à Ninive dont il admoneste les habitants. Ceux-ci se sont vite repentis, et échapperont donc à la punition dont les avait menacés le prophète. Jonas proteste, puis accepte avec résignation le verdict divin. L'opposition entre le désir de l'individu et l'intérêt de l'universel est dépassée: le silence de l'homme remplit l'espace où ne s'affrontent plus le singulier et le pluriel. C'est le même silence qu'oppose l'artiste de Camus. Lui aussi, infidèle à son rôle, se voit obligé, du fait de tout son entourage, d'arrêter de peindre: la collectivité a stérilisé l'inspiration de l'individu. A l'instar de sa mère, cette "sainte laïque", il se montratprêt à soutenir toutes les bonnes causes, il était compréhensif à l'égard de tous -- sa famille, ses amis, ses disciples, ses admirateurs et même plus tard ses détracteurs -- mais son oeuvre en pâtit. Comme le prophète biblique, sa protestation se fair progressivement silencieuse: il cesse d'abord de peindre, puis il s'arrête même de parler. Il ne peur qu'écouter

> la belle rumeur que font les hommes...Elle ne contrariait pas cette force joyeuse en lui, son art, ces pensées qu'il ne pouvait pas dire, à jamais silencieuses... (I, p. 1652)

Le voilà, comme son homolyme biblique, à jamais réfugié dans le silence. Son expérience de la solidarité le conduit à la solitude. La remarque finale de Dieu à Jonas sur la pitié que doivent susciter les habitants de Ninive est accueillie par le prophète avec silence, de même que notre peintre ne réagit plus, effondré sur sa toile. Perplexes tous deux sur leur expérience de la solidarité, les voilà solitaires à jamais.

Il n'est pas interdit de voit dans cet échec de Jonas un autre avatar de Clamence, lui aussi -- selon la belle expression de Paul Viallaneix -- victime d'une chute, par suite de

> l'exercice funambulesque de la pensée du midi

qui le faisait hésiter entre la solitude et la solidarité. Jonas a fui comme le héros biblique, le monde qui voulait le happer. M. Meschamic écrit:

> Jona est trois jours dans le poisson, trois jours dans Ninive. Seul dans le poisson, seul dans Ninive. Ni de la mer, ni du désert, il ne sait s'il sortira vivant.

Le Jonas de Camus est le fils de Meursault -- le solitaire -- et de Rieux -- le solidaire, et il se réalise pleinement sous la forme de cet autre prophète qu'est Jean-Baptiste Clamence, ce juge pénitent qui se veut lui aussi, comme le Jonas biblique, chargé de ramener ses contemporains à résipiscence.

Meursault, on l'a assez remarqué, a eu à la fin de sa vie, la nostalgie du ventre maternel, du recommencement, de la renaissance. Peu avant son exécution, il dit comprendre pourquoi à la fin d'une vie, elle avait pris un "fiancé", pourquoi elle avait joué à recommencer. (I, p. 1209).

La mère, la pureté originelle, l'eau -- qui avaient été aussi les refuges du Jonas biblique, sous la forme du ventre du poisson -- tels sont les éléments qui ont jalonné la nostalgie de Meursault: c'est ce qui l'attire -- cela a été souvent relevé -- dans Marie, dont le nom même évoque la mer, c'est aussi la raison pour laquelle il retire une telle joie des bains de mer -- mais il est intéressant de noter qu'Albert Camus va décrire un paysage édénique aux yeux de Meursault, et que ce paradis terrestre sera, à l'image du Gan Eden, interdit d'accès par une épée flamboyante. Il s'agit maintenant comme nous l'avions indiqué au commencement, non plus d'une thématique biblique expréssément formulée, mais d'une utilisation volontaire ou non, d'une imagerie qui trouve sa référence dans la Bible. Camus d'ailleurs autorise cette évocation, par cette note des Carnets:

> Curieux texte de la Genèse (III, rr): "Et l'Eternel Dieu dit: "Voici l'homme est devenu (après la faute), comme l'un de nous, sachant le bien et le mal. Main maintenant il faut prendre garde qu'il n'avance la main et ne prenne aussi l'arbre de vie, et qu'il n'en mange et ne vive à toujours." Et l'épée de feu qui chasse alors l'homme de l'Eden, "se tournait çà et là pour garder le chemin de l'arbre de vie." (Carnets II, 77).

C'est cette épée de feu que l'auteur de l'Etranger mettra sur le chemin de Meursault au moment où il a découvert un paysage édénique.

> On a encore entendu le petit bruit d'eu et de flûte au coeur du silence et de la chaleur...Tout s'arrêtait ici entre la mer, le sable et le soleil, le double silence de la flûte et de l'eau...Je marchais lentement vers les rochers, je sentais mon front se gonfler sous le soleil...A chaque épée de lumière jaillie du sable, d'un coquillage...mes mâchoires se crispaient...Je voyais de loin la petite masse sombre du rocher...je pensais à la source fraîche derrière le rocher. J'avais envie de retrouver le murmure de son eau, envie de fuir le soleil, l'effort et les pleurs de femme, envie de retrouver l'ombre et son repos. (I, 1165)

Tel est le paysage paradisiaque: l'ombre, le bruit de l'eau et de la flûte, la source fraîche. Il n'est pas inutile de relever qu'en hébreu, c'est la même racine -- TSL -- qui rend les trois composantes de ce paysage: l'ombre -- Tsél -- le son (de la flûte ou de l'eau) Tslil -- et la fraîcheur, la pureté de la source -- Tsaloul -- et il y a certainement ici une de ces rencontres sémantiques, particulières à la langue hébraïque, qui traduisent la cohésion générique d'un concept.

Cependant, ce paysage, l'épée de feu dont Camus parlait dans ses Carnets, citant la Genèse, va en enterdire l'accès.

J'ai fait quelques pas vers la source...j'ai fait un mouvement en avant...
(puis)...j'ai fait un pas, un seul pas en avant. Et cette fois,...l'Arabe a tiré son
couteau qu'il m'a présenté dans le soleil. La lumière a giclé sur l'acier et
c'était comme une longue lame étincelante qui m'atteignait au front... Je ne
sentais plus que les cymbales du soleil sur mon front et...le glaive éclatant
jailli du couteau toujours en face de moi. Cette épée brûlante rongeait mes
cils et fouillait mes yeux douloureux (I, 1166).

L'épée de feu punit les pélerins du Royaume, ceux qui ont osé enfreindre l'interdit de
pénétrer dans l'Eden. Cette démesure se traduit par la mort, et s'il s'agit ici de la mort
de l'autre, en fait, on le sait, c'est lui-même, son bonheur, que Meursault a exécuté. Dure
sanction pour ceux qui se sont permis de tendre à la démesure. Meursault est victime de
son désir d'incursion dans l'au-delà. Comme l'explique M. Claude Vigée,

> la mort est le prix de la démesure, même si celle-ci donne accès au monde de
> la réalité et la démesure, fût-elle...la seult clé capable de rouvrir la porte du
> royaume paternel de la présence. (Les Artistes de la Faim, p. 262).

La nostalgie du sacré jalonne l'oeuvre de Camus, et Meursault apparaît ici puni pour
avoir enfreint ce que se permettront -- ne fût-ce qu'un court instant -- Rieux et Tarrou
dans la Peste, dont le bain sera une sorte de sacrement d'accès, quelque bref qu'il soit à
ce Royaume inaccessible. Mais si pour eux, le paradis n'est pas entièrement inabordable,
c'est parce qu'ils n'oublient pas leurs contemporains, et que, ayant vecu l'experience du
sacré, ils savent qu'ils doivent reprendre la lutte, et

qu'il fallait maintenant recommencer.

Si Meursault est une sorte de "premier homme" -- nom bien biblique d'une oeuvre de
Camus restée inachevée --, si l'on peur faire des héros de la Peste qui luttent contre la
maladie des prototypes de Job qui s'interroge sur le sens de ses malheurs, il faudra
asssurément voir dans Clamence une synthèse de ces personnages, puisqu'il est le prophète
qui, comme il le dit, "annoncera la." Mais ce prophète a -- c'est bien naturel -- des
relents d'apôtre chrétien, malgré la référence çà et là à des prophètes d'Israël. Il
convient de relever, ainsi, que Clamence se compare au première version, au prophète
Jérémie -- qui prêche dans le dexert. Relativement à Jérémie, cette référence est
intéressante, dans la mesure où, déjà -- on l'a noté plus haut -- les Carnets citaient 5
versets de Jérémie menaçant de la peste, et par ailleurs le prêche de Paneloux est
annoncé de la façon suivante dans les Carnets:

Avez-vous remarqué, mes frères, comme Jérémie est monotone. (p. 67).

Quoi qu'il en soit, Clamence se présente ainsi:

Dans la solitude, la fatigue aidant, que voulez-vous, on se prend volongiers pour un prophète. Après tout, c'est bien là ce que je suis, réfugié dans un désert de pierres, de brumes et d'eaux pourries, prophète vide pour temps médiocres, Elie (ici le manuscrit offre comme variante Jérémie) sans messie... (I. p. 1533)

et plus tard, Clamence reprend cette image du prophète Elie, quand, au moment de prendre congé de son interlocuteur, il admire d'abord le vol des colombes qui -- il l'espère, à l'instar de la colombe envoyée par Noé, hors de l'arche, --

apportent la bonne nouvelle. Tout le monde sera sauvé, hein, et pas seulement les élus...Allons, avouez que vous resteriez pantois si un char descendait du ciel pour m'emporter.

L'image biblique du char de feu emportant le prophète Elie est certes presentée avec ironie, mais la référence biblique souligne bien que ce héros de notre temps qu'est Jean-Baptiste Clamence trouve lui aussi son écho dans la Bible hébraïque.

Mais la Bible, avons-nous relevé dès le départ, n'est pas uniquement, pour l'auteur du Mythe de Sisyphe une référence thématique: Camus a un compte à règler avec le Dieu de l'Ancien Testament, et le chrétien qu'il est -- malgré son refus de se rattacher à aucune Eglise -- ne peut s'empêcher de parler de la cruauté du Dieu biblique. Il écrit:

C'est au dieu personnel que la révolte peut demander personnellement des comptes. Dès qu'il règne, elle se dresse, dans sa résolution la plus farouche et prononce le nom définitif. Avec Caïn, la première révolte coïncide avec le premier crime. L'histoire de la révolte, telle que nous la vivons aujourd'hui, est bien plus celle des enfants de Caïn que des disciples de Prométhée. En ce sens, c'est le Dieu de l'Ancien Testament, surtout qui mobilisera l'énergie révoltée...Jusqu'à Dostoievski et Nietzsche, la révolte ne s'adresse qu'à une divinité cruelle et capricieuse, celle qui préfère, sans motif convaincant, le sacrifice d'Abel à celui de Caïn, et qui par là, provoque le premier meurtre. (II, p. 443 et 445).

L'attitude, ici, de Camus par rapport à un thème biblique est empreinte de refus: il s'agit, ici, de refuser la sévérité du Dieu d'Israël, l'arbitraire d'une préférence qui provoque le meurtre. La révolte est justifiée dans la mesure où il y a arbitraire, et c'est ainsi qu'adoptant une lecture chrétienne, Camus comprend l'attitude du Dieu d'Israël. Comment comprendre cet intérêt de Camus pour l'acte de Caïn? Pourquoi se montre-t-il si sévère à l'égard des fils de Caïn? Il est intéressant de relever que, dans les Actuelles, Camus voulant stigmatiser son époque, remarque que l'histoire officielle a toujours été l'histoire des grands meurtriers. Et ce n'est pas aujourd'hui que Caïn tue Abel. Mais c'est aujourd'hui que Caïn tue Abel au nom de la logique et réclame ensuire la Legion d'Honneur (II, p. 400).

Caïn apparaît ici comme le prototype du meurtrier, et, dans son étude sur "Camus et la Bible," Jacques Goldstain relève justement que Camus eût pu noter la réserve que la Bible semble éprouver pour le geste de Caïn, et souligner par là, l'éthique biblique. Golstain note qu'au contraire c'est la révolte de Caïn qui intéresse Camus. Et cela mérite, en effet réflexion.

Il s'agit, maintenant, de nous interroger, à la suite de cette réflexion camusienne -- qui n'est nullement marginale -- sur le sens de l'intérêt de Camus pour le texte biblique et pour cetains aspects de l'Ancien Testament. Assurément, pour lui, il s'agit, comme pour les chrétiens, d'une première présentation de l'histoire religieuse, dont la seconde partie sera illustrée par le christianisme. Le Nouveau Testament répond, nous dit Camus, à tous les Caïn du monde en adoucissant la figure de Dieu...et ce cliché sur l'opposition entre le Dieu cruel des juifs et le Dieu clément des chrétiens -- cliché dont on n'a jamais assez souligné l'ineptie -- expliquera l'intérêt de Camus pour les thèmes bibliques, pour certains schémas tirés de la Bible hébraïque, intérêt qui se double d'une réserve. L'attitude de Camus à l'égard de la Bible est à l'image de son attitude générale: fidèle à la "mesure", il est à la fois désireux et retenu. La Bible le séduit par son style imagé, par l'inspiration poétique et prophétique, par la richesse et la puissance des thèmes qui la composent, et surtout par l'attrait qu'il éprouve pour le sacré, sacré qui habite chaque page de la Bible, mais le Dieu d'Israël, ce Dieu personnel qui punit le méchant et récompense le juste, ce Dieu qui enseigne l'espoir ce "Dieu d'Abraham, d'Isaac et de Jacob," auquel, nous dit Camus,

il faut se soumettre...quand on a achevé, comme Pascal, la carrière de l'intelligence révoltée,

ce Dieu s'oppose trop à la sensibilité camusienne pourqu'il s'y soumette. Albert Camus ne peut accepter une réalité transcendante, qui justifie la souffrance. La seule façon possible d'accepter l'existence de la souffrance, ce serait de devenir Dieu -- comme Caligula ou Clamence qui parle de

l'ivresse de se senter Dieu le père (I, 1547) --

mais il s'agit là d'une attitude fondamentalement opposée au biblisme. L'aventure de la génération de Babel en témoigne assez.

Paul Viallaneix remarque que

ce Sisyphe algérois parlait couramment la langue de la Bible, même lorsqu'il élevait la voix pour contester la Révélation, et ce pourrait être la conclusion de cette brève et nullement exhaustive analyse de l'infuence de la Bible hébraïque sur Albert Camus. Il apprécie l'expérience immanente du sacré,, de l'identification ontologique au monde, que la Bible nous propose, par exemple, en décrivant la nostalgie du pardis originel ou en nous proposant l'aspiration collective d'un peuple à l'expérience de la pénitence, mais cet attrait poétique pour la Bible ne doit pas faire illusion: il ne fait pas de Clamence un croyant, même s'il est devenu Dieu le père. Certes, Camus reste réservé à l'égard de la transcendance, et M. Gay-Crosier a eu raison de relever que la seule transcendance à laquelle se réfère Camus est

une transcendance horizontale au niveau de l'homme, et non une trnscendance verticale qui aboutirait à Dieu (Les Envers d'un échec p. 111).

Peut-être est-ce là le secret de l'intérêt de Camus pour l'imagerie biblique: l'identification ontologique avec un sacré dont il a la nostalgie;

hanté par la révélation précaire d'une réalité sacrée,

selon l'expression de M. Vigée, Camus a peut-être trouvé dans la Bible le seul terrain fertile où pouvait s'alimenter l'"'incroyance passionée" et le sens du sacré qui caractérisent celui qui a écrit, dans L'Envers et l'Endroit:

A cette heure, tout mon royaume est de ce monde... Tout est écrit dans cette fenêtre où le ciel déverse sa plénitude à la rencontre de ma pitié...L'éternité est là, et moi je l'espérais. (II, p. 49).

ON THE IRONIC USE OF THE MYTH OF JOB IN Y.H. BRENNER'S
BREAKDOWN AND BEREAVEMENT

Menachem Brinker

Tel-Aviv University

Job is mentioned explicitly only once in Breakdown and Bereavement. The novel, however, makes additional, very obvious allusions to the Biblical myth, themes and problems. Among the critics who have discussed this novel -- from M. Y. Berdichevsky up to Gershon Shaked -- some have discerned this fact, assigning it various functions. Their views are summarily stated by Shaked, who sees the novel's main protagonist as rendered more profound through its association with the archetypal sufferer. He also sees the novel's earlier reference to Job as giving it "a certain unity superseding its details." Shaked finds that it "gives the main character a significance even before he is fully "realized" in the details of the fable.[1]

In my opinion, the main effect attained by introducing Job into the novel is a totally different one. This becomes clear when we understand the role played by similar allusions in Brenner's other works. I see the main function in these cases as a meta-poetic, rather than a poetic one. The aim of this and similar allusions is that of shedding light on the nature of Brenner's story and illuminating it as a specific literary work rather than elucidating a representational structure within its "world."

In order to give some weight to my hypothesis, however, we must first scrutinize the main instances in which the text refers or alludes to the Book of Job.

A.

Yehezkel Hefetz experiences a severe crisis. While performing an especially strenuous task at the kvutza, he collapses and the resulting hernia which he sees as a wretched, unmanly ailment, gradually pushes him towards a severe psychological crisis, a condition he has already experienced at least once before. One of his friends escorts him to the home of the poor Jerusalem relatives, to which he has been sent. In the course of a visit at the "Physick for the Soul" hospital, he overhears a discussion of his uncle's plight. Not only is this uncle a destitute cripple saddled with two unmarried daughters; now heaven has sent him an ailing relative to burden him even further. This occurs in the second chapter of the story (31).[2] An external analepsis in the first chapter has already informed us that this is the second time that Yehezkel Hefetz has left the kvutza, On the first occasion he emigrated to Europe where he met a poor, gentle girl. After much hesitation and inner conflict, he "pulled himself together and persisted" (22) only to find her one evening "cheating" on him with a student of wealthy parentage (25). He then returned to the kvutza in disappointment and despair, in search of a new life. Now he had been forced to leave it yet a second time.

In chapter 2, Hefetz buys the girdle recommended by the doctor and conducts an animated conversation with his escort-friend, during which his mind dwells upon other things:

> He thought: What an ugly way to suffer ... what an ugly way to suffer.... In the book of Job the Leper it is written: "And he took a potsherd to scrape himself with." ... Only I am not Job: I have no complaints against God. In fact, I have no God. I have nothing to do with God. And even if I could complain -- I'm not complaining and I don't wish to protest. I'm not Job. And I don't sit in ashes, either, but in refuse, in the refuse of my own ugly suffering. Only I don't let go of the potsherd. I can't stop scratching. Yes, a potsherd is probably the one thing I don't do without.... (32)

The comparison with Job results from a verbal association caused by the word "suffering." It ends by establishing an analogy between two sufferers scratching themselves with shards. This analogy obviously disproves the validity of the whole comparison, as it is based on a merely figurative potsherd. Hefetz's suffering is ugly. There is no surrounding aura of theological grandeur. His "potsherd" is no more than his driving need to pick at his mental wounds, to return time and again to his hernia and his crisis, and to keep the tale of his failures ever present, as it were, obsessively, in his thoughts. The main difference between Yehezkel and Job -- an absence of complaints stemming from an absence of faith -- narrows down the common ground between the two to the abstract theme of suffering. The novel develops this crucial difference with regard to another of its characters as well, Hanoch, whose suffering is also compared with Job's through two allusions.

The first of these has to do with Yehezkel's thoughts on Hanoch. Hanoch has been divorced by his wife and banished from Jerusalem, and reaches Safed where he finds work in a flour mill. In obscure circumstances he is somehow taken ill at the mill and for lack of anyone to visit or attend him, he dies a lonely death, far away from his only son, his father and the whole of his family. While following a family Bible lesson, given during his illness, Yehezkel observes Hanoch's father drowsing off and thinks:

> "Haim is sleeping ... and when Haim sleeps his thoughts sleep too. Perhaps he doesn't even see things in his dreams like I do ... but if he were to see his son in a dream, his divorced son Hanoch, Hanoch from the mill whom he was telling us about only yesterday, I'm sure he would tell him: 'Father! Don't listen to what they tell you about the greatness of "the eternal book"! The eternal book -- what does it have to say about all the solitary years that I've spent here by the millstones? What does it have to say about my anguish, my life, and my approaching death? At the very most -- a word here, a word there -- some paradox about the justice of God ... about the justice of what doesn't exist. Or is it that my years simply don't matter at all? That my life

is unimportant, insignificant, undeserving of mention? Two or three years on the job in some forsaken mill ... ah? You say they're nothing to speak of against the background of eternity? The book of eternity passes over them in silence? Eternity?'" (90-91)

In this instance the whole Bible appears in Yehezkel's thoughts as a work incapable of helping Hanoch to understand, justify or accept his suffering. Hanoch's suffering is conceived of by Yehezkel as suffering which isn't "writ in the Bible."

The second allusion to Job occurs in a passage spoken by Hanoch himself. This is a more explicit allusion, as it opens with a quotation from the Book of Job: "Wilt thou ever find knowledge of God" (250). The sentence used by the Biblical Zophar the Naamathite to begin his answer to Job, is stated here by Joseph, Haim's brother, at the end of a grandiloquent sermon on the value of the study of God in Judaism. It reminds Haim of his stammering son, Hanoch, and of the latter's statements on the subject of faith during one of his visits to Jerusalem:

"I'm s-s-saying," Hanoch stammered, "I'm saying ... that if God made all this ... and if He made it so that I shouldn't know about Him -- f-fine, then I don't know. B-b-but why did He make it so I sh-shouldn't know? And how d-do I know it was Him? And what difference does it make whether I say that He did or didn't? I'm asking you what difference ... what difference does it make whether I pray to Him or not ... will He listen to me if I do? Life is hard for those who b-b-believe and h-hard for those who don't ... s-so why b-bother? If t-times are hard ... I'll get by ... I'll get by without Him. Wh-what? You want me to get on my knees and cry 'm-mercy'? It would be out of p-p-p-place...." (251)

After coming upon the memory of this conversation, Haim is overcome with terror. The terror does not stem from an endeavor to ask the questions of Job, but rather due to his awareness that he too is gradually losing his religious faith:

<u>It isn't so ... it isn't so at all ... to breathe is truly impossible ... but there's nothing to hold on to ... only empty space ... and nothing, nothing can ever fill it ... there isn't any God.....</u> (252)

The thematic focus of the three cases where the story recourses to Job and to <u>Job</u> amounts, then, to an emphasis of the far-reaching difference between the world of Yehezkel and Hanoch Hefetz on the one hand, and the world of Job and <u>The Book of Job</u> on the other. Each and every member of the Hefetz family suffers. However, it is not the believers among them, or those who lead observant lives, who are involved in comparisons and allusions to Job and <u>The Book of Job</u>, but rather the two characters who are most conscious of their utter secularism. Their world is one of full awareness of the pointlessness of suffering, and no place is left for a theological problem of any kind. It is a world which has no place for the answers of Job's friends as it has no place for any of Job's questions. Yehezkel and Hanoch's questions on suffering, the means for withstanding it, the point of withstanding it (the point of living), are very different from the ones asked by Job.

Two other members of the family -- the two uncles, Haim and Joseph -- scratch themselves. If, however, the circumstances of these two "scratchings" can at all be taken to be allusions to Job, they can only be construed as detractory allusions, as near parody. In the last lines of the book, Haim the bereaved father, sits on the banks of the Sea of Galilee contemplating the nearby arrival of his grandson, Hanoch's son. He picks up a pebble, "and putting it under his shirt, began to scratch and scratch with great gusto" (310). This takes place at none other a time than that when "a feeling of well-being seeped slowly through the body of the man on land" (310). Elsewhere in the book Joseph gives a lengthy sermon on the tiny stings, the wily Jerusalem mosquitos, who succeed in outwitting their prospective trappers. This sermon is one of the few humoristic passages in the sorry tale of the Hefetz family (187). Besides these two motifs which need not be seen as allusions to Job at all, Breakdown and Bereavement's whole reference to The Book of Job is limited to the instances cited above. Its allusions to Job underline the dividing distance between the Hefetz family and the ancient, archetypal figure of the Biblical sufferer.

The weight of this infiltration of Breakdown and Bereavement by the story of Job should not be underestimated. It must, however, be realized that the poetic function of these allusions is a limited and static one. While it does contribute towards illuminating certain facets of personality in Yehezkel and Hanoch Hefetz, it adds nothing to the plot's evolvement and signifies nothing in the spiritual development of the main protagonist. Its static nature becomes obvious in contrast to Brenner's dynamic use of literary allusions not only in this, but in his other major stories as well.

B.

Many of Brenner's characters -- and that of Yehezkel Hefetz is a prominent example -- repeatedly turn and roll passages and phrases from various texts through their thoughts. The running debate that they keep up with their surroundings (and the echoes of their surroundings within themselves), concerns not only the statements of the stories' other characters, but also the statements of authors and literary characters as well as quotations and excerpts. This phenomenon is especially frequent in Brenner's longer stories whose main line of development lies in the spiritual-ideological development of the protagonist.

There is no doubt that Breakdown and Bereavement is fundamentally such a story, despite the profusion of external events occurring in it. As far as Yehezkel's external fate is concerned, the novel makes it quite clear that the development described by it is merely a segment of a recurring cycle, being spread out for the reader in linear form. Hefetz has already experienced a mental crisis before the series of events comprising this segment (7) and he will become mentally ill again after the events depicted by the novel (3). The decision to end the story "on the verge of peace" during one of the "hours of sun" mentioned by Yehezkel in the chapter before the last (297), is one made by the fictional author, the editor of Yehezkel's diary. It is necessitated by the novel only because we are willing to identify the mental oscillation in Yehezkel's attitude towards his fate rather than this fate itself as the main story. On the part of the "author-editor," this would seem to be an "ideological" decision rather than a "narrative" one. It cannot be justified by the fact that the source notes, written by Yehezkel Hefetz himself, end at this point, as the last section of the novel does not deal with him at all, but with his uncle Haim. Moreover, the editor-author met Yehezkel on a ship where he was again taken ill, and could therefore have ended the story with this meeting. Yet, a kind of narrative justification for this ending may be found in the progress of the hero's ideas: Hefetz is unable to find an answer to his questions on the purpose of life, an answer which might make his life an incline leading towards a goal. The illumination that he achieves towards the end of the novel stems from the idea that life's justification and sense of purpose have to do with sporadic "hours of sun" that are scattered throughout it and not with any final objective towards which it leads. Thus, when the story ends with one of these hours, this constitutes an illustration of the main character's thoughts, and a natural point for terminating this pendulum of mental processes, while still complying with the conventional narrative requirement of linear development. Hefetz's life is a recurring cycle. Yet this cycle contains directional psychological movements. The cycle therefore makes it possible to unfold one of these in linear form, while the linear arrangement of this segment does not deny the cycle.

Hefetz's development involves two central subjects. The first is Hemilin's "theft" of his beloved ones, the sense of failure and inferiority aroused in him by this theft, his jealousy of Hemilin, and -- most important -- the suspicion that the whole of his intellectual life and his moral judgement is being poisoned by his jealousy of Hemilin. His anger at this jealousy is, in fact, greater than his anger at its subject. The second, wider issue is the lack of a clear purpose in life, the lack of a great aspiration which would justify the suffering. The development experienced by Yehezkel with regard to these two subjects is linked up with literary fragments: quotations and passages which he turns over and over in his mind. These signify the spiritual development he is undergoing, so much so that understanding them correctly becomes a necessary condition for the understanding of the development itself.

At the height of his mental crisis, Hefetz conducts an imaginary argument with Hemilin (163-165). The whole argument is, in fact, carried on in quotations from Nietzsche, especially quotations from The Geneology of Morals and Beyond Good and Evil. Two of Brenner's earlier stories include such confrontations between the main protagonist and his rival who has stolen away a beloved's attentions and who subsequently expresses his superiority in Nietzschean language. The first is "In Winter" and the second "Around the Point."[3] In Breakdown and Bereavement, however, this confrontation is placed at the center of the work and it is very clearly an internal confrontation occurring within the character's mind. Hefetz emphasizes that Hemilin could have carried on no such argument with him, being a person untouched by moral dilemmas of any kind, and lacking in general education, excepting that necessary for a medical career. It is clear that Hemilin provokes Hefetz without, himself, committing any provocation. He apparently stole the first girl without knowing anything of her alliance with Hefetz, while the more recent incident -- that concerning Miriam -- is no "theft" at all, as Hefetz has not even summoned the courage to tell Miriam of his feelings, while Hemilin has, in turn, become the object of her longing unknowingly and to no avail. Hefetz's jealousy of Hemilin is thus focused on the ease with which Hemilin attains success with women, and on his freedom from the reflectiveness or the inhibitions so characteristic of Hefetz himself.

Hefetz's imagination transforms Hemilin to a sort of "metaphysical substance" (160-161) whose very existence is an accusation directed against him, which undermines the remnants of his sanity and his inner peace. It is thus that Hefetz comes to invent these dialogues "that never had and never could have taken place" (161). In the course of the imaginary argument, Hemilin accuses Hefetz of a sense of moral superiority which rests on dubious grounds, while describing himself as a healthy person who is free of reflectiveness. Morality and reflectiveness, the advantages of Hefetz and his kind, are no more than a cover for their sickness and for their incapability of making open and easy contact with their surroundings and with life. Hemilin is obviously expressing Hefetz's own suspicions towards himself, here, suspicions which he finds much bitterer than the actual theft of his beloveds' attentions.

Hefetz resists this accusation by claiming full awareness of the fact that he is a mere "part," who by no means presumes to "sit in judgement on the whole." He knows that he is "interested" (164). But he spits both upon philosophy and objectivity as well, since for him this "part" is the "whole." The pathos of the weak-reflective is evident in the claims put forth by Hefetz (who defends not only himself, but Esther too, against the imaginary Hemilin of his thoughts). However, they suggest that Hemilin too is but a "part," affecting an inclusive, indomitable view of the "whole." As regards the validity of his judgements, he who is engrossed in the "satisfaction of his desires" and is altogether lacking in reflectiveness, fares no better than the man who is given to reflection. Furthermore -- Hefetz stresses -- he too, no less than Hemilin, is engrossed in the gratification of his instinctual needs. The only difference lies in the fact that in him it is the "moral instinct" that dominates the rest. Thus, even if this happens to be caused by his illness and his over-sensitivity to suffering, "my motives can't be questioned" for (as he concludes one of the internal dialogues preceding this imaginary argument) "the victorious instincts can't be questioned" (146).

This last phrase which Brenner puts in quotation marks is a summary of one of Nietzsche's aphorisms (no. 200 in Beyond Good and Evil) describing mental illness (decadence) as anarchy resulting from a struggle between conflicting impulses, and health as a condition attained through the predominance of one of these impulses. Hefetz, accordingly receives full "exoneration" at the hands of the very philosophy and psychology that cast suspicion upon his self-evaluation. He beats Hemilin (as well as what is actually his own suspicion towards himself) by beating Nietzsche with Nietzsche. The legalistic Talmudic language in which the whole of the hallucinated argument goes on, creates an overt, amusing parody of the Nietzschean language, so popular at the time among some sectors of the Russian-Jewish intelligentsia. It is, however, important to perceive that Hefetz's own deliberations, presented in his inner monologues and dialogues, are worded in the very style whose devoted incorporation he parodies here. Hefetz's jealousy of Hemilin and the depression it brings upon him are crucial to an understanding of Hefetz's mental crisis, and the defeat of both the jealousy and the depression are vital for his emergence -- albeit a temporary emergence only -- from the mental crisis which is the novel's central subject. One must understand the original context of the slogan concerning "the victorious instincts" in order to understand how it is that Hefetz succeeds in accepting himself. Granted, this acceptance may be lacking in heartfelt pride ("without bravado" 296). Yet it is also without self-deprecation in the face of the Other's scrutiny which he has internalized. The issue is not only psychological and social. Hefetz -- the only central protagonist of Brenner's who is not a professional intellectual; an author, a teacher or a journalist -- is a thinker both despite and of his own will. The thought that his judgement of the hardships of life may be "infected" not only with the usual, necessary form of subjectivity but also by the subjectivity of "we who are ruptured" (162) is one that shakes him to the very depths of his being. Like all of Brenner's central characters -- all anti-heroes and heros of the spirit at one and the same time -- Hefetz needs to know that his judgements on life, both his own and that of his surroundings, are no less valid than those of others, and, perchance, are even more valuable for their having been formulated "in this house at the city's end." Hefetz's acknowledgement of his perpetual critical reflectiveness, a torment both to himself and his surroundings, as a "victorious instinct," allows him to turn this fact of fate and character into a value.

Yet another quotation plays a more dynamic and equally important role in the novel. It is a quotation which penetrates into Hefetz's mind at the beginning of the story, and which he subsequently turns over and over in the course of the book. He returns to it towards the novel's end and uses it in the tentative summary of his life-experience and his resulting convictions. In Chapter Three of Part One, Yehezkel hears his uncle reading and translating from a book before him:

"And whereas experience has taught me ... experience has taught me ... that all ordinary circumstances of life ... all contingent phenomena as we know them are vanity and evil. ... And whereas I have seen ... I have seen ... that all the causes and objects of my fears ... are substantially ... neither good nor evil ... but only as they affect the spirit ... I made up my mind ... my mind ... to inquire after the true good. ... " (37)[4]

Yehezkel "understood nothing of what he heard" (37). Yet a few lines later, due to a chain of ideas aroused in him as he listened to these seemingly indecipherable words, he develops the first symptoms of mental illness: "he was frightened by the glasses of his learned uncle, the scholar Reb Yosef Hefetz" (38). The narrator has already told us that a few days later he was finally taken to a hospital, "though not to one for the physically ill" (38).

Spinoza's words from the first section of the Treatise on the Improvement of the Understanding -- identified simply as The Tractatus in Reb Joseph's discussion -- seep down into the depths of Hefetz's thoughts. From here on echos and fragmentary memories of this text, which Hefetz heard for the first time only to be taken ill and hospitalized soon after, appear at crucial points in the recovery process. The wording is always militantly polemical. Yehezkel rejects the recommendation that he search for "the true good" instead of attaching importance of the "ordinary circumstances of life." As he does not believe in any kind of personal, social or metaphysical "transcendence" which would justify the suffering of existence-on-earth, his recovery must involve the identification in the heart of the "ordinary circumstances of life." Upon returning from the hospital, he contemplates his future and his first steps at work, and he thinks of the need for "finding meaning in the ordinary circumstances of life" (146). (Brenner often emphasizes quotations which define central themes in his protagonists' inner worlds, with double spacing or with quotation marks; in this case he uses both.) Towards the end of the story, as Yehezkel Hefetz is summarizing the events he has experienced during the year, his lips again utter the self same words: "there's meaning enough in the ordinary circumstances of life" (296). The final summary of Yehezkel Hefetz's long-suffering thought is given as these words' immediate sequel, and it has to do with "the many hours of sun, many hours of light, in those thirty years," the thirty years of his life (296).

The Tractatus passage's penetration into the depths of Hefetz's mind, thus plays an active role in the story. It enables him to summarize his experience as to "the true good" in a manner that shows the marks of the preceding debates and deliberations carried on within himself. According to an artistic convention dominating all of Brenner's longer works, the character's life-experience is considered more reliable the more it is placed, through the use of polemic, in opposition to the wisdom offered by "books." Discovering "the true good" within "the ordinary circumstances of life" is the central piece of wisdom arising from the life-experience of Yehezkel Hefetz. As his hours of light have to do with his visits with Hanoch's orphaned son, at the orphanage, Hefetz's declaration concerning "hours of light" attains a climax of the anti-pathetical pathos which pervades the whole of his thought and life.

Yehezkel Hefetz's mental development passes through three stages: failure and crisis; insanity and despair; an acceptance of life as it is and a (temporary) reconciliation with it. The complete Tractatus quotation indicates his transition from the first stage to the second. Fragments of this quotation then accompany Hefetz throughout the second stage. Finally, these fragments' recombination in Hefetz's mind which aligns them in a new pattern, indicates the third and last stage in this segment of linear-like mental development isolated by the novel from the whole of Hefetz's cyclical life. All of this complies perfectly with the fixed manner in which Brenner's stories make use of quotations and quotation fragments, a manner so constantly fixed, in fact, that it comes close to becoming the predominant artistic convention governing these stories. According to this convention, the complete and faithful literary quotation almost always signifies "literature" as opposed to "life," "the exalted" as opposed to "the lowly," ridiculous pathos as opposed to wretched reality, and the unreliable as opposed to the credible. Yet when this quotation is shattered in the mind of the Brennerean character, its broken or distorted form comes to signify the characters' palpitant inner lives and especially their running dialogues with themselves and their surroundings. Brenner's stories are dominated by the convention according to which everything stemming from a literary source must first be shattered, melted down and remolded into a new textual fabric before it is accepted as a genuine representation of life. The inner controversy within the characters' souls lends "life" to such literary quotations and to identifiable echoes of literary situations. During moments at which the characters' contact with their worlds reaches a climax, the literary allusions, made unreliable before in contrast to "wretched life," now become reliable as they serve to heighten this very life. The remolded form of the fragments of the Spinoza quotation -- discovery of "the true good" within "the ordinary circumstances of life" -- this indicates the arrival of the reconciliatory stage of Yehezkel's mental drama, while underlining the pathos of these moments of climax. As this mental drama is the movel's underlying axis of development, the role played by this quotation is highly dynamic and clearly related to the plot's innermost components.

C.

The role played in the novel by the allusions to Job is not even remotely similar to that played by its allusions to Nietzsche and Spinoza. None of Yehezkel Hefetz's internal polemics have anything to do with Job, his friends or the teller of the Biblical story. Subsequently, the poetic function of these allusions is a static and limited one. This, however, is not true of their meta-poetic function.

Poetic function is a property of the elements and motifs that build the plot, the characters, in short the "poetic world" the reader constructs from the text. Meta-poetic function is a property of the elements and motifs active in the clarification of the nature of the text itself as a work of literature (in comparison with other texts and other works of literature). Needless to say, there is a multiplex relationship between these two functions, as the understanding of a story's character (whether, for example, it is "realistic," or "fantastic," a satire or a parody), obviously guides us in the construction of its "world." It is also obvious that some of the text's most central elements serve both of these functions simultaneously. Any element of the story representing a part of its "world" can also, in principle, call attention to <u>the story itself</u> as a type of reality. The text forms the basis of the story's "reality" or "world." However, the same text also characterizes it as a specific literary reality, and defines its place in the world of literature.

Nevertheless, not all the elements of the story share the burden of these functions, either equally or at all. Some of Hefetz's debates with authors, books and quotations are crucial for an understanding of his spiritual and mental development, while the fact that he finds nothing truly in common with Job mainly serves to underline that <u>Breakdown and</u>

Development is, as a story of suffering, very different from the story of Job. Yehezkel and Hanoch's inability to see themselves as modern versions of Job, is a means through which the book as a whole declares the story of Job inappropriate as a model for the kind of suffering described in Brenner's novel. Rejection of the story of Job as a model suited for construing the agony in Breakdown and Bereavement, directs the reader towards a view of the work as a fictional tale inspired by life itself rather than a literary variation on a "classical" theme.

The rejection of literary models is part of the strategy of Brenner's realism. His critics have long been aware of this with respect to the rejection of generistic models. However, this strategy is also active on other levels of the work, most certainly so on that of the participant characters.

Several Brennerean characters direct the reader's attention towards an archetypal character, taken from a "classical" work, with which Brenner's character appears to have something in common. The common aspect, however, is quick to emerge as an abstract theme only. The similarity is disproved, the distance and disconnection between the two characters is underlined, and all that is left of the association is the admonition that the reader refrain from seeing the archetypal character as a model for understanding the Brennerean character.

The role played by Faust and Faust in From Here and There (Mi-kan-oo-mi-kan) is quite similar to that played by Job and Job in Breakdown and Bereavement. Seemingly, its hero decides to immigrate to Palestine as he is reading Faust, and he decides at the time that, unlike Faust, he is unafraid of the "narrow circle." In fact, though, the revulsion aroused in him by his wanderings permeates his reading, dampens his interest in Faust's dilemmas and stops him from finishing Faust for the third time. The story's connection with Faust ends immediately after he has formulated his "glimmer of decision":

> I closed the small, unbound book which was somewhat torn, I lay my head between my knees and gave myself over to my thoughts.

> "I'm no Faust -- I thought -- it's evident that I'm not. Witchcraft will surely bring me no salvation and "the narrow circle," of it I oddly have not fear. I don't know where the wide one is."

> The head came up and the eyes with it. In them, in my eyes, I felt a glimmer which was strange to me, a glimmer of decision [...] I got up to look for some forgotten land to walk down and calculate my eternal account, my world account (1276).

Faust's entry into the story serves only one principle function: that of emphasizing the "low" background of its hero's deliberations. The problems preoccupying him are not the "universal problems" constantly rehashed by world literature. The distance between these problems and his enhances the reader's perception of his problems as "real-life" problems. The dilemmas, the strife of spirit, the thought and even the internal and external speech of Brenner's characters are recognized as reality in contrast to dilemmas, spiritual strife, thoughts and speech recognized as literature. The author subsequently ensures that these last do not stray too far from sight.

D.

Any exhaustive study of the uses made by realism -- and modern narrative in general -- of ancient myths, must take account of the possibility of using myth for meta-poetic purposes. The absence of such a view is a serious disadvantage in Northrop Frye's discussion of myth's relationships with realism and irony, in his Anatomy of Criticism.[5]

Frye sees the myth as determining literature's basic conventions in the manner that tonal scales determine Western music's possibilities. What's more, myth's archetypal images also contain the story's abstract, basic elements. In a way, everything is already predetermined by the myth, and the later modes of narrative art merely establish new principles of combination and displacement. The principles of verisimilitude and probability, those of realism, are an added factor, "outside" these basic elements and conventions, just like the principle adding the possibility of representation in the plastic arts.[6] Accordingly, it is always possible, by virtue of the very definition of literature, to identify a mythical pattern in a realistic work, as the absence of this possibility would remove the work from the realm of literature, transferring it into that of non-literary documentation of reality.

Traces of ancient myths are readily identifiable in Breakdown and Bereavement, and the novel is easily placed in the map of myths delineated by the Anatomy. There is a hero who is turned out of a comparatively high social circle into a lower one, and is then turned out of the lower one as well due to a seizure of mental illness. There is also the story of his return to society after its deterioration, due to the deaths of two of its sons, and the loss of its livelihood on the one hand, and after the banished hero's gradual recovery on the other. Naturally, additional patterns may also be identified in the story.

I am by no means claiming that analyses of this kind are incapable of illuminating any valuable points in Breakdown and Bereavement. However, an analysis of its realism as a series of displacements of mythical patterns and motifs, will not reach the story's crucial levels of significance without a supplementary analysis stressing this realism's overt affront to this myth. It is this affront which prepares the new principles of combination and introduces them as a new, original creation.

Frye describes Kafka's stories as a series of commentaries on the story of Job.[7] A story where an ancient myth is mainly used as a negative background which enhances the story's modernity, clearly may not, in my opinion, be defined as a commentary on this myth.

As seen by Brenner's realism, the myth of Job is not a "structural principle," a "basic unit" or a "convention" in need of a displacement into a new context subjecting it to the added principle of probability. As seen by this realism, the myth of Job is a literary "world" in its own right, whose thematic construal in another, ancient spiritual world was in complete accord with the principle of probability, as it suited the beliefs of this world.

There is no need for realism to perceive itself as a series of commentaries and additions to ancient myths, thus determining, a priori, the secondary status of its principles of verisimilitude. Realism is capable of viewing myth itself in terms of the motifs and patterns it borrows from extra-literary life. This way it changes the meaning of the myth and rather than seeing it as the source of all stories, it turns it into the contrasting background serving some of them. It is possible that the syntactic elements of narrative art belong to a realm which is wider than both myth and realism together. Yet, as I see it, there can be no doubt that displacement of mythical patterns into realism or into the ironic mode, is one which requires dual sight on the part of the critic or the commentator. It is not enough to look from myth to realism and identify mythical patterns in the latter. One must look from realism to myth and perceive how the new story has altered both the meaning and function of the original pattern.

Notes

1. Gershon Shaked, Le-lo-motza, Hakibutz Hameuchad, Tel Aviv, 1973, p. 104.

2. All page references to Breakdown and Bereavement (appearing in parentheses) refer to Hillel Halkin's translation, Cornell University Press, Ithaca, N.Y., 1971.

3. See "Ba-horef" and "Mi-saviv la-nekuda" in the edition of Brenner's stories in two volumes, Hakibutz Hameuchad and Sifriat HaPoalim, Tel Aviv, 1978, vol. 1, pp. 242-253 and pp. 519-520.

4. In this specific quotation and all the following quotations which echo it, I had to change Hillel Halkin's translation. For the same Hebrew words that are repeated in the novel several times, Halkin uses different translations in various places. In order to recognize the repetitions as echoes of the same text, consistency is essential. In keeping with one of the English translations of the Tractatus, I used "the ordinary circumstances of life."

5. Northrop Frye, Anatomy of Criticism, Atheneum, New York, 1968.

6. A criticism of Frye's conception of the principle of probability may be found in Menachem Brinker, "Realism, Conventions and Beliefs," New Literary History, forthcoming.

7. Anatomy of Criticism, p. 42.

ABISHAG

Murray Baumgarten

Kresge College, University of California

In this essay I want to consider whether Auerbach's concept of "fraught with background" can be applied to minor Biblical characters. The character I shall discuss is Abishag, the young woman of Shunem brought to warm King David in his old age, and who reappears in several modern works: a cycle of four poems by Itzik Manger, a long strophic poem of Jacob Glatstein, a short lyric by Rainer Maria Rilke, and in Gladys Schmitt's fine novel, David the King. Looking at these different reincarnations I want to ask how they may help us deal with the question of endings. Does she, in the modern accounts, have a controlling function because she is a Biblical figure? What authority does she confer upon these different modern versions? Perhaps in considering these questions we may also shed light on her function in the Biblical narrative. I begin with her reincarnation in the Yiddish poems.

Perhaps Biblical figures enter Yiddish poetry so comfortably because of the enduring Jewish tradition of translation, aimed at making holy writ available to unlettered folk. There are many early Yiddish versions of the Bible that helped to shape the idiom of Yiddish poetry. It is more difficult to explain how the heroes and heroines of the sacred Hebrew were transformed into the village dwellers of Yiddish literature. In Yiddish poetry, David, Rachel, Naomi, Ruth, and Elijah are not ancient mythic actors; nor are they the protagonists of historical narratives and lyrics who, despite their temporal distance, pronounce stern judgment on an unheroic present, as is the case in so much of modern Hebrew literature. Especially in the poetry of Itzik Manger, the "biblical figures" inhabit the everyday world of the shtetl and the modern town, in an eternal present. The Biblical qualities of their spirit are, as it were, immanent in the texture and daily speech of the folk -- that is, in the subtle mixture of the holy tongue with the secular linguistic realms of German and Polish, the prophetic strains and inflected structure of Hebrew bonded to the mundane vocabulary and analytic syntax of the modern languages.

Flexible, supple, witty, ironic, and playful, Yiddish reaches a remarkable intensity when it deals with Biblical figures: it is as if the Hebrew letters in which it is written reveal its Biblical characteristics even in an adopted vocabulary. Surely this mysterious quality lies behind the declaration of the introspectivists among modern Yiddish poets who, led by Jacob Glatstein, believed that any subject could be Jewish if it were but dealt with in Yiddish. The intensity of Yiddish is especially noteworthy when we encounter a narrative of Biblical events told by characters who, notably in Manger's poetry, have read about the lives of the Biblical characters in the original Hebrew text.

In the very texture of their language these writers confront the general problems of imaginative writing in the modern world, exploring them with a personal, unique, and brilliant intensity. Their poetry echoes the long tradition of Biblical and post-biblical Hebrew lyricism, occupying an unusually wide range that encompasses both folk and high culture. Thus, many of their poems are sung in the street as ballads and yet can enter the consciousness of a people as if they were psalms of a contemporary, skeptical, bitter mode dedicated to the service of an ancient God.[1]

As a character in Yiddish poems, Abishag (I Kings 1:1-4, 15) brings the world-historical Jewish king, conqueror of Jerusalem and founder of it as capital of all the Jews, into the presence of the pintele yid, the anonymous Jew, who makes up the substratum of Jewish life so often unreflected in its national consciousness. The meeting of the two -- great king and little woman at his service -- marks out the area Yiddish literature made its own. How interesting then to find in Glatstein's poem, as well as in Manger's Abishag group, an encounter between two speakers on a not-so-unequal level.

Manger's Abishag knows -- because she has read her story in the Bible -- that for her deeds she will only receive "a shura in Tanach", a line in the Bible:

> A line for her young flesh,
> the years of her youth.
> A line of ink on parchment
> for the whole long truth.[2]

In the previous poem of Manger's cycle, Abishag speaks out in her sleep of all those village things she has left behind in coming to the court:

> Abishag sleeps. She breathes quietly.
> But listen -- in her sleep she speaks,
> and from her dream she breathes
> the scent of calves and sheep.

Having put aside his book of psalms, which he has been wearily thumbing, King David approaches her bed. He overhears her dream speech, and the heroic lutanist hearkens to her village world, of

> A pond, a pine forest,
> a giant village moon,
> an old and pious linden tree
> that watches over mama's house.

Abishag's entranced evocation of the natural world echoes the characteristic Wordsworthian process by which we make nature into our lasting spiritual home. In the previous poem nature bestows remarkable gifts on her. Even at the moment of her departure from this natural realm,

the weary sun at evening
adds to her summer dress
a great and golden blossom.

But now in the king's bedroom, Abishag's sleepy words carry

a sad and haunting tone,
homesickness that draws the king
from his psalter and becomes
its own song.

In a superb lyric moment the full contrast between David and Abishag flashes upon us. It is also the moment of Abishag's triumph, in her simplicity and naturalness, over the world of the court and the city. Her body, which according to the story is to be used only to warm the great king, her youthful being that is to be demeaned into an instrument, asserts its value as body, in making a song of her native realm. By this song she asserts her right to be, even in David's presence.

Manger's poem ends as the old and weary king kisses Abishag and withdraws.

He bends the old white head,
kissing the village-life in her,
kissing the old linden tree
that watches over her mother's door.

Sighing, stroking his beard, David returns to his loneliness and his ancient psalms, thumbing through his psalter. Separated from her by his age, piety, and sophistication, David, the sweet singer of Israel, here accepts, and thus legitimizes, her world, with his gesture marking and recognizing Abishag's integrity and intrinsic value. The young girl has enacted an ironic Cinderella story, leaving a humble hearth for the great modern world of a king,

whose portrait
hangs for years now on the wall
above her mother's bed.

She expects him to be

the prince of her dreams,
young and slender,

and in her excitement of anticipation has imagined herself a fancy lady. Yet she lives through the saddening tale of modern Jewish life in a poem that is not only a criticism of the false allure of the modern world but a comment on urbanization's inevitable effect on simple folk. David's kiss enshrines the value of her transitory village realm. The mighty one has stooped to the humble, the simple girl has spoken to the great king and been hearkened to, the nation has been made whole.

The final poem of the cycle, is a sad letter home, describing Abishag's life with old and pious King David:

> and she herself is "oh, well" --
> She's the king's hotwater bottle
> against the bedroom chill.

The poem concludes with the ironic promise of a line in the Bible as recompense for her young life, but Manger transfigures this seemingly petty reward of posterity by evoking its human meaning:

> Abishag puts down her pen,
> her heart is strangely bitter,
> a tear drips from her eyes
> and falls on the letter.

> The tear erases "mother"
> and erases "linden tree"
> while girlish in a corner
> a dream sobs tenderly.

In focusing his poetic cycle on her, Manger rescues Abishag from her subservient position in the David chronicle. Endowing her with multiple value in having her enact the trajectory of modern Jewish life, he transforms her into a symbolic figure powerfully expressing -- as she lives through it -- the predicament of the modern Jew. The king she serves, whose portrait hangs above her mother's bed, might be Franz Joseph of Austria as well as David of Israel; and she is every village girl who, having left home for the urban possibilities of the modern city, writes home in acknowledgement of the spiritual cost of her journey.

As the modest and simple girl, Manger's Abishag does not reflect the limited yet significant and even heroic role the rabbis assigned to her in Jewish tradition. In the Talmud she receives several lines of bemused conversation, a paragraph of rabbinical discussion emphasizing her holiness and devotion, and linking her to another woman of Shunem, whose hospitable welcome of the prophet Elisha brought her praise and succor. In Jewish tradition she is ancillary to David, and in the later commentaries the rabbis approve of Solomon's decision to eliminate Adonijah's feeble-hearted claim for the Davidic role in denying him Abishag in marriage.[3] Manger rescues Abishag by making her the representative of the folk on whose backs the royal pyramid of power and authority, be it David's or Franz Joseph's, rests. As she sleepily creates her own song out of memories of her village world, Abishag speaks for its creative energy and vitality. Abishag thus becomes a figure of basic human value, not limited to her role in an ancient Hebrew story.

The relationship between David and Abishag is striking, echoing deep male desires, and the actual diminution of woman into man's servant. Yet Jewish tradition is relatively silent on the subject, as if the rabbis had sought to repress a particularly dangerous issue by refusing to explore it. By contrast, Manger and Glatstein bring the question of the place of women in Jewish life to a sharp focus in their poems, allowing us to consider various aspects of the problem while focusing on its sexual center.

The Abishag poems reflect the literary topos, widespread in non-Jewish culture, of the senex amans. In their silence on the subject, the rabbis suggest the extent of their embarrassment at what the Biblical story includes in a matter-of-fact way as part of the history of the Davidic era. Both Manger's and Glatstein's poems echo the Biblical account. Unlike Boccaccio's senescent males or Chaucer's January lusting after May, the Yiddish writers depict a senex amans despite himself. Though Abishag ministers to David and cares for him, the old king -- in that consistent Biblical phrase linking sexuality, self-consciousness, and knowledge -- "knew her not".

The failure of David's masculinity is an apt prelude in the Biblical account to the effort of Adonijah to declare himself king, an action that rouses David to declare Solomon his true heir, as the narrator chronicles the political intrigues of a patriarchal society. In such a world, the power of maleness is the necessary condition for kingly rule, its absence the sign that the crown must pass to a younger, more virile heir. In the poems of Manger and Glatstein David's impotence takes on a personal rather than social value, which enables them to consider Abishag's role in the relationship, rather than passing over it as do the David chronicles.

In treating the relationship of Abishag and David, Manger and Glatstein bring the concerns of nature, the body, and sexuality to a literary tradition notable for the absence of these themes. It is enough for us to recall the peculiar linguistic energy of Sholom Aleichem's world, where speech is a surrogate for nature and the bodily passions, prosaic social experience predominates, and the institutional life of the Jews is so wittily represented, to comprehend the force of the Abishag poems. In effect, Manger and Glatstein figure for us a world in which speech can become song because it expresses the longings and meanings of the body. In Manger's world we have the evocation of these possibilities through their dialectic negation, compressed into a stanza of Abishag's letter:

> Greet the handsome miller
> who works in the mill --
> and the shepherd Oizer, whose
> piping she cherishes still,

she writes home to her mother. It is the miracle of his poetry that from the absence of bodily and spiritual fulfillment Manger can evoke for us its potential promise. For him, as for Bashevis Singer -- notably in his novel The Slave -- it is the body's song that is supreme, possible only when enacted among equals and unavailable to either man or woman when the power of lust and the lust of power degrades man into master and woman into slave. Transforming Abishag into David's equal by allowing her the right of speech, Manger cuts through the sexist knot.

For the vehicle of encounter between old king and young maiden in Manger's and Glatstein's poems is their mutual ability to speak to each other -- an ancient and powerful vision of the deepest force of language as metaphoric and even actual sexual intercourse. As he evokes this image out of their meeting, Manger encompasses the widest possible human experience and symbolically focuses the multiple possibilities for human self-realization within the nation's realm. Part of the power of his images grows out of the social and chronological inequalities that are overcome when the old king and the young maiden respond to each other by allowing their basic human concerns the space in which to be articulated.

In Glatstein's poem,[4] Abishag becomes David's equal in a more intense way, focused even more closely on the links between sexuality and language than Manger's. Here too we have an old king, who calls to her in longing. For him she is "Abishag. Little, youthful, warm Abishag." But now David feels himself close to death, and Abishag comforts him through his long night of despair. Glatstein's poem compresses David's career into a few remarkable and intense lines: the people in the streets will not let him sleep. As he calls out in despair at the bands of Adonijah's supporters who demand the throne for the son, though his old father yet lives, Abishag soothes him. For David, she is the only servant left, as the others all jockey for the succession. Even Bat-Sheva, his beloved,

> Fat Bat-Sheva blesses me with eternal life and
>   with a sly smile watches for my last words.

An antiphonal, strophic dialogue, the poem echoes the great Biblical lyrics in its poetic structure and its free verse. It recounts Abishag's steadfastness as she responds ever more strongly to David's increasingly bitter strictures. At first he tells her, "Cry out into the street: King David has not yet died!" A stanza later he is ready to relinquish the throne:

> Throw my crown into the street, and let whoever
>   wants to catch it!

But as his bitterness grows, Abishag answers him by subtly varying her declaration of loyalty suffused with love. First she soothes him:

> Sleep, my King. The night is dead. We are all
>   your faithful servants.

Then as his hysteria increases, she answers his strident queries,

> Nap, my King. The night is still. We are all
>   your faithful servants.

Glatstein's masterful variation of the refrain, one of the characteristics of his finest poems, is striking.

> Rest, my King. The night is still. We are all
>   your faithful servants,

Abishag says. And later she tells him to dream, concluding the poem.

> Sleep deeply, my King. Day will soon dawn. We
>   are all your faithful servants.

Here I think Glatstein captures certain essential qualities of the Biblical account. We recognize that David is king because songs were sung by and of him. His legitimacy results not only from the power of his sword but the truth of his words. We participate in David's act of remembering the force of those words in the agony of old age, when the memories of triumphs that evoke past glories congeal like blood.

It is his power with words and the power of his figure in words that has made him king. He is the poet of Israel whose singing surges from his being in its commitment to God and people. David reaches out to understand his career, as poet, warrior, and king, calling out to Abishag in one of the climactic lines of the poem: "Abishag, surely songs are truer than sin", as he longs to believe the psalms of his pious youth will stand witness for him at the final judgment.

Glatstein's poem articulates the encounter between David and Abishag through a profound appreciation of the sexual basis of language. Though their consummation is physically impossible, on the level of speech -- an older generation would say, on a spiritual plane -- it is accomplished. In the playfulness and seriousness with which they respond to each other's words, we have almost a model of sexual encounter. The teasing epithets with which David endows Abishag are echoed by the changing refrain with which she answers him, constantly deflecting his attention from his distress, perhaps in order to keep him from letting his wit and consciousness of himself as impotent and senescent lover turn into self-pity. She leads him to a spiritual realization, as he exclaims over the power of song to outface sin itself and overcome the horrors of the wars in which he has engaged.

For a moment we are reminded in this poem, as we are in Manger's, that David the warrior, able even in old age to overcome the incipient rebellion of Adonijah, also has a feminine side -- that of the youthful singer and lover of Jonathan. Glatstein's poem manifests the power of song, echoing David's traditional achievement as the composer of the Book of Psalms, and suggests that it is in David's ability to unite masculine as well as feminine attributes that his enduring value consists.

The past glories of his song are countered here -- at the same moment they are evoked -- in Abishag's singing, for now the village maiden from Shunem sings to David as she rocks him to sleep in a song at once lullaby and pledge of fealty. She is his only servant, his singer and solace, and it is nothing more than her song emanating from the warmth and youth of her being that staves off the death David cries out against. Paradoxically, then, Abishag plays the healing role parallel to that which David, the young lutanist from rural Bethlehem, enacted for King Saul.

For both Abishag and David, poetry is God's gift and brings health and life. Their song encompasses the sad tale of war and politics and transforms it. This bodily speech is not only an artistic creation but a procreative one. It articulates the poet's being and the nation's existence, as in Glatstein's remarkable technical feat it assures him of life at the very edge of death. Thereby his poem enacts the situation of the post-Holocaust Yiddish poet, writing in a tongue that resurrects and gives life to a world most. brutally exterminated; and yet because of his poetic act of witness and reenactment, it is unvanquished.

In the work of European poets, Abishag is given a poem in two short sections early in the first part of Rilke's Neue Gedichte. This relatively little-known lyric is part of an early Biblical group in the collection. "David Singt Vor Saul" and "Josuas Landtag" come immediately after, violating chronology but developing Rilke's thematic concern with the relation of singing, poetry, and knowledge. Abishag also appears in Gladys Schmitt's brilliant novel David, the King and serves there to focus similar themes.[5]

In Rilke's poem as well as Schmitt's novel, Abishag plays a mythic role. The young girl involved with the ancient king of Israel, enacts in both works a metaphysical, even theologically centered role through her physical caring for David. Schmitt recaptures the heroic qualities of the original; her portrait of Abishag has many affinities with Glatstein's poem. By contrast, stressing the extraordinary qualities of the encounter, Rilke reaches for different effects.

His poem does not contextualize Abishag's figure in her village world, as do the other versions; more abstract, it does not locate Abishag within an easily apprehended mundane world as do Manger's witty and playful poems. Rilke's poem -- unlike Manger's, Glatstein's, and Schmitt's novel -- does not give her the right of personal speech. Rather, she serves as the occasion for a profound meditation on themes that reach apotheosis in some of the more famous poems of the Neue Gedichte, "Apollo: Archaic Torso" or "Orpheus, Eurydice, Hermes". Nevertheless, here too we find the remarkable sculptural insight into the intersection of corporeality and spirituality that characterize his greater poems.

For Rilke, the encounter of David and Abishag becomes a symbol of unfulfillment. If she is aching youth, he is immobilized age. Though they meet each other only in the dark, her night is bright and lit by stars while his is cold and unilluminated. David cannot respond to her "unstirred mouth that cannot kiss", even though he is "skilled in the knowledge of women". The poem plays variations on an image from the preceding one, "Eastern Aubade", and figures their meeting in terms of a natural scene of desolation.

But at evening Abishag arched
over him. His mazy being lay
abandoned like the coastline of an infamous ocean
beneath the constellation of her quiet breasts.

He is an isolated coast unable to respond to the call of her star. Three lines later, the
roles reverse and

the green wand of her feelings
did not incline to his ground.
He shivered.

Though Rilke associates David and Abishag by means of these images with the fertility
encounters of heaven and earth common to Babylonian lore, he also reveals their inability
to play the traditional fructifying mythic roles. The gap between her youth and his age is
too great for knowledge -- sexual or cosmic -- and the poem leaves them isolated each
within an appointed realm.

In turning to anthropomorphic images, Rilke clearly shows the difference between
his interest in Abishag and David and the concerns of Manger and Glatstein. For the
Yiddish poets such anthropomorphism is blasphemous, steeped as they are in an iconoclastic tradition. To suggest that David and Abishag play transhuman roles and enact a
shadowy version of the encounter of earth and heaven is to deprive them of their human
freedom. According to Jewish tradition, the human being is in history and therefore able
to perform his own destiny precisely because he is not bound to enact and reiterate the
encounters of the gods. Banishing the pagan idols, he no longer accepts their limitations
as rules for his life, but instead is freed to order the world and thereby realize his true
nature in making use of the divine power with which he has been endowed by virtue of
creation in the divine image. According to very old traditions, central to both Jewish and
Christian thought, it is speech -- logos, the word -- that incarnates the human being's
divinely granted power.

It is the inability of Rilke's figures to make contact with each other that is the
central theme of his poem. Their frustrated striving for a meaningful and self-conscious
relation -- sexual as well as linguistic, two realms that are so often metaphorically
intertwined, parallels Rilke's often desperate effort in the Neue Gedichte to bring Greek
and Hebrew traditions into vital encounter, out of which alone he feels can come the
fructifying speech he seeks. In "Abishag" Rilke enacts the effort to transform the gods of
myth into human figures and thereby marry ancient hellenistic values and the prophetic
speech of the Hebrew Bible. As Rilke brings these two cultures together in the Neue
Gedichte we are reminded of the similar efforts of Franz Rosenzweig and Martin Buber,
which occurred at roughly the same time, to bring into being in their Free Jewish House
of Study at Frankfort as well as in their translation of the Bible into German, a similar
cultural confrontation that would reveal the elements from which the Biblical synthesis

emerged. Though Manger may have met Rilke, and is recorded as having been envious of his fame,[6] his concern, like Glatstein's, was to domesticate Abishag and David in his own world. Manger did not see in their encounter the force of myth but a contact thrust upon two persons by the impersonal forces of history. For him as for Glatstein, it is the speech of the body and its difficulties in a precariously poised world that are worthy of exploration.

It is appropriate here to consider the possibility that, at this point in his career, David is a tragic hero. This is of some importance for our understanding of the common matrix from which these different versions emerge and has as well the further interest that in general the Jewish Testament eschews tragedy. The problem of genre may also be illuminated. We discover that, for Rilke, David's encounter with Abishag yields silence instead of speech. Instead of intercourse, in all its meanings, we have two isolated selves reinforced in their isolation; instead of communication we have -- as Rosenzweig puts it -- "the 'selfication' of the hero's self". As hero, "he yearns for the solitude of demise, because there is no greater solitude than this". So Rilke's is a poem enacting David's effort to reach out, even in his old age, beyond his isolating, royal self and, revealing the trajectory of his grand effort, to express in lyric speech its heroic culmination: silence. If for the moment we follow the distinctions Rosenzweig works out, it becomes clear that in Rilke's poem David is indeed a tragic hero at this moment in his life. "The tragic hero has only one language which completely corresponds to him," Rosenzweig points out -- "precisely keeping silent".[7] Rilke thus charts for us the ways in which David falls into silence and tragedy, at the end of his life, echoing the Biblical account.

For the sharp-eyed narrator of the Book of Kings, as for Rilke, this situation is ironic. Are there any other moments in the Bible in which David, the sweet singer of Israel, is silenced, his being rendered only by speechlessness? We are reminded of Saul's struggle to express himself, which finds an outlet only in certain mute and tragic actions -- the moment, for example, when he tears Samuel's cloak and the prophet draws an appropriate moral from the event: "The Lord has torn the kingdom of Israel from thee this day" (I Samuel 15:28). David's silence, expressed in Rilke's poem, is thus doubly ironic, for was it not in part the fact that David had the gift of speech and song which made it possible for him to supersede Saul?

Rilke's poem meets the Biblical narrative at this point in working out a tragic moment. For Rilke this is conclusion; for the Biblical narrator it is transition. At the level of genre, the Biblical account moves away from tragedy to chart historical patterns -- of continuity amid change, for example -- which Manger and Glatstein suggest but Rilke chooses not to emphasize. In his, as in the Biblical story, we have a tragic mode. As Rosenzweig notes, "In narrative poetry, keeping silent is the rule; dramatic poetry, on the contrary, knows only of speaking, and it is only thereby that silence here becomes eloquent. By keeping silent, the hero breaks down the bridges which connect him with God and the world, and elevates himself out of the fields of personality, delimiting itself and individualizing itself from others in speech, into the icy solitude of self... The heroic is speechless."[8]

Where Rilke thus echoes the Biblical story, the other writers evade the tragic moment, in its classical guise. Instead of silence, we have Abishag's speech that, in Schmitt's novel, defines David's self as well as her own. This is also true of Glatstein's great poem and to a somewhat lesser extent holds for Manger's cycle. These writers find dialogue central in this story and thereby articulate -- instead of Rilke's "drag of the ground" -- the heroism possible in the modern world. Theirs is not a Greek heroism of the closed self but a modern sense of self-interpenetrating world and word in mutual self-articulation, in Wordsworthian interfusion. In Rosenzweig's terms, "the hero of the newer tragedy is no longer a 'hero' at all in the old sense, he no longer 'approaches' the spectator 'rigid as antiquity.' He is tossed with a will, wholly receptive, into the to and fro of the world, wholly alive... every inch a human being."[9] In these interpretations of the ancient story, we have characters in a modern sense, as Abishag emerges from the shadowy quasi-anonymity of the Biblical account into a local habitation now attached to what formerly was little more than a name, coming forward to challenge David with the special intensity of modern life for the heroic role. For Manger especially, Abishag is heroine even more than King David is hero. Instead of lyric hymn, we have the pathos and intelligence of Coleridgean conversation poems; instead of classical Attic tragedy, we have the historical novel.

What the Biblical narrative ignores, these writers restore to Abishag. Manger's cycle in particular frees her from her link to King David and leads us to wonder even about the rest of her life. The paradox of her situation -- though in effect married to King David she remains a virgin -- is resolved by her rabbinic assimilation to the woman of Shunem whose son the prophet Elisha calls back from death with mouth-to-mouth respiration in II Kings 4:1-44. Thus Abishag is given a typical woman's history: marriage, child-bearing, care for her family and sustenance for the wandering prophet, who in the moment of crisis rescues her familial possibilities.

In considering the ways in which Abishag's transition from court-maiden to wife is possible we encounter the Canaanite subtext of the Biblical story. The matter of fact account of summoning a virgin to heat the great King echoes pagan habits that I suspect would have concluded, for a non-Jewish Abishag, in service as a temple prostitute if not ritual sacrifice. In the rewriting of the Canaanite practice, the Biblical narrative evades the pathos of Abishag's status. Consider the contrast with another Biblical tale rooted in Canaanite practice. Jephthah's daughter -- victim of her father's pagan vow -- is granted the right to mourn her virginity. The company of maidens who serve as her choral supporters help her play out the drama of her woman's un-consummation. They grieve at the role imposed on her by the male demands of war, reminding us of Agamemnon's sacrifice of his daughter Iphigeneia which later brings the great Greek king to his downfall. By contrast, Abishag's dramatic possibilities are fewer, while her human situation is more open. If her heroic possibilities are diminished, her psychological complexity and human power are enriched.

Shirley Kaufman's recent poem gives us Abishag in the fullness of her power. As she nurtures and protects the old king, Abishag simultaneously expresses her world-creating force. In this poem she becomes an image, suspended in the mysterious background of the Biblical account, of the range of meanings of woman's sexual being -- despite the male's consistent and all too often willful miscomprehension of it. Like the Spirit of God hovering over the waters of chaos, this Abishag broods over the bitter formlessness of her human lot and thereby rescues it for us.

> She thinks if she pinches
> his hand it will turn to powder.
> She feels his thin claws, his wings
> spread over her like arms, not bones
> but feathers ready to fall.
> She suffers the jerk
> of his feeble legs. Take it easy,
> she tells him cruelly
>
> submissive in her bright flesh.
> He's cold from the fear.
> of death, the sorrow
> of failure, night after night
> he shivers with her breasts
> against him like an accusation,
> her mouth slightly open,
> her hair spilling everywhere. [10]

Similarly, Schmitt's book shows Abishag and David breaking through the gap central to Rilke's poem to form a loving relationship. For the modern novelist, Abishag brings David to his final moment of consciousness -- exactly what Rilke shows to be impossible. Abishag sings to David not only of his glories but his own songs, which she reveals to him as his most lasting legacy to Israel. "I can sing the songs of David," she responds to his query, "even he who is exalted above all the sweet singers in Israel. Nor did they teach me these songs hastily on the night before I departed, that I might sing them before my lord in order to find favor in his sight. Since the day when I first learned what it was to ease the fullness of my heart by pouring my spirit forth from my lips, I sang the songs of David in the fields of Gilead. I know the songs of David as I know the branch that grows across the window near my bed." [11]

Here Abishag expresses one of the deepest, most abiding themes of Jewish tradition by showing how David's psalms have become one with the natural world of Israel, adding a transcendent human value to its beauty. It is as song, as measured breath, that Abishag and David encounter each other. "The vibrant music that was within him rose and swelled. Ah, God, he thought, brushing his lips across her hair, how can I turn my back upon this fair, heavy-headed flower that blooms at the edge of my grave?" [12] In their relationship, David's music is transformed into the natural rhythms of their world.

Through Abishag, David reaches a final understanding of his own role as God's servant and, in Schmitt's novel, learns from Abishag its full meaning. She sings for him, through and with him, the body's song:

> And while she settled him against the heaped cushions, the vibrant music grew within him. The splash and ripple of the spring, the sound of the wind-stirred leaves, the coming and going of her breath -- all these became a party of one broad, endless antiphonal song, rising, swelling, opening out above him, encompassing new voices lifted up from the sands of the desert, from the snow-tipped mountains of Lebanon, from the unknown countries beyond Edom and Moab, from the legendary islands in the western sea. Behold, he thought in wonderment, if my heart had ceased to beat while I lay in the churning darkness, the music would not have lessened.[13]

David's songs -- the psalms of the Bible -- are here, as Jewish tradition has understood them, the very breath of Israel's life. The songs of its messianic king express the gamut of the feelings of all Israel.

In two modern Hebrew poems that focus on Abishag, David appears similarly as king and poet. For Yaakov Fichman, Abishag serves the poet while ministering to the king. For Anda Finkerfeld-Amir, Abishag -- who first rebels against her fate in warming a dying old man -- is recalled to her king's service by his art. In neither poem is contact made between senex amans and maiden. Like Rilke, these Hebrew poets focus on the failure of communication. Both poems conclude with a re-assertion of the importance of the differential status between king and ministering woman.

Both poems are monologues. Finkerfeld-Amir's free verse is stormy and dramatic, while Fichman's, in rhymed couplets, is restrained. In the first we reach a climax when Abishag implicitly wishes her lover dead so that she might be freed of the bondage of his old age. Sharing in the excitement of her desire from the beginning, when she is called to minister to the king, we follow the process by which, first delayed and then rebelled against, her frustrated sexual gratification is transformed into metaphysical longing and happiness through projection onto David's role as redeemer of Israel.

In Fichman's poem we encounter a woman's acceptance of her sexual frustration in serving her king, and the private need is subsumed within the more important public role.

Both poets re-enact the Biblical account from Abishag's perspective. Drawing upon legends in which David is the future redeemer of Israel and the medieval mourner of the destruction of the Temple, both poems nevertheless situate themselves in a Biblical world. They take us back into that realm to capture its eternal human meanings.[14]

In neither, however, do we encounter Abishag as our contemporary. That quality distinguishes Manager's treatment as well as Schmitt's. Her novel is a remarkable achievement -- supple, lithe, breathtaking -- and not least of all its glories is its portrait of Abishag the Shunamite, a fit companion to those of Manger and Glatstein. Her novel captures the way in which David is the center of the messianic imagination of the Jews.

In the encounter with Abishag, she points to the profound meaning in the lines every Jewish child knows: <u>david melekh yisrael hai vekayom</u> (David king of Israel yet lives). With this phrase we return to the problem of endings. Not only for the Jews but, as Professor Frye makes clear in his recent book, for all of western culture the Bible is unending. Not only its theological meanings but the fullness of the experiences it articulates, including that of the strange background in which its characters participate, have no conclusion. Wittgenstein argued that it is not possible for us to get outside of language. I am not the first to claim that for western culture at least there is no way to get outside of the Bible. We are embedded in it as much as, if not more than the other way 'round. At this point in the discussion my students begin to contemplate revolution. What their youth and optimism find difficult is the idea that they too are part of the unfolding of a story they are reading.

This is also to claim that Biblically governed texts engage the reader in ways specific to themselves. Like these versions of Abishag they draw us into a process of interpretation of a special kind. The Biblical Abishag engages us in the hermeneutic activity, in the <u>midrash</u> if you will, of completing her story. It is this process which these modern versions exemplify. To read them is to participate in an activity, at once literary and religious, that leads us back to their Biblical inspiration. For them as for us, the Bible is both source and re-source.[15] We return to the originating material to discover that its mythic focus impels us into playing a game whose purpose is not winning -- that would give it an end -- but to keep on playing. In that spirit, then, not only does King David keep on living but so too does Abishag -- even if all she has is one line in the Bible.

This paradox binds us to the text, engaging us in the continuous and unceasing act of interpretation. It is an aesthetic appropriately parallel to the substance of this testament. As it unfolds the story of a people struggling to grasp the meaning of, and live up to, their covenant with God, so it binds us in narrative terms to the process of reading.

To put it another way, by way not of concluding this by now endless essay, but only of making a transition: in the words of Rabbi Tarfon,

-- though you are not required to complete the task, neither are you free to desist from it.

Notes

1. Hannah Arendt, <u>The Human Condition</u> (Chicago: University of Chicago Press, 1958), p. 166. Some of the materials of this essay are from my <u>City Scriptures: Modern Jewish Writing</u> (Cambridge, Mass.: Harvard University Press, 1982), Chapter 4.

2. Ruth Whitman, <u>An Anthology of Modern Yiddish Poetry</u> (New York: October House, 1966), pp. 20-23. Manger's Abishag cycle is in the <u>Lied un Balade</u> (New York: Itzik-Manger-Comitet, 1952), pp. 254-261. Except where otherwise noted, translations are my own. The four poems are: "Abishag", "Abishag's Last Night in the Village", "King David and Abishag", and "Abishag Writes a Letter Home".

3. Babylonian Talmud, Tractate Sanhedrin 22a, 39b. Also see the entry in Encyclopedia Judaica.

4. Jacob Glatstein, "Abishag", Fun Mayn Gantser mi (Of All My Labor; Collected Poems, 1919-1956; New York, 1956), p. 360, originally published in Fraye Ferzn (New York: Groyer Stodolski, 1926). I have referred to the translation in The Golden Peacock, ed. Joseph Leftwich (London: Ashcombe, 1939), pp. 333-334.

5. Gladys Schmitt, David, the King (New York: Dial, 1946; reissued 1973). For Rilke's poems I have referred to Rainer Maria Rilke, New Poems, trans. J.B. Leishman (New York: New Directions, 1964). "Abishag" is in the First Part, p. 58.

6. See Brian Murdock, "A Yiddish Writer and the German Cultural Hegemony Before World War II", Jewish Social Studies (April 1973), 103-104.

7. Franz Rosenzweig, The Star of Redemption, trans. from the 2nd ed. of 1930 by William W. Hallo (London: Routledge and Kegan Paul, 1970), pp. 77-79.

8. Ibid., p. 77.

9. Ibid., p. 209. The expressive "drag of the ground" I owe to Harold Fisch, who also called my attention to Rosenzweig.

10. Shirley Kaufman, "Abishag", to be published in The Iowa Review, 1982.

11. Schmitt, p. 599.

12. Ibid., p. 600.

13. Ibid., p. 621.

14. Both Fichman's and Finkerfeld-Amir's poems can be found in Lifnim Mishurat Hashur, 119-139. See also M.M. Kaspi, "The Figure of the Aged Lover in Our Literature" in Hebrew), Bisaron, 1976, Vol. 67, pp. 164-174, "The Old Man as Motif in Modern Hebrew Literature," Alei Siach, 1983.

15. See Jack R. Miles, "Radical Editing", in The Creation of Sacred Literature: Composition and Redaction of the Biblical Text, edited by Richard Elliott Friedman, Near Eastern Studies Series, Volume 22, Berkeley & Los Angeles: University of California Press, 1981, p. 98.

"THE LAST PROPHET" -- THE BIBLICAL GROUND OF BIALIK'S POETRY

Hillel Barzel

Bar-Ilan University

1.   The Historical Aspect

Four periods can be distinguished in the relationship between Hebrew poetry and the Bible. In the first, Scripture is regarded as absolutely sacred, as it was in early liturgical poetry (piyut) and prayer. The biblical verse there serves as point of departure for everything said by the liturgical poet (piyutist). The piyut is, as it were, a midrash expounding a point of law, devotion, or legend based on the biblical letters or words or on the Bible in general and as a revered and binding text. In the piyut, composed according to the method of remez (symbolic or allegoric allusion), all the words share a significance deriving from the verse, and the verse becomes a code for understanding the work both in isolation and in context. The second period is characterized by the sharp separation between the sacred poem meant for the synagogue, and the secular poem unrelated to ritual purposes. Sacred poetry, especially in the Golden Age of Spain, drew its inspiration from the sublimest of spheres, for the words and verses of the Bible are uniquely fitted to evoke a sense of the sublime. Secular poetry, on the other hand, based itself as need be on biblical associations, the imagery of the Bible providing a living and constant presence both for the poet and his readers. Writers of the maqama (rhymed prose) even allowed themselves to remove Scripture from its usual reading or understanding in order to achieve a comic effect. The third period, which can be identified with the literature of the Hebrew Enlightenment (Haskalah), beginning with Moshe Haim Luzzatto and Naftali Hertz Wessely, marks the beginning of diversification in the approach to the Bible, determined by the outlook of the poet himself. Luzzatto's "The Samson Story" may suggest a Kabbalistic substructure, with Delilah symbolizing the forces of darkness. Naftali Hertz Wessely takes up the position of an interpreter of Scripture. As he says in his introduction to Songs of Splendor ("Shirei Tiferet"): "This time my heart is roused to follow our fathers of old, to interpret sayings in song." The biblical poems of Mikha Levinsohn represent a personal and romantic approach, which transforms the source into a mirror of ideas and expressions personal to the poet. What Bialik called "war poetry," as well as the polemical poems of Judah Leib Gordon, were intended to represent the prophet and the rabbis as Zealots who endanger the existence of the nation, for the nation needs a material and political basis above all. Elsewhere I have tried to show that even the "innocent" biblical poems of Gordon, such as "The Love of David and Michal" and "Asenath, daughter of Potiphera," which on the face of it do not have a combative ideological intent, nevertheless convey his militant outlook. In the former, there is admiration for the king, while in the underlying layer of the latter poem can be found justification for assimilation, mixed marriages and the attraction of sovereign power.

- 143 -

The fourth period, which begins with Chaim Nachman Bialik, marks an even sharper turn towards the individual-personal approach. Not every poet must contend with the authority of the Scriptures. The relationship between the poet and the sacred source is not necessarily one of tension; it can be natural, as it were, and not overloaded with a sense of deference and commitment. We have before us a phenomenon to which can be applied the term coined by Menachem Azulai with reference to the piyutist school of Saadia Gaon: "biblical saturation." A. Avital's book, Bialik's Poetry and the Bible (in Hebrew), clearly shows how nearly all of Bialik's poetry abounds with allusions to the Pentateuch, the Prophets, the five "megillot" and the wisdom books. But the Biblical texts are invoked loosely, and the poet does not subjugate himself to them.

In sacred poetry, piyut and the poetry of Spain, the Bible is the master and the poet the servant. In the secular poetry in Spain and in the maqama, the poet was free to do as he wished with the Scriptural verses, but was fully aware of the supremacy of the divine and prophetic source. The poetry of the Haskalah continued along this line until the appearance of Judah Leib Gordon. Gordon, "lion" of the Haskalah poets, moves from acceptance of the prophetic books to rejection of them, in the knowledge that he has come to change the world and to fight against convention. Bialik was an enthusiastic admirer of the Scriptures, but treated them according to the demands of the poem in hand. Faithfulness to the scriptural text need not be declared; it is self-evident, but so too is the need for renewed inspiration from the Bible in accordance with the particular character of each poem. Bialik described his relationship to the Bible as follows: "The Bible is always on my desk. And when I am on a journey it comes along with me. I can't put my pen to paper without first dipping into it. This little book -- everything is already said in it. Everything is hidden and anticipated in it. It seems that whatever you want to say and express -- has already been said in it."

It should be noted that Bialik speaks of the Bible as a permanent resource, a constant presence, and of the need to renew contact with it in the writing of any poem. Just as every poem has its own time and experience, so too does it have its own link to the Bible, which gives it power and direction.

Describing the creation of "The Scroll of Fire," Bialik says that one kind of biblical tone asserts itself, suppressing the tone that he originally sought. The subdued tone of the Book of Ruth that Bialik tried to achieve gave way to higher octaves that eventually came to dominate the poem.

This kind of inner mastery, unaccompanied by any disavowal of the magnificence of the source but which stressed the straying from its hidden contents, is a hallmark of Bialik's attitude to the Bible. The tension between a sacred tradition demanding submission as a matter of course and a poet possessing his own singularity, simply disappears. Paradoxically, Bialik restores the relationship to the Bible that was obtained during the almost utopian period of the piyutist of old, who alters the scriptural verses freely and yet accepts their yoke, unaware that in the poem he demonstrates a far-reaching independence with respect to the original, and who in fact, although not in theory, imposes his own authority on it. In the piyut, however, the scriptural verses will appear in the forefront as having exclusive binding force. In Bialik, it is the poet's own emotional imperative which takes over even in those poems which feature a name or citation from the Bible in their title, or those in which the narration derives from the Bible ("The Last Dead of the Desert," "The Dead of the Desert"), or poems in which a biblical figure is foremost, or poems of reproof, which bring together God and his wrathful prophet, such as "Word,"[1] "And I Knew on a Misty Night"[2] or poems such as "The Pool," which cannot be described without reference to a system of Biblical allusions.

It should be stressed that we are speaking of the beginning of a period in which each poet determines his own individual relationship to the Bible. There are poets such as Zalman Schneur, Yonatan Ratosh, and Aaron Amir, who write in explicit opposition to the Bible, contending against what it says. Schneur's "Hidden Tablets" or a poem such as Ratosh's "Eve" are cases in point.

But the personal relationship to the Bible in the case of Bialik was not in a spirit of opposition but rather of harmony.

2.   "On the Slaughter"

In response to calamitous events even God-fearing piyutists wrote in defiance of Scripture. Challenging the verse "Who is like unto Thee, O Lord, among the mighty? Who is like unto Thee, glorious in holiness..." (Exodus 15:11), Isaac Ben Shalom wrote: "There is none like unto Thee among the mute, Still and silent to the grieving..." The verse from the "Song of the Sea," the great victory song of the Jewish people over its enemies at the Red Sea (Exodus 15), is here chosen to describe an opposite situation -- that of a people ravaged and decimated. Menachem Ben Yaakov did the same: "Who is like unto Thee among the mute, my God, You keep yourself in rein; Nations created a tumult in your House, and you kept quiet, Strangers mock your sons and you utter not a word..." In a poem that seemingly denies the tenets of Jewish faith, "On the Slaughter," Bialik, too, uses biblical verses that express the greatness of the Creator in a provocative fashion. "You have an arm with an axe" which refers to the wild hangman, paraphrases the Biblical "You have an arm with might" (Psalms 89:14) that describes the Almighty. This verse appears in Psalms as part of an expression of admiration and awe.

Bialik's poem was written under exceptional circumstances -- a new [c]aqedah, like the [c]aqedah poetry of Crusader times. The title "On the Slaughter" has reference not only to a specific event, namely, the Kishinev Pogrom, but also to a literary genre: the [c]aqedah in which the Jewish people is 'bound' like Isaac. This calls for a poetic response on the part of the Jewish reader, who, like Isaac, is "bound." Many of Bialik's allusions challenge sacred phrases, but I think Avraham Kariv and others were correct in viewing "On the Slaughter" as a reaction appropriate to the nature of the events related. "On the Slaughter" is the first immediate response to the Kishinev Pogrom. The poet's bitterness vents itself in his stand against the Creator and against the biblical verses that ascribe to Him mercy, justice, greatness, etc.

In "In the City of the Killing,"[3] written several months after the same event, the Divine presence and His binding commandments are again manifest: "Get thee up and go unto the city of the killing and come thee to the courtyards...," echoes God addressing Abraham, this time with a sense of certainty about the existence of Him who commands His messenger.

What may be called the "bending of biblical verses" in "On the Slaughter" is totally unlike that in Judah Leib Gordon, or the anti-biblical position in some of Tchernichovski's poetry, or Schneur's, or Ratosh's, which are meant to demonstrate opposition to the biblical world view, or to discover another, deeper truth which the Scriptures have allegedly suppressed or concealed.

Bialik's version is closer to that of those piyutists whose challenge to the word of Scripture issues from full obedience to its content. The devastating event, the ^{c}aqedah, is what calls for the extraordinary and extreme expression of taking a stand in defiance of a verse. Bialik's relationship to the Bible should be defined as phenomenological; it does not depend on an esthetic, intellectual or any other world view. The singularity of the subject to which the poem is devoted is what governs the form of relationship to the biblical verse, the biblical story, or the revered figure from the biblical past.

3.   Poems That Contradict One Another
For that reason it is not surprising to find two biblical poems, "The Last Dead of the Desert," and "The Dead of the Desert" contradicting one another. In the former, written in the Autumn of 1896, the generation that was destined to wander for forty years in the desert, among the mountains, is held in disdain. The dominant term in this poem is "carcasses." The poem speaks of the craving for meat, fleshpots, onions and garlic that debased and corrupted those who had come out of Egypt. The vulture is called upon to share his trophy with the desert wind. Both will overcome those whose end is to rot in their shame: "Around the last dead slave, perhaps tonight/The desert wind with wasteland vulture shall fight." The later poem, written in the Spring of 1903, has none of this. In it, the death of the desert generation does not terminate their immensity, mightiness or their ability to be resurrected. The intonation is not ideological. The desire for redemption, symbolized by the departure from the desert of servitude, or from Abbadon, is the same in both poems, and it matters little whether the poems are interpreted allegorically, mythically, descriptively, or in universal terms. The difference lies in the phenomenon that calls for a spiritual and poetic response. In "The Last Dead of the Desert," the main thing is not the desert, but the change, the going out from the wasteland to the promised land: "Moses dies and Joshua leads," as the poem's motto proclaims. The speaker in the poem is Joshua, the new leader, and it is his point of view that dominates. It is worth noting that in his words, too, one hears the muted echo of fear of those who have remained in the sands, for perhaps they are not altogether dead and the vulture will not overcome them.

> Rise, wanderers, in the wilderness come out!
> With step assured, yet neither cry nor shout,
> And lest the sands with all their sleepers start,
> Let each man's footfall sound but in his heart.

Those who had been called slaves are now referred to as sleepers who can be disturbed and awakened. They are likened to the awakening desert. The stress is not only on the parting from the last of the desert dead, but also from the one who had to die with them, the leader of the generation that went out of Egypt: Moses, the faithful shepherd. Joshua speaks, but the eyes of the new generation are also on the prophet of God who remained atop Mt. Nevo.

In contrast to "The Last Dead of the Desert," other voices are at work in "The Dead of the Desert." The fallen are now observed from a point remote in time. "Come and I will show you the Dead of the Desert," (Baba Bathra, 736), says Rabbah b. Bar Hana, the teller of remarkable tales. He too tells of the dead of the desert by means of a wanderer, tiy'a, who, according to Rashi, is an "Ishmaelite merchant." In Bialik's poem that same tiy'a reappears as the speaker, an old man, solitary, holy, the elder who relates wondrous tales. He is the old man of whom it is said that if he swears by the beard of the Prophet, that is Muhammed; you can believe what he says or take it as a tall tale.

Needless to say, both poems are to be regarded as an expression of the poet's world of emotions and ideas. But the biblical story appears in each of them in a different mold. In "The Last Dead of the Desert," the emphasis is on the change of leadership. The epithets used in the Bible to denounce the deceased generation, their iniquities and quarrelsomeness, are selected in order to justify the new status of the conquering generation. In "The Dead of the Desert," the emphasis is on the rebellion and tempestuousness of the fallen generation as well. The poem is based on the last part of the story of the spies, the act of remorse: "And they rose up early in the morning, and got them up to the top of the mountain, saying: 'Lo, we are here, and will go up to the place which the Lord hath promised; for we have sinned.'" (Numbers 14:40) Bialik puts into his heroes' mouths the call from the Bible:

> Behold us! We will ascend
> With the tempest!
> Though the Lord has withdrawn His hand from us,
> And the ark stands moveless in its place,
> Still we will ascend -- alone!
> Even under the eye of His wrath, daring the
>   lightning of His countenance,
> We will carry with storm the citadels of the hills,
> And face to face in combat encounter the armed foe!

This echoes the Scriptural verses which culminate in: "But they presumed to go up to the top of the mountain; nevertheless the ark of the covenant of the Lord, and Moses, departed not out of the camp. Then the Amalekite and the Canaanite, who dwelt in that hill-country, came down, and smote them and beat them down, even unto Hormah" (14:44-45).

Both poems are inspired by the biblical tale and allude to it, but each expresses a different voice, and emphasizes a different aspect of national and human existence. That too is what accounts for the shift in the Scriptural underpinning. An echo of the curse "Your carcasses shall fall in this wilderness" (14:29) resonates in "The Last Dead of the Desert" while "Lo, we are here and will go up," voicing the remorse of the heroes, even as they are sinners, reverberates in "The Dead of the Desert."

4. Variegation

What has been called a phenomenological approach to the Bible, i.e., a dependence on the spiritual, existential phenomenon that gave birth to the poem, as opposed to a dependence on prior lead assumptions -- apart from an attitude of wonderment with regard to the Book of Books -- introduces variegation into the relationship between great poetry and the Bible. The poem "On the Peak of a Mountain" adopts an allegorical form for depicting the struggle between Christianity, Islam and Judaism. The war between Amalek and Moses hints at a reality beyond it, and its arena, the Mountain of god, becomes a reflection of the world as a whole. The poems of wrath and reproach draw their key images from the words of the prophets. "Surely the People is Grass" presents the contempt of the herald for his audience. The poem "I Knew on a Misty Night" rests on apocalyptical visions, a vision of destruction at the time of judgement. The day of the Lord, as the great and awesome Day of Judgement, is sustained through the levels of the poem. The figure of Moses, the location of whose grave is known to no one, merges with the poetic "I," the story of whose death and the loss of meaning of whose mission and utterances are related in the poem. The clear and expressive introduction of the biblical element into the text is sometimes the key to its content. The story of the expulsion from Eden, and of the accursed Adam exchanged for a blessed boy, sheds light on the nature of "The Pool" and what takes place nearby it.

At times the biblical origin is manifest and dominant, as in "Go Flee, Oh Prophet," and at times it is blended with other sources. In "He Gazed and Died" the leading image comes from mysticism, the men who went to the "fiftieth gate." But it is not only the figure of Moses that is alluded to by way of the Talmudic comments on "No man shall see Me and live," but also whoever stood close to the Absolute -- including Adam in the Garden of Eden, and the High Priest who alone was allowed to enter the Holy of Holies.

Bialik himself related the joy of moving from a constrictive rhythm to a freer, more open meter that evolved under the influence of the Bible. In this context, it is worth quoting Jacob Fichman's description of the creation of "In the City of the Killing." "He wrote several versions but none of them satisfied him. He had most trouble with meter. He had the distinct feeling that none of the meters he had composed previously were suitable. Once he almost completed the poem ["In the City of the Killing"] but he was still dissatisfied and rewrote it through to the end in that same broad, free, sweeping rhythm -- the prophetic rhythm in which he later wrote his great dirge "I Knew on a Misty Night." In this uniquely Jewish meter he subsequently composed not only the poems of reproach and the satirical works ("Word," "Surely This Too," etc.) but also the most sublime elegies -- "Let My Lot Be With You" and the four poems: "My Father," "Seven," "Widows" and "Parting" which put the seal forever on his vision." Even in classifying his works into genres, Bialik adopts categorical distinctions from the Bible: the "scroll" and the "song" -- not poetry as a general category distinct from prose, but "song" as in the "Song of the Sea" or the "Song of Deborah." Bialik writes "The Scroll of Fire" and by means of its title seeks to present it as akin to a biblical "scroll." He himself divides his work into "songs" (shirim), "canticles and ballads" (mizmorim upizmonot) and "poems" (shirot). The association of the great long poems, "The Talmud Student," "The Dead of the Desert," "In the City of the Killing," "The Pool," and "The Scroll of Fire" with a genre whose meaning is to be sought in the Bible, is helpful for understanding those works. But here too one must bear in mind the personal nuance attached to the traditional structures. "Songs" are for marking great events, like the "songs" in the bible, but one should not overlook the personal statement that the poet makes when he categorizes "Jonah the Tailor" as one of the "songs," implying that the humble and mute spirits also deserve to be celebrated in a "song."

Within the vast and shifting variety, there are, of course, preferences. The figure of Moses recurs time and again. That is, in part, a consequence of Bialik's special relation to Ahad Ha^{C}am, who headed the Bnei Moshe order. There is also a circumstantial reason. The poem "On the Peak of a Mountain" was written on the Seventh of Adar, the day of Moses' death. The great castigators, Isaiah, Jeremiah and Ezekiel, have a special place. The figure of Amos, the prophet who emphasizes his humble occupation, "I am a cattle breeder and a tender of sycamore figs," is chosen for "Go Flee, Oh Prophet." But the overall picture is one of change and variety. The Bible does not lead the poet but is always at hand to meet his linguistic, visionary, metrical and aesthetic needs.

5.   The Archetypical Foundation

One element from the Bible which is fixed, solid and unchanging is the identification with situations of mission, especially prophetic mission. This is related to Bialik's conception of poetry manifested in "Revealment and Concealment in Language," which maintains that ideal poetry is characterized by disclosure, in the sense of revelation. The poet who commands powerful words resembles a prophet or primordial man in an unrepeatable situation in which a great truth is apprehended and the word appropriate to it emerges. The prophet granted revelation is therefore the ideal figure for self-reference, the standard for judgement of self, of destiny fulfilled or of failure. The admiration for Moses is in part due to his being the supreme prophet, who stood close to the "fiftieth gate."

But, whereas in the poetics of biblical prophecy there is certainty about the prophet selected to deliver the message of he who sends him, in Bialik, doubt and division predominate. The revelation may take on a mystical form, a standing before an absolute that has no continuation, an unrepeated memory. It is the child who is awarded the wonderful sight that will never again return ("Zohar," "The Pool," "Imps of the Sun," etc.). The adult who wants to return to the wonder of childhood will die on the threshhold of the last gate ("He Gazed and Died"). The poet as one charged with speaking to his people will also appear as a bearer of tidings ("To the Bird," "To the People's Volunteers"), or as one who must accept the decree of silence. He may even pray for muteness: "I will no longer beg or try, I will ask nothing... Let there be for me no dream, no vision, no memory, no hope" ("Who Am I and What Am I?"). Indicative of and related to the choice of vision and fear, or flight from it, is the repeated recourse to the word "prophet" ("Word," "In the City of the Killing," "To One of the People," "And if the Days Should Spin Out"), its rejection ("My Soul Speaks"), or its replacement by other images such as the gravedigger poking among the gravestones and within the graves ("In Front of the Bookcase").

The terms of self-reference are many and varied, in keeping with the unique quality of Bialik's poetry which is not dogmatic or political-ideological in the narrow sense of the term, but is experiential, responding to things in general and to the immediate. But the term that reigns above all is "prophet." He sets out images and figures taken from the world of the prophets: "A little chamber on the roof that man had," to remind us of Elisha ("And If You Find"). Even when the actual term "prophet" is rejected, the notion of mission remains the standard.

The speaker who disclaims the title "prophet" is like Amos, the prophet who announced: "I am no prophet, nor am I a prophet's son" (Amos 7:14). Just as Amaziah urges Amos, "O thou seer, go, flee thou away," thus elicit Amos's response, so too in Bialik's poem:

> What is my sin, what my strength
> I'm not a poet, not a prophet --
> I'm just a woodcutter.
> ("My Soul Bends")

What is unique about those singled out for a mission and called a prophet in Bialik's poems of reproach, is that they deliver the last tidings. This "finality" is not because prophecy will cease in Israel, to be revived again at the end of days, but because of the failure of the generation, leading it towards the grave rather than to vision.

In moments of wrath, the poet's vision is of the pointlessness of prophecy, except for that directly concerned with the end of vision and of everything. In "Go Flee, Oh Prophet":

> Return to my own values and habitat
> Make with the forest sycamores my stay
> But you, decaying moldiness and rot,
> Tomorrow's storm shall fling you far away.

In "Word":

> Wherefore shall we fear death,
> His angel already astride upon our shoulders

And his bridle in our mouth?
With shouts of resurrection on our lips,
And with frolickers' mirth
We gambol to the grave.

In "Surely This Too":

There shall you sit mourning and moping, the world
    without dreary
And dust and ashes in the heart.
You shall stare at the dead flies on the windows
And at the spiders in the desolate corners.

The sense of finality is the result of observing the public to whom the one charged with a mission is to carry his message. But it is not totally unrelated to the sense of ending characteristic of images of dust and graves, as, for example, in "They Shake Themselves Free of Dust":

If I rot in the grave -- as I surely will,
I will dream of you rotting,
And my worm-eaten skeleton will laugh at your misfortune,
And shudder at your shame.

The poem "I Knew on a Misty Night" effectively combines the death of the messenger, ("Like a star I shall suddenly be extinguished") and the end visited upon those to whom he was supposed to have been sent and who now await the last trial of death and annihilation.

The powerful elements in Bialik's self-image are those of the man who is last of those who lament, who rebuke, who pray or curse. "I was the last of the last," or alone under the wings of the Shekhinah in "Alone," meaning, of course, a terminal loneliness. The embracing of the experience of a primal revelation that will never be repeated naturally transforms a first experience into a last. The last tear, the last gleam, the last gnashing of teeth spoken of in "God Did Not Show Me" and other poems are indicative of the self-image of one who sees himself in a situation that points to a final surge of inspired vision.

6.   Contradictory Approaches

The twofold emphasis -- the prophetic and the terminal -- has led to radically different impressions of the prophetic, or even the biblical character of Bialik's poetry. Baruch Kurzweil was perhaps the most radical in drawing conclusions from the finality in "He Gazed and Died," "Who Am I and What Am I?" and "In Front of the Bookcase" and saw the poet as a tragic figure seeking death. In the absence of God all the paths of the I in search of dialogue are demolished. A "messenger whom no one has sent" soon loses all relationships which may substitute for meaningful dialogue, and his refuge is silence -- to be identified with annihilation. The claim to the status of prophet should thus be rejected out of hand even when it appears explicitly in a poem and should be seen as an adornment or figurative embellishment only. The identifications with Moses, the supreme prophet, or the suggestion of kinship with the prophets Isaiah, Jeremiah, Ezekiel are to be regarded as poetic fictions. This extreme formulation by Kurzweil can be seen as an overstatement of the trend which emphasizes the personal dimensions of Bialik's poetry as against the 'public' or 'prophetic' element as in David Frishman.

On the other hand, there is the view which ignored the negative trend (which seems to deny salvation) in Bialik and crowned him with the title of prophet. The broad Jewish public, instead of getting upset by the awful words of denunciation in "In the City of the Killing," ascribed a prophetic sublimity to the poet. Lachover recalls a reader of Bialik who upon reading his poetry of rage called him a "divine poet," that is to say, ranked even higher than a prophet. The difficult problem in the poem in which the voice of God interchanges with the poetic I or with the lord or history is solved simply by that reader: the poet is divine. Paradoxically, he reached the same conclusion as Kurzweil, but by magnifying the poet's metaphysical status rather than by negating it. Even those who adopted a more moderate view, like Lachover, ascribed much importance to the prophetic, biblical aspect. In his interpretation Lachover did not forgo the search for the prophetic figure with whom the poetic I's identification is meaningful and not merely superficial.

The relationship between Ezekiel and the wrathful voice in "In the City of the Killing" is real. So too in the final portion of "My Song." The eating of the dough onto which the mother's tear had fallen is like the eating of the scroll by Ezekiel. What we have is a consecration having a distinctly prophetic character. Certainly, those who, with some caution, put the seal of prophecy on Bialik's poetry (such as Joseph Klausner and Jacob Fichman) were careful to stress his character as prophet, but not as the last prophet.

In his essay, "The Seer in Bialik's Poetry," Shimon Halkin provides a fine description of the two approaches to Bialik, but prefers to set Klausner, who makes Bialik nearly a prophet, against Frishman, who says: "Bialik is whatever you want, but he is no prophet." Halkin places most of the interpreters of Bialik, including Brenner, Lachover, Fichman, Wislavsky, Sadan, Tsemach, Kariv and even Kurzweil on the middle line. He calls that position a matter of "confused truth" but does not propose an unequivocal answer to replace what appears to him as the middle way. D.A. Friedman, who also describes the two poles and tends to favor the radically personal side in Bialik's poetry, mentions Frishman's explanation of the many uses of the term "prophet." The audience and the critics have distorted the situation by saddling Bialik with the term. The public wants a "true prophet," as Bialik said in his poem "To One of The People," but it did not turn to Ahad Haam or other leaders, as Bialik asked, but turned rather to Bialik himself, and made him the prophet! The combination of enthusiastic critics and an enthused public is what led to erosion and to inflationary uses of the concept "prophet" in his poems. Friedman differs from Frishman: "Even Bialik's 'nationalistic' and 'prophetic' poems are not artificial." But he goes on to admit: "We will be closer to the truth if we say that in the publication of the 'prophetic' poems and in the entire 'nationalist' period in Bialik's work, there was a good deal of mutual hypnosis. Who misled whom, it is difficult to say at this time."

7.   Firm Center and Open Ends

The point of departure for assessing Bialik's relationship to the Bible and to prophecy must be the poems themselves with their dominant images. The assumption that the audience and the critics asked for and got a prophet, as Frishman suggests, or that it was a matter of 'mutual hypnosis', as Friedman would have it, is not in keeping with Bialik's readiness to write against the accepted and the expected. The awful denunciations in "Word" and "I Knew on a Misty Night" are not by a poet seeking acceptance and anxious to please. The self-image as "last prophet," with all the implications of that term, should be viewed as a unique self-conception. It is not a closed conception which would perhaps justify Kurzweil's view. Bialik speaks of the last, but at the same time is ready to wait for another prophet, who would come after him. In "It Will not be Wiped":

I believe a prophet will yet appear
Who will force from the eyes of the world
        yet another tear
Who will bellow one more lament to anger the heavens
And hearing it, all mortal beings will be seized by fright.

The end looming in "I Knew on a Misty Night" gives way to the appearance of the divine itself, after the disappearance of the last messenger. The God of vengeance enters the arena with a roar. By the self-image of a lion (lavi) -- close in sound to a "prophet" (navi), -- as noted by Dov Sadan, Dan Miron, Adi Tsemach and others -- finality is thwarted by the everlasting and the returning, triumphant appearance.

The term "belimah" in "He Gazed and Died" as Halkin, Joseph Dan, Eliezer Schweid and many others have noted, is not necessarily nothingness or the void, as Kurzweil understood it, but at most a stalemate, or on a higher level, the Kabbalistic sefirah of belimah, or is derived from the word blom in the sense of stopping or bringing to a halt.

The core of the term "last prophet" is strong and refers to a binding calling, a longing for the infinite, to divine voices calling on him, to silence as the infinite, a feeling of sublimity and of eternity. The stars may be extinguished, but the heavens and certainly what is above them, exist forever. But beyond the core is the region of the messenger, whose mortal qualities lead him to helplessness and to a desire for non-being. The last prophet is the point of the infinite's encounter with the finite. The last prophet exists by virtue of the sense of mission created in him by God, history and the people. This feeling itself is stable and nourished by the spiritual tradition of the past, at the center of which stands the Bible. For the poet of reproach, the prophets are not merely useful working fictions but figures with whom he can identify without losing the freedom of his word.

8.   Conclusion: Phenomenological Approach, Stable Self-Image

What has been defined as a relationship determined by force of special experience shows the difference between the poem and the fabric taken from the Bible. This diversity exists in all aspects of the poem: its title, the quotation upon which it rests, its allusions, phrases, idioms. The language of Bialik's poetry (not his folksongs or songs for children) is 'high' biblical and does not skip over any book in the Bible -- Torah, Prophets and Hagiographa. The use of the sources is functional, dynamic and not ornamental.

On the other side, there is his self-conception as messenger and as seer. The ambivalence in Bialik's poetry appears here as well. The tidings of rebirth and death interchange, permanent consecration appears alongside a vanished revelation. But the messenger and the obligation to the sender are the fixed core. From their mutuality stems the glorification of the mission and its prophetic mold. And this is so even in a time of hopelessness; how much more in a time of national rebirth and of a search for renewal.

Notes

1. This poem is translated as "The Last Word" in Selected Poems of Bialik, ed. Israel Efros (New York: Bloch Publishing Co., for Histadruth Ivrith of America, 1965).

2. This poem appears as "Out of the Depth" in the Efros anthology.

3. This poem is translated in the Efros edition as "The City of Slaughter."

ONE HUNDRED YEARS OF SOLITUDE BY GABRIEL GARCIA MARQUEZ, OR GENESIS REWRITTEN

Marta Morello-Frosch

University of California, Santa Cruz

Several critics have pointed out the presence of Biblical allusions in the García Márquez novel One Hundred Years of Solitude[1] and the similarity of the story of the Buendía family to the Biblical concept of the history of man from Genesis to Apocalypse. It has also been observed that the narrative refunctions the main topics of the chronicles of the Spanish conquest of the New World:[2] its perilous expeditions, its early settlements, their growth, the slow inroads of progress in these isolated worlds, and eventually their survival or demise. Recorded history, what can best be called official history, or that told by the conquerors, and Biblical reference, are the textual allusions that dominate this Colombian saga. In this sense García Márquez follows a well established tradition in Latin American letters, since one must remember that the so-called New World of the XVI and XVII centuries did not begin ad ovum Leda, but ad ovum Columbus (con el huevo de Colón) that is to say, with the discovery. This historical event brought together Spanish imperial political designs and divine justification -- in precisely that order -- to what was to be one of the most amazing enterprises of the civilized world: the conquest and colonization of the so-called Indies. Therefore, by bringing together Biblical and historical references in this essay, I am merely foregrounding this familiar context of Latin American self-conscious discourse about its origins and its professed ends. I will mostly concern myself with the components of scriptural nature: oracular prophesies, a quest for knowledge, scourges, etc., because it is an undeniable fact that the history of the Buendía family parallels scriptural patterns closely. But I need to point out also that the peculiar function of these Biblical allusions is to provide an analogy for Latin American history as well. In this sense, G. M. uses the Biblical background, and the echoes of chronicles, as an ideal though no longer viable epic of man. The word of the Book and the word of History become then misleading models, yet create reader expectations as texts whose authority is at once known and set into question. For G. M. will call attention to the dissimilarities between the original text and the Buendía saga, to the incongruities of the latter in light of the former. This ambivalence to the target text allows G. M.'s characters to both invoke and deconstruct the canonized text, in an effort to refunction it and make it relevant to their historical circumstance.[3]

One could thus well say that García Márquez places his own discourse in the space created between the alluded texts and a reading of his own, thus releasing the mechanics for a critical re-examination that would undermine the validity of two all-important texts: the secular scripture: the national history of the country; and the holy one: the epic man. While the absolute authority of such texts is questioned, they are not declared entirely void. Rather, García Márquez revitalizes both versions through a reprocessing that posits various other readings and significations. Hence, while the texts may seem to be subverted in their traditional values, and while the 'circular' reading that the novel itself initially suggests may seem to be superficially negative, the modern text articulates a composite discourse, itself neither eternal nor absolute but serving a marker that allows for disruptions of a single traditional reading.

García Márquez's novel is, therefore, a rewriting of scripture and history designed to recognize the difference between the target texts and the newly proposed one. It thus leads to a recognition of variances, of a set of dynamic situations which disrupt the apparent repeatability of the authoritative texts. The re-reading is, ultimately, an invitation to recognize disruptions in traditions, to reassess one's mental constructs as reflected in our readings of texts, and to defer our judgement so that the above noted differences will not invalidate or close the next discourse, but re-open it to a dialectic with the past and future. As readers, we observe how the characters in the novel repeat histories we know, yet the text is never the same. So if history, or our narrative of it, seems to repeat itself, García Márquez foregrounds its variants so that his own novel becomes one different historicized version of the strife of man to prevail, in this instance in a remote town close to the Atlantic coast of Colombia.

Since the author has managed to write the saga of the Buendías against two textual models, the Bible and the history of Colombia, the concept of rewriting -- re-escritura -- implies a re-reading of both authoritative texts, allowing the implied readers to delve into a world of shared allusions to their culture and national past. At the same time that García Márquez deliberately places his discourse in the space between the two well-known texts, he proceeds to "open" these by thwarting the reader's all too natural expectations, through modifying the original significations of the two models, and thus freeing the modern receptor from the shackles of a closed tradition, yet without severing his other ties with the past. What the new text really manages to do is to act at once diachronically, in that García Márquez revitalizes previous old texts, and synchronically, in that he criticizes, modifies and disrupts such a tradition, at a given point in time, suggesting new significations.

Both Biblical and historical texts appear in the novel as given and prior to the events the fiction will narrate. It is very revealing, then, that against the background of two authoritative narratives that speak of epic deeds, of religious and secular guests, García Márquez's fiction takes 383 pages to present the exhaustive activities of a group that is never delivered in the Biblical sense and is unable to deliver itself from historical bondage.

Let us begin to analyze the concept of Genesis that the novel assumes. After killing a friend who has offended him by casting doubts about his manhood, José Arcadio Buendía sets off eastward, away from the coast that is civilization, in order to resettle elsewhere with his wife and some of his neighbors.

That was how they undertook the crossing of the mountains. Several friends of José Arcadio Buendía, young men like him excited by the adventure, dismantled their houses and packed up, along with their wives and children to head toward the land that no one had promised them. [4]

This modern Adam feels banished from his Arcadia. His very name designates his loss and future quest. But while Arcadias have no history, José Arcadio has one, whose effects have prompted him to flee. He has killed a man, almost a brother since the victim was his friend (Cain motif) and he has also committed a social transgression by marrying his first cousin Ursula. Afraid of the consequences of this union on his progeny, the young couple has avoided sexual contact. Thus the comment by his friend was not totally unfounded, although misdirected.

At the origin we find, then, not a chaos that has to be ordered by Divine design, but a social and religious transgression that causes pangs of conscience as the ghost of the victim -- a non-threatening but pathetic vision -- recurrently visits the young couple. Their departure, therefore, is partly atonement for the bloodshed, and a wish to recommence, and, at the same time, a turning back on a history of violence, of cock fights, of pirate raids on a coast that still recounts terrifying tales of Sir Francis Drake and his bands of marauders in the sixteenth century. There is no pure origin here, as even Arcadio's ancestors have never enjoyed peace. But José Arcadio, a carpenter by trade like the Biblical Joseph, will try again, and turning himself into a young patriarch, sets the march eastward in search of a new beginning, of a new land where, he hopes, he can start civilization anew. His is an enterprise more akin to that of Robinson Crusoe than to a Biblical patriarch, despite his name and profession, despite the explicit analogies to the Bible and the similarity of the initial situation: in this case, transgression, fear of punishment, and self-imposed banishment from their home town. José Arcadio, unlike his Biblical predecessor, carries the memory of his past, and there is also the strange absence of God in his mission. No one has promised a New Jerusalem to these people, whose transgression and punishment is of a very social nature, the result of an order that pits interdiction against limited social realities. For José Arcadio and his present wife Ursula had been meant to be man and wife by the only social possibilities afforded by the community where they dwelled.

Although their marriage was predicted from the time they had come into the world, when they expressed their desire to be married their own relatives tried to stop it. They were afraid that those two healthy products of two races that had interbred over the centuries would suffer the shame of breeding iguanas. There had already been a horrible precedent. An aunt of Ursula's married to an uncle of José Arcadio Buendía had a son who went through life wearing loose, baggy trousers and who bled to death after having lived forty-two years in the purest state of virginity, for he had been born and had grown up with a cartilaginous tail in the shape of a corkscrew and with a small tuft of hair on the tip. A pig's tail that was never allowed to be seen by any woman and that cost him his life when a butcher did him the favor of chopping it off with his cleaver. (p. 28)

The misplaced interdiction is, like the European ideal and models -- historiography included -- an example of the fate of Latin American peoples, destined to be described, prescribed and historicized by the unknowing Other; to be recorded by an alien voice -- even that of the Bible -- that does not account for isolated villages, and subsequent endogamous mating practices.

It is obvious, therefore, that García Márquez is writing his version of genesis, by displacing certain formulaic structures, some familiar narrative situations, and inserting them into a roughly credible new Colombian context, which itself has its own textual paradigms: fear of invasions, precariousness of life on the coast, social interdictions that cannot be obeyed in the face of opposite social realities. If the original Biblical text cannot be frontally attacked in its orthodoxy, the narrative lays bare the incongruity of the model in this Colombian setting. It reveals bare the artificial nature of its interdiction, as opposed to the 'natural' course of things as they have historically prevailed in the village. The practice of culture is thus in conflict with the 'nature' of the word, rendering the last a cause of dysfunction and conflict. There is a displacement of one code by another, an argument and counter-argument that allows the spectre of Biblical punishment to determine historical action.

García Márquez's version is, in this instance, a deforming type of imitation, defined by its differences from the original, differences that render the prior reading incongruous. The modern narrative is, therefore, both dependent and antagonistic vis a vis the target text.[5] It shows, thus, the possibility of other geneses of a non-sacred origin, and the possibility of a man-devised renaissance in the most literal sense. In the case of the Buendías, this will be a departure against one's already established past, without previous promise of a redeeming future. Yet the novelist insists on using the familiar reference, on refunctioning the old literary text, on juxtaposing it to historical fact, and on creating signification precisely because the new version cancels out a good part of the original. Why use Biblical reference then, one may ask? By so doing, García Márquez posits a new concept of imitation, an imitation that distances the original, that turns it into something new and different. His allusion therefore exerts the effect of ostrenanye upon the original by both invoking and destroying audience expectation, and thus promoting new 'readings' of the original text. The modern novelist has managed thus to decode the Biblical narrative and encode it in a new discourse which makes any continuity of reading incongruous. The original text has been refunctioned for a new audience, which is induced to find all the new relationships that the embedding of the old text in its own particular time may suggest. If the knowledge of sin is not enough to restrain the historically inevitable practice of endogamy, the memory of the sacred interdiction is enough to inhibit further transgression, and prompts to a desire for a new -- if not guiltless -- beginning elsewhere.

The founding of the town, Macondo, is enriched by Biblical allusions that transform its original functions.

> ...the night on which they camped beside the river, his father's host had the look of shipwrecked people with no escape, but their number had grown during the crossing and they were all prepared (and they succeeded) to die of old age. José Arcadio Buendía dreamed that night that right there a noisy city with houses having mirror walls rose up. He asked what city it was and they answered him with a name that he had never heard, that had no meaning at all, but that had a supernatural echo in his dream: Macondo. On the following day he convinced his men that they would never find the sea. He ordered them to cut down the trees to make a clearing beside the river, at the coolest spot on the bank, and there they founded the village. (p. 32)

But any similitude between this tropical settlement and the New Jerusalem of the Bible will be the stuff of José Arcadio's dreams only. For while in Revelations (21:18) the undefiled city is presented as a cube, symbolic of perfection, José Arcadio will find in the humble shade of a circus tent, his own cube of perfection: a gigantic piece of ice brought by the gypsies that he and his sons will touch in amazement. In turn, Macondo will enjoy its own particular purity in the heavenly signing of its many birds, and in the youth of its population. For years the town will have no cemetery. Death and historical time, from which the settlers had fled, will temporarily be left behind, so that the young patriarch,

> José Arcadio Buendía, who was the most enterprising man ever to be seen in the village, had set up the placement of the houses in such a way that from all of them one could reach the river and draw water with the same effort, and he had lined up the streets with such good sense that no house got more sun than another during the hot time of the day. Within a few years Macondo was a village that was more orderly and hard working than any known until then by its three hundred inhabitants. It was a truly happy village where no one was over thirty years of age and where no one had died. (p. 18)

This new version of paradise as a socialized settlement is based on equity and a sense of shared wealth and efforts, not on a cornucopia of gifts freely given by a benevolent God. García Márquez's paradise is strictly man-designed, and it induces a cross-reading of its model and subsequent utopias so closely associated to the European view of the New World as an Eden. If this text suggests a new image of the subject, man, as a historical and social being, it would seem that in its self-reflexive nature, he has assumed the responsibility of gift-giving and the distribution of both gifts and effort, having arrived at a new workable model for the origins of man as an ethical being. If the Biblical model induced recognition of the concept of Eden as a locus amenus, as the abode created to the measure of man, the new version would suggest reflection on this model and reprocessing of it in specific historical circumstances, as we mentioned above. The heuristic function of this procedure would elicit a change of opinion upon an analysis of the proposals within the modern text.

If the initial rewriting of genesis may suggest the possibility of a new beginning, albeit a modified one, for man, and thus the emerging of José Arcadio Buendía, the erstwhile avenger, as a young and fair patriarch, one must not forget that he carries with him as we said, his sense of history; that like our own analogue, Robinson Crusoe, José Arcadio is not going to create a new era, but to repeat and prolong the deeds of his past. He may have chosen an Edenic site for his kin, and an Adamic role for himself, but he carries the sin of history: his sense of time -- reflected in his memory of the past -- and his thirst for knowledge. The latter will be stimulated by Melquiades, an old gypsy sage, a mixture of alchemist, prophet and historian. Melquiades will be the one who actualizes José Arcadio's latent curiosity, turning the active patriarch into an obsessive experimenter, with negative results for his paradise.

> That spirit of social initiative disappeared in a short time, pulled away by the fever of the magnets, the astronomical calculations, the dreams of transmutation, and the urge to discover the wonders of the world. From a clean and active man, José Arcadio Buendía changed into a man lazy in appearance, careless in his dress, with a wild beard that Ursula managed to trim with great effort and a kitchen knife. There were many who considered him the victim of some strange spell. (p. 19)

José Arcadio's malady is reflected in his quest for knowledge and of an extension of his self-chosen confines. This prompts him to reach out, to initiate another perilous crossing to where civilization, this time on the positive side of history, is, and away now from Macondo's newness and concomitant lack of history. As he encounters the sea to the north, José Arcadio feels discomfited by the notion that Macondo is surrounded by water on all sides, that it is, in fact, an extended island. José Arcadio's mistake is one of proportions, positionality, or optics that deform his view. There is water to the west and to the north, and indeed to the east also, but only across a whole continental mass. Historically and geographically Macondo is not an island,[6] and it can be reached by gypsies, armies, exploitators of the soil, and the railroad. Melquiades, a suitable modern version of the Biblical priest Melchisedek, brings with him the Promethean will to knowledge that eventually will cause José Arcadio's madness and demise. The patriarch will be defeated by his abortive efforts at alchemy, and at producing the daguerrotyped figure of God, and not by the hardships of his pioneering efforts. Like his Biblical predecessor, José Arcadio will be deranged by a restless and unsatisfied mind. Yet it is pertinent to see that García Márquez actualizes the Biblical model into the context of his fiction, transforming Melquiades into a purveyor of knowledge. For he is a gypsy, and a member of a cursed race, one of a group of wanderers who come and go, who transcend the limited and no longer Edenic boundaries of Macondo. These outsiders bring with them the fantasy of flying carpets, the reality of circus freaks, and the visionary enticement of scientific discovery and progress. For Macondo is the archetypal underdeveloped Latin American town, and from its own perspective, knowledge, and certain forms of desirable or at least non-destructive or non-exploitative progress can only come from outsiders who are, like the Buendías themselves, outcasts. This reflects a deeply critical view of the prevailing concept of progress as coming from centers -- national or foreign -- where those enfranchised by knowledge dwell. It would seem appropriate then that Melquiades assume the role of oracular historian in the narrative. His version of history, like his role as purveyor of knowledge, modifies the traditional coupling of the concept of history and authority. For Melquiades is, as we said, a wanderer without a specific group mission, neither an actor, nor a creator of Macondo's history, merely its prophetic chronicler, since it is he who relates the entire story and eventual demise of the Buendía clan in manuscripts that no one manages to decipher until the very end of the book.

Melquiades' oracular projection therefore is an enigma, hence it does not serve the role of justification for action, as a manifest divine direction would, for the characters in the story. It speaks of a future that, when the script is deciphered, is already fore-closed.[7] Yet through his written yet unread prophecy, the Buendía saga becomes a story already told (written), yet unknown (unread). Fiction -- the events in the novel -- turn into a re-enactment of words in the prophecy, as the characters exist first in Melquiades' parchments, and subsequently, in the narrative, actualizing his prophecy in a new discourse that will end with the incest of the last member, who produces an offspring with a pig's tail. By then, Macondo has suffered through several Biblical-type scourges: the pestilence of insomnia and the pestilence of forgetfulness. Both are designed to leave man's consciousness trapped into an unmovable present without a past -- or sense of history -- and without dreams and the capacity to project a future. In this instance, Macondo suffers two curses that immerse it -- in opposite fashion -- into the abyss of pure present, of utter rapture, of an unsettling discontinuous sense of being. But Macondo will recover from these plagues, to fall into another type of present... that of repetition and the illusion of sameness by circular action. Critics have alluded often to the recurrence of names in the Buendía family tree.[8] While these create the appearance of permanence or intermittence, the senseless acts of war and other violence these people perpetrate and suffer are obvious reminders that their system is in dire need of change, and that their Eden, in fact, has become a Babylon. For if God has promised the Buendías nothing, their demise comes as no surprise, as the repetitions intensify the mistakes and negative traits of the family, heightened by the strong endogamous impulse of its members.[9] The Buendías seem unable to relate to the other, as the incestuous beginnings suggest. Furthermore, they understand, in their Edenic insularity and isolation, that all singular historical events are a mere variant of what they have already experienced. This is not an altogether incorrect perception; yet a variant is not an absolute repetition. Human events -- like textual readings -- are precisely that, a chain of subtle differences that allow for modifications and historical disruptions.

A flood of more than Biblical proportions separates the book into two parts that are similar in structure but have opposite thrust. In the first, there are some signs of an impending apocalyptic end that go unheeded by most everybody but the priest, yet the family grows in numbers while it diminishes in vitality. In the second part, the recluses seem to augment their numbers yet the mark of non-productivity of the family members is never countered by their capacity to rebuild, as they no longer create. Moreover, several characters engage in time-killing enterprises: one fashions little metal fish to melt them subsequently and recommence; another takes forever to weave her own shroud. Their activities become increasingly centripetal and self-reflexive in nature. Eden has become almost a benign cage for them until the floods come and with them the destruction of the town and the ancestral home. But the rains that last four years, eleven months and two days do not arrive as either expected punishment or purification, since after the flood, the last two surviving Buendías commit incest and close with this union and their eventual death, the century of solitude the novel recreates. The narrative closes then upon itself, as the end marks the Apocalyptic destruction and the final point of an historically defined period: one hundred years.

If we return to our initial concept of re-reading texts, we can observe that despite the quantitative expansion of both family and town, their growth has not provided openings for other forms of association, or rather for association with "others". Links have taken place largely among the clan's kin. Obsessed with guilt, and an ancestral curse, they have turned inward. Theirs has not been a providentially inspired enterprise, as they have run away from fear, not towards salvation. In historical terms, they have paid the wages of sin and repetition. The family members have been condemned to solitude because their impulse is essentially backward-looking, nurtured by a memory and a sense of guilt that weigh negatively on their consciousness. However by appropriating known authoritative texts, García Márquez has established for us a different kind of mnemonic path: what we read and what we remember synchronically are at odds, yet the appropriation of older texts thus provides us with a dynamic conflictual opposition. The authoritative texts, far from framing the new one, constitute a borderless composite discourse that at once affirms that these different versions of genesis are Apocalypse not identical, and that they are, nonetheless, inseparable from the original model, since readers and characters alike carry with them the burden and blessing of memory and historical consciousness. The hope lies in perceived differences or critical re-readings, which as we said initially, will not produce stasis or repetition; quite the contrary, they will suggest queries, variances, and ultimately deny the possibility of reading one single, absolute and final sense in every event. Thus, One Hundred Years of Solitude, by appropriating Biblical analogues, tells the story of the Buendía family, while questioning at the same time the purity of their origin, raising the possibility or impossibility of having had other types of origins. Yet Macondo must disappear because the thoughts and actions of their inhabitations are biologically, socially and historically self-reflexive, as they rebuild on the same basis. Unable to restructure their lives, they exhaust themselves in incest. Despite the Biblical model, there was no possibility of revelation for Macondo, nor the promise of a better life beyond, as the Buendías could not read critically their past texts and were thus condemned to solitude.

Notes

1. Crete Evans Miller, "The Ironic Use of Biblical and Religious Motifs in Las tierras flacas and Cien anos de Soledad", Dissertation Abstracts, June 1976. Ms. Miller traces different religious references in the text, and notices their narrative variances, paying particular attention to the ironic treatment of them. Julio Ortega, "Gabriel García Márquez/Cien anos de Soledad" in Asedios a García Márquez, Editorial Universitaria (Santiago, Chile, 1972), pp. 74-88, treats some Biblical topics, particularly the search for Paradise, as secular endeavors. José Miguel Oviedo: "Macondo: Un territorio magico y americano" in Asiedos a García Márquez, pp. 89-105, treats the topic of the fall of man. Several critics have analyzed the mythical resonances in the novel, Biblical motifs included as such. We are attempting in this essay to discuss the use of Biblical references as authoritative texts.

2. Among the critics who have analyzed the treatment of historic material on García Márquez either as referent, as discoursive model or ideological determinant, the following three have contributed solid and not coincidental works: Carlos Blanco Aguinaga "Sobre la lluvia y la historia en las ficciones de García Márquez" in Narradores Hispanoamericanos de Hoy (Chapel Hill, 1973), pp. 55-71, reissued in De mitologos y novelistas (Turner, Madrid); Iris Zacala, "Cien anos de soledad: cronica de Indias", in Homenaje a Gabriel García Márquez, ed. H. Giacoman (Las Americas Publishing Company, New York, 1972) pp. 199-212; and Sergio Benvenuto, "Estetica como historia" in Recopilacion de textos sobre García Márquez (La Habana, Casa de las Americas, 1969), pp. 167-175. In this essay we take historical reference as a given.

3. This is very much like the use of text in a parodic quotation or 'cross reading' as stated by Margaret A. Rose in Parody/Meta-Fiction. Coom Helm (London, 1947), p. 49.

4. Gabriel García Márquez, One Hundred Years of Solitude, Trans. Gregory Rabassa, Avon Books (New York, 1971), p. 31. All quotes from this edition.

5. There is therefore a juxtaposition of messages in the same code. We as readers need to check-up whether we use the same code, or if we are making similar readings. Thus the text performs here almost a meta-linguistic function. See Roman Jakobson, "Linguistics and Poetics" in Style and Language, ed. T. Sebeck (Massachusetts, 1968), p. 353.

6. See Blanco Aguinaga, Op. cit., p. 59.

7. See José Miguel Oviedo, Op. cit., p. 92.

8. Blanco Aguinaga and Oviedo among others.

9. Josefina Ludmer, Cien anos de soledad: una interpretación, Tiempo Contemporáneo (Buenos Aires, 1972).

HARD TIMES IN PARADISE:
AN EXAMPLE OF AN INVERTED BIBLICAL PATTERN

Efraim Sicher
Ben-Gurion University of the Negev

The medieval Church taught that the blessed state of Eden could be regained only in the hereafter, through the grace of God and the sacrifice of Jesus; the fault of disobedience in the Biblical Garden of Eden had condemned mankind to a condition of sinfulness. However, the myth of a hypothetical terrestrial Paradise persisted. This was characteristically located in some far-distant, inaccessible spot, walled off from the misery of actual social disorder to which it was the antithetical model of moral and aesthetic harmony. To enter utopia one had to conform to certain behavioral rules; as in the pact with the Devil, freedom was exchanged for happiness. In modern Europe the city was projected as the model of a new Eden, but the cost of moral and physical imprisonment prompted a questioning of its desirability. Two themes in the biblical myth became relevant to the treatment of the problem of the new urban consciousness: the genesis of injustice and misery in everyday life and the rebellion of the will against a beneficent Creator.

If man was exiled from Eden for the sin of eating from the tree of knowledge, this was an act of disobedience which made possible the distinction between good and evil and hence enabled moral choice. To Reason Romanticism opposed the individualistic and iconoclastic will to act beyond the physical and metaphysical constraints of conventional society; Jonah and Hamlet had known, each in his own way, that rebellion meant flight and exile, but now alienation specified self-exile from both city and civics.[1] Moreover, any pastoral ideal of a return by the individual to a hypothetical idyllic state of affairs, which since Rousseau had involved flight from the communality of a corrupt urban civilization, became a parody by the mid-nineteenth century as the industrial metropolis polluted, despoiled and eventually uprooted Nature.[2] Nevertheless, while Dostoevsky's Notes from the Underground provide a satire on, among much else, the Confessions of Jean-Jacques, the Rousseauesque negation of urbanity is essential to the Underground Man's spiteful contempt for society. To deny the dehumanizing effects of urban living the underground man looks to Adam's example of disobedience and dreams of revolting against a planned utopia which is closer to Babel than to the Eden it purports to be: he has in mind both the narrow mentality of conventional society and the revolutionary ideals of socialism. Neither allows the common herd to go beyond the restricting boundaries of physical and metaphysical walls.

The post-Fall predicament of sin and suffering is, after all, surely preferable to conformity with the totalitarian dogmatism of the Church or State which has taken on the sins of man and given in exchange promises of utopian happiness, but which permits no freedom of conscience, or rather no pains of conscience that remind man he is a responsible, thinking individual, which perpetrates evil in the name of a confining, closed socio-economic system. In the modern city there can be no place for individual will, no deviation, no movement forward. When Jesus, the divine re-embodiment of Adam, comes again in the "Legend of the Grand Inquisitor," in Dostoevsky's Brothers Karamazov, he is arrested as a subversive dissident. The Church preserves only those elements of Jesus' teachings which can be transformed into a mystery religion capable of captivating the will of the masses; in Dostoevsky's scheme of things the Church has been superceded by the city-state, which continues to use the same questionable utopian ends to justify similarly ruthless means.[3]

The modern transformation of the Eden story is characterized by a negative portrayal of the corrupt prison-paradise ruled by a Benefactor who takes charge of the human soul.[4] For the heirs of Dostoevsky the demonic Grand Inquisitor is a Machiavellian Gradgrind of rationalization and his realm is the city. Here one should remember that the archetypal City in Russian literature is the Imperial capital St. Petersburg, canonized (more than Dickens' London and Coketown or Balzac's Paris ever were) as a literary convention of an analytic-critical model of society.

An example of how St. Petersburg's stonehearted granite obliterated the pastoral idyll in the name of Tsarist autocratic ambition and state expediency can be found as early as Pushkin's Bronze Horseman: Nature takes its revenge with an apocalyptic Flood, but the real victim is poor Evgenii, the Adamic hero, who loses his loved one and his sanity. Gogol, of course, cloaks St. Petersburg in a phantasmagoric mist, but in the early works of Dostoevsky its hostile climate becomes mythicized into something much more sinister. It is true that Dostoevsky was infatuated for a while with utopian socialism, but after his traumatic experience at the gallows he recoiled at any institution or ideological system which justified the means by the ends. His Notes from the Underground (1864) were, in part, a response to the novel Chernyshevsky had written in prison the year before and which had so much effect on Lenin, What Is To Be Done? Vera Pavlovna's fourth dream in Chapter 16 of Chernyshevsky's novel is a vision of the machine age, a Fourierist vision of life in huge phalansteries of aluminum and steel, of which there had been hitherto only one pale intimation, the Crystal Palace on Sydenham Hill in London.

The Crystal Palace was officially opened at the Great Exhibition of 1851 in London's Hyde Park. On display were the glorious achievements of modern industrial engineering, the achievements of the victorious British Empire. The keynote was universality, science, civilization and, of course, the Victorian gospel of labor. The Crystal Palace itself made an enormous impact as an architectural as well as literary metaphor of the far-reaching sociological and economic changes wrought by the Industrial Revolution in England.[5] Built of iron and glass, using standardized prefabricated units, the Crystal Palace could be easily adapted to a ready symbol of utopian ideals. In 1854 the Crystal Palace was removed and rebuilt on Sydenham Hill where it was rearranged by capitalist entrepreneurs as an Aladdin's Cave of Civilization; ironically perhaps, this "indestructible" wonder burnt down in 1936.[6] Chernyshevsky enthusiastically recommended the Crystal Palace to the Russian readers of the leading journal Notes of the Fatherland as the supreme attainment of modern science and art and he later visited it himself in 1859.

Very different was Dostoevsky's reaction when he saw the Crystal Palace in 1862. In Summer Notes of Winter Impressions (1862-1863) he conceded that the power of the British Empire to subjugate people around the world into "one herd" was impressive, but this triumph frightened him because it was too finite, too final in its attainment of an ideal. Dostoevsky presented the Crystal Palace as an apocalyptic nightmare of a sort of Tower of Babel where Baal was worshipped. The masses saw escape from the rigid oppression, in the name of utopia on earth, by a mechanized, all-pervasive system not, in religious salvation but in the depravity and gin-shops of the Haymarket and Whitechapel.[7]

All are content in Chernyshevsky's future crystal palaces. Physical and moral health have been perfected. Happiness pervades daily labor. All are free, but all conform to the guidance of Big Sister. The criteria of this utopian Eden are utility and advantage, not all that far removed, perhaps, from the political economy of Coketown. However, as Dostoevsky's underground man protests in his attack on rational egoism, humankind never saw the advantage in good. The underground man denounces Buckle's view that "civilization" is ameliorating the human condition, that aggression and strife can be curtailed. The rationalization of history into laws in Buckle's History of Civilisation in England (1857-1861, Russian translation 1863) threatens to formulate the "laws of nature" like a logarithm table, leaving nothing to chance and excluding the possibility of individual action. The mathematical image of 2 x 2 = 4 (so dear to Mr. Gradgrind in Dickens' Hard Times) is associated by Dostoevsky's paradoxical anti-hero with the confines of the Crystal Palace which, like the geometrically regular walls of the modern city, imprison body and soul. Eden, the modern city and the utopian Crystal Palace are coterminous spatial metaphors opposed by the irrationality of the underground man's 2 x 2 = 5.

In the name of free choice the underground man refuses to become a piano key, a mechanical cog in the works -- here the underground man alludes to Diderot's Reve de d'Alembert. The purpose of existence is to prove that "I" am "I" and not a piano key. Unlike Rousseau, the underground man sees humankind as fundamentally destructive and lacking in moral sense. Man seeks to create and to perfect, but will not rest easy in the anthill of planned utopia which allows no pain or suffering, no doubt or denial, a glass-house in which one dare not poke out one's tongue, let alone throw stones. The crystal palace is the Eden of both socialism and modern technology for the underground man who derides it as a chicken coop and equates it with the misery of the tenement slum. These metaphors of enclosure and the bestial imagery (anthills, chicken coop, herds) were to be repeated and developed in Dostoevsky's later works, though he certainly did not consider the underground man's retreat from society as anything but a way out to nowhere. However, equally detestable to Dostoevsky was the irrevocable finality of the offical Church's version of salvation, which was also a means of building "walls," and it is from religious language that the underground man borrows his atheistic prayer that he may lose his right hand if he adds one brick to the New Jerusalem.

Raskolnikov, in contrast to the underground man, does dare to overstep the walls of conventional morality in Crime and Punishment and he actually pokes out his tongue in a St. Petersburg restaurant called "The Crystal Palace." Yet his will to act has proved nothing, although he manages to break through several psychological and physical barriers (including the old pawnbroker's door and her skull). He has failed to rise above his wretched poverty, he has failed to become a Napoleon. Rather he must expiate his guilt through compassion with those who suffer. The breakthrough to this humbling experience is also a significant spatial metaphor: prostration to the ground in St. Petersburg's most squalid quarter, the Haymarket. Sonya, the prostitute, follows Raskolnikov to Siberia and it is only there that she succeeds in teaching him through Christian love to overcome his egoistic pride. Again, the institutions of the Church and State, as well as the demonic power of an absolutist idea, are negated because they each in their own fashion posit Utopia as both a possible and a desirable Eden.

The closed contours of the urban false Eden provide a metaphor once more for a refutation of the premise that the needs of man are reducible to simple equations and square roots in Evgenii Zamyatin's dystopian fantasy We (first English publication, 1924).[8] In the thirtieth century the Crystal Palace utopia has been built. Society has been integrated into the One State[9] and its citizens are uniformed members subordinate to the will of the all-powerful, Socratically-bald Benefactor, quite plausibly a caricature of Lenin. The enclosing glass of the Crystal Palace reflects the coldness of its inhumanity, as well as the transparent lack of privacy, while the integrality of its ideology, emphasized time and time again by closed geometric forms, speaks for the finality of Eden rebuilt. The last problem unsolved by the One State is the vestige of man's animal origins, his irrational, primeval instincts. These are unaccounted for in the modern Planned Economy, or in the American industrial managerial system of Taylor, which won praise from Lenin's wife, Krupskaya,[10] but is here satirized by Zamyatin.

The modern Adam is D-503, the builder of the spaceship The Integral which will bring mathematically uniform, rationalized utopia to the rest of the galaxy. However, the rational has not completely stifled the second, equally necessary half of human nature, the irrational, which surfaces even in the real number system, in the irksome and irresoluble value of $\sqrt{-1}$. $\sqrt{-1}$ is personified by none other than the modern Eve, I-330, I being the mathematical symbol of $\sqrt{-1}$, but also "I" as in the self, as opposed to the collective we, also "I" as in the "I" that comes from the Devil: "we is from God," she says, "I is from the Devil." She is involved in some mysterious way with S-4711, the biblical serpent and "fallen angel," who turns out to be a double agent.[11] The science-fiction Eve (like Milton's) gives Adam a taste of the forbidden fruit (in this case "venomous green" bootlegged liquor) and after the Fall sex becomes sinful and guilt-ridden. D- realizes the duality of the self, which makes him a true progeny of Dostoevsky's "doubles."[12] I- entices D- beyond the walls of the City State, into the "imperfect," "chaotic" past, into nature, to join the rebels, the self-styled MEPHI, the heretics pledged to Mephistopheles. They breach the walls of the new Eden but in the end unfreedom prevails and the walls are repaired. The imagination, man's last freedom and the last obstacle to total rationality, is removed by surgical operation. Henceforth even thinking beyond the bounds set by the State is to be impossible.

The Benefactor tells D-503 in his Et tu Brute? speech that the ancient dream of Heaven has been fulfilled -- Edenic peace on earth -- but in common with Dostoevsky's Grand Inquisitor he claims the role of crucifier as both the most difficult and the most important. Instead of Jesus' response of a kiss in The Brothers Karamazov, D- laughs, expressing the absurd but necessary revolt of the irrational in the face of reason. As a Jesus-figure this thirty-two-year-old Adam is primarily a heretic in the midst of an apocalypse that allows no possibility, unlike Dostoevsky's dystopian visions, of religious salvation. The atrophy of the totalitarian neo-Edenic city-state, guarded by walls and neo-Platonic Guardian-Angels, can only be opposed, in Zamyatin's formulation of revolution, by the dynamic forces of energy. Zamyatin incorporated his ideas on heresy and revolution into Julius Robert von Mayer's thermo-dynamic concept of entropy as "the tendency of the universe's energy toward rest," as the gradual dissipation of energy, in the form of heat, from concentrations capable of work in hot bodies toward a passive energy equilibrium among warm bodies incapable of work.[13] Transferred to a sociological model, entropy represented for Zamyatin the universal tendency toward spiritual death, while solar energy stimulated spiritual or corporeal activity which disrupted the tendency toward cooler equilibrium, toward philistine stagnation.[14] In his essay "On Literature, Revolution, Entropy and Other Matters" (1923), Zamyatin defined revolution as part of an ongoing, non-infinite process, during which two dead stars collide and a new star is born; revolution is non-bounded and hence appropriately associated in We with non-bounded spatial metaphors, with the unenclosed world outside the Wall of the city-state. Revolution and entropy in Zamyatin's analysis are thesis and antithesis of the Hegelian law of historical process. As soon as the fire of revolution cools into entropy there is social and thermo-dynamic dissipation of energy. The result is ossification, absolutism, dogma. It then needs new heretics -- a Galileo, a Jesus, an Einstein -- to blow up the walls of the totalitarian state and its bounded cosmology.[15]

In We, I-330 is painfully executed under the Bell Jar and D-503 undergoes lobotomy, a form of surgical crucifixion, but D-503 has implanted in the womb of his "legal" mate, his other, god-given Eve, O-90, a future, vernal sapling which will sprout on the other side of the Wall. All is not quite hopeless, for Zamyatin has shown that Eden is not foolproof, that the Fall is inevitable and essential unless man is to lose completely his humanity, his natural duality, his will to sin, his basic freedom of the soul -- that darkening of the glass which can be attained only after the Fall from Grace, from the clarity of the Crystal Palace.

This then is the sombre warning of Zamyatin, writing at the beginning of the nineteen-twenties, after the First World War had regimented the masses into uniformed numbers, after Revolution had shaken Russia, at a time when technocracy threatened to mechanize daily life. Like Dostoevsky's warning it is directed not only at the dangers facing Russia; it too derives much from Zamyatin's impressions of English society while working as an engineer in Newcastle shipbuilding yards in 1916, impressions which

Zamyatin incorporated into his short novel The Islanders. At the same time Zamyatin was responding to the utopias of his literary master, H. G. Wells,[16] though the fear of technology as means to utopia and enslavement of mankind was shared by Forster's "The Machine Stops," Capek's R.U.R. and other fictional fantasies which use science to construct a critical social model.[17] Not that the advantages of industrial technology are undesirable in themselves, as Dickens stressed in Hard Times, but the uses to which they may be put threaten human freedom. The myth of Eden is not so much negated (in the sense that Eliot's Wasteland may be seen as anti-Edenic), as it is inverted. Zamyatin's inversion of the biblical and christological myth directly inspired Orwell to write 1984[18], which incorporates the basic mythic structure of We and applies it to a critical satire of contemporary society -- Britain in 1948. For Orwell, however, the main motivation of Big Brother was power and his ministry Fear, but again freedom of thought is shown to be one of the greatest enemies of the System. On the other hand, Jack London's Iron Heel (1907), which Zamyatin must have known as one who helped popularize London in Russian translation, posited an oligarchy which violently repressed the proletarian revolution, but did not use the Edenic myth except as a passing reference.[19] Huxley's Brave New World does bear striking similarities to We, especially the Jesus figure in the guise of a modern noble savage, but Huxley denied he had previously even heard of Zamyatin's book; if the real model for an inverted Eden myth in both Dostoevsky and Zamyatin was England then it is perhaps hardly surprising that it should also be met in the place of its genesis. In any case Dostoevsky, Zamyatin, Huxley and Orwell are all working in a tradition of social utopias that stretches from Plato through Rousseau to Fourier.[20]

Notes

1. For a survey of the long history of positive alongside negative conceptualizations of urbanity see George Steiner, "The City Under Attack," Salmagundi, 24 (1973).

2. This was less true of North America, a virgin Promised Land that still promised a new Adamic beginning (see inter alia Leo Marx, The Machine in the Garden, New York, 1964; R.W.B. Lewis, The American Adam, Chicago, 1955).

3. Compare Newman's view of the Church ravaging the mind of man and overriding interpretation of the Bible.

4. A paradigmatic motif of a Benevolent Citizen who introduces knowledge of sexuality and violence and thus causes a breakdown of adolescent innocence is discussed in Robert L. Jackson, "Chekhov's Garden of Eden, or the Fall of the Russian Adam and Eve: 'Because of Little Apples,'" Slavica Hierosolymitana, 4 (1979), 70-8, and the same author's "The Garden of Eden in Dostoevsky's 'A Christmas Party and a Wedding' and Chekhov's 'Because of Little Apples,'" Revue de Littérature Comparée, 3-4 (1981), 331-41. There can be little doubt that the Benefactor or "Big Brother" figure was part of reaction to the European Enlightenment and "Benevolent Despotism."

5. See Asa Briggs, Iron Bridge to Crystal Palace: Impact and Images of the Industrial Revolution, London, 1979.

6. For crystal as an Edenic motif cf. the crystal stone in The Romance of the Rose, crystal windows in the Land of Cockayne and the crystal mirror in Paradise Lost, IV, 264. An important property of crystal is its clarity, toughness and regularity of form, but also relevant here is its popular use for divination: hence its suitability as a symbol for a future-oriented, regularized, rationally ordered society.

7. Jacques Catteau has pointed out that Dostoevsky first determined his image of utopia as a palace of marble and gold, which was all very well except for the cost of liberty, an image found in a fragment of the second chapter of Notes from the House of the Dead (1860), written before he had visited the Crystal Palace, symbol for Dostoevsky of the ugliest bourgeois values and of the walling-in of spiritual freedom ("Du palais de cristal à l'âge d'or où les avatars de l'utopie," in Jacques Catteau (ed.), Dostoievsky, Paris (1972), 176-195).

8. Much has been written on Zamyatin's imagery, but only one article deals directly with biblical references in We (R.A. Gregg, "Two Adams and Eve in the Crystal Palace: Dostoevsky, the Bible, and We," Slavic Review, 24, 4 (1965), 680-7). Unfortunately, Gregg does not adequately discuss the inversion of the Eden myth or its relation to anti-utopian models (although R.L. Jackson has included We in his study, Dostoevsky's Underground Man in Russian Literature, The Hague, 1958, 150-7).

9. Literally, "United State," a hint, perhaps, in the direction of the North American continent (cf. references below to bootlegging and Taylor).

10. N. Krupskaya, "Sistema Teilora i organizatsiya raboty sovetskikh uchrezhdenii," Krasnaya nov, 1 (1921), 140-6.

11. S-4711 makes D-503 think of yet another biblical myth, the Binding of Isaac, the archetypal "test" prefiguring the legend of Jesus; the sharp teeth of the X-shaped I- also imply the pain of crucifixion as well as suggesting the temptation of forbidden fruits (note her seductive "smile-bite").

12. Sex with I- leads to a Fall, but in terms of ascendancy, an experience akin to flying, which lifts D- to a seventh heaven beyond the sphere of the State; appropriately it is the spaceship Integral, mathematical symbol of the State's uniformity, which the revolutionaries hijack in an abortive attempt to prevent the expansion of the rule of reason (finity) to outer space: at this point flight from the City gets airborne, if only for a moment. At the same time the Fall brings D- knowledge of death, D- finds himself capable of killing Yu- out of jealousy and revenge, but, like Raskolnikov's "act," this is shown to be no more justified than the State's morality in killing one in the name of many.

13. E. Zamyatin, Julius Robert von Mayer, Berlin, 1922, 56; quoted in A.M. Shane, The Life and Works of Evgenii Zamyatin, New York, 1968, 46-7.

14. An important influence on these ideas was no doubt Frank C. Eve's essay, "In the Beginning: An Interpretation of Sunlight Energy," Atlantic Monthly, 131 (1923), 664-77; translated into Russian in a journal edited by Zamyatin, Sovremennyi zapad, 4 (1923).

15. Zamyatin goes on to apply this theory to contemporary literature and "neo-realism," which he talks of in terms of non-Euclidean geometry. Hence Zamyatin's

basic dystopian thesis -- that there can be no final revolution, just as there can be no final integer -- is built into both the imagistic and mythic framework of We.

16. See E. Zamyatin, Gerbert Uells, Petrograd, 1922. Cf. Wells' story "The Door in the Wall" which fantasizes a return in time through a "door in the wall" to an atavistic garden of childhood innocence. In We the "door in the wall" is also a passage in time, via the municipal Museum of the Ancients. (See also Christopher Collins, "Zamyatin, Wells and the Utopian Literary Tradition," Slavonic and East European Review, 44 (1966), 351-360; and D.J. Richards, "Four Utopias," Slavonic and East European Review, 40 (1962), 220-8.)

17. The influence on Zamyatin of Jerome K. Jerome's "The New Utopia" has also been suggested (E. Stenbock-Fermor, "A Neglected Source of Zamyatin's Novel We," Russian Review, 32 (1973), 187-8), though Jerome, like Zamyatin, would have read Dostoevsky's The Possessed. See also George Kateb, Utopia and its Enemies, New York, 1963. The warnings of the dystopian novelists did not deter twentieth-century builders of "garden-cities;" indeed, the Crystal Palace has no small part in the story of modern architecture (see Lewis Mumford, The City in History, London, 1961; R. Fishman, Urban Utopias in the Twentieth Century, New York, 1977).

18. See George Orwell's essay on Zamyatin in Tribune, 4.1.1946, and Isaac Deutscher's response "1984: The Mysticism of Cruelty," in his Heretics and Renegades, London, 1955, 35-50. Cf. G. Beauchamp, "Of Man's Last Disobedience: Zamyatin's We and Orwell's 1984," Comparative Literature Studies, 10 (1973), 285-301; and E.J. Brown's rather disappointing little book, Brave New World, 1984 and We: An Essay on Anti-Utopia, Ann Arbor, 1976.

20. The mathematical and scientific imagery of Zamyatin's work (apart from more obvious allusions) may refer to Plato's recommendations for the education of the Guardians (though cf. John White, "Mathematical Imagery in Musil's Young Törless and Zamyatin's We," Comparative Literature, 18 (1966), 71-8). Plato was reformulating a foundation myth in the search for the origin of injustice; Plato talked in terms of a city-state, regulation of sex, selective breeding and a common good; Plato, moreover, explicitly states that there is to be no further innovation or revolution in the ideal state. It is therefore perhaps not surprising that Zamyatin and Huxley should both use The Republic in an inversion of a basic European Christian foundation myth, the story of Eden with its prefigurement of the second coming (a second "revolution"), in their critical science-fantasy models of the modern city.

THE AMERICAN DANIEL AS SEEN IN
HAWTHORNE'S THE SCARLET LETTER

Sharon Deykin Baris

Bar Ilan University

Critics have suggested that American literature describes a nation of the New Heavens and the New Earth and that the national literary hero is, in R.W.B. Lewis' phrase, "the American as Adam."[1] Alternatively, in keeping with the felt Power of Blackness so famous in American works, there has been seen what Ursula Brumm has called a prevalent and "strange phenomenon in American literature" of figures who express abysmal despair when their optimism encounters failure; these are what she terms "negative Christ figures" as heroes.[2]

More subtly, as recent studies have theorized, it is not simply the setting or the hero which is Biblical in American writing, but rather the action within the work; the overall shape of the work itself reflects Biblical influence. Perry Miller, who first turned attention to the American penchant for Jeremiads amongst the country's earliest settlers, had seen this form as expressive of a pervasive national condition of anxiety.[3] More recently David Minter and Sacvan Bercovitch have shown that the writers of Jeremiads proffer their works "not as mere lament but rather as a mode of constructive activity, a form of creative endeavor."[4] The Jeremiad, in its wider implications throughout American literature, links the failures of experience to a redemptive end; by joining lament and celebration, the Jeremiad yet reaffirms the American mission.[5]

But I shall posit another powerful Biblical influence at work within the American imagination. It may even be argued that there is one other Biblical figure who stands behind the Adams and the Jeremiahs, controlling their expression in the New World culture. The figure I shall turn to denominates not the subject, nor the dynamic action of American expression, but rather, guides and conditions an awareness of the other two. I find this pervasive and focal figure in the Book of Daniel, and its apocryphal supplement Susannah and the Elders. The Biblical Daniel is both a prophet of the apocalyptic and also a proponent of the hermeneutic; he knows the secrets of the End as well as the writing on the wall. Daniel's dream is the source for the assumption that American is a privileged world, and in his deciphering action he is the type for Americans' ongoing habit of reading everywhere about them the proofs of their given origin.[6] Daniel's powerful example initiated both the dream and the interpretive behavior to support it.

The fundamental links between Daniel and America are historical and religious. The Protestant Reformation in Europe had revitalized the millennialist dream of a New Kingdom on earth in an End of Days -- in keeping with the prophecies of the Four Beasts of the Book of Daniel and the Book of Revelation. Since the time of Jerome the beasts had been seen by Christian exegetes to be four successive monarchies or dominions of power in the history of the world, the last being Catholic Rome.[7] According to the Protestant exegetes these beasts were yet to be supplanted by a Fifth Beast or Fifth Monarch. Their claim was for a new hegemony which would supplant the old religious dominions and which would fulfill the promise of the End of Days to bring the Protestant New Jerusalem to a New Earth.

But physical, historical and political conditions conspired to lend a specifically American dimension to the Dream of the End.[8] Almost coincident in time with the Protestant Reformation a new continent had been discovered; this seemed to have been foretold by the Book of Daniel, since the continent itself, like the meaning of Daniel's visions, had been "sealed" and "shut up until the time of the end." The monarchies, furthermore, were seen to follow a westward course, as empire succeeded empire. The coincidence of the western continent's opening just at that time seemed to complete the promise of this fateful trend.[9]

Inherent in the actions of the story of Daniel, in the personality of the hero himself, and in the very shape and structure of the book, moreover, were discerned certain significant clues and examples for the New World Protestant condition. For Daniel, in a strange king's court, had been the nonconformist, willing to suffer captivity and trial for his belief; was this not the position of the Protestant Reformer? Calvin himself had used Daniel as his example. In his "Commentaries on the Book of Daniel" he praised the "indefatigable constancy of holy men in pursuit of piety which invites us with a loud voice to imitate them"; Puritans, said Calvin, "ought not to consider it a grievance to be thrown into the furnace of trial while profane men enjoy the calmness of repose."[10] In America Roger Williams later preached a similar message: "God's people were and ought to be non-conformitants...and to practise truth (as Daniel did, for which he was cast into the lyons' den)..."[11] But most fundamentally Daniel's example was suited to that Errand into the Wilderness which the Puritan mission became. As Perry Miller observed, "Every effort, no matter how brief is addressed to the persistent question: What is the meaning of this society in the wilderness?...Who, they are forever asking themselves, who are we?"[12] If life was to be an ordeal, a razor's edge existence which struggled to be "in this world but not of it," then the self-interpretive demands were momentous.[13] The example of Daniel might somehow encourage one to keep reading the signs of the wilderness experience and to reframe them in a boundless context. The Puritan could be the Daniel to read the writing on the wall of the daily paths whilst he could also be the Daniel to consider their implications in another register, that of the Time of the End.

Testimony to the powerful attraction of Daniel lies in the numerous early Puritan sermons devoted to The Book of Daniel. The first book published in America was the Bay Psalm Book, in 1639. But within a few years, two sermons were published, in 1644 and 1646, both expounding the "Prophecie of the Book of Daniel."[14] All over New England, until mid-nineteenth century and even thereafter, such sermons were preached. In Boston, in 1842, the very decade of Hawthorne's writing <u>The Scarlet Letter,</u> there appeared the following title for an essay published in the "Christian Review":

REMARKS ON THE BOOK OF DANIEL, in Regard to the Four Kingdoms, especially the Fourth; The 2300 Days; The Seventy Weeks; and the Events Predicted in the Last Three Chapters.

-- by Irah Chase, D.D. Professor of Ecclesiastical History[15]

It is significant that the figure Daniel, or some pattern evocative of the Daniel story, appears repeatedly in the great works of American literature. Many instances are suggestive -- overtones, perhaps, derived from this fundamental interpretive basis -- such as the prevalence of mysteries, clues, detectives, riddles, even hieroglyphs.[16] Yet I suggest that there are several carefully delineated uses of the Daniel figure as well. Three great authors, Melville, Hawthorne, and James, all make subtle use of the Book of Daniel; each author evokes, if briefly yet most significantly, a scene or a cluster of images derived from that book in order to convey the sense of an impending entrapment, a limitation or dangerous captivity which might be avoided by the central figure who ought to interpret, come to judgment and "save" the situation. In each case, I believe, the author uses that Daniel reference to consider some fundamental national cultural condition derived from the American premise, and to question certain attendant assumptions about American origin.

Amongst the many literary examples which might be given, I shall here mention two colorful stories in particular. Hawthorne's short tale, "Rappaccini's Daughter," as I have suggested elsewhere, is a retelling of the apocryphal story of Susannah and the Elders.[17] Hawthorne conjures up the richness of a medieval hortus conclusus setting -- complete with the porta clausa -- within which to portray Baglioni and Rappaccini as the two evil elders of that favorite medieval apocryphal rendition of Daniel; young Giovanni, like a Daniel, is asked to enter that garden world to judge and to save, by reading the symbols so richly offered there. In another story of a young interpretive Daniel, Henry James's "The Pupil" becomes a kind of Captivity Narrative.[18] Here again only the young man who enters the court or household, could possibly bring the tale to a happy end by deciphering the polyglot language shared amongst this strange family.[19] But Pemberton fails, in the crisis, to offer a vision of the very End of Days, although little Morgan asks him to do just that: to take him away, to escape, "to live with him for ever and ever."[20]

In Melville, too, the Daniels abound; Ishmael as Daniel is a subject worthy of a full study in another forum. But what can here be noted is the way that in the early novel Mardi Taji's declaration "All tars are Daniels!" is an exuberant claim; yet in the later works the hints of a Daniel become darker and more tragic. In Melville's last novel Billy Budd, finally, I suggest that the author may be trying to eradicate all signs of a Daniel at work in the American world. Only the Dansker might be a prophet-seer in this novel, but he is an anti-Daniel who refuses to comment and thus to save Billy -- even as Vere, his diametric opposite, insists upon wilfully misinterpreting, only to condemn the young sailor. The two powers for Melville seem to cancel one another out, in a kind of "sinister dexterity"; it is as if the influence of Daniel may be exorcised. But the very "emphasized silence" of any saving interpretive view lies at the core of this work; that silence is so strongly felt as to suggest Daniel's enduring power or attractive potential, even when he fails to speak. And so it is that in such modern works as Doctorow's The Book of Daniel or Bellow's Henderson there are symptoms that the dream of Daniel is alive and well in America today.

As an instance of the way in which an awareness of Daniel may help in understanding a major work of American literature, it may be appropriate to consider Nathaniel Hawthorne's The Scarlet Letter. The story takes place "on the edge of the Western wilderness"; if the Westward Course of History is implied, that hint serves to highlight the momentous setting Hawthorne has chosen for the drama that he presents.[21] For here will be enacted the struggle between two putative, contending American Daniels who must read before them a text in the shape of the mysterious figure, Hester. She will challenge them to understand themselves and the new world that they all share.

In the first chapter of The Scarlet Letter a subtle equation is established. As the woman Hester makes her dramatic entrance through the oaken door, so the narrative itself, at the same moment issues "from that inauspicious portal." The Puritan townfolk have gathered around the door to behave as an audience, and we are to recognize the suggestion that Hester, like the very tale itself, is an artifact, a performance, or a kind of imaginative text -- her 'A' may be a synecdoche of a larger message -- which awaits several varying and intensive kinds of criticism by both the reader and the American audience Hawthorne has gathered.

But Hester's meaning, as her name connotes (Hester, hidden), is not clear and requires careful exegesis. The setting complicates responses. From the first Hawthorne posits a Utopian world; Hester might have entered a land with garden-of-Eden connotations, and her significance might thus have been more predictable, as in an ideal Garden or hortus conclusus setting she may have been an Eve-Mary-Esther figure.[22] But the author thereafter immediately points out that here is a terrain of burdocks as well as of roses, that Hester inhabits a world of prisons as well as of dreams, and that she is indeed, a fallen woman. The crowd that confronts her, therefore, is a public which must create new interpretive contexts in order to derive fresh meanings when they consider a woman named Hester-Esther, and the complex garden-America wherein she dwells.

If Hawthorne seems strangely innovative in dramatically presenting the meaning of America as a text presented for interpretive behavior, one may recall the precedent of that very first American sermon, given by Governor Winthrop himself (the novel's own Winthrop!) upon the deck of the flagship Arabella:

> He shall make us a praise and glory that men shall say of succeeding plantations, the lord make it like that of New England. For we must consider that we shall be as a city upon a hill, the eyes of all people are upon us...we shall be made a story and a by-word through the world...[23]

Hester, like Winthrop's America, finds "the eyes of all people" upon her; she is indeed the story and by-word of the townfolk. Her story will consist of the versions of her meaning these Americans will provide throughout the novel.

Chapter two, then, shows Hester standing before the crowd as one who must play "her part"; and they in turn are "spectators" with a "verdict of public sentiment" as they "intently fasten" their eyes upon her. This chapter is not about Hester, nor is it descriptive of the typical Puritan community. Rather it is a provocative rendition of interpretive reactions. Hester is "revealed" upon a "pedestal of shame" to witnesses below; the scene is overtly dramatic, and we are prepared for the appearance in such an audience mood, of a definitive or significant interpreter.

So it is that in the ensuing chapter Chillingworth appears in the town square to stand "on the outskirts of the crowd." This man who is repeatedly described as a "presence in the crowd" enacts many of the town's critical interpretive tendencies. As we shall see, the very gestures of the town and Chillingworth are notably alike. He confronts a tableau in the market-place which is remarkably similar to the one implicit, in both bold outlines and subtle connotations, in the earlier story, "Rappaccini's Daughter." But if the Apocryphal story of Susannah and the Elders had been implicit in the earlier tale, now the references are overtly declared: A young woman stands charged by the leaders of the community; her past is questionable, and testimony cannot or will not be brought to clear her. Early in Chapter III, Chillingworth leans over to ask a townsman about the mystery they behold, and the source is directly stated: "Of a truth friend, that matter remaineth a riddle and the Daniel who shall expound it is yet a-wanting" (p. 49).

Of course Chillingworth would be a drastically altered Daniel. Although both Daniel and Chillingworth appear as strangers in a scene of trial and mystery, the Biblical hero, a holy-spirited "youth" had willingly and energetically stepped forth to pronounce his judgments and save the girl.[24] Chillingworth is old, deformed, and hardly the warm impetuous youth required. (All that is precisely his problem!) And it must be noted that, whilst Daniel had no possible connection with the accused woman, Hester is, after all, Chillingworth's wife.

Yet there are certain parallels which seem to hold: for this fallen Susannah is indeed "saved" by Chillingworth, the stranger, in an oddly inverted way. The Puritan magistrates had not given Hester the death penalty only because her husband was presumed dead; and now he does not, after all, controvert that assumption. More directly evocative of the Biblical Daniel himself, furthermore, are the stories Hawthorne tells of Chillingworth's recent past. He has been a wanderer held "sorely against his will" and now has been brought hither to be "redeemed out of captivity" (p. 49). His personal captivity narrative but prepares us for ensuing feats of interpretive behavior, and again, the Daniel evocations are present. Chillingworth does focus his attention upon the "solution of a mystery" concerning a symbolic hieroglyph, and as he avows, in his inquest he uses "other senses" than his fellow-men possess (p. 58). He insists that he shall "read" the hidden meaning of the letter -- if not upon a wall, then upon a human heart. At last when the riddle-solving stranger does pull aside the veil of mystery -- the vestments upon the suffering minister's bosom -- to see an actual symbol there, Hawthorne declares, "A revelation, he could almost say had been granted to him" (p. 103).

Having set up Chillingworth in terms evocative of a Daniel, however, Hawthorne then repudiates him as such. He suggests that Chillingworth's interpretive behavior reads not the fate of a kingdom, but a devilish form of identity. His revelation if not "from a celestial source" may be from that "other region." If Hester is the text of the American plantation awaiting the interpreter to "save" her, then in Chillingworth there may be an especially threatening potential which Hawthorne recognizes.

Chillingworth, like the town he represents, characteristically points his finger; he gazes "at" the object he scrutinizes. He lays his long finger on the scarlet letter, and he tells Hester that she had been the very first "object" to greet his eyes when he entered the town. If Hester is to be, as he declares, a "living sermon" to be thus understood, then his exegetical method is objectivist in the extreme. Both the townfolk and the physician point "at" the woman, and both conceive of the truth of inquiry to be something absolute, unmoving and fixed, like a treasure to be uncovered or an iniquity to be "searched out" in order to be "dragged into the sunshine." Both keep the text-as-thing Hester in a "sphere by herself," isolate, autonomous, alone. So Chillingworth declares as he ominously departs from the prison interview: "And now, Mistress Prynne, I leave thee alone, alone with thy infant and thy shame!" (p. 59).

A brief dumbshow here is significant. Chillingworth, upon entering the town and recognizing Hester, had first raised his finger and then motioned to her by placing that finger in a silencing way upon his lips. In the ensuing scene he fulfills the suggestion of this gesture when he binds her to silence with an oath. What Hawthorne suggests is that before such an audience Hester as a performer is unable to "speak out." She does indeed react to the leaden infliction of the town's eye upon her with the "glazed eyes" and "stony crust of insensibility"; when the townfolk stare "at" her, it becomes her habit never to respond (pp. 60, 65.) When the magistrates urge Hester to declare herself in the marketplace, the only sound which finally echoes is another's voice: "She will not speak, she will not speak!" (p. 54).

What concerns Hawthorne about these American interpreters is two-fold. The effect of such an objectivist critical stance is stifling not only for Hester or the American plantation when seen as a text-as-object, but also for those Americans themselves who engaged in such a critical process. Again Chillingworth is instructive as an example. For in order to impose his silence upon Hester, he must be as one who has "withdrawn his name from the ranks of the living"; he and his name are chill and dead (p. 59). The townfolk and their jailer named Brackett are iron-visaged and frosty. Hawthorne makes a joke about the "grave forefathers"; but he is deeply troubled by the probability that not only may the text-America be limited, frozen by such attitudes, but the people in turn, may be stultified by their reading habits (p. 80).[25] For such persons, be they materialists, scientists or old-fashioned religionists (for Hawthorne's purposes these all were the same), all managed to distance themselves from the truth they observed -- it existed in their view as autonomous, unchanging, and requiring no vital action or transaction with themselves.

There has been much talk of Hawthorne's modernity. Frederick Crews perhaps led the way in showing the depth and wisdom of modern psychological insights available in Hawthorne's texts.[26] More recently Frank Kermode, in an essay entitled "Hawthorne's Modernity," discusses certain aspects of the author's narrative technique.[27] What I should like to add is the dimension of Hawthorne's insight into the world of hermeneutics as well. For he recognized in his fellow Americans a wide range of interpretive tendencies, and his analysis may have, in many cases, adumbrated the lengthy articles of such modern journals as "Critical Inquiry" and others which flourish today.

For if, as Quentin Anderson has recently observed, there were post-modernist qualities in some of Hawthorne's contemporaries -- men like Whitman, Thoreau, Emerson -- yet what may have been most brilliantly perceptive on Hawthorne's part was his twofold ability to delineate these stances and to fathom their deeper effects.[28] Hawthorne saw the pitfalls for those American critics he knew. Chillingworth's richly suggestive interpretive drama but adumbrates the negative warnings of such critics writing today as Stanley Fish, Norman Holland and others when they declare, "Reading is not the discovery of meaning, but the creation of it"; "A sentence in the text is not an object, a thing-in-itself"; "We cannot extricate meaning" from a "text in supposed isolation," and so on.[29]

But Hawthorne pushed his questioning further. For Dimmesdale, too, is put forward as a potential Daniel. In many ways Dimmesdale is compatible with the positions discussed by today's subjectivist critics. He "longs to speak out"; it is his intense desire to join with Hester. That is his terrible goal, as he feels her to be calling for his active response -- which indeed she does in the governor's mansion when she demands, "Speak thou for me!" And together they confirm, "Thou shalt not go alone!" (pp. 84, 141, 143).

In the crisis at the center of the novel we are imaginatively returned to the commanding scene of the Daniel come to judgment in the marketplace. May Dimmesdale be the Daniel who can supply the "magic touch to effect the transfiguration" of Hester? Unlike the physician, this minister Dimmesdale is both "young" and "holy spirited" in the style of the Biblical Daniel. Like his Biblical prototype he sees a most significant hieroglyph; -- and indeed it is upon the very walls of heaven. Like a prophet he seeks to give a "new moral interpretation to the things of this world" (p. 112). In the shadow of a dream, we are told, he has a revelation, and in further contrast to his enemy, he sees a vital future, for there is "early grass" and "freshly turned earth." There is talk of a majestic idea, and of the destiny of nations, an aura of hope and future for Dimmesdale's "upward gaze" (p. 113).

But Hawthorne tests the validity of the "new life" of this second Daniel and of his insurgent interpretive views, with a brilliant structural device. There is a strong sense of doubleness in this work which the author uses not only to emphasize but also to question the two Daniels and their two kinds of judgment. Several critics have commented upon the formal clarity noticeable in the novel; it has been considered variously a three part, a four part, or even a five part form, and in each instance the view is suggested, as John Gerber long ago argued, of a strong correlation between "form and content" in this work.[30] But the novel's most apparent design ought to be seen as focusing upon the two contending Daniels, each struggling to impose his view upon the world of the book. This novel is divided into two main sections, each dominated by its own Daniel -- and they stand in increasing tension with one another.[31] Hawthorne makes conscious use of a systematic parallelism in these two parts to force a series of comparisons and contrasts. The Daniel implications and the doubling structure are fused to grant this novel its power and meaning.

The parallelism suggested is numerically re-enforced: 3-13; 4-14; 8-18; and so on. There are key terms and specific gestures which are repeated in this design of architectonic contrasts. In Chapter 3 the iron-visaged and bracketed sages staidly appeared, but in 13 their "rigid wrinkles" relax into "something almost of benevolence." In both Chapters 4 and 14 the physician lays his long forefinger upon the scarlet letter. Whereas in Chapter 4 Hester had been "still as death" in Chapter 14 she refuses to remain silent any longer and will no more play her "false part." In Chapters 5 and 6 Hester had stood apart like a ghost, and Pearl had made lifeless puppets for playthings; she had thrown weeds at her mother's breast. But in Chapters 15 and 16 Hester actually seeks out a "privacy beneath the sky" and Pearl's playful contrivance has become the green 'A' of life, which she then tries on herself. In the catechism of Chapter 8 the old Mr. Wilson had asked Pearl "Canst thou tell me, my child, who made thee?" In Chapter 18 Dimmesdale exclaims that he feels himself "all made anew!... This is already the better life!"

In Chapter 19 the expectations aroused by this pattern of systematic renewal, rekindling, and rebirth have brought about an awareness of an imminent climax. The powerful inner demands of the book have seemed to work toward the validation of Dimmesdale's Daniel vision. The minister may, indeed, promise the "better life!" But suddenly, significantly, all is shockingly set askew by the appearance of Pearl in the forest. Once again there is a brief but meaningful dumbshow. Again there is the gesture of the pointing finger. Suddenly, now, in the wrong half of the novel, Pearl repeats Chillingworth's gesture, indeed in a chilling way. What is it now that so distresses Dimmesdale?

Pearl, we recall, is the child of natural impulse -- she is the expression of the private relations of her own parents. But she is also, in the world at large, a "guilt and torture" for Hester -- a reminder of fact, undeniably, palpably there. The minister had hoped to see his own history on the page of nature, as he had above the midnight scaffold. He had hoped, in modern critical terminology, to see "only the fantasy which he had created from the materials of the story."[32] This is, indeed, just like the "perpetual Messiah" which Hawthorne's neighbor Emerson had evoked, claiming that there should be no "consciousness," no "prison" of other people's public watching eyes.[33] Here is the crux of Dimmesdale's redemptive interpretive vision as Hawthorne understood it. If there is to be a New Kingdom for such a man, it can be only the invincible rule of what Quentin Anderson has called an American "Imperial Self."[34] For Dimmesdale cannot have an audience. He shrieks only at night when the town cannot respond; he can walk naturally only when he does not "deem himself liable of notice." When he speaks to Hester he is like a man "reluctant to have witnesses," and he is true only when "seen by her own eyes" (pp. 135, 136, 141). Dimmesdale can only bear to be seen as he is not, and he keeps his inward version of reality to himself. No public realm and no separate text for him is admissible. In modern terms he "cannot extricate an objective reality from his subjective perception of it," seeing only the unity of his imperious version writ large upon the cope of heaven.[35] We may but realize that there is a kind of humorous relevance to Norman Holland's description: "the unity we find in literary texts is impregnated with the identity that finds that unity."[36] Was Hester's problem merely that of Dimmesdale's too passionately "filling the gaps" of her suggestive text?[37]

Hawthorne shows that if Chillingworth's objectivist extreme denies any flexibility and vitality for an absolute, discrete text, then it is also true that Dimmesdale's version which denies the existence of any text independent of the reader may be nonetheless killing. Indeed they may be opposite sides of the same coin. Hawthorne does, we note, cause these two American Daniels to dwell together in an uneasy household in the center of the town. Both, as Hawthorne has dramatically shown, have denied in their critical stance, the humanizing factors of life.

The pointing finger of Pearl in the crisis of the forest reminds Dimmesdale of the doubleness of the hieroglyph Pearl is. In this sense, adultery has been the perfect crime for Hawthorne's purposes: the private passion gives issue, in time -- nine months, seven years -- and place -- Boston -- to a very real child. To be a true Daniel, Dimmesdale must read not only the idealized hieroglyph on the cope of heaven, but must also recognize the earthly pearl who has issued from his humanity as well.

He must hurry back to town to renegotiate his stance, to retranslate his private vision in terms of the public world. The journey itself is the drama of his efforts. Finally, he finds himself in his lonely room, in the throes of his own 'critical inquiry.' We are reminded by this scene of another lonely room, another interpretive crisis. In the Custom House Introductory the narrator had picked up the rag of scarlet cloth in the shape of the hieroglyph 'A'. Here was the text he would try to fathom. First he used a coldly factual approach -- he held the letter away, and it measured "precisely three inches and a quarter in length." But then he placed it directly upon his breast, where it burned him. So he "let it fall upon the floor" (p. 28). Here is, in essence, the interpretive drama Hawthorne will play out in the novel. But if neither approach meets approval in that custom-house chamber, then, the introductory narrator avers, we must find some way of converting the "snow images" into real men and women (p. 31). Hawthorne's hope is for some "true relation" with the audience to give life not only to the idea of America, but to the real men and women who dwell there. As Dimmesdale emerges from his chamber that drive toward a "true relation" with his text impels his declarative actions.

Once again the imaginative power of the original Daniel-judgment scene is invoked for the last, definitive crisis. We return to the market place again, for the great drama of salvation. Dimmesdale, Chillingworth, Hester (as ever, upon her pedestal) and Pearl -- all take their places. The Daniel is clearly still "a-wanting." Dimmesdale, amidst the expectations of the crowd, and of the demands wrought by the novel's shape and pattern, delivers his sermon. Like a Daniel, he envisions a "high and glorious destiny" for New England. Here I suggest that we are not given the substance of his words -- a subject such as Eden or Adam; nor are we given the way he presents it -- as in the Jeremiad -- because in keeping with the Daniel pattern evoked throughout, we are meant to focus our interest instead, upon the various and significant responses that the sermon elicits.

They are tremendous. First Hester and Pearl, then Chillingworth, join Dimmesdale on the platform. But that is hardly all. For in the final chapter, entitled "Revelation," everyone in fact, seems eager to join in the great interpretive outpouring: a hugely responsive action! All feel conjoined to partake in the message and its mission. Might this be proof, at last, of the true national Daniel Dimmesdale has finally become? That might be a possible version of the end were it not for two details now significant in terms of the interpretive gestures we have noticed. To Hester's final plea, Dimmesdale but responds, "Hush, Hester, hush." He may never, we feel, allow her her own expression. He cannot, even in these last moments, acknowledge the personal plea which she so urgently proffers.

And then there are the townfolk. In following Dimmesdale's example they seem also to be very wrong-headed and opinionated. Is this supposed to be some "interpretive community," and are we to trust the great responsive outpouring after all? It is possible to feel that Hawthorne shows these many "versions" to be but a larger rendition of a tendency to impose meanings upon the scene -- that after all, Hester in the end will become an "artifact consumed" by readers, in consensus. This assumption is enforced when we are succinctly told: "the wearer of the scarlet letter disappeared" from Boston (p. 184).[38]

But the existence of Hester, the meaning of her text, finally must not be denied. Hawthorne brings Hester back in a forceful restatement of her enduring challenge. She speaks about a "new truth to be revealed," and so saying, "she glanced her sad eyes downward at the scarlet letter," in recognition of the focus, the text, she must yet be (p. 186). The shift, then, is suddenly to the graveyard for the scene of the final reading of the letter 'A'.

There seem to be, in the last scene, two lone figures left to contemplate that letter. One might be the "curious investigator" who would "perplex himself with the purport." Perhaps the reader of the first half of the novel had been just such a figure. For like Chillingworth he had stood apart, fascinated by the text before him, wondering "at" the outcome of the story. But the powerful structural demands of Hawthorne's work then transformed the reader, as it were, into a second kind of responsive figure. Forced subtly but urgently to participate "in" the comparisons, to anticipate the contrasts engendered by the novel's architectonic patterns, this reader feels the very agony of the second part. Finally, however, he senses the dangers to Hester of both these interpretive roles. As that fictional observer is asked to recognize the two Daniels that he has been, then, we must see ourselves at last as remnants of the readers that we have been.

Hawthorne has led us, in the intricate pathways of the book, to see potentials and yet dangers in both the American interpretive selves he has drawn. In the end he asks us, his own readers, to accept the lesson of the whole. When we weigh the meanings, and create our own difficult versions, then we may be converted into real men and women -- such as those he has sought to envision. Confronted by these imperfect Daniels the reader has been challenged to transcend Chillingworth's sense of a harsh and impersonal necessity and Dimmesdale's inescapable isolation, and to step forth into his own sense of the world. Then, perhaps, he shall be the true Daniel, come to judgment to save America.

Notes

1. R.W.B. Lewis, The American Adam (Chicago: University of Chicago Press, 1955), p. 111.

2. Ursula Brumm, "Christ and Adam as 'Figures' in American Literature," in The Puritan Imagination, ed. Sacvan Bercovitch (Cambridge, England: Cambridge University Press, 1974), p. 211.

3. Perry Miller, The New England Mind: From Colony to Province (Cambridge, Mass.: Harvard University Press, 1953); and Errand into the Wilderness (Cambridge, Mass.: Harvard University Press, 1956), pp. 1-15.

4. David Minter, "The Puritan Jeremiad as a Literary Form," in The Puritan Imagination, p. 53.

5. Sacvan Bercovitch, The American Jeremiad (Madison: University of Wisconsin Press, 1978), p. 11.

6. Edgar Dryden, "Writer as Reader: An American Story," Boundary 2, III, 1 (1979), 189-195, supports the suggestion that "American Literature is a fiction that exposes the idea of a privileged world." For a discussion of the "hermeneutics of the American Self," see Sacvan Bercovitch, The Puritan Origins of the American Self (New Haven: Yale University Press, 1975).

7. Ernest Lee Tuveson, Millennium and Utopia (Glouster, Mass.: Peter Smith, 1972).

8. J.F. Maclear, "New England and the Fifth Monarchy: The Quest for the Millennium in Early American Puritanism," William and Mary Quarterly, XXXII (975), 223-260.

9. See discussions of Manifest Destiny and the Westward Course of Empire in Ernest Lee Tuveson, Redeemer Nation (Chicago: Chicago University Press, 1968); and Conrad Cherry, ed., God's New Israel (Englewood Cliffs: Prentice-Hall, 1971).

10. John Calvin, "Commentaries on Daniel," selections, in On God and Political Duty, ed. John T. McNeill (Indianapolis: Bobbs-Merrill, 1956), pp. 89, 90.

11. Roger Williams, "The Bloudy Tennet of Persecution," in Perry Miller and Thomas H. Johnson, eds., The Puritans (New York: Harper Torchbook, 1963), Vol, I, P. 220).

12. Perry Miller, Errand into the Wilderness, p. 10.

13. Perry Miller, Introduction to John Cotton, in The Puritans (New York: Anchor Books, 1956), pp. 172-173.

14. Ephraim Huit, "The Whole Prophecie of Daniel Explained, by a Paraphrase," 1644; and Thomas Parker, "The Visions and Prophecies of Daniel Expounded," 1646. These sermons are cited by J.F. Maclear, "New England and the Fifth Monarchy."

15. Similar essays, sermons, lectures include: "New Heavens and New Heath: Marriage Supper of the Lamb," by Nathaniel Hervey, Boston, 1843; "Remarks on the Book of Daniel," by Samuel Osgood, New York, 1794; "The Prophecy of Daniel Literally Fulfilled," by Nathaniel Cover, Boston, 1843; and numerous others.

16. John T. Irwin, American Hieroglyphics (New Haven: Yale University Press, 1980), discusses the American fascination with hieroglyphics, signs, symbols.

17. See my essay, "Giovanni's Garden: Hawthorne's Hope for America," Modern Language Studies, XII (Fall, 1982), 75-90.

18. I discuss this story as an American Captivity Narrative, with Daniel as the hero, in "James's Pupil as American," an unpublished paper.

19. It is interesting here to note that the Writing on the Wall was also a polyglot system for Daniel to decode. See Daniel, Ezra, Nehemiah, Introduction and Commentary by Judah J. Slotkin (London: Soncino Press, 1951) p. 45, f. 25. The Book of Daniel, too, is polyglot; see Introduction, p. xii.

20. Henry James, Selected Fiction, ed. Leon Edel (New York: E.P. Dutton, 1953), "The Pupil," p. 474.

21. Nathaniel Hawthorne, The Scarlet Letter (New York: Norton Critical Edition, 2nd Edition, 1978), p. 46. Hereafter all references will be to this edition and pages will be given in brackets within the text.

22. The name Hester serves in a double sense. The medieval versions of Queen Esther saw her as a figure of Mary and thus of Eve in the garden; here this enforces the implications of the novel's opening scene. But her name in Hebrew implies "hidden one" -- as Hester in this novel, surely will be. See Murray Roston, Biblical Drama in England (Evanston, University of Illinois, 1968), p. 723. Sacvan Bercovitch refers to this doubleness, citing Roston as well. Bercovitch says of Hester, "She is the hidden one who emerges as the star of the new age" Puritan Origins of the American Self, pp. 177, 242.

23. John Winthrop, "A Model of Christian Charity," quoted in Perry Miller and Thomas Johnson, The Puritans, p. 199.

24. Susannah and the Elders, 44. Of course the most famous literary expression of the "Daniel come to judgment" is found in Shakespeare, The Merchant of Venice: Shylock exclaims, "A Daniel come to judgment; yea a Daniel!" (IV, 1, 213).

25. Hawthorne seems to go to elaborate lengths to develop this double-entendre. He describes Governor Bellingham's head, above that wide, stiff ruff, as looking like John the Baptist's. Then he speaks of his "aspect, so rigid and severe, and frostbitten with more than autumnal age..." This, in connection with the "grave" forefathers, is Hawthorne's way of suggesting that such a man is not only severe, but "severed" from life, as well; and that in walking "foremost" he represents the others, p. 80.

26. Frederick C. Crews, The Sins of the Fathers (New York: Oxford University Press, 1966).

27. Frank Kermode, "Hawthorne's Modernity," Partisan Review, XLI (1974), 428-441.

28. Quentin Anderson, "The Employment of Literature in the United States," Annual Samuel Paley Lecture in American Culture and Civilization, given in Jerusalem, May,

1982. This lecture will appear as an essay in a forthcoming volume of Prospects, ed. Jack Salzman (New York).

29. See these various views expressed in a survey of recent criticism, by Steven Mailloux, "Reader-Response Criticism?" Genre, X (1977), 413-431.

30. John Gerber, "Form and Content in the Scarlet Letter," New England Quarterly, XVIII (1944), 25-55.

31. Two other readers have, most recently, divided the novel as I do, into two opposing parts. See Sanford Pinsker, "The Scaffold as Hinge," College Literature, V (1978), 144-145; and John Carlos Rowe, "The Internal Conflict of Romantic Narrative: Hegel's 'Phenomenology' and Hawthorne's The Scarlet Letter, MLN, VC (1980). Whereas Pinsker's Note attributes no meaning to the doubling he sees, Rowe's division of the work is in many ways applicable to mine: he sees the first half as exhibiting the quality of allegorical externality; the second is one of "psychological realism." He sees the text, thus, as divided between "the ideal and the actual, the universal and the individual," 1210, 1225.

32. Norman Holland, 5 Readers Reading (New Haven: Yale University Press, 1975), pp. 121, 122. This process of transformation "of fantasy into a coherent and satisfying meaning" is described in Steven Mailloux, "Reader-Response Criticism?" cited above.

33. Ralph Waldo Emerson, Nature, Selections from Ralph Waldo Emerson, ed. Stephen E. Whicher (Boston: Riverside Edition, 1957), p. 53; "Self Reliance," p. 149.

34. Quentin Anderson, The Imperial Self (New York: Random House, 1971), describes "American modes of psychic self reliance." Americans respond to "imperious inward demands," pp. 124, 84.

35. Norman Holland, "Transactive Criticism," Criticism, 18 (1976), 340.

36. Norman Holland, "Unity, Identity, Text, Self," PMLA, 90 (1976), 816. Both this reference and the one above are in Mailloux, "Reader-Response Criticism?"

37. See Wolfgang Iser, "The Reading Process: A Phenomenological Approach," New Literary History, 3 (1972); and "Indeterminancy and the Reader's Response in Prose Fiction" in Aspects of Narrative, ed. J. Hillis Miller (New York: Columbia University Press, 1971). Iser speaks of the "gaps" in the text that the reader must fill, in a creative act of reading. See also Mailloux, above.

38. Stanley Fish, "How to Do Things with Austin and Searle," discusses the "act of banishing" in Shakespeare's Coriolanus. Although in our case no one "commands" Hester to disappear, she is in effect overruled by the consensus or the shared interpretive authority of these crowd members. The crowd's way of imposing multiple versions upon Hester's meaning, in effect does away with her own single privileged text. This is what Hawthorne contradicts in bringing Hester back to town. Fish's essay appears in Is There a Text in This Class? (Cambridge, Mass." Harvard University Press, 1980), pp. 197-245.

"AMERICAN ISRAELITES": LITERALISM AND TYPOLOGY
IN THE AMERICAN IMAGINATION

E. Miller Budick

Hebrew University

In his seminal study, <u>Puritan origins of the American Self</u>, Sacvan Bercovitch argues that a crucial element in American Puritan interpretation of biblical texts was a "kind of literalism... undreamed of" by any but the early Americans. "The Puritan colonists," Bercovitch explains,

> loudly proclaimed their orthodoxy, but when they announced that "America" was a figural sign, <u>historias</u> and <u>allegoria</u> entwined, they broke free of the restrictions of exegesis. Instead of subsuming themselves in the <u>sensus spiritualis</u> they enlisted hermeneutics in support of what amounted to a private typology of current affairs. They were not only spiritual Israelites... They were also, uniquely, American Israelites, the sole reliable exegetes of a new, last book of scripture.[1]

Bercovitch's insights into Puritan attitudes toward typology, expressed here and in earlier essays,[2] represent a profound and significant contribution to contemporary understanding of America's literary and philosophical ancestry. Nonetheless, it would be unfair to generations of previous Americans to forget that the radical, antitypological literalism to which Bercovitch and other modern critics point us has not only not escaped critical notice, but has, I would submit, featured prominently in one major stream of response to the deficiencies and liabilities of the American imagination. During the Puritan period itself, for example, as Bercovitch points out, Roger Williams fought strenuously against the New England delusion that America was more than a "figural Israel." America, Williams argues, was neither the "new found land of Canaan," nor were the Americans God's chosen people incarnate. New England Puritans, he suggested, seemed to be peculiarly out of touch with covenantal history. They seemed to be under the dangerous misapprehension that, in Williams' words, "the letter [is] yet in force, and <u>Christ Jesus</u> the <u>mystical</u> and <u>spiritual King of Israel</u> is not yet come."[3] The Puritans, in other words, were from Williams' point of view, oddly anti-Christian, even Arminian. They functioned as if the New Testament had not yet replaced the Old, as if Christ had not yet secured grace for humankind.

Nor is Williams alone in his condemnation of what Bercovitch characterizes as the Puritans' literalistic and antitypological mode of perception. This very problem, I would argue, constitutes a recurrent motif in American Literature.[4] It appears as a central concern in no less than five important works of American fiction, each of which is significantly different from the others in terms of its overall themes and structures, but each of which makes recourse to the same biblical type, the sacrifice of Isaac, with the same glance backward at the literalistic, antitypological cast of Puritan hermeneutics. The five works which I would like to discuss are Charles Brockden Brown's Wieland, Hawthorne's "Roger Malvin's Burial," Melville's Billy Budd, Sherwood Anderson's "Godliness" and Flannery O'Connor's "A View of the Woods." Although many critics have noted, in their separate analyses of these works, that one story or the other contains a version of the Old Testament narrative of the binding of Isaac, and while one critic has even remarked on the recurrence of this biblical episode in all five works,[5] no one, I think, has yet described the stories' uses of the biblical materials or explained what the stories may be concluding about a certain quality of the American imagination and its conception of self and nation.

Let me begin my investigation with Brockden Brown's Wieland, which is chronologically the earliest of these works, the first major work of American prose fiction (Gothic or otherwise) to have a lasting impact on the American audience, and the first work of fiction, I would suggest, to grapple with the Americans' tendency to conceive of Americans' history as a "new last book of scripture."

Without a doubt the most striking action of the novel is Wieland's Abraham-like, God-inspired sacrifice of his family. This is the event which spurs Clara to write her memoirs. It is the event against which we measure all of the lesser evils, misapprehensions, rationalistic errors, and religious crises which punctuate the novel. The event's centrality, then, is clear. But what has been far from clear is how Brown intends us to understand Wieland's divinely inspired action. Thus, one critic has argued with great cogency that the novel is an "enlightenment sermon against credulity and religious fanaticism," while another critic, with equal plausibility, has claimed that the book is in fact a diatribe against enlightenment complacency, an allegorical narrative in which a godless eighteenth-century world is made to acknowledge the essentially Calvinistic terms of human existence.[6] In both of these readings (and in other readings as well), the sacrificial act seems to be for Brown a way of testing what the author himself labels "the moral constitution of man."[7] The book's major concerns, then, would appear to be universal and timeless. The Americanness of the tale would seem to consist only in the special relevance of religious fanaticism and/or enlightenment rationality for the American nation in the eighteenth century.

Yet it seems to me that Brown's "American Tale," as the novel is subtitled, has a distinctly American quality which cannot be dismissed either as local color or as window dressing for a universal message. The novel's central tension between faith and reason (between Wieland and Pleyel or between Wieland's own rationalistic inclinations and his fanatically spiritual ones, or between Pleyel's desire to believe Clara and his inability not to believe his senses) does not represent an archetypal debate between two antithetical human impulses. Rather the novel's linking of American religious fanaticism with American rationalism represents an insistence on the common history of the two, a claim that both originated jointly in the peculiar facts of America's antitypological habit of mind as it evolved from Massachusetts Bay of 1632 to the New England of Brown's own day.

The issue with which the novel deals is precisely the issue which toppled the American theocracy in the seventeenth century and which represented for Brown a continuing and troubling force in eighteenth-century America. It is the issue of visible sanctity, the existence of a community of saints (secular or religious) who could know and be known to one another and who could thus establish the pure Church of Christ in the new world.[8] During his testimony at the murder trial, Wieland is made to raise explicitly the problem of visible sanctity. Wieland argues:

It is strange: I am known to my judges and my auditors. Who is there present a stranger to the character of Wieland? Who knows him not as a husband, -- as a father, -- as a friend? Yet here am I arraigned as a criminal. I am charged with diabolical malice! I am accused of the murder of my wife and my children!

It is true, they were slain by me: they all perished by my hand. The task of vindication is ignoble. What is it that I am called to vindicate? ...You charge me with malice; but your eyes are not shut; your reason is still vigorous; your memory has not forsaken you. You know whom it is that you thus charge. The habits of his life are known to you; his treatment of his wife and his offspring is known to you; the soundness of his integrity, and the unchangeableness of his principles, are familiar to your apprehension; yet you persist in this charge... Think not that I speak for your sakes... I make not an effort to dispell your illusion; I utter not a word to cure you of your sanguinary folly; but there are probably some in this assembly who have come from far; for their sakes, whose distance has disabled them from knowing me, I will tell what I have done, and why.

It is needless to say that God is the object of my supreme passion.[9]

Wieland's assumption is that because he is "known" to the community as a good husband and father, that because they "know" him to have a "single and upright heart," that therefore Wieland is what he claims to be, an enactor of divine purposes, an instrument of divine will.

Like many a Christian before him, Wieland has spent his days "search[ing] for the revelation of that will." Like many another of the faithful, he craves to prove himself through "sacrifice." But a Puritan American, Wieland wishes this experience visualized. He wants to have visibly revealed to him the sanctity which me feels certain he possesses. When Wieland prays, "Oh that I might be admitted to thy presence! that mine were the supreme delight of knowing they will," we might imagine that Wieland is asking no more and no less than what any devout observer might request, a chance to prove himself faithful to the divine commandment. But no sooner has Wieland articulated his fervor to know God's will than he expresses his equally strong need "of performing it" in a very "direct" way: "blissful," he says, is the "privilege of <u>direct</u> communication with thee, and of listening to the <u>audible enunciation</u> of thy pleasure."[10] The difference between Wieland's prayer and the prayer of any religious Christian might be one of nuance, but in the context of what occurs, Wieland's special criteria of divine intercourse must not be ignored.

Wieland's prayer is answered, as psychologists of wish fulfillment would not be surprised to discover, in the materialization of the vision he so desires:

> I opened my eyes and found all about me luminous and glowing. It was the element of heaven that flowed around. Nothing but a fiery stream was at first visible; but, anon, a shrill voice from behind me called upon me to attend.[11]

As spirituality is made visually and audibly manifest for Wieland, Wieland, because he believes in the absolute correspondence between appearance and reality, because, in other words, he believes in visible sanctity, responds to the vision by literally murdering his wife and children in sacred sacrifice to his deity.

Wieland's behavior is an exaggeration of Puritan precepts, to be sure. None the less it expresses a disposition of mind which is consummately Puritan and which represented an actual danger within the Puritan world itself, a danger which the Puritans themselves intermittently recognized. To formulate the crisis which Wieland dramatizes for us in the Puritans' own language, Wieland expresses the antinomian tendency of the Puritan imagination, repressed but latent in all orthodox Puritanism and brought to its fullest expression historically by Anne Hutchinson and the Quakers.[12] This antinomianism is enacted for us in Brown's novel in all of the grotesque horribleness in which the highly pragmatic founding fathers knew it would result. Thus Wieland concludes his statement before the court in the following manner:

> "My motives have been truly stated. If my judges are unable to discern the purity of my intentions, or to credit the statement of them which I have just made; if they see not that my deed was enjoined by heaven, that obedience was the test of perfect virtue, and the extinction of selfishness and error, they must pronounce me a murderer.
>
> "They refuse to credit my tale; they impute my acts to the influence of demons; they account me an example of the highest wickedness of which human nature is capable; they doom me to death and infamy. Have I power to escape this evil? If I have, be sure I will exert it. I will not accept evil at their hand, when I am entitled to good; I will suffer only when I cannot elude suffering.
>
> "You say that I am guilty. Impious and rash! thus to usurp the prerogatives of your Maker! to set up your bounded views and halting reason as the measure of truth!

"Thou, Omnipotent and Holy! Thou knowest that my actions were conformable to thy will. I know not what is crime; what actions are evil in their ultimate and comprehensive tendency, or what are good. Thy knowledge, as thy power, is unlimited. I have taken thee for my guide, and cannot err. To the arms of the protection I intrust my safety. In the awards of thy justice I confide for my recompense.

"Come death when it will, I am safe".[13]

Essentially, what Wieland is arguing is that "justification" precedes "sanctification," that election to the divine community of saints puts the saved individual out of reach of human law (the "civil authority," as Williams refers to it) and makes him immune to moral judgement.[14]

America's Puritan ancestors, interested in realizing a federal as well as a spiritual authority in New England, had realized the primary entropic danger which antinomianism posed to the Puritan theocracy. Therefore, they strove energetically to guard against it.[15] But the American Puritans could only barely glimpse that the real and ultimately effective danger to the theocracy was not simply the potential anarchy of antinomianism but the very concept of visible sanctity which underlay both the antinomianism which they rejected and the federal theology to which they subscribed.

In American history itself, the ultimate breakdown in covenant (or federal) theology occurred when visible sanctity no longer represented a viable mechanism for realizing its political and moral objectives. In the Salem Witch Trials of 1692 the American Puritans discovered that sanctity could no longer be proven on the basis of appearance, for, as the argument ran in 1692, if a devil could assume the guise of a saved person, then how could witches be distinguished from saints?[16] Wieland, the saint-as-murderer, poses the same problem of spectral evidence that bedeviled the seventeenth-century Salemites. Wieland himself inadvertently points us to this problem in his final words to Clara:

Neither thee nor myself have I cause to injure. I have done my duty and surely there is merit in having sacrificed to that all that is dear to the heart of man. If a devil has deceived me, he came in the habit of an angel. If I erred, it was not my judgement that deceived me, but my senses. In thy sight, Being of beings! I am still pure. Still will I look for my reward in thy justice![17]

When devils can parade as angels, when the senses must interpret nonsense data, then sanctity must be relegated to the realm not of the visible, but, as St. Augustine had always recognized, and as Roger Williams had reiterated, to the realm of the spiritual community of God's invisible church.

Wieland's story thus dramatizes and interprets for us the evolution and demise of the American theocratic ideal and of the visible sanctity of which it was founded. But Wieland is not a seventeenth-century Puritan. He is an eighteenth-century rationalist. Thus Wieland also suggests how the tendencies of thought which first established the dangerous covenants of the new world and defended them, survived the demise of Puritanism and resurfaced as enlightenment reason and eighteenth-century nationalism. For Wieland's heinous deeds have two significant antecedents in the novel. The first, of course, is the inheritance of his father's indubitability of sense-data to which Wieland also refers in his defense testimony. These are the two causes of what Clara identifies as an "erroneous or imperfect discipline" and while the two might appear to derive from diametrically opposite sources, both the theological assumptions and experiences of the elder Wieland and the education and predisposition of the younger Wieland converge in the consolidation of one overriding principle: that one can depend upon the validity of outward and visible signs as indicators of inward and spiritual grace.[18]

Thus, for example, when Theodore Wieland is first accosted by his wife's voice on his way to the Temple (the novel's first prototype of the divine voice articulating wild injunctions), he argues for the "testimony of [the] senses," and he presents the universe in an unambiguous disposition of either/or alternatives which are reminiscent of Puritan bifurcations and disjunctions. "I must deny credit to your assertions," he tells Pleyel and Clara, "or disbelieve the testimony of my sense... One Thing... is true: either I heard my wife's voice at the bottom of the hill, or I do not hear your voice at present" (italics added).[19] What is true must be true at all places and times. The evidence of one's senses is unchallengeable. One must credit the voice in the flame as being an accurate spokesman of the divine and not a deviant or satanic pretender or a psychotic longing after divinity.

The question Brown is asking is, simply, what if the appearances one witnesses are motivated by spirits which are evil rather than good? What if the voice is not Catherine's but Carwin's, the vision not a manifestation of the divine, but rather the foggy emanations of an overheated imagination? Or, to put the question in the terminology of the Puritan debate on spectral evidence, can the devil assume the body of a saint? And, if so, what, then, is the meaning of visible sanctity, of sense evidence? By forcing external reality to conform to an internal and highly subjective image of reality, Wieland disallows the possiblility both of human error and of divine inscrutibility. He does not grant the necessary and ultimately saving distance between divine perfection and human fallibility and depravity.

Wieland's father, for all his apparent religious fanaticism, does not suffer from the same errors that afflict his son. It is important, therefore, to consider the case of the elder Wieland and of his failure to perform the act of ultimate sacrifice if we are to understand the behavior of the son, specifically if we are to understand how Wieland extends the seventeenth-century world of sense-data. If one looks carefully at the biography of the elder Wieland it is possible to perceive in the fictional persona the portrait of an historical figure, a man whose insights into the problems of visible sanctity and antitypological exegesis are, as we have already noted, crucial for the development of the American imagination.

Although the historical Roger Williams is in many ways different from the fictional Wieland senior, enough similarities can be adduced from the text to suggest that the elder

Wieland is intended, in some oblique fashion at least, as a version of the earlier Puritan dissident.[20] Wieland, like Williams, is theologically and temperamentally a Puritan of the most rigorous variety (Wieland is a self-proclaimed descendant of the French Camisards, a fanatical minority group of Calvinistic Protestants). He is a man whose fanaticism is so extreme that his church ultimately becomes, like Williams', a solipsistic church of one. And like Williams, Wieland comes to America as a converter of the Indians.

But Wieland senior is not simply an earlier version of his son, just as Williams is not a model of Puritan vices, and the examples of these two men point to a failing in the American Puritan imagination which is exposed by Theodore Wieland and the majority of the Puritans, but which they themselves do not exhibit. Whatever the senior Wieland's quirks of personality, for example, he is benevolent and charitable, a mild human being of "invincible candor" and "invariable integrity." Furthermore, despite his relationship equally as intense as his son's, he does not allow himself to obliterate the distinction between the figural and the literal. Therefore, he himself is unable to fulfill what he also believes to be the ultimate divine command, the commandment which the son eventually does fulfill.[21]

In other words, the elder Wieland (like Williams) recognizes what Theodore Wieland cannot understand -- that the visible church of man (even of one saintly man) and the invisible church of God are ever two and separate, or, as Williams had put it, that "only the spiritual Israel and the seed of God, the new born, are... one."[22] The antitypological moment of Christian history -- the birth and resurrection of Christ -- has already occurred, and we, as the Israelites before us, stand in a typological -- or figurative or spiritual -- relationship to biblical truths.

By the time Theodore is confronted with the same theological choices that his father faced, the safeguards of typological thought had wholly fallen away. But they have done so, in Brown's view, not only because of the invidious antitypological attitudes of the Puritans themselves, but also because of the substitution of a wholly anti-Puritan world view (a liberal Christian or deist or rational enlightenment world view) which still retained the Puritans' faith in the American as savior (political, moral, humanistic) but without a proper respect and reverence for the kind of saviors of whom the Americans, even as a national entity, could only be the barest of types. This new breed of American hubris and egomania emerged out of the separation of church and state argued for by none other than Roger Williams.[23]

If the history of the older Wieland demonstrates the same dialectic that Williams himself articulated vis-a-vis Puritan literalism, and thus suggests a specific criticism of Puritan modes of perception, it also helps us to see (and this is crucial for the development of Puritan habits of mind into the eighteenth century) how the arch-enemy of antitypological thinking became a force in enabling the development of another, equally dangerous kind of American literalism. For if Williams corrected some of the sins of the fathers, he provided no formula for insuring a lasting influence for true religious reverence and belief in the world of secular reason. He found no way of integrating his Calvinistic orthodoxy with this religious toleration, and therefore, he left the path open to the secularization of an enlightened American which would merely substitute the senses and reason for the soul as the arbitrators of wisdom and salvation. Within the novel itself, the elder Wieland's self-destructive obsession provides his children with no religious instruction and thus opens the way for the abuses of purely secular, rationalistic learning.

Wieland the elder and Williams represent a consummate, solipsistic individualism which is shared by Puritan and non-Puritan American alike. Within the Puritan community itself it surfaced either as antinomianism (in the Puritan dissidents) or an antitypological literalism and as belief in the community of the elect (the federal position). Amongst Franklin, Jefferson, and the other founding fathers of the American republic, individualism emerged in the form of deism and Jeffersonianism, the democratic ideal on which the nation was built. And later in the nineteenth century, it would appear again, this time as Emersonian self-reliance, Whitman's song of the self. But in the eighteenth century, Brown suggests, American moral consciousness found itself in a horrific breach which could only be conveyed in a story of Gothic horror. Reawakened fanaticism loomed on one side, threatening to repeat the perils of Puritan history. Atheism and self-deification haunted the other side, veritably catapulting the nation into apostasy. And to some large extent, Brown believed, both religiosity and secularism were infected by the same destructive literalism which in the novel poisons both Wieland and Pleyel. America's secular reason had served, not to save the Americans from the dire implications of their fanatical Puritan past, but to push them further over its brink. Thus the antinomianism which was so guarded in the Puritans themselves reaches its fullest expression, first in eighteenth-century enlightenment, with its liberalized, atheistic theologies, and later, in the nineteenth century in the transcendentalist radicalization of liberal theology in which the self substituted for God as the organizing center of creation. The ultimate implications of Franklin's or Emerson's individualism and self-reliance, Brown wishes to suggest, might be as murderously problematic as the Puritans' belief in visible sanctity. As Bercovitch points out, "Early New England rhetoric provided a ready framework for inverting later secular values... into the mold of a sacred teleology." Or as one critic has suggested, the line from Edwards to Franklin, or for another critic, from Edwards to Emerson, is not as oblique as we might think.[24] This is precisely Brown's point.

Wieland the younger, untutored in theology, fails to understand that the covenant between God and man is no longer direct and personal. Christ has interceded on man's behalf. The Old Testament has been supplanted by the New. The covenant with Abraham has been replaced by the covenant of grace. Therefore, only the deity himself can enact the sacrificial act. In fact, even in the Old Testament type on which Wieland presumably bases his actions, the human sacrifice is never consummated. Abraham is never made to complete the binding of Isaac. The sacrifice remains, as it were, in suspended animation until the coming of the divine son, Christ himself.

Thus Wieland's act can be seen as the consummate expression of American hubris and misconceived religious passion, an atrophy both of proper religious understanding and of human sensitivity. In literally reenacting the sacrifice of the son, in literally imagining himself the heir of Abraham, as Bradford and Winthrop and others had literally imagined themselves heirs of Moses, Wieland does not play Abraham to his family's Isaac, but rather vaunts himself into the role of God and plays deity to his Christ-crucified family.[25] The Old Testament story is about Abraham's reverence and respect for God. His is the sacrificial willingness which ultimately does pave the way for human salvation. But Wieland's rehearsal of the biblical episode is a disastrous closing of the gap not only between the Old Testament and the New, type and antitype, but between the self and God. Wieland is arch-antinomian, and Arminian to boot. He is the ultimate literalist. The consequence of his deed, therefore, even though the deed itself is a logical extension of his Puritan theology, is, as the more guarded Puritans had always suspected it would be, a lethal blow against Puritan holiness. Thus, dialectically, Wieland is also consummate secularist or pagan. He is an American rationalist who has eliminated God and grace from his universe altogether.

Reuben Bourne of "Roger Malvin's Burial," Captain Vere of Billy Budd, Jesse Bentley of "Godliness," and Grandfather Fortune in "A View of the Woods" are all shown as suffering from a similarly mistaken notion of the direction of Christian history. All of them are unable to accept that the time for direct communion with God is over. They have forgotten that mankind has been condemned, by that momentous disregard for divine interdiction in the Garden of Eden (and all these stories, including Wieland, deal with the problem of the fall), to dwell throughout its mortal existence in a frail and vulnerable world from which it can be saved only by grace. All of them, therefore, interpret their life's experiences literally, seeing themselves not as types but as antitypes.

Thus Reuben, for example, can imagine no road to salvation except to murder his own son. The more readily available and logical forms of penitence, such as confessing his sin to Dorcas and to the community, or at least pursuing an honestly remorseful relationship with his God within the structures of the mortal church, are closed to him. He cannot understand that the self does not exist in direct relationship with the Almighty and therefore he believes the Puritan rhetoric which conflates America with Israel and which makes American "current events," as Bercovitch puts it, a transcript of biblical affairs.

But "Roger Malvin's Burial," Billy Budd, "Godliness" and "A View of the Woods" do not simply restate the problems which are so complexly approached in Wieland. Each of these works of fiction delves into new aspects of the problem, and thus each one deepens our understanding of America's imaginative inheritance from the Puritans. "Roger Malvin's Burial," for example, does, like Wieland, raise the issue of visible sanctity, but it examines this problem in relation to another issue which is implicit in Wieland but not really developed there: the issue of Puritan historiography. The Puritans' special brand of historical interpretation and its connection to visible sanctity is described by Bercovitch as follows:

the national covenant emphasized the Lord's promise to Abraham, which materialized in the Israelite state; after the Hebrews' apostasy, the promise was renewed, this time in aeternum, by Christ to His Church. The Renewal antitypes the earlier agreement; historically it establishes a developmental connection between two elect communities. Seen in this double aspect, the New World theocracy becomes a collection of saints whose public contract reflects the progress of human history and by the same token is mystically foreordained like the covenant of grace... This correspondence between Israel and the "new Adam" (and by extension between the "new Israel" and the "second Adam") can be made to serve, from the standpoint of historical typology, as an implicit justification of the New England doctrine of a "visible" church-state.[26]

As many critics have already pointed out, battles such as Lovell's Fight, on which the story is based, were seen by the Puritans in this double aspect, both as types of the evercontinuing battle of the saints for Christendom, which had in a sense already been "antityped" and won in Christ's death, and as America's special continuation of Christian history as the battle moved from the Old Testament to the New to the American continent. The Americans' interpretation of the Indian wars, in other words, was not just a providential or typological rendering of historical realities, but the colonists' literalistic attempt to make American history the history of Christianity. In the case of Lovell's Fight, Cotton Mather himself, we find, preached a sermon in which the typological relationship between the Old Testament and the New and the antitypological, special historiographic relationship between the Old Testament and America is carefully spelled out. (Ely Stock's discussion of the Mather text is quite complete, and I will not try to summarize or elaborate here.)[27] For our purposes, what is even more remarkable about Mather's sermon is that it analyzes the historical-antitypological relationship between America and Israel specifically in relation to the story of the binding of Isaac, drawing out its typological foreshadowing of the sacrifice of Christ and, as the Americans saw it, its prefiguring of the founding of the American theocracy.

One way of interpreting "Roger Malvin's Burial," therefore, is as a rounding out of the biblical episodes on which the tale is based and which were, in fact, the deep infrastructure of the Puritans' federal theology. In this view, the story can be seen as confirming the need for sacrifice, for only by the Americans' reliving of biblical moments could they earn their right to the promised land. In other words, like Wieland, the story can be read as an affirmation of the antitypical relationship between the protagonist's killing of his son and Abraham's sacrifice of Isaac, or God's of Christ, out of which salvation emerges.[28]

Before we reject this interpretation of the story, as indeed every moral criterion within the work prompts us to do, let us note a further element in "Roger Malvin's Burial" which appears in Wieland as well and which can be seen as confirming the straight-forward, tale-as-allegory reading of the story. Like Wieland, "Roger Malvin's Burial" not only invokes the issues of type and antitype, but it also develops its own internal set of typologically related moments which are linked to each other in precisely the same relationship and in precisely the same chronology as the original Old Testament and New Testament events. Thus, early in "Roger Malvin's Burial," the narrator raises the possibility of Roger's (the "father's") "sacrifice" of Reuben (the "son") on the "rock." This sacrifice, like the sacrifice of Isaac, is not completed. It is only metaphorically enacted by Reuben's willingness to die for his "father." Later in the story, when the theme of "sacrifice" is again raised, on the same "rock," it is indeed effected, and Cyrus, like Christ (and like all the Wielands) dies.[29] Furthermore, all this occurs, of course, within the context of a providential interpretation of history in which Roger Malvin himself, self-proclaimed patriarch of the race, pronounces the importance of Reuben's carrying forward the national covenant with which Roger entrusts him.

Is the story, then, as some have suggested, an allegory of Christian history which confirms the Americans' special rendering of covenant theology, of providence, and of the antitypological relationship between American and the chosen people? The answer, as I have already begun to suggest, must be an emphatic no. Reuben's sacrifice of Cyrus, as many commentators have already remarked, is a deed which springs from psychosis, not from faith. It is an act of desperation of a moral coward who has fallen out of communion with his God, not a beatific moment effected by a saint who has discovered a way of bringing his belief to meaningful expression. For if there are similarities between the plot of "Roger Malvin's Burial" and the Old Testament and New Testament stories which is echoes, there are also significant differences. Most importantly, in the Old Testament type a clearly mortal Abraham treats with a just as clearly divine God. In granting God the absolute authority and reverence due Him, Abraham is rewarded with human-like consideration. Analogously, in the New Testament antitype of the same performance, a wholly divine God treats with his equally divine son and the sacrifice is effected within a realm of existence which is only tangentially, covenantally, related to human affairs. In other words, in the Old and New Testament versions of the sacrifice of the son, in both of its typological and antitypological avatars, the lines of distinction between the human context and the divine, between the Old Testament and the New, and between the covenant with Israel and the covenant of grace are clearly drawn.

In "Roger Malvin's Burial," however, they are horribly intermingled and blurred. The results are catastrophic. Because Reuben cannot understand that there is only one antitype, Christ and the crucifixion, he can wildly imagine the possibility of his own enacting of antitypological events. He cannot see that the "sacrifice" of Cyrus will be just as "useless" as his own death would have been, that neither of the sacrificial moments of his life, first with his "father" and later with his son, is antitypological, either in a personal, biographical sense or in a national, religious one.[30] In other words, he cannot see that the sacrifice of Cyrus is not, nor ought it to be, the antitype of the interrupted sacrifice of himself. Nor can he see that it is not the logical extension of the type and antitype of Isaac and Christ.

Much has been made of the biblical allusions which abound throughout "Roger Malvin's Burial" and which seem, upon careful investigation, not to confirm one another in any coherent pattern of biblical allegory but rather to contradict and even negate one another.[31] I would suggest that the story employs myriad biblical echoes precisely in order to emphasize Hawthorne's preference for a conventional typological interpretation of scripture as opposed to a historical, antitypological one. Hawthorne uses his biblical allusions in order to make the point that eighteenth-century humankind (along with its seventeenth-century and nineteenth-century relatives) lives in a world in which access to the divine occurs only through Christ. The inability to preserve the distinction between the human and the divine, or between metaphoric and literal experience, can lead to a perception of reality in which the self is vaunted into the role of savior and God is diminished to simply one more character in the ongoing unfolding of providential history which has culminated in America. The letter killeth, as St. Paul put it, and in literalistic America, that killing was in danger of becoming more than metaphoric.

Thus, when Reuben's conscience, "a continual impulse, a voice audible only to himself," commands him to go forth and redeem his vow, the Puritan anti-typologist Reuben can only imagine that this voice is a "supernatural power [calling] him onward." Reuben, the author tells us, is "unable to penetrate to the secret place in his soul, where his motives lay hidden." And unable to see and respect the difference between his mortal self and the indwelling spirit of the divine which he believes to characterize that self, Reuben conflates the self and God and imagines himself a biblical patriarch, if not the deity incarnate.[32] Had Reuben a true understanding of typological relationship he would not have had to pursue so disastrous a course. But theological education has gone astray of its purposes and, as we shall now see, it is at Roger Malvin's (and the founding fathers') feet that we shall have to lay the body of the murdered Cyrus.

As Hawthorne perceptively acknowledges, it is every man's dream to be a "patriarch" to his people; to be "dimly glorious" and "godlike."[33] But for Reuben, under the pressure of his Puritan beliefs, this fanciful craving for lofty ideals become a desire literally to reenact patriarchal events. This impulse for patriarchal and ultimately divine experience originates, however, in Roger and not in Reuben. It is Roger who instills within Reuben the fervor for the covenantal relationship to the land which ultimately makes the confession of his sins impossible. Godlike, he articulates for Reuben the course of providential history (including the meaning of the battle). Scholastically, Roger relates the typological episode in his own immediate biography which entitles Reuben to leave him in the wilderness, even though he admits to himself the "wide dissimilarity between the two cases."[34] But Roger Malvin is not God. He is not even an Old Testament patriarch. He is a frail, albeit noble human being who, no sooner has he spoken the words of prophetic wisdom and encouraged Reuben on his course, than he lays upon Reuben the burden of guilt which causes Reuben to distort his understanding of biblical texts and to murder his own son. "'And Reuben,' added he, as the weakness of mortality made its way at last, 'return, when your wounds are healed and your weariness refreshed, return to this wild rock, and lay my bones in the grave, and say a prayer over them.'"[35]

When Reuben thinks back on their parting in the woods, he cannot remember Roger's wavering. He can remember only the "kind and generous" man who had not a thought of his own welfare.[36] Thus he is bound to an ideal which in fact never really existed.

Reuben errs because he imagines that he and Roger and Cyrus are literally reenacting the moment when the covenant is granted to Israel-America. Hawthorne, however, forces us to recognize that they are, instead, only human beings involved in a mortal dilemma which has certain ethical overtones and which corresponds to a variety of different biblical moments and events which range from the binding of Isaac to the selling of Joseph to the redemption of Israel through Cyrus. Roger and Reuben's failure to recognize the multiplicity of biblical referents in their situation, in other words, their tenacious antitypological literalism, precipitates the tale's tragic conclusion.

Billy Budd, of course, is not an American story in the same way that Wieland and "Roger Malvin's Burial" are. The action of the story takes place on a British ship in a situation fraught with special significance for British and European history. And yet the devices of the story and its conclusion are so similar to those of Wieland and "Roger Malvin's Burial" that it merits a place in our discussion. In fact, it is precisely because Melville adapts a consummately American theme to a non-American circumstance and, in addition, develops the aspects of the motif relating to the fall which are less highly developed in Wieland and "Roger Malvin's Burial," that the tale becomes so intensely interesting.

Scholars have long recognized the Calvinistic influences in Melville's fiction, especially in Billy Budd. The story is veritably a treatise on the three central tenets of Calvinistic theology -- innate depravity (suggested in the novel by the inherent imperfections of both Claggart and Billy); determinism (the "fated boy" is an "angel of God" yet "the angel must die"); and the salvation of mankind through Christ (represented in the story of Billy's death). In fact, the final sermon delivered by Vere is explicitly compared to a "Calvinistic text" to which the sailors listen like "a seated congregation of believers in hell."[37]

Melville's view of the universe, in other words, as it emerges in the story, seems to be fundamentally Calvinistic. But the events which transpire on board the Indomitable derive their special meanings, I would argue, not because they are the inevitable consequences of a (villainous) Calvinistic God, but because they are the handiwork of a very mortal, very deficient captain who seems disposed to act as if he himself were responsible for rectifying original sin and personally determining the course of human salvation. Vere acts as if he were God, and a Calvinistic God at that.

We are not provided with an abundance of information concerning Vere, but the evidence which we are given suggests that he is a dry, egocentric literalist, a man who, like Wieland and Reuben Bourne, is all too likely to see the universe and himself in the Puritans' antitypological, special historical terms. Thus we are told that Vere prefers to read history and biography, and that "in his love of reading he found confirmation of his own more reserved thoughts." He is a man of "settled," "positive convictions," "which he forefelt would abide in him essentially unmodified so long as his intelligent part remained unimpaired." "In illustrating any point touching the stirring personages and events of the time," Vere, we discover, "would be as apt to cite some historic character or incident of antiquity as he would to cite from the moderns."[38] Even Vere's name is a clue to the way Melville wishes us to associate him with the exegetical tradition. It is only an accident of language which stirs a relative to call him "starry Vere." The name itself signifies nothing. And yet this is how Vere is known to us, as the "starry Vere," as if he were reincarnated from Marvell's "Upon Appleton House," and antityped some concept or formulation in that earlier work.

These intimations about Vere's egocentricity and his typological view of historical events are confirmed for us in the action of the story. Vere conceives of himself as the center of law and order on the ship. Therefore, he manipulates events from beginning to end and catapults the characters into the tragedy that ensues. It is Vere who stages the confrontation between good and evil; Vere who conducts the trial against innocence; Vere who sentences mortal humanity to death. Melville stresses throughout the story that Vere is under no legal obligation to conduct the affairs of the case in this way. In fact we are told explicitly that duty may well require that he defer the trial to the "admiral" and the naval courts,[39] or at least to try Billy by a jury of his peers. Certainly Vere is restricted under the legal system as to how active a role he can assume in a trial for which he is simultaneously "sole witness," prosecutor, and judge. Vere knows this. But "a sense of the urgency of the case overruled in Captain Vere every other consideration."[40] Therefore, he stages the trial as to reap maximum benefit from his rank, even deviating from custom to do so.[41]

Vere is convinced that events on the Indomitable have national, if not cosmic, significance. For this reason, he forsakes the strict letter of military and civil law. He speaks of the mutiny on the Nore as if it were indeed a type of mutiny upon the Indomitable, even though mutiny has not been proven on his ship and is indeed not in the offing. "In Adam's fall/We sinneth all," read the New England primer. "Billy's intent or non-intent is nothing to the purpose," explains Vere.[42] Neither is his guilt or innocence, for Billy, in the end, is hanged for the mutiny on the Nore, for the original disobedience, as it were, and not for any mutiny or insurrection or murder of which he himself is guilty.

Because of Vere's general sense of typological cosmic relationships and because of his special, antitypological historiography, law and order on Vere's ship become the natural and necessary culmination of law and order outside the ship (the law and order of the nation, for example, or beyond that, of God). Vere and his ship are for him anti-typical. He proceeds, therefore, as if his judgement and his judgement alone will determine the outcome of national and Christian history. But Vere forgets that the fall has already been atoned for, that the mutiny on the Nore has been put down. The critical action of the story, in other words, can be understood in terms of the competition between a typological and an antitypological interpretation of human events, which is to say, in language more familiar in Melville criticism, as a conflict between a literalistic definition of Billy's crime as murder or a more human consideration of it as inadvertent manslaughter. The two sets of terminologies -- the one biblical-exegetical, the other human-legalistic -- are, as we shall see in a moment, not unrelated.

The issue of typology opens the story. In the preface Melville introduces us to the subject of mutiny, not simply in its specific historical context upon the Nore but as a generalizable, universal phenomenon, as "Revolutionary Spirit," the "Spirit of [the] Age" in which the term revolution comes to signify not only revolt against tyranny but the very cycles (revolutions) of tyranny and freedom themselves.[43] The French Revolution and the Great Mutiny are presented as types of one another, and as we are led into Melville's discourse on the "handsome sailor" which begins the story proper, we are made to realize that these revolts are also types of another mutiny or revolution, that original, antitypical insurrection in the garden of Eden.

The consequences of that original, prelapsarian mutiny are, of course, known to all of us, and they are clearly recorded in the primary allegorical level of Billy Budd itself: God (represented in the story by Vere) punishes sinning Adam and the rest of innocent mankind (both represented by Billy) with death, but in condemning mankind to death God also provides for its redemption in Christ (again represented by Billy). In the Old Testament-New Testament sequence of events (and in Melville's allegory), the fall leads directly to the resurrection, Adam to Christ. In fact, the two events and their two major figures have significant typological connections within the Christian tradition. Adam and Christ are both innocents, favored sons of God, bound to Him in special covenantal relationships, and Christ is referred to in theological writings as the "second Adam."

But in Melville's story Adam is Christ. The fall, consequently, is the resurrection. It may be, as many critics have argued, that Melville is collapsing typological distance and distinction in order to accentuate the particularly vicious character of Christian history. He may be condemning God Himself for a strikingly cruel masterminding of a gothic cosmic plot.[44] And yet, I think that the fault, according to Melville, is not with God, but with Vere and with the special kind of literalistic, anti-Christian imagination he embodies. The tragedy of Billy Budd is precipitated not because of the contours of Christian history in which a God may work in mysterious ways, but because of a failure in theological imagination by an individual who would ignore redemption as the primary fact of Christian history after the fall. In Christian history, Adam and Christ are not one and the same figure. The fall and the resurrection, therefore, are two very different events, and their relationship to one another is carefully controlled by Christian typology and Christian history. It is Vere's failure to understand these controls and his subsequent blurring of type and antitype that precipitates the crisis. For Vere sees Billy and mutiny not as types but as antitypes, and herein lies the problem.

In order to make this point, Melville provides us not with one type-antitype relationship (the relationship between the fall and the resurrection), but with two. After Vere has sentenced Billy, Melville writes that Vere, "letting himself melt back into what remains primeval in our formalized humanity, may in the end have caught Billy to his heart even as Abraham may have caught Isaac on the brink of resolutely offering him up in obedience to the exacting behest."[45] The second type of Christ, Isaac, contains within him the theological and human message that Vere cannot understand and therefore does not heed. Mediating between the one type (Vere and Billy) and the other type (Abraham and Isaac) is the true antitype, God and Christ, and it is the existence of this antitype which invalidates Vere's compulsion to sacrifice his "son" in order to expiate for a sin and a rebellion which have already been atoned for by Christ's death. The crucifixion opens up the universe once more to compassion and love, the same compassion and love which God Himself chose to demonstrate to Abraham and which Vere chooses to ignore.

In Billy Budd Melville is exploring a particular aspect of the Americans' historical antitypologizing which is treated in Wieland and in "Roger Malvin's Burial" as well, but which is developed with special care in Billy Budd and which had special implications for America's role in the international community. As R.W.B. Lewis has so thoroughly demonstrated, the American desired to see himself as the Adamic creator, the new man in a new Eden.[46] But he also wished to see himself as Christ, as savior. For the American, then, America was Eden. But it was also Canaan. The American was Adam. The American was Christ. America's role, therefore, in the international community was to be both prophetic and evangelical. But presenting his version of America's wildly erring, historical, antitypological conception of self on a British ship, with a British cast of characters, Melville is suggesting that the American passion to export salvation may have issued not in the resurrection of Christian faith but in its repeated crucifixion. For another revolution which is related to the French Revolution and the Great Mutiny but which is left unnamed in the preface is, of course, the American Revolution. If America did antitype anything at all, it might be neither creation nor redemption but disobedience itself. Thus the story, in Melville's words, is about a "crisis in Christendom."[47] It is about the ever-constant, ever-present threat of rebellion which is directed not against the king nor against the navy but by the civil authority against the authority of God Himself.

By the time "Godliness" and "A View of the Woods" are written, we have moved forward a few generations. The "father" figures are now grandfathers, who stand in an even more oblique relationship to biblical events than did their ancestors. The social conditions are no longer those of a nation and culture being thrust into civil and religious consciousness. Rather they are of a highly industrialized, modern, materialistic society trying to preserve wealth and progress. The issues of the stories, therefore, are somewhat different from those in Wieland, "Roger Malvin's Burial" and Billy Budd, and yet both stories focus on characters who are remarkably reminiscent of Wieland, Reuben, and Vere. Both Grandfather Bentley and Grandfather Fortune long for patriarchal authority and divine election. Both view their lives providentially. Both quest after visible confirmation of their sainthood, and both believe that they themselves, within their own person and in their progeny, will secure God's covenant for the land. Grandfather Bentley and Grandfather Fortune, in other words, are latter-day antitypologists of the sort we have already met, and Anderson's and O'Connor's stories represent still another significant manifestation of a continuing theme in American literature.

These stories, however, do more than launch America's heritage from her Puritan ancestry into the twentieth century. They also reflect on the causes and consequences of American materialism and relate that materialism to elements of America's antitypological and historical literalism. The development of Jesse Bentley's religious fanaticism, for example, is an object lesson in the relationship between greed and an historical-antitypological reading of nation and self. Jesse's ancestors in Winesburg are characterized by a different kind of religious passion altogether:

As they worked in the fields, vague, half-formed thoughts took possession of
them. They believed in God and in God's power to control their lives... The
churches were the center of the social and intellectual life of the times. The
figure of God was big in the hearts of men.[48]

But Jesse forgets the bigness of God and the intermediating and saving power of the
church. He begins instead to appropriate these things to himself. He forgets that man is
puny and that Christ's church, and not the self, secures salvation. Consequently, he
confuses material signs with spiritual meanings, or, to put the problem in the language of
the story, he allows avarice and self-interest to interfere with and determine his
relationship to God. The issues at hand, as in the following passage, are again those of
visible sanctity and federal theology:

Jesse's mind went back to the men of the Old Testament days who had also
owned lands and herds. He remembered how God had come down out of the
skies and talked to these men and he wanted God to notice and talk to him
also. A kind of feverish boyish eagerness to in some way achieve in his own
life the flavor of significance that had hung over these men took possession of
him. Being a prayerful man he spoke of the matter aloud to God and the sound
of his own words strengthened and fed his eagerness... "Oh God, create in me
another Jesse, like that one of old, to rule over men and to be the father of
sons who shall be rulers."[49]

But the motivation for such palpable, visible expressions of sanctity is located, according
to Anderson, not in pure religious feeling, but in avarice and greed:

A fantastic impulse, half fear, half greediness, took possession of Jesse
Bentley. He remembered how in the old Bible story the Lord had appeared to
that other Jesse and told him to send his son David to where Saul and the men
of Israel were fighting the Philistines in the valley of Elah. Into Jesse's mind
came the conviction that all of the Ohio Farmers who owned land in the valley
of Wine Creek were Philistines and enemies of God. "Suppose," he whispered
to himself, "there should come from among them one who, like Goliath the
Philistine of Gath, could defeat me and take from me my possessions"...
Jumping to his feet, he began to run through the night. As he ran he called to
God... "Jehovah of Hosts," he cried, "send to me this night... a son. Let Thy
grace alight upon me. Send me a son to be called David who shall help me to
pluck at last all of these lands out of the hands of the Philistines and turn
them to Thy service and to the building of Thy kingdom on earth".[50]

"Thy service" and "the building of Thy kingdom on earth" are inextricable from the "fear"
of "defeat" and the "greediness" for one's own worldly "possessions" which so fire Jesse
Bentley with religious passion.

Jesse's failure, like Wieland's, Reuben's and Vere's before him, is, in moral psychological terms, a failure in humility. In more sophisticated theological terms, it is a failure in faith, a failure in typological sensitivity. Jesse cannot accept that biblical times are over, that he is Jesse Bentley, grandfather to David Hartley, brother of Enoch. As in "Roger Malvin's Burial," the biblical allusions in the story are sufficiently askew to prevent a neat paralleling of scriptural events. Thus, while Jesse sees the citizens of Winesburg as Philistines, it is Jesse himself who is seen as Goliath when David shoots him with his slingshot. Jesse acts as if he were Saul, king and defender of the Israelites and spiritual father to David, his heir apparent. But he is Jesse, David's physical ancestor; not his father, but his grandfather.

Jesse, in other words, is not the biblical figure he thinks he is. Nor, we are meant to see, is he Abraham, nor is David Isaac, although this possibility is also raised in the story. When Jesse first takes David into the woods to pray, he becomes so possessed of his Old Testament visions of himself as biblical patriarch that he terrifies his grandson who then hits his head and falls unconscious. Jesse's response to David's hurt is human and sympathetic (he cradles the "boy's cut and bleeding head... tenderly against his shoulder")[51] but it also reveals a total lack of understanding of what has occurred. He cannot see that David's terror is derived from his own ranting and raving about the biblical patriarchs. He does not realize that his religious fanaticism has not only not transformed him into that other Jesse whom he so desires to be but has made of him a "dangerous" usurper of the body of the "kindly" grandfather whom David loves.[52]

For these reasons, Jesse cannot forebear taking his grandson into the woods again on a related but even more disturbing mission, one which results not in physical injury to David but in psychological and physical injury to Jesse himself. Jesse's failure to perceive the meaning of the first encounter in the woods is like a failure in typological sensibility. That is, Jesse cannot see concealed in the first moment a hint of what the second antitypological moment would have to be. His error in the second excursion into the woods, however, is literally a failure in typological knowledge, for the need to sacrifice the lamb (and by extension, the son or grandson who is identified with the lamb)[53] has already been eliminated in Christian history by the antitypological occurrence of the sacrifice, the crucifixion of that other lamb, Christ, which is itself typed in the story of Abraham and Isaac, in which the ram is killed in Isaac's stead. In attempting literally to reproduce biblical events, Jesse effectively severs himself from the covenant of grace. David strikes him down with his slingshot and then disappears, forever.

Grandfather Fortune in "A View of the Woods" is a similarly erring antitypologist who has failed to acknowledge that the climax of Christian history has already occurred and that the only true antitype is the crucifixion of Christ. Fortune seems to believe that he and his granddaughter Mary can conduct themselves as if the covenant of works is still in effect. Therefore, he thinks that if he can only separate himself and his sole acknowledged offspring from those mortal Pitts who have contaminated his world, he can reestablish Eden without the intervention of any external savior.

But, of course, as we see from the beginning of the story to the end, Fortune himself is fallen. His Eden consists of parking lots and huge monster machines, and only Christ can redeem him. Fortune is given a chance to acknowledge the true nature of the postlapsarian world and its only true savior. Before he takes his granddaughter into the woods to whip her and ultimately to sacrifice her, he sees the woods "as if someone were wounded behind [them] and the trees were bathed in blood."[54] But this vision of Christ and salvation does not penetrate his warped religious sensitivities. When at the end of the story he gazes at his dead granddaughter, a "little motionless figure with its head on the rock,"[55] slaughtered as her prototype Isaac was not, he has in fact translated cautionary vision into vivid reality. The woods, now, really are bathed in blood, but the blood of Mary Pitts will not bring salvation. The point is that Grandfather Fortune has not recognized the bond of flesh which unites mortal men and fixes their destiny in Christ. Or, to put the problem in the story's own dramatic structure, he is not willing to yield the child to her mortal, earthly father, and by implication, to place her destiny in the hands of her immortal father who has already seen to her salvation by sacrificing his own son. Fortune insists upon molding the "clay" himself,[56] both in terms of the child and in terms of the land to which the child is intimately related in his mind. Thus, Fortune forfeits his right both to the child and to the land, precisely because he imagines that it is within his power to secure and bestow salvation. Fortune falls for reasons similar to those for which Adam himself fell, for presuming to knowledge to which he is in no way entitled. He is damned, like Satan, for playing God.

O'Connor, of course, is a Catholic and not a Protestant writer. "A View of the Woods," therefore, can be seen as opening up the patterns of the American imagination to new and different kinds of scrutiny. It also suggests that the peculiarly Puritan problems of the past had, by the twentieth century, become truly national concerns, affecting not only New England Protestants, but midwesterners, southerners, Catholics, and other Americans as well. The antinomian literalism of American historiography and antitypological thinking was not simply a particular instance of a universal problem. For Brown, Hawthorne, Melville, Anderson, and O'Connor (in these stories, and, I would claim, in other of their works as well) the implications of the Fall and of the Resurrection had special relevance to the American experience precisely because the Americans insisted on a literalistic reading of Christian and American history.

The American Adam, the Americans believed, would not fall. He would redeem the original Adam, and the original Abraham too. He would redeem Christ himself. Therefore, when the American Adam did fall, as indeed he must in a postlapsarian universe, he fell, according to our writers, with a force that threatened to shake the foundations of "Christendom" itself. According to the Puritans, Adam's fall had abrogated the covenant of works. But God, in his divine wisdom and mercy, had another covenant in the offing, the covenant of grace which is typed in the Old Testament in the covenants with Abraham and Moses.[57] The fall of the American Adam threatened to annul that second covenant as well. It threatened to abolish grace and thus eliminate salvation. It is this that all five writers have perceived.

American history, these writers thus insist, was not the antitype of Christian history. Christian history had already found its penultimate climax in the resurrection of

Christ. It promised its ultimate finale in his second coming. American history, on the other hand, was a linear affair. It might, every now and again, have parallels in Christian history. It might even intersect with it or have typological affinities with it. But American history could never transcend its own earthly limitations. It could never usurp the authority of the divine historiographer who authored American history and divine history both. In fact, whatever spiritual meaning American history might have, derived from the infusion of spiritual grace which Christ's death had secured for humanity as a whole. For America to imagine itself Christ, or worse, for America to imagine itself God the Father, was to find itself bereft of the only covenant that mattered, locked out of grace and effectively denied salvation.

Notes

1. Sacvan Bercovitch, Puritan Origins of the American Self (New Haven: Yale University Press, 1975), pp. 112-113.

2. "Typology in Puritan New England: The Williams-Cotton Controversy," American Quarterly, 19 (1967), 166-191.

3. From "The Bloody Tenent Yet more Bloody," quoted in Bercovitch, "Typology in Puritan New England," p. 177. See Bercovitch's discussion of Williams in Puritan Origins, passim. and Perry Miller, Roger Williams: His Contribution to the American Tradition (New York: Atheneum, 1966).

4. Issues similar to the ones discussed here are treated by Michael Colacurcio, "Visible Sanctity and Specter Evidence: The Moral World of Hawthorne's 'Young Goodman Brown,'" Essex Institute Historical Collections, 110 (1974), 259-299 and in my essay "When the Soul Selects: Emily Dickinson's Attack on New England Symbolism" American Literature, 51 (1979), 349-63.

5. See Rosemary M. Laughlin, "Godliness and the American Dream in Winesburg, Ohio," Twentieth Century Literature, 13 (1967), 97-103 for a discussion of the motif in all five works.

6. See e.g. Harry R. Warfel, Charles Brockden Brown: American Gothic Novelist (Gainesville, Florida: University of Florida Press, 1949) for a rationalist interpretation and Michael T. Gilmore, "Calvinism and Gothicism: The Example of Brown's Wieland," Studies in the Novel, 9 (1977), 107-118 for a moral-allegorical reading.

7. Charles Brockden Brown, "Advertisement," Wieland; or, The Transformation: An American Tale (New York: Doubleday, 1962), p.7.

8. On the issue of visible sanctity, see, for example, Edmund Morgan, The Visible Saints: The History of a Puritan Idea (New York: Cornell University Press, 1963).

9. Wieland, pp. 187-188.

10. Wieland, pp. 188-190. Italics added.

11. Wieland, p. 191.

12. For comments on the antinomian crisis in Puritan history, see Perry Miller, The New England Mind: From Colony to Province (Boston: Beacon Press, 1953), passim. and Cotton Mather, Magnalia Christi Americana or the Ecclesiastical History of New England, ed. Raymond Cunningham (New York: Ungar, 1970), pp. 130-133.

13. Wieland, p. 201.

14. On this aspect of antinomianism see Miller, The New England Mind: The Seventeenth Century (Boston: Beacon Press, 1953), pp. 26-28 and 49 ff.: "Sanctification flowes from justification; Being justified, we are sanctified" (p. 49).

15. Miller, The New England Mind: From Colony to Province, specifically treats the ways in which antinomianism posed a threat to federal New England.

16. On the Salem Witch Trials and their effect on the American theocracy, see Miller, The New England Mind: From Colony to Province, pp. 192-196.

17. Wieland, pp. 253-254.

18. Wieland, p. 11. Wieland may thus be seen as an interpretation of the Great Awakening, where the Enlightenment and Puritan sensibility converged.

19. Wieland, p. 41.

20. Perhaps Brown's insistence in the "Advertisement" on "historical evidence" is related to the elder Wieland's evocation of Roger Williams. His later statement -- "If history furnishes one parallel fact, it is a sufficient vindication of the writer; but most readers will probably recollect an authentic case, remarkably similar to that of Wieland" -- may refer to the tale's alluding to the story of Isaac and Abraham. On Roger Williams' life, see also Cotton Mather's Magnalia Christi, pp. 126-1230 and Perry Miller's biography, Roger Williams.

21. This commandment is never specified in relation to Wieland's father, but the accumulated evidence of the story -- the allusion to the elder Wieland's temple as the "rock," the statement that the commandment is "transferred... to another," and the fact that the elder Wieland, though a "dreamer and a fanatic," finds himself unable to execute it -- suggests that it is precisely the sacrifice of the son, or of the family, which the younger Wieland finally does bring to a conclusion. Wieland, pp. 19-20.

22. Williams, quoted in Miller, Roger Williams, p. 151.

23. On Williams and the separation of church and state, see Miller, Roger Williams, passim.

24. Bercovitch, Puritan Origins, p. 136; John F. Lynen, "Benjamin Franklin and the Choice of a Single Point of View," The American Puritan Imagination: Essays in Reevaluation, ed. Sacvan Bercovitch (Cambridge: Cambridge University Press, 1974), pp. 173-195 (on the line between the Puritans and Franklin); and Perry Miller, "From Edwards to Emerson," Errand into the Wilderness (New York: Harper-Row, 1956), pp. 184-203.

25. On Winthrop and the early Puritan fathers' identification with biblical figures, see, of course, Bercovitch, Puritan Origins of the American Self.

26. "Typology in Puritan New England," p. 182.

27. "History and the Bible in Hawthorne's 'Roger Malvin's Burial,'" Essex Institute Historical Collections, 100 (1964), 279-296.

28. On the debate about whether the story is intended to confirm the need for sacrifice or oppose it, see, among others, Burton J. Fishman, "Imagined Redemption in 'Roger Malvin's Burial,'" Studies in American Fiction, 5 (1977), 257-262.

29. "Roger Malvin's Burial," The Centenary Edition of the Works of Nathaniel Hawthorne, ed. William Charvat, Roy Harvey Pearce, and Calude M. Simpson (Columbus: Ohio State University Press, 1974), pp. 338, 339, 344, and 346.

30. "Roger Malvin's Burial," p. 346.

31. See, for example, Ely Stock, "History and Bible in 'Roger Malvin's Burial;'" W.R. Thompson, "The Biblical Sources of Hawthorne's 'Roger Malvin's Burial,'" PMLA, 77 (1962), 92-96, and, especially for its argument about the story and history, Robert Daly, "History and Chivalric Myth in 'Roger Malvin's Burial,'" Essex Institute Historical Collections, 109 (1974), 99-115.

32. "Roger Malvin's Burial," pp. 350 and 356.

33. "Roger Malvin's Burial," p. 352.

34. "Roger Malvin's Burial," p. 342.

35. "Roger Malvin's Burial," p. 344.

36. "Roger Malvin's Burial," p. 346.

37. Billy Budd, Sailor, ed. Harrison Hayford and Merton M. Scalts, Jr. (Chicago: Chicago University Press, 1962), pp. 99, 101 and 117.

38. Billy Budd, pp. 62-63.

39. Billy Budd, p. 102.

40. Billy Budd, pp. 104-106.

41. Billy Budd, p. 104.

42. Billy Budd, p. 112.

43. See Preface, printed in Billy Budd, Foretopman in Herman Melville: Selected Tales and Poems, ed. Richard Chase (New York: Holt, Rinehart, 1966), pp. 289-90.

44. The most penetrating and thoroughgoing analysis of this is Laurance Thompson's Melville's Quarrel with God (Princeton: Princeton University Press, 1952) in which his chapter on Billy Budd is entitled "Divine Depravity" (pp. 355-414).

45. Billy Budd, p. 115.

46. R.W.B. Lewis, The American Adam: Innocence, Tragedy, and Tradition in the Nineteenth Century (Chicago: Chicago University Press, 1958).

47. Billy Budd, in Herman Melville: Selected Tales, p. 289.

48. "Godliness," Winesburg, Ohio (New York: Viking, 1960), p. 71.

49. "Godliness," pp. 69-70.

50. "Godliness," pp. 72-73.

51. "Godliness," p. 86.

52. "Godliness," p. 85.

53. "Godliness," pp. 100-101.

54. Flannery O'Connor, "A View of the Woods," Everything that Rises Must Converge (New York: Farrar, Straus & Giroux, 1965), p. 71.

55. "A View of the Woods," p. 80.

56. "A View of the Woods," p. 58.

57. See Perry Miller's chapter on "The Covenant of Grace" in The New England Mind: The Seventeenth Century, especially p. 377.

HENRY JAMES AND THE SEAL OF LOVE

David H. Hirsch

Brown University

Henry James is justly credited with having invented, developed and brought to fruition what is called the "international theme." It seems to be less commonly apparent that the international theme was almost always no more than a platform for a love story. Perhaps because his characters seem so far from passion and from erotic impulses, James is not known as an incisive anatomist of sexual or romantic love. Nevertheless, James drew both themes and imagery from that most erotic, and yet at the same time most spiritual, of poems, The Song of Songs. The Song of Songs and the Garden of Eden narrative of Genesis II inform and give depth to the love motif in The Portrait of a Lady (1881) and The Wings of the Dove (1902).

The Portrait is a novel about a young American girl, Isabel Archer, who comes to Europe on the invitation of a benevolent aunt with a very wealthy banker husband and a son (Ralph Touchett) who is seriously afflicted with tuberculosis. In Europe, Isabel is pursued and proposed to by various eligible bachelors, including a rich American businessman and a British lord. On his deathbed her rich uncle is persuaded by his son Ralph to leave Isabel a handsome bequest. Subsequently, Isabel rejects the opportunity to make a brilliant match, and marries instead an aging American aesthete and dilettante (Gilbert Osmond) who has been living in Italy, and who may or may not be marrying her for her newly acquired fortune, but who would certainly not have married her without it.

Dorothy Van Ghent has perceptively linked one movement of the plot to the Fall of Man described in Genesis. She observes that:

> The postulate of wealth and privilege is, in revised terms, that of the second chapter of Genesis (the story of Adam in the garden) -- that of the optimum conditions which will leave the innocent soul at liberty to develop its potentialities -- and, as in the archetype of the Fall of Man, the postulate is significant not as excluding knowledge of good and evil, but as presenting a rare opportunity for such knowledge. It is her money that draws Madame Merle and Osmond to her; so that her "freedom" is actualized as imprisonment, in a peculiarly ashen and claustral, because peculiarly refined, suburb of hell. Isabel's quest had, at the earliest, been a quest for happiness -- the naïvely egoistic American quest; it converts into a problem of spiritual salvation, that is, into a quest of "life"; and again the Biblical archetype shadows forth the problem. After eating of the fruit of the tree of knowledge of good and evil, how is one to regain access to the tree of life?[1]

Having perceived this much, however, Van Ghent digresses into the imagery of "seeing" and does not really return to the questions of "spiritual salvation" and renewed access to the "tree of life."

Nowhere are these questions addressed more directly than in the two deathbed scenes of the novel. In the first of these scenes, Ralph persuades his dying father to make Isabel rich, which means, according to Ralph's definition, to settle on her enough money to enable her "...to meet the requirements of... [her] imagination."[2] Ralph then adds that Isabel "has a great deal of imagination." But having been set free to meet the requirements of her imagination, Isabel disappoints. She binds herself into a loveless marriage that results in her incarceration, as Van Ghent puts it, in a "refined... suburb of hell." This first deathbed scene serves one more purpose, a purpose ultimately related to the lovelessness of Isabel's marriage, and one that has received scant notice from commentators on the novel. Ralph presents the request to his father as one of disinterested curiosity. He senses some great potential in Isabel which he would like to nurture so that it can expand to its fullest. To use his own metaphor, he wants "to put a little wind in her sails" (p. 158). But Mr. Touchett senses that his son is motivated by something more than disinterested curiosity. Three times in this scene, Mr. Touchett challenges Ralph with being in love with Isabel. The first two times Ralph denies it. The third time he neither denies nor affirms. When his father asks Ralph why he can't wait until he has inherited the money, and then give it to Isabel himself, Ralph answers, "Ah, dear father, I can't offer Isabel money!" Whereupon the old man shrewdly observes, "Don't tell me you're not in love with her!" (p. 159). At this point, Ralph no longer denies.

In a later scene, after Isabel has announced her engagement to Osmond, Ralph tries to dissuade her from falling into this, as he sees it, stifling marriage. When Isabel challenges him with having gone too far in his denunciation of Osmond as "a sterile dilettante," he answers pathetically, "I've said what I had on my mind -- and I've said it because I love you." When Isabel then accuses him of not being "disinterested," he replies, even more pathetically, "I love you, but I love without hope" (p. 286). Dorothea Krook and Ora Segal have pointed out that Ralph is in love with Isabel, but they treat the relationship more from the standpoint of James's technique than of his theme. "In sum," writes Segal, "since Ralph finds his spectatorship sufficiently absorbing and rewarding, his love for Isabel, though it intensifies the passionate interest he takes in her history, does not obscure his vision by detracting from his disinterestedness."[3] But this disinterestedness is puzzling in itself. He gives up half his inheritance for Isabel; he is totally committed to watching Isabel develop and to being part of that development. He expects her to fulfill his "charming vision of [her] future" (p. 291). He is, in fact, "disinterested" in only one sense: sexually.

If Ralph's love of Isabel is revealed by the first deathbed scene, the second reveals that Isabel is in love with Ralph, a phenomenon that has, for the most part, escaped the notice of commentators.[4] In this second scene it is Ralph himself who is dying. Isabel, who has clipped her own wings by marrying Gilbert Osmond, has been waiting for Ralph to recover sufficient strength and consciousness so that he may speak to her. When the long-awaited moment finally arrives, the most intense, and perhaps most important, dialogue in the novel ensues. In the course of the dialogue, Ralph says:

"You've been like an angel beside my bed. You know they talk about the angel of death. It's the most beautiful of all. You've been like that; as if you were waiting for me."

"I was not waiting for your death; I was waiting for -- for this. This is not death, dear Ralph."

"Not for you -- no. There's nothing makes us feel so much alive as to see others die. That's the sensation of life -- the sense that we remain. I've had it -- even I. But now I'm of no use but to give it to others. With me it's all over." And then he paused. Isabel bowed her head further, till it rested on the two hands that were clasped upon his own. She couldn't see him now; but his far-away voice was close to her ear. "Isabel," he went on suddenly, "I wish it were over for you." She answered nothing; she had burst into sobs; she remained so, with her buried face. He lay silent, listening to her sobs: at last he gave a long groan. "Ah, what is it you have done for me?"

"What is it you did for me?" she cried, her now extreme agitation half smothered by her attitude. She had lost all her shame, all wish to hide things. Now he must know; she wished him to know, for it brought them supremely together, and he was beyond the reach of pain. "You did something once -- you know it. O Ralph, you've been everything! What have I done for you -- what can I do to-day? I would die if you could live. But I don't wish you to live; I would die myself, not to lose you." Her voice was as broken as his own and full of tears and anguish.

"You won't lose me -- you'll keep me. Keep me in your heart; I shall be nearer to you than I've ever been. Dear Isabel, life is better; for in life there's love. Death is good -- but there's no love."

(pp. 469-470)

Much of this dialogue borders on incoherence. Such near incoherence is, of course, in keeping with the dramatic situation, since the utterances of both Isabel and Ralph are made in anguish. It is their unguardedness that is revealing. What does the dying Ralph mean when he says, "I wish it were over for you?" Does he mean merely her marriage, or does he mean life itself?[5] What does Isabel mean when she says, "I would die if you could live. But I don't wish you to live; I would die myself, not to lose you?" The first sentence is a most powerful expression of love: Isabel would change places with Ralph, i.e., she would die in his place. But the next two sentences are puzzling. Why does she say that she does not want Ralph to live? In what way will her dying enable her not to lose Ralph? This last sentence suggests that they will be (can be?) joined only in death.

Various themes have been suggested for this novel, including "betrayal," "the importance of wealth," "the search for freedom," "the conflict of American innocence and

European corruption," and, corollary to this, the fall from innocence. But, as the second
deathbed scene makes clear, these themes are subsidiary to the motif of love against
death. When Ralph tells Isabel, "you won't lose me -- you'll keep me. Keep me in your
heart," he is echoing the Shulamite's request to her lover in v. 8:6 of The Song of Songs:
"Set me as a seal upon thy heart, as a seal upon thine arm; for love is strong as death..."
Among the many interpretations of this verse one holds that "the maiden cannot bear any
separation from her lover. She therefore pleads to be as close to him as his seal."
Another interpretation holds that the maiden "...entreats him to set her as a seal upon his
heart, etc. [as] an allusion to her hope that she abide forever in his memory." Both these
commentaries apply here. Ralph himself explicates his own allusion to The Song of Songs
by telling Isabel, "I shall be nearer to you than I've ever been," which means, presumably,
that after his death he will abide (that is, continue to live) in her memory.[6]

Immediately following this deathbed scene and Ralph's ensuing demise, there is a
concluding anticlimactic encounter between Isabel and another rejected would-be lover,
the American businessman, Caspar Goodwood. Goodwood tries to persuade Isabel not to
return to her (as Goodwood perceives him) ogre-like husband in Rome.

> "You don't know where to turn. Turn straight to me. I want to persuade
> you to trust me," Goodwood repeated. And then he paused with his shining
> eyes. "Why should you go back -- why should you go back to that ghastly
> form?"
>
> "To get away from you!" she answered. But this expressed only a little
> of what she felt. The rest was that she had never been loved before. She had
> believed it, but this was different; this was the hot wind of the desert, at the
> approach of which the others dropped dead like mere sweet airs of the garden.
> It wrapped her about; it lifted her off her feet, while the very taste of it, as of
> something potent, acrid and strange, forced open her set teeth.
> (p. 480)

James's description of Isabel's revulsion forces us to note not only that Isabel is in love
with a dying man, but that she loves him most intensely at the very moment of his dying.
In the description of her revulsion from Goodwood there is an inversion of the erotic
imagery of The Song of Songs. Whereas the Shulamite and her lover speak of love in
imagery of gardens and fountains, and hands dripping with myrrh, Isabel's reaction to love
is described in the image of a scorching desert wind that overpowers the sweet airs of the
garden. Later, in the same scene, as Goodwood continues to press his case, the
description of Isabel's thinking switches from the imagery of the hot desert wind to the
imagery of drowning.

> She had wanted help, and here was help; it had come in a rushing
> torrent. I know not whether she believed everything he said; but she believed
> just then that to let him take her in his arms would be the next best thing to

her dying. This belief, for a moment, was a kind of rapture, in which she felt
herself sink and sink... This however, of course, was but a subjective fact as
the metaphysicians say; the confusion, the noise of waters, all the rest of it,
were in her own swimming head.

(p. 481)

Here again, there is a reversal of the lush, erotic, life-engendering love imagery of The
Song of Songs. In the biblical book, it will be recalled, the sealing of love is followed by
the verse, "Many waters cannot quench love,/Neither can the floods drown it..." Whereas
in The Song "many waters cannot quench love," in James's novel the thought of love is
associated precisely with drowning and with the noise of waters as an overwhelming chaos.

Ever since James's novel appeared critics have been disturbed by the indeterminate
nature of the object of Isabel's quest. Some of the possibilities that have been suggested
as the object of her quest are freedom and fulfillment of her potential as a unique
individual. But underlying the restlessness of her questing and overriding all the other
possibilities there seems to be a desire to overcome the human condition of mortality. At
first, Isabel seems to represent the life force itself. When she makes her first appearance
in the novel, for example, she breaks into the setting of afternoon tea, a setting described
in terms of a parodic or de-sacralized religious ritual.

Under certain circumstances there are few hours in life more agreeable than
the hour dedicated to the ceremony known as afternoon tea. There are
circumstances in which, whether you partake of the tea or not -- some people
of course never do, -- the situation is in itself delightful. Those that I have in
mind in beginning to unfold this simple history offered an admirable setting to
an innocent pastime. The implements of the little feast had been disposed
upon the lawn of an old English countryhouse, in what I should call the perfect
middle of a splendid summer afternoon. Part of the afternoon had waned, but
much of it was left, and what was left was of the finest and rarest quality.
Real dusk would not arrive for many hours; but the flood of summer light had
begun to ebb, the air had grown mellow, the shadows were long upon the
smooth, dense turf. They lengthened slowly, however, and the scene expressed
that sense of leisure still to come which is perhaps the chief source of one's
enjoyment of such a scene at such an hour. From five o'clock to eight is on
certain occasions a little eternity; but on such an occasion as this the interval
could be only an eternity of pleasure. The persons concerned in it were taking
their pleasure quietly, and they were not of the sex which is supposed to
furnish the regular votaries of the ceremony I have mentioned. The shadows
on the perfect lawn were straight and angular; they were the shadows of an old
man sitting in a deep wicker-chair near the low table on which the tea had
been served, and of two younger men strolling to and fro, in desultory talk, in
front of him.

(p. 17)

If anything, the reader seems, here, to have stumbled onto a sterility cult: an old dying man, a young dying man, and a functionless lord, all engaged in desultory talk; a ceremony lacking female votaries; a dying day. The religious terminology is striking: "dedicated," "ceremony," "innocent pastime," "little feast," "eternity," "votaries." Isabel arrives on a scene of impending darkness, and darkness clings to her throughout the novel.[7] In the midnight vigil in which she meditates on her failing marriage, she thinks of herself as being enclosed "...in the house of darkness, the house of dumbness, the house of suffocation" (p. 60), recalling Koheleth's declaration that "The heart of the wise is in the house of mourning; but the heart of fools is in the house of mirth." The penultimate scene, in which Isabel rejects Goodwood with total finality, takes place, as does the opening scene of the novel, at dusk. When he kisses her in desperation she is overcome by blinding destructive light (analogous to the hot wind) and, again, by sensations of sinking and drowning. But she then finds relief and freedom in darkness.

> He glared at her a moment through the dusk, and the next instant she felt his arms about her and his lips on her own lips. His kiss was like white lightening, a flash that spread, and spread again, and stayed; and it was extraordinarily as if, while she took it, she felt each thing in his hard manhood that had least pleased her, each aggressive fact of his face, his figure, his presence, justified of its intense identity and made one with this act of possession. So had she heard of those wrecked and under water following a train of images before they sink. But when darkness returned she was free.
>
> (p. 489)

The ending of the novel has puzzled critics because Isabel's freedom is paradoxical. She is free, but she returns to her seeming incarceration with Gilbert Osmond. She returns to what the reader must assume is a death in life. For Isabel, and for James, love is not as strong as death.[8] I should like to add a word of caution here. I do not mean to say, as Dennis L. O'Connor does, that in rejecting Goodwood Isabel is choosing "renunciation over communion," or that "Goodwood and Osmond symbolize the choice between love and death, tumescence and entombment, intimacy and spectatorship." On the contrary, I would hold that both Osmond and Goodwood offer only barrenness, but in different ways. Goodwood's insensitive, brutal lust is as repugnant as Osmond's insensitive, decadent aestheticism. O'Connor, like so many commentators on the novel, downgrades Ralph's role, seeing in him only a suggestion of "the price of narcissistic renunciation." But since O'Connor does not acknowledge that Ralph is in love with Isabel, it is not quite clear just what O'Connor thinks Ralph is renouncing.[9] I should also point out that sex and eroticism are not synonymous. Goodwood's sexuality is sterile precisely because it is lacking in that sensitivity, tenderness, self-effacement, and love that would make it erotic in the sense that the lovers in Canticles are erotic.

In her excellent study, God and the Rhetoric of Sexuality, Phyllis Trible summarizes verses 8:6-7 of The Song of Songs in relation to the Garden of Eden as follows:

Love redeemed meets even death unflinchingly. Although the threat of death belonged to the creation of Eros (Gen. 2:17), it was through human disobedience that death became the disintegration of life. Harmony gave way to hostility; unity and fulfillment to fragmentation and dispersion. In the closing movement of the Song of Songs, this tragedy is reversed. Once again, eroticism can embrace the threat of death. The woman says:

> Let me be a seal upon your heart,
> Like the seal upon your hand.
> For love is fierce as death,
> Passion is mighty as Sheol;
> Its darts are darts of fire.
> A blazing flame.
>
> (8:6)

But she does more than affirm life as the equal of death. She asserts triumphantly that not even the primeval waters of chaos can destroy Eros:

> Many waters cannot quench love,
>   neither can floods drown it.
>
> (8:7, RSV)

As a "garden fountain, a well of living water [mayïm hayyïm]" (4:15, RSV), a woman in love prevails over the many waters (mayïm rabbïm) of chaos. With such assurances, the poetry moves inexorably to its consummation.[10]

Far from being strong as death, and redemptive, eroticism is for Isabel (and probably for James) a destructive force. Instead of the "living waters" of The Song of Songs 4:15, love remains the bottomless deep [the tehom] of Genesis 1:2. We may glean some hint of the reason for this dysfunction of both erotic and spiritual love in James from a passage in Robert Gordis's foreword to his edition of The Song of Songs:

> When the Song of Songs is studied without preconceived notions, it emerges as a superb lyrical anthology, containing songs of love and nature, of courtship and marriage, all of which reveal its spiritual character. The two Greek terms, eros, "carnal love," and agapé, "caritas, spiritual love," reflect a dichotomy that has entered into classical Christian theology. The classical Hebrew outlook, on the contrary, finds it entirely proper to apply the same root, 'ahabah, to all aspects of love.[11]

For James and his characters, eros and agapé remain separate. The extent of this separation, and its inverted relation to The Song of Songs, becomes apparent in one of the narrator's descriptions of Isabel's mind. The narrator mentions Isabel's theory "...that a woman ought to be able to live to herself, in the absence of exceptional flimsiness, and that it was perfectly possible to be happy without the society of a more or less coarse-minded person of another sex." The narrator then continues:

> Deep in her soul -- it was the deepest thing there -- lay a belief that if a certain light should dawn she could give herself completely; but this image, on the whole, was too formidable to be attractive. Isabel's thoughts hovered about it, but they seldom rested on it long; after a little it ended in alarms. It often seemed to her that she thought too much about herself; you could have made her colour, any day in the year, by calling her a rank egoist. She was always planning out her development, desiring her perfection, observing her progress. Her nature had, in her conceit, a certain garden-like quality, a suggestion of perfume and murmuring boughs, of shady bowers and lengthening vistas, which made her feel that introspection was, after all, an exercise in the open air, and that a visit to the recesses of one's spirit was harmless when one returned from it with a lapful of roses. But she was often reminded that there were other gardens in the world than those of her remarkable soul, and that there were moreover a great many places which were not gardens at all -- only dusky pestiferous tracts, planted thick with ugliness and misery.
>
> (p. 55)

While this garden of Isabel's consciousness contains "a suggestion of perfume and murmuring boughs," nevertheless its "lengthening vistas" are a far cry from the lush erotic garden imagery of the Song, with its pomegranates and all manner of precious fruits and myrrh and aloes. Isabel is a garden eternally locked.[12] She will never say, as does the Shulamite, "I rose to open to my love, and my hands dripped with myrrh" (5:5). In another meditation, this one explicitly centering on her relationship to Osmond, her bluebeard husband, Isabel thinks: "Her mind was to be his -- attached to his own like a small garden to a deer-park. He would rake the soil gently and water the flowers; he would weed the beds and gather an occasional nosegay. It would be a pretty piece of property for a proprietor already far-reaching" (p. 355).

It is tempting to link Isabel's frigidity and sexual dysfunction with James's own obvious problems, but since such connections have already been made elsewhere, I shall not dwell on them here. I should prefer to connect this failure of love with the motif of the liebestod[13] and of unconsummated love that was still traditional in Western thought, and especially in the novel, at the time that James was writing his Portrait. From the middle ages on, eros is not only divorced from agapé, it is wed to thanatos. As Denis de Rougement puts it, in his study of Love in the Western World:

> Love and death, a fatal love -- in these phrases is summed up, if not the whole of poetry, at least whatever is popular, whatever is universally moving in

European literature, alike as regards the oldest legends and the sweetest songs. Happy love has no history. Romance only comes into existence where love is fatal, frowned upon and doomed by life itself. What stirs lyrical poets to their finest flights is neither the delight of the senses nor the fruitful contentment of the settled couple; not the satisfaction of love, but its passion. And passion means suffering. There we have the fundamental fact.[14]

The theme of Portrait is the failure of love, with the theme of "love and death" more adumbrated than realized; in The Wings of the Dove, which critics have often seen as a novel continuing and bringing to fulfillment the themes of the earlier novel, the motif of love and death is clearly at the center of James's consciousness. I cannot agree with Lyall H. Powers, however, that "Ralph's love for Isabel serves the same function, ultimately, as Milly's for Densher: the means of salvation."[15] Certainly, it is not clear in Isabel's case that she achieves "salvation," and few commentators on the novel seem to come away with the impression that Isabel is "saved." The case for redemption is stronger in the case of Milly Theale and Densher, but I shall argue that Densher is no more "redeemed" than Isabel. Nevertheless, the parallels between Touchett-Archer and Theale-Densher are undeniable. But in the later novel, James has managed to bring his subject into clearer focus. Powers finds that "it is perhaps permissible to say that... Ralph assumes a Christ-like role."[16] Ralph's role and his personality do at times seem Christ-like. Yet it is Isabel, not Ralph, who is associated with the image of the dove, which is the "type" of Christ. In trying to dissuade Isabel from marrying Osmond, Ralph says: "You seemed to me to be soaring far up in the blue -- to be, sailing in the bright light, over the heads of men. Suddenly someone tosses up a faded rosebud -- a missile that should never have reached you -- and straight you drop to the ground" (p. 285). It is also Isabel, as many commentators have pointed out, who embodies "innocence," one of the qualities of the dove. In The Wings of the Dove there is no split between the dove imagery and the Christ imagery. Both revolve around Milly Theale. Moreover, she is in the center of the action. The unbeloved lover is now in the foreground, and that is the one thing that makes the novels very different in tone and effect.

The Portrait is, as Segal notes, written "in the tragic key."[17] But The Wings of the Dove seems to be written in the key of pure terror, albeit a terror brilliantly muffled. It is universally accepted, these days, that Milly Theale is modeled, like Isabel, on James's cousin, Minnie Temple, whom he may have been in love with, and who died very young. But while it is true that Milly's initials match Minnie's, and while it is true that both died young, there is, nevertheless, a more likely model. The seed of The Wings of the Dove is first recorded in James's Notebooks in November 1894 and, as initially conceived, the seed is very terrifying indeed. The note begins:

Isn't perhaps something to be made of the idea that came to me some time ago and that I have not hitherto made any note of -- the little idea of the situation of some young creature (it seems to me preferably a woman, but of this I'm not sure), who, at 20, on the threshold of a life that has seemed boundless, is suddenly condemned to death (by consumption, heart-disease, or whatever) by the voice of the physician? She learns that she has but a short time to live, and she rebels, she is terrified, she cries out in her anguish, her tragic young despair. She is in love with life, her dreams of it have been immense, and she clings to it with passion, with supplication. "I don't want to die -- I won't, I won't, oh, let me live; oh, save me!" She is equally pathetic in her doom and in her horror of it. If she only could live just a little; just a little more -- just a little longer. She is like a creature dragged shrieking to the guillotine -- to the shambles.[18]

Those who have read the novel will recognize instantly how thoroughly James muted the terror when he came to write the novel some years later.[21] To some extent, this muting may be attributed to the difference between the artful fiction and the naked idea. But it is also possible that the unmuffled terror of the notebook entry is owing to Henry's recent direct exposure to the reality of death. During the years 1891-1892, Henry's chronically invalid sister, Alice, who had made her home in England since 1884, was dying of cancer. It was Henry who saw her through the last stages of her illness. As Leon Edel describes it, "This was the first time that Henry had watched someone through the hours of death -- and someone close to him.... He looked on now with .. helpless hurt and suffering..."[20]

Early in 1894, Henry read one of the four privately printed copies of Alice's diary, which contained her impressions and thoughts during the nearly three years of her terminal illness. On May 25, 1894, Henry wrote to William that:

As regards the life, the power, the temper, the humour and beauty and expressiveness of the Diary in itself -- these things were partly "discounted" to me in advance by so much of Alice's talk during her last years -- and my constant association with her -- which led me often to reflect about her extraordinary force of mind and character, her whole way of taking life -- and death -- in very much the manner in which the book does. I find in its pages, for instance, many things I heard her say. None the less I have been immensely impressed with the thing as a revelation of a moral and personal picture. It is heroic in its individuality, its independence -- its face-to-face with the universe for-and-by herself -- and the beauty and eloquence with which she often expresses this.[21]

James adds that the Diary "...puts before me what I was tremendously conscious of in her lifetime -- that the extraordinary intensity of her will and personality really would have made the equal, the reciprocal life of a 'well' person -- in the usual world -- almost impossible to her -- so that her disastrous, her tragic health was in a manner the only solution for her of the practical problem of life..."

This notion of the "reciprocal life of a 'well' person" set against the ebbing life of an invalid enters into the novel whose seed was planted exactly six months after his epistolary tribute to Alice's courage in the face of death. In the novel, Kate Croy, a healthy and beautiful (but also poor) young woman, tries to arrange a marriage between her dashing (but also poor) lover, Merton Densher, and the dying American millionairess, Milly Theale, who is also in love with Densher. Once again, James returns to the theme of love and death, but with sharper focus. In the later novel, with his experience of Alice's lingering death behind him, James reflects the traditional Western schism between _eros_ and _agapé_ even more devastatingly than he had in the earlier novel. Kate, who is young and vigorous, embodying (as Isabel Archer did), the life-force itself, is spiritually diseased. "She saw herself as handsome, no doubt, but as hard, and felt herself as clever but as cold..." Kate is ready to barter love for money. On the other hand, Milly, who is wasting away physically, loves selflessly, but with a love that is necessarily disembodied.[22]

If in her dying, however, Milly resembles Alice James, in her yearning for love she resembles the Shulamite of The Song of Songs. If Alice is the life model, the Shulamite is the literary-mythic model. In the later novel, James permits his literary source to rise to the surface, giving it the prominence of the title of the novel. Numerous critics have identified the title as an allusion to Psalm 55: "And I said, O that I had wings like a dove! for then I would fly away and be at rest."[23] Dorothea Krook cites also the two verses preceding this one, which describe Milly's situation precisely: "My heart is sore pained within me: and the terrors of death are fallen upon me. Fearfulness and trembling are come upon me, and horror hath overwhelmed me."[24] But the critics overlook the connection between James's dove imagery and The Song of Songs. While it is correct to say that the psalm provides an apt description of Milly's psychological condition, it is the dove imagery in the love song that allows full resonance to the pervasive dove symbolism in the novel.

Twice in the biblical book, the Shulamite's eyes are compared to doves, and three times she herself is compared to a dove. The qualities of the beloved that may be inferred from these metaphors and similes are modesty, beauty, purity, perfection, lovingness, warmth. The beloved is apostrophized as a dove in outbursts of passion, as in 5:2: "Open to me, my sister, my love, my dove, my undefiled; for my head is filled with dew, my locks with the drops of the night." When we juxtapose the biblical metaphor to the Jamesian, the pallor and coldness of the latter are immediately apparent. In James's novel, it is Milly Theale, the dying woman who loves but is not loved in return, who is the dove. Interestingly, it is not a lover who calls Milly a dove, it is her female rival, Kate Croy. In one of their conversations Kate tells Milly, "Oh you may very well loathe me yet." When Milly, shocked, inquires, "Why do you say such things to me?" Kate replies:

"Because you're a dove." With which she felt herself ever so delicately, so considerately, embraced; not with familiarity or as a liberty taken, but almost ceremonially and in the manner of an accolade; partly as if, though a dove who

could perch on a finger, one were also a princess with whom forms were to be
observed. It even came to her, through the touch of her companion's lips, that
this form, this cool pressure, fairly sealed the sense of what Kate had just
said. It was moreover, for the girl, like an inspiration: she found herself
accepting as the right one, while she caught her breath with relief, the name
so given her. She met it on the instant as she would have met revealed truth;
it lighted up the strange dusk in which she lately had walked. That was what
was the matter with her. She was a dove. Oh wasn't she?[25]

All the eroticism is screened out in James's use of the figure of the dove. The qualities
that we impute to Milly as dove are vulnerability and the potentiality of self-sacrifice.

It is well known that allegorical interpretations of The Song of Songs, both Jewish
and Christian, made a very early appearance. I shall not be concerned directly with the
Jewish allegorical interpretations, which are not immediately relevant. The Christian
interpretations, according to Marvin H. Pope, "were progressively influenced by
Hellenistic Roman" ideals. Origen, writes Pope, "combined with Platonic and Gnostic
attitudes toward sexuality to denature the Canticle and transform it into a spiritual
drama free from all carnality."[26] At the core of Origen's influential commentary lay the
Gnostic notion of "the divine Spirit as the exclusive bridegroom of the devoted soul..."
The bride/dove becomes the soul and the bridegroom becomes Jesus/divine Spirit. This
widespread understanding of The Song of Songs is reflected in James's use of the dove
imagery, at least in part. Milly is a denatured Shulamite, for unlike the Shulamite she
stands for a purity that is already physically sterile. The allegorical readings of the
Canticle depend on the completion of love. The spirituality of the bride becomes
meaningless in the absence of the total love of the bridegroom. But in James's novel, love
is short-circuited, as is required by the Pagan myth of the liebestod. Milly loves a man
who does not (at least, at first) love her. Kate Croy, on the other hand, sets material
considerations above love, postponing love for money. Kate's patience and her willingness
to suppress love in favor of financial security is in sharp contrast to the eagerness of the
Shulamite, who laments, "By night on my bed I sought him whom my soul loveth."

F.O. Matthiessen has written that "It is startling to realize that the subject of The
Wings of the Dove is precisely what Poe formulated as the greatest possible subject for
poetry, the death of a beautiful woman."[27] Just as Isabel loves Ralph most intensely
when he is dying, so Densher comes to love Milly totally only after she is dead. What
James does, in the later novel, rather oddly, is to conflate Hezekiah's "sickness unto
death" with the Shulamite's being "sick with love."[28] The narrator never names Milly's
sickness. Her physician, Sir Luke Strett, intimates that she can live if she wills herself
to. He apparently tells her friend and travelling companion, Susan Sheperd Stringham,
that happiness will prolong her life. As Mrs. Stringham and her friend Lady Maud
Manningham discuss Milly's illness, they consider the question of whether love can sustain
Milly:

"The point is will it cure?"

"Precisely. Is it absolutely a remedy -- the specific?"

"Well, I should think we might know!" Mrs. Stringham delicately declared.

"Have you never, dearest, been in love?" Susan Sheperd enquired.

"Yes, my child; but not by the doctor's direction."

Maud Manningham had spoken perforce with a break into momentary mirth, which operated -- and happily too -- as a challenge to her visitor's spirit. "Oh of course we don't ask his leave to fall. But it's something to know he thinks it good for us."

"My dear woman," Mrs. Lowder cried, "it strikes me we know it without him. So that when that's all he had to tell us -- !"

"Ah," Mrs. Stringham interposed, "it isn't 'all.' I feel Sir Luke will have more; he won't have put me off with anything inadequate. I'm to see him again; he as good as told me that he'll wish it. So it won't be for nothing.

"Then what will it be for? Do you mean he has somebody of his own to propose? Do you mean you told him nothing?"

(p. 247)

What Susan Stringham has failed to tell the physician is that the particular object of Milly's love is Merton Densher, who, as Milly knows, loves Kate Croy, though she does not know that they are secretly engaged. When Kate tells Densher that she and her aunt are returning to England, leaving Milly in Venice, Merton asks, "You leave her here to die?" Kate answers, "'Ah she believes she won't die. Not if you stay. I mean,' Kate explained, 'Aunt Maud believes'" (p. 310). When Milly finds out from an unsuccessful suitor that Densher and Kate are engaged, the sickness of love turns into the sickness unto death, and like Hezekiah, she "turns her face to the wall." Four times this sentence is repeated.[29]

As was the case in Portrait of a Lady, death is stronger than love, and jealousy truly turns out to be "as cruel as the grave." In one of Poe's "death-of-a-beautiful-woman" stories, Madeline Usher returns from the grave to destroy her brother. Milly Theale does not return from the grave in her own physical person, but she does return figuratively to quench erotic love. In the resolution of James's novel, Milly dies, bequeathing her fortune to Merton Densher. Her will is a message from the grave, assuring her triumph over her rival Kate Croy, the penultimate triumph of death over love.[30] In the novel's final scene, Kate and Densher try to get their new relationship sorted out. Densher offers to marry Kate if she renounces Milly's money. He makes it clear to her that she cannot have both himself and the money:

His look at her had a slow strangeness that had dried, on the moment, his tears. "Do I understand then -- ?"

"That I do consent?" She gravely shook her head. "No -- for I see. You'll marry me without the money; you won't marry me with it. If I don't consent you don't."

"You lose me?" He showed, though naming it frankly, a sort of awe of her high grasp. "Well, you lose nothing else. I make over to you every penny."

Prompt was his own clearness, but she had no smile this time to spare. "Precisely -- so that I must choose."

"You must choose."

Strange it was for him then that she stood in his own rooms doing it, while, with an intensity now beyond any that had ever made his breath come slow, he waited for her act. "There's but one thing that can save you from my choice."

"From your choice of my surrender to you?"

"Yes" -- and she gave a nod at the long envelope on the table -- "your surrender of that."

"What is it then?"

"Your word of honour that you're not in love with her memory."

"Oh -- her memory!"

"Ah" -- she made a high gesture -- "don't speak of it as if you couldn't be. I could be in your place; and you're one for whom it will do. Her memory's your love. You want no other."

He heard her out in stillness, watching her face but not moving. Then he only said: "I'll marry you, mind you, in an hour."

"As we were?"

"As we were."

But she turned to the door, and her headshake was now the end.

"We shall never be again as we were!"

(p. 403)

Kate states explicitly what both of them have come to realize. Love is dead. Oscar Cargill summarizes a widely accepted reading of this ending which presents James's denouement in a positive light:

Densher had discovered too much about Kate Croy for her to live with him: he is generous to be sure, for he knows her tantamount to a murderess; but he does not hold himself above her -- they have been partners, though he the lesser one, in crime. But he is determined to expiate his share, while she is not. Their parting has for long been inevitable; she, seeing that love is dead, characteristically terminates the relationship. But he is infinitely richer from the relationship, for he is now a man capable of love and not any longer the slave of passion. It is Tristan who learns what love is and not Iseult of the White Hands.[31]

I must disagree with this widely held assessment of Densher's new condition. Far from being capable of love, Densher has been transformed from a slave of _eros_ to a slave of thanatos. He is still a slave of passion because he still suffers. But now he has become the consummate romantic hero precisely because his love can never be consummated and his suffering must remain eternal. In a strange way this triumph of sterility and death is the outcome of James's reallegorizing of the Christian allegorical interpretation of The Song of Songs. The Christian allegory suppresses eros in favor of agapé. James concretizes this division by dividing the female protagonist of The Song, in whom bodily and spiritual love are fused, into dual female protagonists -- Kate Croy, who is full-bodied fleshly love, and Milly Theale, who is disembodied spiritual love. Merton Densher then becomes the victim in a conflict between forces of fleshly love and spiritual love that strips him of his own freedom of action. Whoever wins, Densher is doomed -- either to physical sterility or spiritual barrenness.

Notes

1.   The English Novel: Form and Function (1953; rpt. New York and Evanston: Harper and Row, 1961), p. 214.

2.   Henry James, The Portrait of a Lady, ed. Leon Edel (Cambridge, Mass.: The Riverside Press, 1956), p. 158. All further references to the novel are to this edition and appear in the text.

3.   The Lucid Reflector (New Haven and London: Yale University Press, 1969), pp. 37-38.

4.   Annette Niemtzow mentions in passing Isabel's having "...to reconsider her visits to Ralph Touchett, her beloved cousin..." But I don't think she is talking about "beloved" in the sense I have in mind. At least, she does not develop her essay along that line. See "Marriage and the New Woman in The Portrait of a Lady," American Literature, 47 (November 1975), p. 380. In The American Henry James (New Brunswick, New Jersey: Rutgers University Press, 1957), Quentin Anderson writes that Isabel's "love for [Ralph] had led her to make the journey" to visit him on his deathbed, and he observes, further, that "Ralph's love will be her real inheritance..." (p. 190).

5.   If, as Niemtzow argues in the above cited essay, James believed that the marriage vow was indissoluble, then the marriage and the life would be inexorably coterminous.

6.   Robert Gordis, The Song of Songs and Lamentations: A Study, Modern Translation and Commentary (New York: Ktav Publishing House, Inc., 1974), p. 74. Leon A. Feldman, R. Abraham b. Isaac ha-LEVI Ta Makh Commentary on The Song of Songs (Assen, The Netherlands: Van Gorcum, Ltd., 1970), p. 187.

7.   For a more comprehensive presentation of the imagery of darkness in the novel see R.W. Stallman's much neglected essay on the novel in The Houses that James Built (n.p.: Michigan State University Press, 1961). He writes that "She is a creature of darkness..." (p. 14). In arguing for the importance of houses rather than gardens in the novel, Stallman writes, "All the houses Isabel inhabits or visits... are dimly-lit interiors..." (p. 11). I must disagree with his contention, however, that the garden imagery is totally eclipsed by house imagery, and that "All the crucial events in our heroine's career occur

in houses -- not in gardens" (p. 16). Though Stallman's essay is brilliant and packed with insights into the novel, his reading of the novel tends to underestimate James's ambivalence toward characters, situations, and moral dilemmas. In fact, crucial events occur both in houses and in gardens.

8.   Niemtzow argues very convincingly that Isabel's return to Osmond may be explained by Henry's adoption of his father's views on the sanctity and permanence of the marriage vows. While the argument is convincing, however, it does not alter the fact that commentators have perceived the ending as a return to a death-in-life for Isabel.

9.   "Intimacy and Spectatorship in The Portrait of a Lady," The Henry James Review, II (Fall 1980), pp. 25, 26, 32. Stallman, too, calls attention to some of Isabel's less admirable qualities, calling her James's "pretentious, imperceptive, and self-deluded heroine" in The Houses that James Built, p. 32. Q. Anderson suggests that Isabel finds reflected in Osmond the salient defect in her own character, "absolute or spiritual greed" (p. 188).

10.   Phyllis Trible, God and the Rhetoric of Sexuality (Philadelphia: The Fortess Press, 1978), pp. 160-161. The translation Trible uses here when RSV is not specified is H.L. Ginsberg, The Five Megilloth and Jonah (Philadelphia: Jewish Publication Society, 1969), p. 16.

11.   Gordis, p. x.

12.   Both Stallman and O'Connor link Isabel to Diana, chaste goddess of the hunt. O'Connor goes on to say that "...her innermost self suggests a virgo intacta" (p. 26).

13.   Oscar Cargill identifies and discusses the presence of the liebestod motif in The Wings of the Dove in The Novels of Henry James (New York: The Macmillan Company, 1961), p. 338. Charles Samuels discusses the idea without using the word in The Ambiguity of Henry James (Urbana, Chicago, London: The University of Illinois Press, 1971), pp. 72-75. After summarizing several James stories "with affinities to The Wings of the Dove," Samuels concludes that they "...cluster about a life denial that is neither satiric nor tragic but morbidly sentimental" (p. 74).

14.   Denis de Rougement, Love in the Western World (1956; rpt. New York, Hagerstown, San Francisco, London: Harper and Row, 1974; orig. pub. 1940), p. 15.

15.   "The Portrait of a Lady: The Eternal Mystery of Things," Nineteenth Century Fiction, 14 (September 1959), p. 152. See also Q. Anderson, p. 190.

16.   Powers, p. 152. Charles R. Anderson maintains that "the great theme of The Wings of the Dove [is] the power of love in mortal conflict with the power of money." This way of stating the theme seems to me to put the emphasis in the wrong place. The "power of money" is one of the fields on which the struggle between love and death is carried on. Person, Place and Thing in Henry James's Novels (Durham, North Carolina: Duke University Press, 1977, p. 174.

17.   The Lucid Reflector, p. 55

18.   F.O. Matthiessen and Kenneth B. Murdock, eds., The Notebooks of Henry James (New York: George Braziller, Inc., 1955), p. 169.

19. While it is true that James softens the dread of Milly's dying by pushing her offstage for the last third of the novel, the horror does peep through at times, as in the following bit of dialogue between Kate and Densher:

> It came out in Kate's face that there were several questions on her lips, but the one she presently put was: "Is it very terrible?"
>
> "The manner of her so consciously and helplessly dying?" He had to think a moment. "Well, yes -- since you ask me: very terrible to _me_ -- so far as, before I came away, I had any sight of it. But I don't think," he went on, "that -- though I'll try -- I _can_ quite tell you what it was, what it is, for me. That's why I probably just sounded to you," he explained, "as if I hoped it might be over."
>
> (p. 355)

F.O. Matthiessen, in Henry James: The Major Phase (1944; rpt. New York: Oxford University Press, 1963), p. 54, writes that James's "...most effective combination of [pity and terror] was in The Wings of the Dove." He mentions, but does not develop, the "themes of love and death" on p. 67.

20.   Henry James: The Middle Years: 1882-1895 (Philadelphia and New York: J. Lippincott Company, 1962), p. 301.

21.   Leon Edel, ed., Henry James Letters (Cambridge, Mass.: The Belknap Press of Harvard University Press, 1980), III, pp. 480-481. I am not arguing that the thought of Minnie Temple is not in some way present in James's portrait of Milly, but I would insist that Minnie is only one component. Matthiessen, who argues the Minnie Temple model extensively in The Major Phase, quotes selectively from Notes of a Son and Brother James's assertion "...that he had sought there [Dove] 'to lay the ghost by wrapping it... in the beauty and dignity of art'" (p. 47). The phrase that Matthiessen omits, and that no one has yet explained, is, "a particular occasion aiding." What more natural than for James to conflate the two dying women as models for Milly. Cargill comments on the name Kate Croy: "That a Kate should be placed beside the two Millys is not surprising, for Minny's older sister was Katherine..." (p. 378). By a remarkable coincidence, another Katherine played a very important role in Alice's life. Katherine Peabody Loring, who sailed to England with Alice, later became her nurse and constant companion during her illness. It was Katherine Loring who arranged to have the diary privately printed, and then sent copies to Alice's surviving brothers.

22.   I must disagree with those critics who take the position that the diseases with which Ralph and Milly are afflicted are both physical and spiritual. Such a contention tends to oversimplify the resonances of disease as metaphor. Q. Anderson locates what he calls "moral illness" in Densher, p. 271.

23.   See, for example, Ernest Sandee, "The Wings of the Dove and The Portrait of a Lady: A Study of Henry James's Later Phase," PMLA, 69 (December 1954), pp. 1073-1074. F.O. Matthiessen writes that "The four [symbols] that furnished titles for

[James'] books are biblical allusions, to which he proceeded to give concrete embodiment with little reference to the Bible," The Major Phase, p. 72. For a dissenting opinion on Matthiessen and for a comparison between Milly and Hilda in Hawthorne's The Marble Faun, see Marius Bewley, The Complex Fate (New York: The Gordian Press, Inc., 1967), pp. 31-54. Milly, like Isabel, has had her detractors.

24.   The Ordeal of Consciousness in Henry James (Cambridge: Cambridge University Press, 1962), p. 195.

25.   Henry James (J. Donald Crowley and Richard A. Hocks, eds.), The Wings of the Dove (New York: W.W. Norton & Co., Inc., 1978), p. 171. All further references to the novel are to this edition and appear in the text.

26.   The Anchor Bible, Song of Songs: A New Translation with Introduction and Commentary (Garden City, New York: Doubleday & Company, Inc., 1977), p. 115.

27.   The Major Phase, p. 50.

28.   See 2 Kings 20:1-11; Isaiah 38:1-8. On Poe's use of this same motif of "the sickness unto death," see the present author's "The Pit and the Apocalypse," The Sewanee Review, LXXVI (Autumn 1968), pp. 632-652.

29.   The biblical phrase appears in 2 Kings 20:2 and Isaiah 38:2; in the novel on pp. 331, 333, 357, 359.

30.   Compare Q. Anderson's comment, cited in footnote 4, that "Ralph's love will be [Isabel's] real inheritance." Anderson does not elaborate, but the parallels in these two key James novels are unmistakable, and are a very clear indication that Poe's influence on James is stronger and more pervasive than James himself was willing to admit, and than most critics are ready to concede.

31.   Cargill, p. 373.

TRANSLATING BIBLICAL RHYTHM

Henri Meschonnic

Paris-VIII (Vincennes) University

1. Hebrew Rhythm versus Greek Sign

In choosing this subject, I shall not discuss what is biblical in modern literature; instead, I shall try to show how biblical rhythm is still modern and can even appear as an undiscovered theoretical object, which can also renew the translation of the Bible, and thus take its place as a device in contemporary poetics.

All statements that I shall make must be placed in the context of my background as a poet and translator, and in the context of my work in progress; I have undertaken, in the wake of so many others, to translate the Bible anew, into French, attempting, thereby, to make something new. I am referring to my translation of Les Cinq Rouleaux, the "Five Scrolls"; and of the book of Jonah in Jona et le signifiant errant, "Jonah and the erring signifier." One additional contextual reference point is my theoretical work on rhythm, which came out last April under the title of Critique du rhythm, Anthropologie historique du langue ("Critique of Rhythm, an Historical Anthropology of Language"). These works offer a context of demonstration for what I shall not be able to develop in detail, here.

The importance of my subject is such, indeed, that in so short a space I can only hope to give an idea of the scope of the problem, with one or two examples. I will not speak as a specialist in comparative literature, but as a poet and as a linguist. I shall analyze various translations in order to show what is at stake in them, what is shown and what is hidden, so that translating the Bible eventually appears to be not merely a literary process, but an enterprise of utopia: Utopia with its metaphysical and even political interest, in the broad sense of "political," and this, in two ways.

A new translation of the biblical text, and verse, into French is my first concern, but I am sure that the point of view I shall try to expound can be extended and applied to other languages and literature as well. A new French translation has to face a problem which is proper to French. The challenge is to produce a translation that would act in French as a part of French literature, and would be a meeting, thus far never achieved, between the poetics of Hebrew verse and the poetics of modern French writing. That challenge stems from the literary non-existence of the Bible in French, as compared with the cultural and political existence of the Bible in English in the King James version, or in German with the Luther translation.

Certainly, the fact that in both these instances the success of the translation has been linked to a specifically Protestant outlook on the Bible, as compared to a Catholic outlook, is an important event. But can the cultural factor be everything? Can it be the only factor determining that difference? There are, necessarily, linguistic and poetic elements involved too. It is a demonstrable fact that purely ideological translations are unsuccessful. They are unsuccessful in that they last briefly, and being worn out with the aging of language, merge into other translations, which will last as briefly. A successful translation, on the other hand, acts as an "original" work, and outlasts the aging of its own language. Fitzgerald's Rubaiyat of Omar Khayyam is a well known example.

That leads to the question of whether a specifically Jewish way of translating can be conceived, and what, on the basis of previous Jewish translations, it might be. The paradox holds in the following hypothesis: if, as an answer to that challenge, a French poetical Bible is possible, perhaps it can only be a Jewish one.

Compared to Catholic and Protestant translations, which all work on the side of meaning, in the dualistic frame of the sign, the striking phenomenon one can observe is a Jewish reaction, which could be named Aquila's complex, after the literal translation of Aquila into Greek: bereshit=in the beginning=in te kephale=in the head. Thus some Jewish translations, at least into French, have thrown themselves into the other extreme of the sign, form understood as the servile copy of the signifier, the pidgin French of Edmond Fleg and Andre Chouraki. But the other extreme of the dual partition of language, far from breaking through the frame of the sign, remains a prisoner of it. It even strengthens it, for it can only lead to preferring meaning to form, if anything has to be lost. And it is that dual frame as a whole which the theory of language has to get rid of.

The second, main, and broadest interest of the subject lies in the theoretical effect of biblical rhythm on the general theory of language and meaning.

To start with, I invoke a sentence by Abraham Ibn-Ezra, which can serve as a motto both for the general theory of rhythm and for whatever can be said about the Bible. It says: "Any comment that is not on a comment of the accents you will not want it and you will not listen to it."[2]

I would infer from this that, in the general state of present linguistics and theory of language, it is perhaps urgent to reverse the common hierarchy that makes meaning the main consideration in language. Meaning entails the race for meaning, the reduction of language to meaning -- themes, message, communication -- which implies the dual split between form and meaning, and the reduction of language to instrument. Thus the philosophy of ordinary speech, together with pragmatics, make the language of literature a deviation, a language outside common language. The sentence by Abraham Ibn-Ezra shows that, from an empirical point of view, the last thing that counts in language is meaning. At least, according to the way one usually speaks of meaning. Intonation, for instance, counts far more, to say nothing of mimicry, gestures, relationships, situation, and so on.

Language is not accessible apart from the ways of speaking about language. And these ways are historical. Therefore they constitute an inescapable grid. Any model of description is such a grid. The primary fallacy a cultural grid can produce is to make one believe there is none. Being invisible, it is taken for the very nature of things. The usual model of the sign is such a grid.

To refer to rhythm or to meaning, necessarily implies referring oneself to, and situating oneself in, a history which is, as far as we are concerned, the history of western Greek and Christian dualism, the dualism of the linguistic sign, which is the pattern of a whole anthropology. That anthropology opposes body and soul, the letter and the spirit, form and meaning, of which a variant is the opposition between rhythm and meaning as well, since it opposes language and life, the rational and the irrational, prose and poetry, or words and actions -- all aspects of dualism linked together, if they do not make one paradigm. Together they characterize the self-centered logic of identity towards the indefinitely rejected other side of the mirror, the well-known strength and weakness of our civilization. In that anthropology, <u>duality is totality</u>.

But a linguistic model is never just a linguistic model. The dual pattern of the sign acts also as a political pattern. For in the same way that the signifier, having no meaning by itself, being just the bearer of the signified, retracts before the signified, in the social contract, as Rousseau drew its scheme and as it functions in our democracies, the minority is in the position of the signifier, and the majority is identified with the general will; it does not rule because it is the greater number, but because it is the Sovereign. If the dual pattern of the sign is so well established, compensating in extension for the efficiency it lacks in comprehension, it is just for epistemological reasons, but for pragmatic and political reasons. A theological scheme still reinforces the political one. It appears at its best in Hegel's <u>Spirit of Christianity and its Fate</u>: Judaism has the position of the signifier, and Christianity has the one of the signified. It is at a time the new religion and the truth of both, retaining and outdoing the religion of the past, the first sketch of Hegel's <u>Aufhebung</u>.

The place and definition given to rhythm by the sign, in linguistic as well as in semiotics, belongs to that grid. So the question of rhythm appears to be the hidden side of the sign. To realize that in nearly all activities of language rhythm carries much more than its traditional and formal definition limits it to, brings one to alter the definitions both of rhythm and of meaning, and their relationship.

For that, one simply has to take language as speech, integrating into the empirical, historical activity of subjects in their language all that which the dual pattern of the sign describes as two separated entities, without restraining language to the logical or rhetorical aspects, which are but a part of it. The trouble with the studies that specialize in those aspects, as stimulating as they may be, is that they perfectly accommodate themselves with the dual grid of the sign. In fact, they find their place in it, therefore contributing to maintaining it unchanged. But that might be the main reason for the difficulties they have in dealing with literature.

To displace the usual relationship between rhythm and meaning implies a radical move from <u>totality</u> to <u>infinity</u> -- which is nothing but the empirical condition shared both by history and by meaning. That move is also a move from linguistics, or semiotics, or pragmatics, as I know them, to an historical anthropology of language. By that I mean an empirical study where body, voice, gesture are understood as inseparable from meaning, and where all the organizing marks of the signifier contribute to meaning, and may be more important to meaning, or rather to the activity of language than the traditional, lexical idea of meaning. In other words, orality, as including all that (and no more in the sociological sense, restricted to the absence of writing), is the main support and medium of meaning. That orality is sociality, as Marcel Mauss long ago demonstrated, is indicated in Hebrew by the word miqra for designating the Bible. For miqra says reading, not Scripture, and reading aloud and together, the two being reciprocal conditions. More generally, it is the integration of rhythm and meaning into one another that makes intonation, and prosody (by which I mean all the consonant and vowel organization) essential to meaning. Conversely, it is quite significant that linguistics once excluded intonation from meaning as "suprasegmental."

Rhythm, no longer conceived as the formal alternation of the same and the different, the weak and the strong syllable or position, symmetry versus asymmetry, can be understood as the specific organization of speech, of all the marks of speech, subjective and cultural, in any given speech. Rhythm is an aspect of historicity. Although rhythm can have conflicting, and various, relationships with lexical meaning, it can no longer be opposed to, and separated from, meaning. It is elementary, for instance, that pauses in speech have to do with meaning. Meaning is in rhythm as language is in the body, the individual body, with its history. But that body is also the body social. Again Mauss had, in the thirties, pointed to the most physiological "practices of the body" as being cultural. The same reciprocity holds for language.

Although there is no rhythmical void anywhere in language, any more than there is a semantic void, the Bible does not stand here as one example among many. It is not even a particular, or privileged example. Rhythm in the Bible plays an exemplary part because it functions in a unique way. To my knowledge, it is unique in its systematic codification of rhythm, and by the virtue of the specific organizing role that rhythm plays. And it is unique in the theoretical effect that codification can have on the general theory of sign. That effect does not seem so far to have attracted due attention, for good reasons. For the Bible, through the theory of rhythm that can be drawn out of it, can unsettle the tradition of sign, and contribute to a reconstrual of the theoretical status of the relationship between body and language. The threefold status of the sign (linguistic, theological and political) and its dual scheme have made the whole history of the western outlook on the Bible a history of efforts to reduce the primacy of rhythm to its own dualism. These efforts have not succeeded, although they have been going on for more than two thousand years.

2.   Rhythm versus Parallelism

The Bible has no metrics. Definitions of poetry through verse, of poetry as opposed to prose, and of prose with regard to verse, are not relevant when applied to the Bible. A metrical definition of biblical poetry is no longer possible; thus our western ideas of prose, verse and poetry do not work in dealing with the Bible. It is an old scandal which centuries of clever attempts have failed to cover up. Herein lies the interest of biblical rhythm for poetics.

Rhythm in the Bible figures the central place of rhythm in language. Instead of that, it has been placed in a margin-like position by the sign, which is the position of the Jew himself, which he fails to recognize, as he has accepted the order of the sign.

The failure of the usual ideas of prose and poetry, when they are applied to the Bible, lies in the lack of formal criteria. Poetry then takes on a vague and exalted meaning, dissolving into religiosity; poetry and prose seem to merge into one another. The very first endeavors to see the Bible as poetry, or to see poetry in the Bible, were Greek, and therefore metrical. Josephus saw hexameters in the song of Moses. The Bible could not be less beautiful than the Greek models. Since the latter were in meters, so the former also had to be in meters. For centuries, metrical readings forced the text into a pseudo-symmetry which systematically disregarded the text as it was. Devaluating the text was apparently a strategy towards origin, and actually towards symmetry and the sign. Biblical criticism, as if it were the philological side of an anti-Jewish theology and general attitude, has been constantly biased against the Massora -- the establishment of the vowels and of the cantillation of the text.

James Kugel, who has written masterfully on the history of "the idea of biblical poetry,"[3] has shown that parallelism was a rhetorical substitute for metrics, since the classical attempts to discover biblical metrics had failed. He is the first one to have recognized that Robert Lowth, in 1853, did not discover parallelism, but invented it. Still, since that date, parallelism has become the commonly accepted paradigm of biblical verse, and is unquestioningly believed to be the constant and fundamental law of biblical poetry. Even Benjamin Hrushovski, in an opening "Note on the systems of Hebrew Versification" for the recent Penguin Book of Hebrew Verse, writes that "the basic principle is parallelism."[4]

Parallelism has been defined as a division of the biblical verse into two halves that respond to each other, according to three types. In the first type, the second half is synonymous with the first one, and it is supposed to repeat it with other terms, such as

Who shall ascend into the hill of the Lord?/or who shall stand in his holy place? (Psalm XXIV, 3)

The second type is the one in which the second half says the opposite of the first one, such as

For the Lord knoweth the way of the righteous:/but the way of the ungodly shall perish (Psalm I, 6)

According to a third, mixed and controversial type, the second half completes the first one, as in

Thou preparest a table before me/in the presence of mine enemies: thou anointest my head with oil;/my cup runneth over (Psalm XXIII, 5)

Nobody can deny that there are parallel sentences, or symmetry in words, repetitions of sounds. Yet the idea of repetition of meaning, which is fundamental to parallelism, is not in accord with a linguistic analysis of synonymy. Repetition reinforces the term that is repeated. It emphasizes. Moreover, the rhetoric of repetition is universal. It in no way distinguishes poetry from prose.

Yet, probably because it lends to easy formalization, that stereotyped notion of parallelism has grown into a general idea of poetry. Through folk-lore studies and ethnology of the previous century and the present one, the scope of parallelism has been extended in space and time. Secondly, by virtue of the formal character of structuralism, and in the work of Roman Jakobson in particular, parallelism as a theoretical concept took on the appearance of the essential feature of poetry. I intend to show that parallelism is not a crucial factor in identifying such pseudo-objects as biblical "poetry" or biblical "prose," nor, in a more general sense, in distinguishing poetry from prose.

Though the extension of parallelism is no doubt impressive, the thoroughness with which it is understood is less certain. Kugel has shown how the three types of parallelism can be analyzed into about a dozen types. But, mainly, parallelism is linked to the repetitive style throughout the Bible. The beginning of Genesis, for instance, and chapter II in Exodus, are organized into parallel oppositions, even though they are generally printed, and treated, as "prose." There are more parallelisms in Leviticus, XX than in Jacob's blessing. But convention sees poetry in the latter passage, and prose in the former.

Kugel noticed that there is no term for poetry in the Bible, nor for parallelism. Poetry came later, with Greek words. The word shira does not stand for "poetry," but for a song of praise. It is through its resemblance to the Arabic word shi^{c}r that it took on the meaning "poetry" in the Middle Ages. The Bible knows the opposition only between the sung and the spoken -- a state previous to metrics, which one also finds in XIIth century Russian literature. Kugel establishes that both "prose" and "poetry" are alien to the biblical world and constitute a "Hellenistic imposition."

Nor for the whole world of traditional Jewish interpretation were there poetry or parallelisms. Since all traditional Jewish interpretation is devoted to the analysis of differences, it cannot see those synonymous parallelisms. Its hermeneutical reasons are more in keeping with modern linguistic analysis than are the rhetorical assumptions of synonymous repetition. Cantillation, too, without which the text cannot be conceived, hinders the perception of parallelism.

When readers started to see poetry in the Bible, the opinion was circulated that the original meters had got lost. But it is remarkable that for Judah Halevi, in The Kuzari, there is no meter, only song: "It is obvious that a tune is independent of the meter, or of the lesser or greater number of syllables."[5]

With parallelism there has developed a biblical stylistics. More recently, biblical semiotics has appeared -- that is, the application of literary semiotics to biblical texts. But there is still no biblical poetics. In spite of efforts to renew biblical stylistics, it remains stylistics, and not poetics.[6] That is, it refers to langue (according to Saussure) rather than parole; it refers to structure, but not to the more fruitful notion of system (for it takes structure and system as being equivalent, not realizing their radical difference in attitude towards subject and history). Poetics, in the way I understand it, starts when system is applied to speech, to enunciation (according to Benveniste), integrating both the subject and its history.

Terence Collins tried to renew stylistics from the point of view of syntax.[7] He classified verses according to their grammatical structures, showing that many are not built upon parallelism. But although his analysis is quite useful and interesting, it says nothing of prosody, or of rhythm, which seems to leave it open to subjective interpretation.

The same goes for M. O. O'Connor's Hebrew Verse Structure,[8] entirely based on the idea of parallelism and where there is not a word about the te^Camim, as if they did not exist, and had nothing to do with Hebrew verse structure.

It is, then, ironic that biblical rhythmics are inscribed in the text, as visible and hidden as the letter in Poe's Purloined Letter. It is a group rhythm in a language with word stress. A system of accents regulates the junctions and the pauses, governing the cantillation of the verse and therefore regulating the meaning, in so far as meaning depends on joining or not joining such and such a word. That system of accents goes back to archaic hand signs, a cheironomy, as some of the names of the accents show -- one of the reasons to ignore them is their later being set to written form.[9] Cantillation is mentioned in the Talmud, and called ne^Cima: "every one who reads without ne^Cima, on him what is written says, and I too gave them laws that are not good" (Megillah 32, at the end). There is an allusion to hand signs in Berakhot 62 a: (why is the right hand preferred) "R. Akiva says because one sees by it the te^Camei torah" and Rashi comments: "I saw in readers coming from the land of Israel." Without going into detail here, even the distinctions between the three books of Job, Proverbs, and Psalms (te^Camei Emet), which are regulated by a system other than the one regulating the other twenty-one books, as it is purely technical and musical, has nothing to do with a distinction between "prose" books or "poetical" ones, or "poetical" versus historical ones. Those are later and rhetorical categories. It is also clear that the division between Tora, Nevi'im and Ketuvim has nothing to do either with poetry or prose. Whatever the variations of melody, according to various rites, places and periods, the hierarchy and the rhythmical value of the accents has been constant. One has to remember that the word ta^Cam means both "taste" and "meaning." The sensory metaphor implies both the corporal nature of meaning, and the comprehensive character of oral meaning, different from meaning as belonging to a word.

As the whole Bible is made of verses, and every verse is regulated by the te^Camim, all one can say about the Bible is that it is all verse. But since it is verse in such a special sense, and since no part of the text escapes from it, that does not mean it is poetry. On the contrary, it makes it impossible to enter into our Hellenistic, and modern, notions of prose or poetry. The verse is the only rhythmical unit.

That overall presence of rhythm is disturbing. Judah Halevi in his Kuzari already noticed that "it mostly connects when it should stop and stops where it should go on" (II,

72). That may also explain the usual disregard of the accents, since grammar -- and not rhythm -- is commonly taken for the law of meaning, not recognizing that rhythm is just as important, if not more important, in making sense. A similar problem is presented by sixteenth-century punctuation. Stage punctuation in Shakespeare's edition is disregarded, because by the standards of logical punctuation, it is considered faulty, the caprice of printers. Perhaps the most famous case in the Bible of the primacy of rhythm occurs in Isaiah (XL, 3), translated in the King James Version: "The voice of him that crieth in the wilderness, Prepare ye the way of the Lord," with a pause after wilderness, whereas the Hebrew has a major pause after "crieth"; a zaqef qatan after qol qore//and then bamidbar/panu derekh ladoni, with a zaqef gadol after bamidbar. That accent, when it follows immediately after zaqef qatan, is always weaker. In Hebrew the passage has a historical and terrestrial meaning, related to the exile of Babylon: it calls to open a way into the desert to go back to Jerusalem. But split after "wilderness," it takes on the messianic and Christian calling, as it is quoted in Mark (I, 3), where it is related to John the Baptist, and in Matthew (III, 3) and John (I, 23).[10]

The criticism made by James Kugel of classical parallelism may be termed a structuralist one, in the sense that it is linguistically and logically quite effective. The essence of parallelism in the Bible, compared to parallelism in Ugaritic texts, is shown to be emphasis. But this presents a difficulty, since it amounts to maintaining the principle of parallelism, forgetting that parallelism is linked to the distinction between prose and poetry, which was recognized as irrelevant to the Bible. To keep parallelism is to keep that distinction, though irrelevant. Kugel concludes that "parallelism is the only meter of biblical poetry" (p. 301), which retains the essential strategy of Robert Lowth. Even if Kugel takes parallelism in a "nontraditional manner," he is led then to underestimate the te^{C}amim, for, as he says in a footnote, they "often obscure the parallelism" (p. 191, n.44).

But it seems to me that parallelism and the te^{C}amim are two radically opposite, incompatible principles. The principle of te^{C}amim is the one of Judah Halevi, the one of the biblical signifier, not only from a semantic point of view, but as an anthropological principle, integrating body and language into one orality. The other principle is that of Greek rhetoric, and of the theory of sign. It has conspicuously enough led to a misunderstanding of the signifier in general, and particularly of the biblical signifier. This is widely demonstrated by the weak ways of translating that have to be related to their linguistic principle. Both from the point of view of how language works, and of the efficiency actually achieved, that principle, together with its consequences, ought to be put into the museum of out-of-date and ineffectual theories. That is, of course, if the epistemological point of view were the only one in cause. In any case, I do not see any comparison, any Hegelian conciliation between the two. The technical aspects of the problem should not mask what is theoretically at stake. Yet, one of the effects of parallelism is precisely to mask the problem. That is why I am here on the side of Judah Halevi, not of parallelism.

3. Two examples

The practical aspect of translation will show the differences. The first example I take is from Deuteronomy (XI, 30). I have chosen it because, unlike Isaiah (XL, 3), it does not have any striking difference in meaning due to change of rhythm. The difference might even pass unseen. Actually, it has passed unseen. Yet, that is precisely what can allow us to see, almost independently of meaning, what a mode of signifying is, how it changes the tone and character of one and the same sentence. I have also chosen that verse because it is one of the rare passages where Rashi comments on the te^{C}amim. Here is the verse with the names of the accents:

halo'-hémma   /be^{C}éver hayyarden /
   geresh   munah   revi^{C}i
'aharei   dérekh   mevo'   hashshemesh //
   pashta   yetiv   munah   zaqef qatan
be'érets   /hakena^{C}ani // hayyoshev ba^{C}arava ///
   azla   zaqef qatan   tifha   atnah
mul   /hagilgal   // 'étsel   /'lonei moreh////
vetiv zaqef qatan   tifha   merkha sof pasuq

Every relatively minor disjunctive accent is marked with one bar. It determines a rhythmical group: zaqaf qatan, an important accent, is marked with two bars; atnah, which means "rest," and is the main division in the verse, is marked with three bars; sof pasuq, "end of the verse," with four. The conjunction accents (munah, merkha) are not marked.

The importance of accents has been stressed by Rashi, which indicates their consequence for that passage. I translate his note: "and the accentuation of the reading [that is, of the Bible: veta^{C}am hamiqra] shows that there are two things for they have been pointed out with two accents; aharei is pointed with pashta and derekh is pointed with mashpel and it has a dagesh. And if aharei derekh were one phrase aharei would have been pointed with a conjunctive accent [mesharet] with shofar hipukh and derekh with pashta and rafé." In other words, the pronunciation would not have been the same: derekh would have been dherekh, since rafé indicates the "soft" pronunciation of the consonant, and dagesh the "hard" one. Mashpel is another name for yetiv, "pause." What is implicit in Rashi is that the disjunctive accents here -- and this verse is unusually filled with disjunctive accents -- are essential both to grammar and to meaning. More effectively, rhythm is essential here to the mode of signifying (the way the thing is said, by whom, to whom, and in what circumstances), which requires another mode than a linked one, a conversational tone.

But no translation I know has listened to that rhythm. For brevity's sake I shall quote only three English translations. The King James Version:

Are they not on the other side Jordan, by the way where the sun goeth down, in the land of the Canaanites, which dwell in the champaign over against Gilgal, beside the plains of Moreh?

This rendering has no concordance with the rhythm of the original, but the translation has kept the initial phrasing of the emphasis, and it has a metrical rhythm of its own. It remains, to this day, the nearest approximation to the tone of the original. That is not the case with the New English Bible, which aims at a plain, conversational style:

(These mountains are on the other side of the Jordan, close to Gilgal beside the terebinth of Moreh, beyond the road to the west which lies in the territory of the Canaanites of the Arabah.)

I leave aside detail problems, such as elonei (more), which as far as I know, is the plural construct of a word which means "oak-tree," neither "plains" nor "terebinth." The character of the New English Bible depends on the displacement of the last group to the second position, the reduced number of commas, the insertion of an explanatory word (mountains) taken and repeated from the end of the preceding verse (which mentions "mount Gerizim" and "mount Ebal"). The emphasis of the phrase "are they not" is replaced by its positive meaning, but the emphasis is lost. In the same way, the signified is split from the signifier in "the road to the west," substituted for the setting sun. Even the adding of parentheses tends to explain, implying that the text was not clear enough, or that the reader of the New English Bible is considerably less intelligent than the reader of the King James Version, and of the original. That systematic disregard for the signifier shows the strategy of meaning, and is obviously meant for efficiency's sake. It is characteristic of the methods and theory elaborated by Nida and biblical committees.[11] It aims at a "dynamic equivalence." Actually, it restrains language to an impoverished idea of meaning. It is no surprise, since it is linked to an equally poor idea of "form," identified with archaism, because it is the King James Version, and not the Hebrew text, which is the starting point of comparisons. The idea of meaning which prevails here unites the theory of information, the stimulus-response behaviorist idea of meaning, and lastly also generative grammar. That eclectic epistemology works havoc with translation, and with the Bible in particular, for it considers it as a mere support for an ideological message, and action. Its pragmaticism is the final outcome of the linguistic and theological (Christian) dualism. It strikes out all cultural, historical, linguistic distances, and rhythm, in order to achieve the same reaction as would a message in the language of the receptor. Being natural, that apparently innocent aim, is in fact intended for, and most effective upon the various aborigines for whom hundreds of such translations are fabricated, from English as a Source Language. That kind of translation succeeds when the natives say, as Nida quotes it, "I did not know that God was speaking my language." But conversion may not be the only aim for the theory of translation. And such a theory, when it deals with literature, fails to recognize its specific activity, for the signifier is more than Nida's "formal equivalence."

A third translation is that of the Jewish Publication Society of America:[12]

--Both are on the side of the Jordan, beyond the west road which is in the land
of the Canaanites who dwell in the Arabah -- near Gilgal, by the terebinths of
Moreh.

Although it does not displace the last group, that translation shares, to a lesser degree,
the same technique as the New English Bible. It does not add the "mountains," but adds
"Both," and transforms "are they not" into the affirmative voice. The sunset also becomes
the west. In spite of its use of dashes, it no more respects Rashi and rhythm than the
others, though it should, being Jewish. Thus it is not faithful to its own tradition, though
it proceeds with the conscience of being "faithful," as its preface says. The improvements
it claims to have achieved are philological, or archeological. They concern "accuracy,"
and the recasting of an obsolete state of language into an idiomatic, "natural," up-to-date
speech. That idea of the "natural" obliterates the fact that there are a great many ways
of being natural. Every mode of signifying is natural to its purpose and situation. The
claim of being natural conveys some linguistic ingenuousness. It also covers the
well-known separation between ordinary speech and literature. It is there that its
pragmatic bias for efficiency is hampered by an over-simple idea of language, its
blindness to poetics.

    Other translations I might quote would not add much, although each one has enough
in it to show where it stands. I shall just present a translation which does nothing more
than to keep exactly to the te^{c}amim, to the rhythm of groups and words. It proposes a
system of equivalences, with blank spaces, which amount to the raising intonation. It is,
of course, but an approximation, which leaves out, here, the musical value and retains
only the pause value, and the semantic one. In accordance with my experiments in
French, I use a medium blank for the medium disjunctive accents, a bigger blank for the
more important ones, such as zaqef qatan, an indentation inside the verse for atnah. One
can often observe a relationship between the oral and the visual in modern typography.
The verse would run:

Are they not beyond the Jordan   behind   the way   where
the sun goes down   in the land of the Canaanite
who lives   in the Arava
       Facing   the Gilgal   near   the oaks of Moreh

The extremely, and unusually, broken rhythm is here essential to the importance of the
message, for it implies the rhythmical marks, and so increases the semantic weight of
every marked term. Translating the Bible with its rhythm, and in its rhythm, is not more
difficult than translating within the frame of the sign. It is just a different program, for a
different purpose, another way of being in the language. And even for a pragmatic aim of
efficiency, rhythm is more efficient than the absence of rhythm.

The second example I take from Jonah (II, 9), because of its very tight prosodic and rhythmical organization, and because of the way prosodic and rhythmical organization are linked to meaning. The verse is from Jonah's prayer, in the belly of the whale, after the sailors prayed vainly to their own gods, and after it turned out that only the God of Jonah proved to be efficient in calming the tempest. The verse, towards the end of that prayer, opposes the false gods to the true one, and urges the idol-worshippers to forsake their faith:

meshamrim / havlei-shav /// hasdam / ya^{c}azovu ///

    <u>tifha</u>   <u>atnah</u>   <u>tifha</u>   <u>sof pasuq</u>

As it is a violent statement against idolatry, meaning, in the dualistic sense, is not the only element involved. The effect works through the oral character of the verse: its pauses, but also the prosodic equation that opposes the syllable numbers on each side of <u>atnah</u> (3-3/2-4), the links between the signifiers, the /m/ in <u>me</u>sha<u>m</u>rim-hasda<u>m</u>, the <u>sh</u> in me<u>sh</u>amrim-<u>sh</u>av, the /v/ in the coupling ha<u>v</u>lei-sha<u>v</u> and ya^{c}azo<u>v</u>u. Those are not repetitions of mere sounds, but interactions between signifiers, that strengthen their bonds. The prosodic element plays its part in the metaphor <u>havlei-shav</u>, where <u>hevel</u> is concretely the vapor produced by breath about to vanish in the air, out of which Jerome made the <u>vanitas vanitatum</u> of <u>Ecclesiastes,</u> and it is the name of Abel; <u>shav</u> is emptiness, falsehood, and qualifies the false prophets. The two words linked together -- literally something like "vapors of falsehood" -- are a kind of superlative, more than an imprecation, than a definition. But, instead of that signifier, translations usually have either put the signified, as the <u>King James Version</u>:

They that observe lying vanities forsake their own mercy

or even the referent, that is the mention of the gods or idols implied, as the <u>New English Bible</u>:

Men who worship false gods may abandon their loyalty.

There are many interpretations for <u>hesed,</u> but the context seems to favor the meaning of faith, or cult, and ya^{c}azovu is an imperfect jussive, not an indicative. I translated into French as

    Veilleurs de   vent buée
       Leur foi   délaisseront

and would venture to propose in English something like

> Watchers of   wind and blur
>   Their faith   shall relinquish

after which I will certainly not conclude, for the question of rhythm is so vast, that it cannot but remain open. It is intensely polemical, because what it shows is still a scandal, and perhaps the most stimulating question in language, and so I shall put it in a scandalous way, saying that rhythm is the Jew of sign, and that rhythm is the utopia of meaning.

Notes

1. Henri Meschonnic is a poet and professor of linguistics at Paris-VIII (Vincennes) University. He has published three books of poetry: Dédicaces proverbes, 1972; Dans nos recommencements, 1976; Légendaire chaque jour, 1979. He is also the author of five volumes of essays on poetics, Pour la poétique I-V (Gallimard, 1970-1978). Volumes II and V pay special attention to the poetics of translation. In addition, he has written on the theory of language in Le Signe et le poéme (Gallimard, 1975), and has translated from the Hebrew Bible in Les cinq Rouleaux (Gallimard, 1970), and Jona et le signifiant errant (Gallimard, 1981). His latest book is Critique du rhythme, Anthropologie historique du langue (Paris: Verdier, 1982).

2. William Wickes, Two Treatises on the Accentuation of the Old Testament (New York: Ktav Publishing House, 1970), p. 4. There are two volumes in one (1881, 1887), with a prolegomenon by Aron Dotan, who appraises the work as a classic.

3. James Kugel, The Idea of Biblical Poetry, Parallelism and its History (New Haven: Yale University Press, 1981).

4. T. Carmi, Ed., The Penguin Book of Hebrew Verse (London: Allen Lane, 1981), p. 58.

5. Judah Halevi, The Kuzari (New York: Schocken Books, 1974), p. 125.

6. The book of Luis Alonso Schokel, Estudios de poética hebrea (Barcelona: Juan Flors, 1963), in spite of its title, is a study in stylistics.

7. Terence Collins, Line-Forms in Hebrew Poetry, A Grammatical Approach to the stylistic study of the Hebrew Prophets (Rome: Biblical Institute Press, 1978, Studia Pohl, Series Major).

8. M. O. O'Connor, Hebrew Verse Structure (P.O.B.275 Winona Lake, Indiana 46590: Eisenbrauns, 1980).

9. For the details, see Wickes' book, already quoted, from which I take the following references.

10. It is not the only case when the Hebrew text has a historical meaning, and its translation into Greek has a metaphysical one. Another typical case is the phrase taken as a title by René Girard for his book Des choses cachées depuis la fondation du monde

(Grasset, 1978), "Things hidden since the foundation of the world," which follows Matthew (XIII, 35), which in its turn translates Psalm LXXVIII, 2. But where the New Testament Greek refers to a cosmic dimension, which reestablishes the sacred, the Hebrew says, as the King James Version correctly translates: "I will utter dark sayings of old." The Hebrew refers to human memory, to the knowledge of the Elders, which always has to be interpreted. Both are completely different worlds.

11. Eugene A. Nida, Toward a Science of Translating (Leiden: E. J. Brill, 1964); Eugene A. Nida and Charles R. Taber, The Theory and Practice of Translation (Leiden: E. J. Brill, 1969).

12. The Torah, The Five Books of Moses (Philadelphia: The Jewish Publication Society of America, 1962, 1967).

INDEX